The Reluctant Crusade

A Study from the Center for Korean Studies
University of Hawaii

The *Reluctant Crusade*

AMERICAN FOREIGN POLICY
IN KOREA, 1941–1950

James Irving Matray

UNIVERSITY OF HAWAII PRESS
Honolulu

Library of Congress Cataloging in Publication Data

Matray, James Irving, 1948–
   The reluctant crusade.

   Bibliography: p.
   Includes index.
   1.   United States—Foreign relations—Korea.   2.   Korea—
Foreign relations—United States.   3.   United States—
Foreign relations—1933–1945.   4.   United States—Foreign
relations—1945–1953.   5.   Korea (South)—Politics and
government—1945–1948.   6.   Korea (South)—Politics and
government—1948–1960.   I.   Title.
E183.8.K7M28   1985   327.730519   85–1079
ISBN 0–8248–0973–4

We acknowledge with thanks permission from the publishers to reprint portions of
this book that appeared in *Diplomatic History* 2 (Spring 1978): 181–196 (Scholarly
Resources, Inc.); *Pacific Historical Review* (Pacific Coast Branch of the American Historical Association); and *The Historian* (Phi Alpha Theta International Honor Society in History).

To Karin

The activities of the U.N. in Korea have been described as "the reluctant crusade." . . .

Korea's significance is not the final crusade. It is not finally making valid the idea of collective security. . . .

In Korea the Russians presented a check which was drawn on the bank account of collective security. The Russians thought the check would bounce. They thought it was a bad check. But to their great surprise, the teller paid it. The important thing was that the check was paid. The importance will be nothing if the next check is not paid and if the bank account is not kept strong and sufficient to cover all checks which are drawn upon it.

Dean G. Acheson
June 29, 1951

Contents

Acknowledgments

Every historian knows that research and writing would be impossible without the help of countless people, especially archivists, colleagues, family, and friends. I was fortunate in that wherever I traveled to do research, the staff members of these institutions were not only competent but also uniformly pleasant and eager to provide assistance. In particular, John Taylor, William Cunliffe, and Edward Reese at the Modern Military Branch of the National Archives devoted a great deal of time and energy to removing barriers to an expeditious search for documents. Nancy Bressler at the Princeton University Library kindly granted access to the Dulles papers even though she was involved in reclassifying these materials. At the MacArthur Memorial Library, Larry Redford's efficiency ensured that none of my limited time was wasted. I also want to thank numerous unnamed people at the Library of Congress, the University of Virginia Library, Clemson University Library, and the Diplomatic Records Division at the National Archives.

I owe a special debt of gratitude to the Harry S. Truman Library Institute and its director Benedict Zobrist for awarding me research grants during 1976 and 1982. During my three visits to Independence, Dennis Bilger assumed primary responsibility for helping me and spent many hours uncovering and bringing to my attention significant documents. His professional skill and warmth are characteristic of the entire staff at the Truman Library, making it an outstanding research institution. Also, I am grateful to the College of Arts and Sciences Research Center at New Mexico State University for its continuing financial support.

This study began in 1974 as a dissertation project under the direction of Norman A. Graebner at the University of Virginia. I am deeply indebted to Professor Graebner for his guidance and assistance not only in completing this book but throughout my graduate and subsequent professional career. His sincere concern for my personal progress continues to provide a source of inspiration and a model for emulation. His comments on style and content were invaluable. The late Edward E. Younger read parts of the original manuscript and reminded me of the importance of balance and objectivity in historical interpretation.

More recently, I have had the good fortune to receive encouragement and advice from George C. Herring of the University of Kentucky. Without Professor Herring's help, the revised dissertation might never have appeared in print. John Lewis Gaddis of Ohio University provided valuable suggestions for revision and offered reinforcement when I needed it most. Michael C. Sandusky's comments were helpful in the final stages of revision. I also am grateful for permission to use material initially appearing in *Diplomatic History, The Pacific Historical Review,* and *The Historian.* Damaris Kirchhofer deserves credit for excellent editorial advice. My thanks also to the staff at the University of Hawaii Press for their help in preparing the manuscript for publication.

Finding inexpensive housing while researching in Washington, D.C., is difficult at best. Thus I am especially grateful that, while a graduate student, I was able to stay at the home of Tony Lerner and his family. Since 1980, my colleagues here at New Mexico State University, especially Joan M. Jensen and Monroe L. Billington, have helped me in times of frustration. Finally, this book is dedicated to my wife Karin in appreciation for her innumerable sacrifices. Without Karin's understanding, encouragement, and unfailing devotion, I never could have completed either a doctoral program or this book. If I am a success, most of the credit ultimately belongs to her.

Abbreviations

AMG   American Military Government in Korea
DPRK   Democratic People's Republic of Korea
ECA   Economic Cooperation Administration
GARIOA   Government Aid and Relief in Occupied Areas
JCS   Joint Chiefs of Staff
KMAG   Korean Military Advisory Group
KPG   Korean Provisional Government
KPR   Korean People's Republic
MDAP   Military Defense Appropriations Program
NSC   National Security Council
OSS   Office of Strategic Services
PKMAG   Provisional Korean Military Advisory Group
ROK   Republic of Korea
SANACC   State–Army–Navy–Air Force Coordinating Committee
SKIG   South Korean Interim Government
SKILA   South Korean Interim Legislative Assembly
SWNCC   State–War–Navy Coordinating Committee
UNCOK   United Nations Commission on Korea
UNRRA   United Nations Relief and Rehabilitation Administration
UNTCOK   United Nations Temporary Commission on Korea
USAFIK   United States Armed Forces in Korea

The transliteration of Korean names in the text is based on the McCune-Reischauer System, except for those widely accepted and familiar spellings such as Syngman Rhee, Kim Il Sung, Pyongyang, and Seoul.

Introduction

Just before dawn on June 30, 1950, President Harry S. Truman received an urgent telephone call from Secretary of the Army Frank Pace. South Korea, Pace explained, could not prevent North Korea from conquering the entire nation without immediate help from American ground troops. In reply, Truman authorized the use of combat forces to prevent a Communist triumph in the Korean War. That the president would even consider sending American soldiers to fight on this distant Asian peninsula surely would have startled countless citizens in the United States a decade earlier. Although American involvement in Asian affairs had increased steadily after the Civil War, the United States rarely contemplated the direct application of military power. An exception was the Philippines, yet even there Washington had begun a retreat from its commitments after World War I. But Japan's attack on Pearl Harbor had inaugurated a process of change in the way American leaders assessed the role of the United States in international affairs. Truman's commitment of ground troops in Korea marked the climax of a fundamental transformation in American foreign policy from restrained involvement to global interventionism.

Axis aggression convinced most American leaders that the United States could not follow an isolationist foreign policy after World War II without jeopardizing the nation's security.[1] "We cannot withdraw from participation in the political and economic decisions affecting other parts of the world," one American official wrote in 1944, "without thereby losing a share in the control of our own future. We shall either help to stamp our pattern on world affairs or have someone else's pattern imposed on us."[2] Soviet behavior in Eastern Europe during the last year of World War II seemed to confirm the accuracy of this assessment. Yet the United States embraced this new activist approach in foreign affairs only with great uncertainty and reluctance. Ultimately, it was the perceived threat of Soviet ideology and power that pushed the United States further from its isolationist past. After 1945, a basic trend in world affairs was Washington's increasing willingness to assume primary responsibility for maintaining global peace and stability. It was significant, however, that the United States implemented policies for countering the Soviet challenge all of which emphasized the importance of restraint.

American involvement in Korean affairs prior to the outbreak of war in 1950 both reflected and played a crucial role in this broad shift in foreign policy. Korea was, admittedly, only a small part of the American vision for postwar global reconstruction during World War II and immediately thereafter. Yet Washington's response to instability in Korea typified its overall approach in Asia following the defeat of Japan. President Franklin D. Roosevelt pledged in the Cairo Declaration of 1943 that the United States would help supervise the restoration of independence and self-government to a nation previously the recipient of scant American attention. A stable Korea presumably would act as an economic and diplomatic partner for the United States in the postwar world. In September 1945, following American military occupation of the southern half of Korea, Washington had an opportunity to implement its plan but experienced difficulties from the outset. Not only did Korea face the complex task of social, political, and economic readjustment after years of Japanese colonial domination, but many Koreans resisted American advice and demanded immediate and complete independence.[3] Still worse, the Soviet Union had occupied the northern half of the Korean peninsula and American concern over Moscow's intentions hampered an unemotional assessment of Korea's problems.

American negotiations with the Soviet Union for Korea's reunification during 1946 and 1947 failed miserably. Much like Germany, Korea emerged after World War II, in the words of Frank Baldwin, as a "hostage to strategies and ambitions of the cold war" rather than a liberated nation.[4] Truman's policy in Korea mirrored the pattern established in Eastern Europe, as the United States refused to accept Soviet intransigence but lacked sufficient power to force a settlement on American terms. Without an overall plan for dealing with Soviet obstructionism, American foreign policy manifested considerable irresolution during the early years of the Cold War.[5] But this situation changed significantly with George F. Kennan's formulation of the containment policy and its subsequent application in Europe during

1947. At the time, Kennan was U.S. chargé d'affaires in Moscow and considered an expert on the Soviet Union.

Kennan's containment strategy had a powerful impact on the Truman administration because it provided a method for countering the Soviet challenge without requiring an unqualified commitment of American power. Containment promised to halt Russian expansion and preserve American security at the relatively low cost of economic, technical, and military assistance.[6] If smaller nations could provide for their own defense with American aid and advice, a positive guarantee of military protection would not be necessary. Kennan's strategy thus would permit the United States to foster international stability without necessitating an increase in defense spending or the sacrifice of American lives. More important, containment promised ultimate victory in the Cold War without requiring a resort to war. Although success would not emerge quickly, Moscow's defeat would occur eventually in "either the breakup or the gradual mellowing of Soviet power."[7]

Containment would facilitate as well the realization of Truman's goal of national self-determination. The Soviet Union, Truman believed, exploited postwar economic distress to foster civil strife that allowed Communist minorities to seize power and prevent freedom of choice. Kennan's formula assumed that nations would reject communism if the United States denied the Soviets an environment conducive to expansion.[8] The strategy appeared especially successful in Western Europe, largely because the Soviet Union never seriously challenged American interests there. In Asia, on the other hand, Truman's policy encountered vexing difficulties from the start, particularly in China.

Nevertheless, Truman retained confidence in the ultimate promise of containment. By 1948, Korea had emerged as the test case of his Asian policy, as the administration prepared a three-year program for economic and military aid. American objectives in Korea were far more grandiose than most observers realized at the time. Arthur C. Bunce, the American economic advisor in Korea, indicated the nature of Washington's expectation when he expressed his hope in one revealing letter that the South Korean leaders "will institute a whole series of necessary reforms which will so appeal to the North Koreans that their army will revolt, kill all the nasty Communists, and create a lovely liberal democracy to the everlasting credit of the U.S.A.!"[9] Containment in Korea aimed at inflicting a major defeat on the Soviet Union and scoring a crucial victory for national self-determination. For Truman, containment would act as a liberating force. At least that was the hope.

Containment in Korea never reached the level of success that Truman and his advisors anticipated. By the beginning of 1950 South Korea still remained politically divided and economically weak and the future of containment as a liberating force in Korea seemed in doubt. At this juncture, North Korea attacked South Korea and shattered the theoretical foundations of American foreign policy. Containment now appeared inadequate, for the challenge of Soviet ideology and power was not only economic but also military in nature. Faced with Stalin's apparent drive for world conquest, the administration concluded that the United States could not, without grave risk, limit its commitment to preserve international stability. As one State Department official warned dramatically in the autumn of 1950, "though the fire be distant at the moment, if it is not extinguished it will surely spread and will ultimately threaten our own homes."[10]

American policy toward Korea from 1941 to 1950 presents an excellent case study for understanding how the United States reluctantly adopted a thoroughly internationalist approach in foreign affairs after World War II. Despite Korea's secondary importance for American national security during these years, Truman and his advisors nevertheless looked to this nation for clues regarding the extent to which the United States should be involved in world affairs. Korea therefore played a pivotal role in the postwar transformation of American foreign policy. Prior to the Korean War, American leaders accepted a series of assumptions that permitted a restrained course in diplomacy and reflected the continuing influence of an isolationist past. Consequently, Washington's dispatch of American ground forces came after the United States had labored long and hard to limit its commitment for military action in Korea and elsewhere in Asia. Military intervention constituted more than an admission that Washington's policy in Korea had failed, however. Truman's decision to commit combat troops signaled the adoption of a new globalist course in international affairs and the final abandonment of an isolationist tradition in American foreign policy.

CHAPTER 1

An End to Indifference

World War II ended a tradition of American indifference toward Korea. This policy shift was both surprising and significant because the United States previously had seen no national interests worth defending on the Korean peninsula. Before 1941, Korean affairs had been the exclusive concern of closer and more powerful neighbors—Russia, China, and Japan. Korea was, in fact, the strategic focal point of northeast Asia. As a result, the Korean people had been the long-suffering victims of great power rivalry throughout most of their history.[1] Japan eventually established complete political and economic control over Korea shortly before the outbreak of World War I, thereby removing the peninsula, at least temporarily, from the arena of international conflict.[2] In the wake of Japan's defeat in World War II, however, Korean affairs again involved a contest for influence among great powers. The only difference was that in 1945 the United States emerged as a principal competitor in the struggle to determine Korea's destiny.

An American desire to expand trade opportunities in the Pacific was the central feature of early relations between the United States and Korea. Although some Americans had pointed to Korea's commercial potential before the Civil War, Secretary of State William H. Seward made the first earnest attempt to open contacts with the "Hermit Kingdom." In 1866, he dispatched the *General Sherman* to Korea, but after the ship ran aground, Koreans boarded the vessel, burned it, and murdered the crew. Seward's successor, Hamilton Fish, tried to negotiate a commercial treaty with Korea in 1871, but he failed as well.[3] Ultimately, it was Sino-Japanese competition for dominance over the peninsula that led to the establishment of formal diplomatic relations between the United States and Korea. To offset rising Japanese political influence, China facilitated the negotiation in 1882 of the Korean-American treaty of friendship and commerce.

This agreement provided for the exchange of diplomatic representatives, protection of navigation rights, extraterritoriality, and most favored nation status in commercial affairs. One additional provision would have particular importance in the future: The two nations promised that in the event "other powers deal unjustly or oppressively with either government, the other will exert their good offices, on being informed of the case, to bring about an amicable arrangement."[4]

American diplomatic representatives in Korea labored diligently during subsequent years to expand commercial opportunities while striving to remain uninvolved in the ongoing Sino-Japanese rivalry. When China and Japan finally went to war over the peninsula in 1894, Korea appealed to the United States to fulfill its obligations under the treaty of 1882 and intervene in the dispute. Accordingly, the American ambassador in Tokyo notified Japanese authorities that the "President will be painfully disappointed should Japan visit upon her feeble and defenceless neighbor the horrors of an unjust war." But words alone would not preserve Korea's sovereignty. The militarily superior Japanese easily defeated China, eliminating Chinese influence from the Korean peninsula.[5] After the Sino-Japanese War, Washington instructed its diplomats in the Korean capital at Seoul not to interfere in Korea's internal affairs. This commitment to a policy of noninvolvement became stronger as Russia began to challenge Japanese hegemony in Korea. Despite pressure from American Minister Horace N. Allen to reverse Washington's policy, the United States remained indifferent to Korea's fate.[6] This approach properly reflected the extent of American interests in Korea, however, since the peninsula was neither politically nor economically vital to the United States.

In February 1904, Japan staged its surprise attack on the Russian fleet at Port Arthur, thus initiating the long-anticipated Russo-Japanese War. Japan's military victory was quick and complete, confirming its preeminent position in Korea. Realizing that the United States could do little to preserve Korea's freedom, President Theodore Roosevelt decided to acknowledge Japanese control in return for important concessions in other areas. In the Taft–Katsura agreement of 1905, the United States recognized Japanese hegemony in Korea, while Japan accepted American dominance over the Philippines. Before the end of the year, the United States had closed its embassy in Seoul and terminated official relations with Korea.[7]

Japan formally annexed Korea in 1910, systematically integrating the peninsula into its imperial structure during the next decade. Yet the Korean people did not accept dictation meekly. Despite brutal repression, Koreans continually staged demonstrations protesting Japanese imperialism.[8] Washington studiously avoided involvement in such revolutionary activities. In April 1919, for example, the State Department advised its consular representatives in Korea to "be extremely careful not to encourage any belief that the United States will assist the Korean nationalists in carrying out their plans."[9] Thereafter, Americans conducted only some missionary work and desultory trade. Although Korean patriots never forgave the United States for its policy of silence regarding Japanese subjugation of Korea, Japan's close regulation of all outside contacts with Korea left Washington no other choice.

Following World War I, several Koreans sought to enlist foreign support for the liberation of their nation. As Korean exiles scattered to China, the Soviet Union, and the United States, a number of groups emerged, each forwarding a variety of tactics and strategies for achieving Korea's independence.[10] From the outset, factionalism was the dominant characteristic of the Korean independence movement.[11] Certainly the most well-known organization was the self-styled "Korean Provisional Government" (KPG), formed by Korean leaders in the aftermath of the abortive March First Rebellion in 1919.[12] But many Korean radicals became disenchanted with the KPG's reliance on diplomacy and propaganda as primary weapons in the fight for independence.[13] Young Koreans in particular favored a more direct and violent strategy. As a result, Communist revolutionary ideology emerged as a popular and powerful force not only among Korean exiles but inside Korea itself.[14] This lack of unity in outlook and purpose in the Korean liberation movement made common action under a single leader impossible.

After the outbreak of World War II, Korean exile leaders intensified their efforts to procure American support for Korea's liberation. Almost immediately, several groups appealed to the State Department for recognition and assistance. Invariably, each harped on the need for vigorous steps to halt Japanese imperialism, as well as Korea's readiness for independence. One especially active Korean exile was Han Kil-su, representative of the Sino-Korean People's League. In May 1941, Han urged the United States to prohibit Japanese use of the Panama Canal while restricting oil shipments to Japan and freezing Japanese assets in the United States. He also pledged that a Korean guerrilla army, fighting in northern China, would continue to combat Japanese expansion. To encourage resistance efforts, Han suggested that Washington issue a public statement advocating Korea's independence and applauding Korean military action.[15]

Kim Ku, now president of the KPG and living in exile in Chungking, challenged the legitimacy of Han Kil-su and all other exile groups. Only the KPG, he claimed, was worthy of recognition and material assistance from the United States and China. Cho So-ang, the KPG's foreign minister, appealed to Secretary of State Cordell Hull on several occasions for the extension of Lend Lease aid.[16] The United States rejected this and all other Korean requests for recognition and support, maintaining strict impartiality toward all rival exile factions. President Roosevelt and his advisors recognized that aid to the Koreans would not be sufficient to counteract Japanese expansion. It might even increase Japan's aggressiveness and lead to open hostilities with the United States, which Roosevelt still hoped to avoid.

Japan's attack on Pearl Harbor forced the United States to alter its Asian policy and devise a strategy that would promote peace and security in the Pacific after the end of World War II. The success of its postwar policy in Asia, however, would require the emergence of a stable government in Korea capable of self-defense and worthy of international diplomatic support. Roosevelt and his advisors saw that in the absence of positive measures to achieve such a result, competition for influence and control in Korea would resume. Korea's future depended upon the ability of the Allies to cooperate in the negotiation of an agreement that would protect the interests of all nations directly involved in the peninsula. Thus, the Roosevelt administration came to advocate an international trusteeship for Korea in an effort to eliminate this strategic area as a potential source of tension and conflict in the postwar world.[17]

William R. Langdon of the Division of Far Eastern Affairs provided the foundation for Roosevelt's wartime policy toward Korea during February 1942. In a key memorandum, Langdon noted that the vast majority of Koreans were illiterate and poor, politically inexperienced, and economically backward. After forty years of Japanese domination, only older Koreans could even remember freedom. One can pinpoint the origins of American support for a Korean trusteeship in Langdon's observation that "for a generation at least Korea would have to be protected, guided, and aided to modern statehood by the great powers." He went on to suggest that the United States should sponsor those Korean exiles with proven ties inside Korea, such as the guerrilla forces located in Manchuria, and avoid being "stampeded" into recognition of any "shadow organization." Even an American promise of postwar independence would be ill advised, Langdon argued, since it "would only do the Korean cause harm, give the Japanese and their allies a good laugh, and irritate our own friends if we promised independence to one Asiatic people as we were being pushed out of our own possessions in Asia by the Japanese." In any event, Langdon recommended that the administration formulate a definitive policy on Korea only after consultations with China and the Soviet Union.[18]

Roosevelt undoubtedly was aware of the contents of Langdon's memorandum. In a radio address on February 23, 1942, the president referred to the Korean "experience of enslavement" under the Japanese. He then guaranteed that the promise of national self-determination enunciated in the Atlantic Charter applied "to the whole world." Significantly, this statement corresponded precisely to Langdon's recommendation that the United States, "until the situation becomes clearer, not go beyond referring . . . to the third principle for a better world proclaimed in the joint Anglo-American declaration of August 14, 1941, namely our 'respect of the right of all peoples to choose the form of government under which they will live' and our 'wish to see sovereign rights and self-government restored to those who have been forcibly deprived of them'."[19]

Roosevelt's Korea policy demanded impartiality and delay during the first year of American involvement in World War II. Korean exiles in the United States and China opposed this position, however, and sought positive American action for Korea's liberation. On December 9, 1941, Kim Ku formally asked the United States to extend recognition and Lend Lease assistance to the KPG. Simultaneously, Syngman Rhee (Yi Sŭng-man), the KPG's official representative in Washington, applied intense pressure on the administration to force an abandonment of impartiality.[20] From the outset, then, the KPG was determined to play a significant role in the evolution of wartime American policy toward Korea.

Kim Ku's request was hardly unique. Countless demands for recognition from exile groups representing other nations poured into the State Department. In response, the administration announced that it did not intend to recognize any "free movement" and warned all exile leaders not to attempt to divide the American people. The United States government also urged its citizens not to participate directly in the efforts of these foreign representatives to obtain support.[21] Thus, despite numerous pleas from the Koreans, Washington rejected all requests for assistance.[22] In refusing to recognize the KPG, American leaders avoided setting a dangerous precedent requiring similar action elsewhere in Asia.[23] More important, the Roosevelt administration believed that the success of trusteeship in Korea depended upon respect for the principle of national self-determination.

Several other questions suggested the need for caution. For example, none of the Korean exile groups had strong organizational backing inside Korea. Furthermore, factional disputes between rival leaders prevented unified action even after Pearl Harbor. During discussions with State Department official Alger Hiss in December 1941, Rhee discounted Han's influence in the Korean independence movement. Only the KPG, he insisted, deserved American and Chinese recognition. In reply, Hiss offered yet another cogent reason for delay. The United States could not alter its policy of impartiality until Washington had consulted not only China but also the Soviet Union. Moscow, Hiss continued, held a major interest in the fate of Korea but could not engage in consultations until it was at war with Japan. Stanley K. Hornbeck, division chief for Far Eastern Affairs, summarized Washington's attitude when he observed that recognition of any exile group "might involve responsibilities which in the light of later events it might have been better for this government not to have assumed."[24]

Rhee was able, however, to persuade several private American citizens to sponsor the KPG's cause. John W. Staggers and Jay Jerome Williams, two Washington businessmen, exerted notable pressure on the administration to alter its stance. While ruling out recognition, the State Department encouraged Staggers and Williams to maintain contacts with the KPG and keep the administration informed of Rhee's activities. Staggers evidently interpreted this suggestion as tantamount to unofficial recognition. In January 1942, he instructed Han to channel his activities through Rhee's Washington-based Korean Commission. The United States, Staggers asserted, had recognized Rhee as the legitimate representative of Korea's government in exile. Han immediately requested verification. Undersecretary of

State Sumner Welles quickly disavowed Staggers' allegations and reaffirmed American impartiality.[25]

Leaders of the KPG then decided upon a direct appeal to the American people. On February 28, 1942, a three-day "Liberty Conference" opened in Washington, D.C. Speakers demanded immediate recognition of Kim Ku's regime as the legitimate representative of the Korean nation. After attending the conference, Langdon and Hornbeck dismissed the entire affair as a "publicity stunt."[26] Yet the administration apparently concluded that its Korea policy now required public clarification. At a press conference on March 2, Undersecretary Welles confirmed that the State Department had the Korean matter under consideration and would announce any change in policy. The United States regarded all free movements with "utmost sympathy," Welles declared, but the Korean case involved certain complex problems that required caution and delay.[27]

Korea simply could not generate sufficient public interest to force a change in Roosevelt's policy. One person who would not take no for an answer was James H. R. Cromwell, the former American Ambassador to Canada. In a letter to Cordell Hull, Cromwell explained that Rhee's followers had developed "a blueprint for revolution by arson" and therefore deserved American assistance. The KPG would not implement its plan, however, until the State Department recognized it as "the de facto government of the Republic of Korea."[28] This resort to blackmail failed to alter Washington's policy. Hull's reply emphasized that the administration was determined to avoid any action depriving captive peoples of the right to freedom of choice. Moreover, American recognition was not necessary if the KPG genuinely wanted to demonstrate its devotion to the Atlantic Charter. In July, Hull announced publicly that the United States endorsed the efforts of all exile groups willing to fight for their nation's freedom.[29]

Undaunted, Cromwell now raised the issue with his old friend Adolph A. Berle, the assistant secretary of state. If the United States sponsored a systematic campaign of sabotage and subversion inside Korea, it could build a "bonfire" in Japan's backyard at very low cost. "Adolph," Cromwell pleaded, "you are about the only firecracker I know in the State Department—why don't you do it?" On July 31, Berle referred Cromwell's proposal to the Joint Intelligence Committee. Although the committee's report advised against recognition of the KPG, it stressed the importance of maintaining contacts with the various Korean exile groups. At some future date, the

United States might adopt Cromwell's plan; the report therefore recommended soliciting the comments of General Joseph Stilwell in China.[30]

For Stilwell, Cromwell's scheme was utterly infeasible. The KPG had few contacts inside Korea and its ability to spark a rebellion was dubious at best. Such an operation, Stilwell believed, would be a waste of money, provide no tangible benefits, and entail grave political risks. Army Chief of Staff General George C. Marshall concurred, observing that it would be "doubtful policy to blindly pick some group . . . , thus antagonizing other groups" which might emerge later. As a result, American military leaders rejected Cromwell's plan, informing Berle on September 24 of the decision. They urged Berle to explain to the KPG's supporters that limited American assistance alone could not produce a revolution in Korea. Even if an uprising did occur, Japan would have little trouble suppressing such a poorly organized rebellion.[31]

American diplomats and missionaries fleeing Korea during the summer of 1942 substantiated Stilwell's assessment. They dismissed promises of independence or recognition as pointless in view of the totality of Japanese control in Korea. Arthur B. Emmons III, the American vice-consul in Korea, was among those being repatriated to the United States aboard the Swedish vessel *Gripsholm*. After his arrival, Emmons submitted a memorandum emphasizing the improbability of a Korean uprising against Japan. The isolation and economic straits of the average Korean produced incredible political apathy. Emmons went on to remind the administration that the Korean peninsula was situated in a precarious geographic position between China, Russia, and Japan. Korea would emerge after World War II as the object of a dangerous international rivalry, he warned, "unless such pressure could be neutralized by some effective form of international agreement to which Far Eastern Countries concerned would give their sincere effective support."[32]

China's close relationship with the KPG reinforced Roosevelt's commitment to nonrecognition. In January 1942, Clarence Gauss, the American ambassador to China, reported that Chiang Kai-shek exerted undue influence over the KPG and Kim Ku. Cho So-ang, Gauss explained, was evasive and secretive when questioned about the KPG's financial resources.[33] Moreover, Washington began to receive reports that the Chinese intended to recognize the KPG and extend a promise of postwar independence. Replying to a request for confirmation, Gauss stated that although the rumors were accurate, Chiang opposed precipitate action.[34] Then Chinese Foreign Minister T. V. Soong suggested in a letter to Roosevelt dated April 8 that the Allies issue a joint declaration promising Korea postwar independence and extending formal recognition to the KPG. Soong proposed as well that the Allies train and equip a "Korean People's Army" capable of conducting sabotage and espionage operations inside Korea. This Chinese *démarche* caught the administration off guard. Undersecretary Welles instructed Gauss to impress upon Chiang the importance of delay, since "parallel and cooperative action . . . would be desirable so far as practical."[35]

In all probability, Welles consulted Hornbeck regarding Soong's proposals. In a memorandum dated April 11, Hornbeck confessed deep misgivings about issuing a promise of postwar independence for Korea. Some form of "dominion status" would be necessary after the war, he contended, because Korea would be incapable of immediate self-government. Hornbeck also believed that "the work of the peacemakers be not impeded by hampering antecedent commitments to a greater extent than is necessary." For the present, he advised delay.[36] Welles followed Hornbeck's recommendations closely in responding to Roosevelt's request for comments on Soong's letter. Recognition of any single exile group, he insisted, would be premature, while a promise of independence would "lack reality." Welles acknowledged, however, that the plan for creating an irregular Korean army possessed some merit. Furthermore, the Allies should attempt to foster unity within the Korean exile movement.[37] Welles subsequently convinced other members of the administration that it would be unwise to adopt a more positive course with respect to Korea. On April 15, the Pacific War Council formally endorsed the State Department's position.[38]

China's attitude toward Korea reflected Chiang's fear of Soviet intentions in Asia. He was well aware of Soviet and Chinese Communist support, both financial and moral, for the Korean guerrillas fighting in northern China. After Moscow entered the war against Japan, Chiang expected Stalin to utilize the Korean exiles in Siberia and Manchuria to control Korea's postwar development. Even before receiving the American response to Soong's initiative, Chiang called publicly for immediate Allied recognition of the KPG.[39] Secretary Hull, in a memorandum to Roosevelt, worried that if China recognized the KPG, the Soviet Union would sponsor its own group.

Given China's geographic and historic association with Korea, however, the secretary of state thought the United States should not
object strongly to whatever policy Chiang decided to follow. Nevertheless, Hull instructed Gauss to impress upon the Chinese that the
administration would not endorse China's recognition of the KPG.
Washington had decided that the Korean exile movement not only
lacked unity but had "little association with the Korean population
in Korea."[40]

Washington's reticence compelled Chiang to reconsider his position. In May, Gauss informed Hull that the Chinese had decided to
postpone action until the KPG was sufficiently representative of the
entire Korean exile movement to warrant Allied recognition.[41] In all
probability, both American and Chinese leaders then explained to
the Koreans that unity was a prerequisite for international support.
Han Kil-su quickly submitted to the State Department a plan for
military and political consolidation. It provided, in part, for the creation of a "unification committee" composed of representatives from
both the KPG and the guerrilla forces in northern China.[42] Although
Hull doubted whether the Koreans would be able to cooperate, he
forwarded Han's proposal to Gauss for comment. The ambassador
shared Hull's pessimism about the prospects for success. Subsequently, rivalry and friction within the Korean independence movement persisted and all efforts for cooperative action collapsed.[43]

Curiously, Chinese involvement with the Korean exiles at Chungking caused the Roosevelt administration to view China as a greater
threat than the Soviet Union to Korea's independence. Chiang and
T. V. Soong, however, never ceased emphasizing China's determination that Korea would emerge as a free nation after the war. Chinese
leaders insisted that they sought international responsibility, not
domination, in the postwar world.[44] Yet the United States found
ample reason to question China's motives. In October 1942, Kim Ku
granted Chiang control over the KPG's military force in return for
financial aid. Rumors spread that the agreement also bound "Korea
to China in any postwar scheme in the Orient."[45] American diplomats at Chungking immediately probed the KPG for information
about the terms of its arrangement with Chiang. Cho So-ang
explained to Vice-Consul O. Edmund Clubb that the KPG's financial limitations necessitated dependence on China. Kim Ku could
terminate the relationship, he suggested, if the United States agreed

to extend Lend Lease assistance.[46] Such incidents merely increased American suspicion of China's expansionist intent and reduced the likelihood of American backing for the KPG.

Roosevelt and his advisors believed that China would play a key role in the success of postwar American policy in Korea and elsewhere in Asia. State Department official John Carter Vincent argued, for example, that the United States should rely on Chiang to encourage the KPG to broaden its support.[47] At the same time, the administration recognized that China had to develop internal strength if it expected to help with the preservation of peace in the Pacific. In a letter written to Chiang (which Roosevelt revised and approved), Owen Lattimore, an expert on Asia and Roosevelt's special advisor to Chiang, stressed the importance of China acting as a "policeman" in Asia. China's participation in the postwar reconstruction of Asia was essential, but the United States would not permit Chiang to dominate any of China's neighbors. Moreover, Lattimore reminded Chiang that the views of the Soviet Union were extremely important. As a result, "it would be undesirable to exclude Russia from such problems as the independence of Korea," because this would merely create tension and spawn mistrust among the Allies.[48]

China's apparent determination to reestablish its preeminence in Korean affairs added urgency to the task of formulating a specific program for trusteeship. During the autumn of 1942, the Division of Far Eastern Affairs proposed that a committee comprised of representatives from China, New Zealand, and the United States develop a united policy on Korea. This committee would seek "to cooperate with the Korean people in setting up and establishing a national government of Korea and . . . to assist in forming a temporary trusteeship under which there would be given advice and technical assistance." State Department officials also proposed measures for coordination with the Soviet Union.[49] If all went well, the major powers would agree to a trusteeship arrangement and thereby ensure the postwar sovereignty of Korea.

Wartime policy toward Korea illustrates Roosevelt's emphasis on Allied cooperation as the crucial requirement for the preservation of American security interests in Asia. In one address, the president pointed to the Philippine experience as a model for the future development of small nations in Asia. American policy toward the Philippines had been based on two important factors. The first is that there be a period of preparation, through the dissemination of education and the recognition and fulfillment of physical and social and economic needs. The second is that there be a period of training for ultimate independent sovereignty, through the practice of more and more self-government, beginning with local government and passing on through various steps to complete statehood.[50]

Roosevelt insisted that the stability of independence depended on training and experience in self-government.

Significantly, the Institute of World Affairs provided something of a trial balloon for Roosevelt's trusteeship policy for Korea. In December 1942, that organization recommended just such a plan, but the Korean exile reaction was immediate and hostile. The KPG and Rhee denounced the proposal as Japanese-inspired and promised to resist any postwar mandatory status. Kim Ku declared that Korea "must secure her . . . absolute independence," arguing that Korea's political experience was of longer duration than Japan's. Cho So-ang reminded the administration that trusteeship "does not accord with the Atlantic Charter, is against the will of 30.000.000 [sic] Koreans and ever endangers peace in Eastern Asia." The State Department provided Roosevelt with reports of these protests. Thus, the president knew at an early date that the most vocal Korean exiles opposed the heart of his Korea policy.[51]

Trusteeship offered little to the KPG, but Kim Ku still had reason for optimism. Late in 1942, Rhee had established a close relationship with Colonel Preston Goodfellow of the Office of Strategic Services (OSS). Together, Rhee and Goodfellow drew up a plan to train and equip one hundred Koreans for espionage and sabotage activities inside Korea. Goodfellow then urged the State Department to recognize the KPG and adopt the program, asserting that any delay "might be of benefit to the Soviet Union in any plans the latter might have in respect of Korea."[52] But State Department officials quickly rejected Goodfellow's scheme, doubting both the unity and the ability of Kim Ku's regime. Moreover, the administration feared that "to try to steal a march on the Soviet Union . . . might create fresh difficulties."[53]

Surprisingly, Great Britain registered greater opposition to Roosevelt's policy in Asia than either the Soviet Union or China. In November 1942, Prime Minister Winston Churchill had made it quite clear that the British Empire would remain intact following World War II.[54] Accordingly, Lord Halifax, British ambassador in Washington, submitted a proposal pertaining to Allied policy in colonial areas to the United States in February 1943. Halifax recommended that the Allies issue a declaration promising total destruction of the Axis aggressors and the creation of world peace in the postwar era. He then noted that while some colonial peoples were sufficiently advanced to ensure their own security and prosperity, others required experience in self-government and international guidance prior to independence.[55]

Britain therefore proposed that the Allies designate "trustee" nations to develop social, economic, and political institutions in the less advanced colonial areas in the interests of world peace and commercial activity. Colonial policy was an important item on the agenda for Anglo-American discussions when, in March 1943, British Foreign Minister Anthony Eden visited Washington. While in the United States, Eden conferred primarily with Roosevelt, Welles, and presidential advisor Harry Hopkins. But Hull was interested in discussing the Halifax proposal on colonial peoples and met with Eden privately on March 22. After Eden had summarized the British position, Hull countered that any colonial policy had to emphasize the development of sufficient experience in self-government to guarantee complete independence without external interference of any kind. Hull believed that the British proposal did not go far enough in this respect.[56]

Hull then offered an alternative plan stressing maximum local participation in self-government and rapid realization of independence. During discussions with Roosevelt that same day, Eden expressed concern over too broad an application of trusteeship and overreliance on China's role in postwar affairs. Hopkins noted the divergence of opinion between Britain and the United States when he stated later that "it becomes clearer all the time that Eden thinks very little of a trusteeship and would rather have the full responsibility in the hands of one country."[57] On March 27, Roosevelt conveyed to Eden his general approval of Hull's proposal. The president declared that the Allied policy toward dependent peoples had to possess universal applicability. Roosevelt advocated international control over Indochina and the Japanese-mandated islands. Furthermore, "Korea might be placed under an international trusteeship, with China, the United States and one or two other countries participating."[58] Eden reacted favorably to Roosevelt's comments but said that Hull's proposal was not the final word. Hopkins privately voiced optimism, thinking that Britain would not demand a restoration of colonial rule in all areas. Hull agreed. On March 29, he acknowledged that his proposal was subject to revision.[59]

In reality, the American proposal deeply disturbed Eden, who worried about its wider implications for the British Empire. Eden decided nevertheless to hold his criticism in reserve until a later date. In his public evaluation of the conference, Roosevelt claimed that discussions had produced Anglo-American agreement in virtually every area. Yet his inability to announce any specific policy decisions indicated the inconclusive nature of the results. On March 29, Welles discussed the outcome of the Anglo-American negotiations with T. V. Soong. The United States and Britain, he explained, intended to treat China as a major power after the war. Roosevelt and Eden also had agreed to trusteeship for Korea, but the specific features of the plan would await consultations with the Soviet Union.[60]

Despite the ambiguous results of the Roosevelt–Eden discussions, the United States proceeded with the development of comprehensive plans for a trusteeship system. In April 1943, the State Department finished a specific proposal providing for machinery to implement, supervise, and finance a program of international control. The memorandum discussed positive guarantees for international respect regarding the principle of a commercial "open door" and then made reference to Korea, among other areas, as suitable for the application of trusteeship. Korea was "to be temporarily administered by the Council, anticipating independence probably with close economic ties with China."[61] Although the administration had linked American policy firmly to trusteeship, it never vocalized the decision. The State Department would issue only a formal promise that the Allies intended to strip Korea from Japan and accord it national self-determination after the war.[62]

Allied military victories in the Pacific during 1943 forced the United States to consider more seriously the impact of Soviet entrance into the war against Japan. In August, Hornbeck prepared a memorandum outlining Soviet objectives in the Pacific, which accentuated the importance of Russian national security. As in Europe, Stalin's paramount political objective was to establish political dominance over neighboring countries. Hornbeck then observed that Moscow maintained close ties with a group of Korean guerrillas in Siberia and thus possessed an excellent instrument for exploiting unrest and exerting Soviet influence in postwar Korea. In a letter to Hull, Hornbeck referred to the likelihood of conflict in Korea after World War II:

> The future of Korea . . . will, it is believed, be of paramount importance to Soviet Russia and to China. The Soviet Union may be expected to exert efforts to assure that the future government of Korea is favorably disposed and ideologically sympathetic to the Government of the U.S.S.R. Such a policy, if vigorously pursued by the U.S.S.R., would almost certainly conflict with Chinese policy in regard to Korea.

Soviet agreement to trusteeship, not to mention that of China and Britain, thus assumed added importance. While Roosevelt and his advisors favored trusteeship for moral reasons in certain areas, strategic considerations were to dominate American thinking with respect to Korea.[63]

For Rhee, Stalin's expansionist ambitions demanded immediate American recognition and assistance for the KPG. In a letter to Roosevelt, Rhee pointed out that "the danger of Russian expansion, so feared and dreaded by the United States forty years ago, has not entirely disappeared."[64] Chiang too stated his anxiety over Soviet aspirations with increasing frequency during 1943. He feared that Stalin would exploit postwar unrest in Korea to achieve total sway. To avoid such a result, China exhorted the United States to join in a tripartite conference with Britain to devise an agreement guaranteeing Korea's independence. For Soong, trusteeship provided the best means to attain this objective. In private discussions with Hull, Hornbeck insisted that a neutral Korea was essential for peace and stability in Asia and would require Soviet-Chinese agreement. During the autumn of 1943, the Roosevelt administration concentrated on achieving an accord among all four major powers for a Korean trusteeship.[65]

Hull resumed his struggle to convince the British of the wisdom of trusteeship at the first Quebec Conference in August 1943. After twice refusing to discuss the matter, Eden finally stated his disapproval of the emphasis on "independence" in the American proposal. Several British dominions preferred continued imperial ties, despite the liberty to request independence at any time. Hull reassured Eden that the United States did not favor immediate independence but believed it necessary to emphasize freedom as the ultimate goal. Eden stood his ground and British antipathy toward Hull's proposal continued for the balance of the war.[66]

In October 1943, Hull traveled to Moscow for a meeting of the Allied foreign ministers. Prior to his departure, Roosevelt instructed his secretary of state to pursue a definite agreement favoring wide application of the American trusteeship proposal.[67] The president hoped that through publicizing the plan, popular support would force British, Chinese, and Russian compliance. Thus, on October 29, Hull raised the issue of dependent peoples and distributed his proposal. He regretted that there would not be enough time to discuss colonial policy in depth. Eden reminded Hull that Britain had registered its opposition to the American plan just three days earlier. Soviet Foreign Minister V. M. Molotov, on the other hand, agreed that the issue was of vital importance and deserved study and discussion.[68] As a result, the other Allied leaders could expect the United States to raise the issue of trusteeship during the upcoming meetings at Cairo and Teheran in November 1943.

Roosevelt was determined to obtain British and Chinese consent for a three-power trusteeship for Korea at Cairo and was confident of Chiang's support.[69] On November 23, however, Chiang strongly endorsed the issuance of an immediate statement promising Korean independence. This statement apparently revived Roosevelt's apprehensions, since he conveyed fears regarding China's "wide aspirations" to Churchill the following day. Roosevelt suspected that Chiang sought military occupation of Korea at the end of World War II.[70] Despite such anxieties, Roosevelt, Churchill, and Chiang agreed to issue the famous Cairo Declaration, which promised the liquidation of the Japanese Empire and the restoration of Chinese sovereignty over Manchuria and Formosa. With respect to Korea, the Cairo Declaration stated that the Allies, "mindful of the enslavement of the people of Korea, are determined that in due course Korea shall become free and independent."[71] Although the declaration avoided specific references to trusteeship, the Allies unquestionably had indicated an intention to impose on Korea an interim period of international supervision.

Many scholars have faulted Roosevelt for including the phrase "in due course" in the Cairo Declaration, contending that the United States should have satisfied Korean demands for immediate independence. "The proviso," Bruce Cumings writes, "reflected only the paternalistic, gradualist element of the trusteeship idea that deemed no colonial people fit to run their own affairs without a period of tutelage."[72] In reality, the president recognized that postwar peace and stability in the Pacific depended upon the support of Britain and China for joint action in the reconstruction of Korea and other nations. Nor did Roosevelt seek to dominate the peninsula, as Cumings contends. Roosevelt realized that Chiang's aspirations in Korea would alarm Stalin. He therefore pursued an international trusteeship to reassure not only Britain and China but also the Soviet Union and thereby preserve Korea's independence.

Thus, Roosevelt left Cairo for Teheran intent upon gaining Stalin's assent for the Cairo Declaration and a Korean trusteeship. On November 30, Stalin said that although he could make no commitments, he approved of the Far Eastern communiqué. Roosevelt later avowed that Stalin had agreed specifically that "the Koreans are not yet capable of exercising and maintaining independent government and that they should be placed under a 40 year tutelage." Roosevelt must have been pleased about his Korea policy when he left Teheran; the Allies now appeared united behind trusteeship.[73]

Upon his return to Washington, Roosevelt announced that the Cairo Declaration involved "the restoration of stolen property to its rightful owners and the recognition of the rights of millions of people in the Far East to build up their own forms of self-government without molestation."[74] Despite the president's promise of eventual independence, the Korean exile movement was thoroughly dissatisfied with the Cairo Declaration and demanded clarification of the phrase "in due course." Kim Ku charged that Allied policy toward Korea was insulting and disgraceful because it envisioned a continuation of outside control.[75] Such criticism of American policy was unjustified. All indications pointed to Korean unpreparedness for independence and to the probability of Sino-Soviet disagreement over the best means of reconstructing the Korean nation. Trusteeship afforded the dual benefit of ensuring that the Koreans could protect their own sovereignty and security while reducing the likelihood of conflict among great powers in a strategic area. It was specious to argue that Korea's long history of self-government negated forty years of Japanese colonialism.[76]

Early in 1944, the State Department began to develop concrete plans for the occupation and administration of Korea. In March, the Inter-Divisional Area Committee on the Far East produced three papers dealing with American policy aims in Korea.[77] Hiss and Clubb were principally responsible for the proposals dealing with occupation and administration. The first paper stressed that Korea had been subject to Japanese rule for decades and exiles had doubtful local support and negligible administrative experience. The largest group of exiles were Soviet-trained and imbued with Communist ideology, numbering approximately thirty-five thousand compared to one thousand located at Chungking. If the Soviet Union entered the Pacific war, the paper predicted that it would occupy a large portion of the Korean peninsula.[78]

The second paper recommended that since the United States, Britain, China, and the Soviet Union each possessed legitimate interests in Korea, all four nations should participate in the occupation and administration of the country. The Allies had to avoid one-power control at all costs. If zonal division proved unavoidable, the occupying nations should fashion a unified administration as quickly as possible. Although the paper called for military responsibility over civil affairs in the American zone, it offered no details pertaining to the proposed trusteeship. The third paper, which dealt with the utilization of Japanese technical personnel, would have considerable importance later. It postulated that the Allies might not be able to maintain industrial operations with Korean and military personnel alone. Thus, the United States intended to permit Japanese technicians to continue to function where security allowed and qualified Koreans were not available. Events soon demonstrated that the paper was mistaken when it speculated that "politically undesirable results of the use . . . of Japanese technical . . . personnel can to a great extent be controlled and will be more than offset by the practical need for the use of such personnel."[79]

On May 3, 1944, the State Department Postwar Programs Committee discussed and approved the three papers with only minor alterations. The committee members generally agreed that an international trusteeship was "absolutely necessary" for Korea because of past competition among the great powers over the strategic area. The only change advised that the United States should not accept an exclusive mandate in Korea under any circumstances.[80] Simultaneously, the administration reaffirmed its policy of impartiality toward the exile movement. It denied the KPG's request for representation on the United Nations Relief and Rehabilitation Administration (UNRRA), arguing that it would exploit this concession for political gain. American leaders believed that "the efforts of each faction are directed toward obtaining political capital, prestige and monetary assistance for that faction and not for the benefit of a concerted effort directed toward liberation of Korea."[81] Despite constant prodding from the KPG during the spring of 1944, Washington would not recognize the Kim Ku regime.[82]

China's behavior after the Cairo Conference eliminated any lingering doubts within the Roosevelt administration about the wisdom of its Korea policy. Reports from Chungking revealed that Chiang, in an effort to foster unity, had threatened to terminate Kim Ku's subsidy unless the KPG ended its factional divisions.[83] Such highhanded treatment drew criticism from not only the Koreans but also American diplomats in China. Clubb told Chiang that the United States would not tolerate interference in the rights of China's neighbors to determine their own destiny. Only cooperation, not unilateral acts, he admonished, would guarantee China's security in the postwar world. Foreign Service Officer John S. Service was far more distressed about Chiang's preoccupation with Soviet expansionism. Observing that the generalissimo's obsession was producing divisions in the Kuomintang, Service warned that Chiang was weakening China and contributing to economic deterioration, thus forcing the people in Korea and on Formosa to turn to Moscow as a last resort.[84]

By the summer of 1944, Soviet agreement to a specific trusteeship agreement for Korea also had assumed added importance. In July, Roosevelt approved General Douglas MacArthur's plans for the invasion of the Philippines and the final assault on Japan. American military leaders had convinced Roosevelt that Soviet participation in the Pacific war would render the defeat of Japan infinitely easier. Yet, despite Stalin's concern for Soviet security in Asia, Moscow would not enter the war against Japan until victory in Europe was certain. The OSS noted ominously that if, at the moment of Soviet entry, "the trend in Europe is toward competition among the powers, a corresponding competition can hardly fail to arise in the Far East." Stalin would not accept, for example, a Korean government more favorable toward China than toward the Soviet Union. Given Chiang's determination to reestablish preponderant Chinese influence in Asia, the report advised that Sino-Soviet conflict in Korea was highly probable.[85]

Washington's dilemma was clear. The United States desired Soviet entry into the war against Japan, but it feared that China would be unable to cooperate with Moscow for the preservation of peace and security in the area. Hull believed that trusteeship, while reassuring the Chinese, would prevent any undesirable political ramifications stemming from Soviet participation in the Pacific war. He therefore intended to delineate Allied policy on dependent peoples at the Dumbarton Oaks Conference in August 1944. American military leaders, afraid that discord among the Allies would delay Soviet entry and thereby prolong the Pacific war, forced Hull to postpone action on colonial policy. The War Department observed pessimistically that any trusteeship agreement would be irrelevant, since "the fall of Japan will leave Russia in a dominant position on continental Northeast Asia, and . . . able to impose her will in all that area."[86]

State Department officials manifested greater optimism about the future of American policy in Korea, but they saw the need for more positive steps. Assistant Secretary Berle now implored the administration to approve and implement Rhee's plan for the creation of a Korean espionage army. If the United States utilized the KPG, he argued, it not only could hasten the defeat of Japan but also forestall Soviet mastery in postwar Korea.[87] Hornbeck, on the other hand, accepted the Soviet occupation of Manchuria, Mongolia, and Korea at the end of the war as an unavoidable probability. To check further Stalinist expansion, he advocated providing Chiang with sufficient military aid and diplomatic support for the creation of a strong China. Since the United States and Britain would be concentrating on defeating Japan, only China could construct a barrier to Soviet aggression elsewhere in Asia.[88]

China's internal political and economic problems, however, undermined the logic of Hornbeck's strategy. As early as May 1944, Roosevelt suggested during a cabinet meeting that Chiang's regime would not survive for the duration of the war. Perhaps worse, Chiang's expansionist ambitions continued to alarm American representatives in China. Langdon, now consul general at Kunming, reported that the Chinese were more interested in establishing hegemony in Tibet, Mongolia, and Korea than fighting Japan.[89] Allied agreement still seemed the best method for preserving postwar peace. By August 1944, the administration was contemplating an Allied conference to reach agreement on military government in the territories recaptured from Japan.[90]

In October 1944, Moscow satisfied American desires for a Soviet commitment to enter the Pacific war. Stalin informed the American ambassador to the Soviet Union, W. Averell Harriman, that Moscow would declare war on Japan within three months after the defeat of Germany. He then asked Harriman what concessions Russia could expect in return for participation in the war. Harriman quickly alerted Roosevelt that China's future would be in jeopardy if the Allies disagreed on the postwar reconstruction of Asia. Secretary of War Henry L. Stimson seconded this assessment, pointing out that only firm agreements would provide a sound foundation for the postwar peace settlement and guarantee American security in the Pacific.[91]

American military strategy thus played a critical role in the administration's deliberations regarding Korea during the first month of 1945. The Joint Chiefs of Staff (JCS) even recommended that the Soviets occupy the entire peninsula at an early date to prevent Japanese reinforcement of the home islands prior to the American invasion. Despite Admiral William D. Leahy's vigorous dissent, Roosevelt endorsed Russian participation in the Pacific war at the earliest possible moment to ensure a quicker and less costly victory. Consequently, the Roosevelt administration rejected any action that might arouse Soviet suspicion of American intentions. Trying to limit Stalin's participation in the postwar reconstruction of Asia would only undermine China's position and place Korea's independence in doubt.[92] As Roosevelt left for his meeting at Yalta with Churchill and Stalin, his main objective was to confirm plans for Soviet entry into the Pacific war while gaining an Allied agreement that would produce a strong China and an independent Korea.

State Department officials had drawn specific plans for Korea in preparation for the Yalta Conference, which followed the recommendations of the Pacific War Council reports formulated during the spring of 1944. This briefing paper placed a high priority on inter-Allied participation in the occupation and civil administration of the Korean peninsula, suggesting a four-power trusteeship if the Soviet Union entered the Pacific war. The achievement of a detailed agreement was essential if the Allies expected to avoid prolonged occupation or any delay in granting independence. The paper pointed out, however, that it "would seem advisable to have Soviet representation on an interim administration regardless of whether or not the Soviet Union enters the war."[93]

Thus, on February 9, 1945, Roosevelt raised the issue of Korea during discussions with Stalin at Yalta and proposed a three-power trusteeship. The president pointed to American experiences in the Philippines and surmised that the Korean trusteeship would last twenty to thirty years. Stalin responded that the shorter the duration the better. He then inquired about the stationing of foreign troops on the peninsula. After agreeing that there should be no foreign military forces stationed in Korea, Roosevelt mentioned the "delicate" matter of possibly excluding the British from participation in the Korean trusteeship. The president believed that there was no necessity for British inclusion in the arrangement. Stalin disagreed, pointing out that Churchill would be offended and might "kill us."[94] Roosevelt and Stalin thus agreed to a four-power trusteeship for Korea in addition to the concessions the Soviet Union received in return for participation in the Pacific war. Roosevelt undoubtedly left Yalta confident that Soviet-American agreement had enhanced the likelihood that both China and Korea would be independent and sovereign nations at the end of World War II.[95]

Scholars have debated at length the wisdom of the Yalta agreement on the Far East. With the benefit of hindsight, many have argued that Soviet participation in the Pacific war was unnecessary. Some writers have termed Roosevelt's failure to consult China as "unpleasant and immoral"; others have charged that the president "gave away" too much.[96] Regardless of the larger aspects of the Yalta agreements, one can hardly find fault with the Korean arrangement. All Korean experts in Washington agreed that Korea was not sufficiently prepared for self-government, and American experiences with the exile movement added credence to this conclusion. More important, Korea represented a particularly difficult problem for the administration because Washington harbored conflicting fears of British imperialism, Chinese expansionism, and Soviet communism. Roosevelt speculated that Allied support for trusteeship would permit Korea to develop enough political skill and experience for the maintenance of independence.

Strategic considerations dictated American advocacy of a Korean trusteeship and underlined the realism of the policy. In view of past Sino-Soviet competition for control in Korea, only an Allied agreement could encourage an atmosphere of stability in that area. Success would depend upon mutual trust, harmony, and cooperation which would be impossible if Korea obtained sovereignty and independence prematurely.[97] Trusteeship would foster Allied cooperation and coordination, thus ensuring Korea protection until it developed the capacity for self-direction. Roosevelt was aware that the Korean exiles violently opposed trusteeship, but all the facts at his disposal and the strategic nature of the peninsula demanded a period of preparation prior to full independence.

Roosevelt therefore listened to his experts on Korea and adopted the realistic policy of pursuing Allied endorsement of a Korean trusteeship. Without such an agreement, almost certainly Korea once again would become the victim of a great power rivalry.[98] The United States then would have to apply considerable military power to guarantee Korea's independence. By 1945, Roosevelt refused to divert any resources from operations contributing directly to the defeat of Japan. The president also remained committed to Allied cooperation as the basis for peace in the postwar world. After forty years of Japanese domination, Tyler Dennett concluded early in 1945, Korea had emerged as "a test case in international cooperation and international good faith."[99] American indifference toward Korea was at an end.

CHAPTER 2

Captive of the Cold War

Wartime negotiations among the Allies suggest that a Soviet-American dispute over the fate of postwar Korea was far from inevitable. At Yalta, Roosevelt and Stalin agreed that since Korea would be incapable of self-government after liberation from the Japanese Empire, a four-power trusteeship would provide the best method for removing the peninsula from the arena of great power rivalry and conflict. Both Washington and Moscow appeared to share the common goal of creating stable economic and political conditions in postwar Korea and favored cooperation and coordination to achieve this result.[1] Roosevelt's Korea policy was realistic because it acknowledged that the Soviet Union, by virtue of its superior military position on the Asian mainland, could occupy Korea unilaterally at the end of the war. The president believed that national self-determination in Korea was possible only if the Allies managed to satisfy divergent national interests in this strategic area and fashion a new balance of power underwriting Korea's independence.

For Stalin, the preservation of Russian national security in northeast Asia was of much greater importance than the fulfillment of idealistic principles. He would not permit the emergence of a Korean government hostile to the Soviet Union under any circumstances. Yet the Russian leader had good reason to believe that Soviet-trained Koreans, not to mention domestic Communists and those returning from exile in China, would exercise strong influence in any postwar Korean provisional government.[2] Stalin's opposition to the maintenance of foreign troops in Korea during trusteeship implied that he expected significant popular appeal for communism and the Soviet Union in Korea after World War II. Although Stalin may have sought direct domination over Korea as a war aim, no conclusive evidence exists to substantiate this contention.[3] It is quite possible that Stalin's support for trusteeship was sincere, since he believed the arrangement would not prevent Moscow from having decisive influence over the development of postwar Korea.

Unfortunately, neither Roosevelt nor Stalin anticipated that the defeat of Japan would follow so quickly after Allied victory in Europe. Consequently, the Allied leaders had not discussed trusteeship in detail at Yalta. They had decided instead that a five-member committee, composed of representatives from member nations on the proposed Security Council of the United Nations, would meet prior to the San Francisco Conference to discuss the terms of an international trusteeship system.[4] Chiang, however, remained uneasy about Russian ambitions in Asia and therefore resisted any further delay on the trusteeship issue.[5]

During conversations in Washington, the Chinese advocated immediate recognition of the KPG and adoption of a plan for three-power military administration of Korea after liberation; there would be Soviet participation once Moscow entered the Pacific war. State Department official Joseph Ballantine replied that the United States was willing to exchange proposals but would not alter its policy of nonrecognition. Vincent advised newly appointed Secretary of State Edward R. Stettinius, Jr., that Sino-Soviet discussion "of the future position of Korea should be avoided if possible and, in any event, should be 'purely exploratory'." Final determination of Allied policy on Korea required simultaneous consultations between all nations with legitimate interests on the peninsula.[6]

Soviet behavior in Eastern Europe shortly after Yalta frightened the Roosevelt administration and appeared to substantiate Chiang's warnings. Growing American fears of "sovietization" soon would undermine and ultimately destroy Washington's confidence in the advantages of a Korean trusteeship. Syngman Rhee acted quickly to cultivate and exploit this emerging Soviet-American rift and thereby encourage the United States to provide positive assistance to the Kim Ku regime. He notified the administration that Moscow intended to dominate Korea and had created a "Korean Liberation Committee" in Siberia for this purpose. Rhee's attempt to equate Korea with Poland was unmistakable. He demanded an immediate investigation and reiterated the wisdom of extending recognition to the KPG.[7] When the State Department ignored his advice, Rhee charged that Roosevelt had agreed at Yalta to permit Soviet dominance over postwar Korea. "It is not the first time," he bitterly reminded the

Roosevelt administration, that "Korea was made a victim of secret diplomacy."[8]

American leaders did not dispute the accuracy of Rhee's assessment of the strength of the Korean Communist movement. Sources indicated that Moscow had trained and equipped more than 100,000 Korean guerrillas for the liberation of Korea. American intelligence reports also revealed that the Chinese Communists had created a "Korean Revolutionary Military-Political School" at Yenan to train Korean leaders for the postwar administration of Korea.[9] Although the KPG persistently claimed that it was the strongest and best-organized resistance group, such information provided abundant contrary evidence. Kim Ku's regime still manifested extreme factionalism, while its principal leaders appeared preoccupied with the pursuit of personal ambition and financial gain. Consequently, the administration persisted in its refusal to recognize the legitimacy of any Korean exile group.[10] American leaders hardly welcomed the prospect of a Communist victory in Korea, but they confronted the fundamental problem of being unable to find a capable and popular exile group worthy of aid and support.

Trusteeship and impartiality thus remained the hallmarks of Roosevelt's Korea policy. Yet Stimson and Secretary of the Navy James V. Forrestal harbored serious doubts about Roosevelt's entire approach toward the reconstruction of colonial areas. American responsibility for dependent peoples and power for action, they argued, lacked specificity. Both men worried that the United States would surrender areas of strategic importance in the Pacific but other nations would not follow suit. During a cabinet meeting on March 9, 1945, Roosevelt dismissed these arguments and reaffirmed his support for a system of trustee nations deriving authority from the proposed postwar international security organization. Three weeks later, Stettinius flatly insisted on discussing the trusteeship issue at the San Francisco Conference.[11]

Washington envisioned the inclusion of Korea in this larger trusteeship formula. As a result, the State Department rejected all requests for Korean representation at San Francisco.[12] In the meantime, the administration was formulating a specific program for the occupation and interim administration of Korea. During November 1944, Roosevelt had created the State–War–Navy Coordinating Committee (SWNCC), comprised of assistant secretaries from each department, to improve civil-military consultation on major policy questions. By the following March, the SWNCC had completed work on a series of papers dealing with the treatment of the Korean population during occupation, the utilization of Koreans and Japanese in the military government, and the deportation of Japanese to their home islands. The SWNCC also discussed the composition of the occupation force and the relationship between the temporary military administration and the future international supervisory authority. By April, American plans for the transition period between liberation and trusteeship were virtually complete.[13] That same month, Roosevelt stated publicly that the United States not only advocated postwar international control over Japan's mandates but intended to participate in these trusteeship arrangements as well.[14]

Roosevelt's hope for postwar peace and security in Korea depended entirely upon the maintenance of Allied cooperation and mutual trust. Understandably, Stalin's determination to achieve hegemony in Eastern Europe caused Roosevelt to question the Soviet leader's willingness to fulfill Allied agreements. Nevertheless, when Roosevelt died on April 12, he still was optimistic about the chances for continued Soviet-American cooperation despite sharp differences over such issues as the fate of Poland.[15] If the future of Soviet-American relations in Eastern Europe appeared uncertain, however, American policy toward Korea remained intact.

Whether Soviet aspirations in Asia would have become a source of serious concern in Washington had Roosevelt lived will always be debatable. But Harry S. Truman's assumption of the presidency marks a distinct turning point in American policy toward Korea. Almost from the outset, the new president expected Soviet actions in Asia to parallel Stalin's policies in Eastern Europe. Although no clear relationship existed between the two areas, Truman preferred to view Soviet expansionism as an unchanging force in postwar international affairs. Less than one week after taking office, Truman reversed Roosevelt's position on the territorial trusteeship issue and adopted the Stimson–Forrestal approach. Washington now would resist any detailed discussion of the machinery for an international trusteeship system at the San Francisco Conference.[16] This decision signaled the beginning of Truman's search for an alternative in Korea that would eliminate any opportunity for Soviet expansionism.

Truman responded to postwar instability in colonial areas in a thoroughly predictable fashion that reflected his deep devotion to the American tradition of political liberalism. Like most Americans, the new president assumed that liberated peoples, if given a free choice, would opt to follow the American model for political, economic, and social development in reconstructing their nations. Convinced of American altruism and the superiority of its political system, Truman hoped to use the power and influence of the United States to foster the emergence of democracy and economic development in colonial areas.[17] In theory, the realization of the Wilsonian dream of world-wide democracy, the ultimate goal of Truman's approach, would produce an international system of maximum stability. More important, if nations shared American values and institutions they would be more likely to act in partnership with the United States after World War II. In practice, however, Truman's policy toward colonial areas came to focus almost exclusively on sponsoring governments that favored the achievement of American objectives regardless of their affection for democratic principles.

For Truman, Soviet actions in Eastern Europe demonstrated Stalin's determination to prevent the realization of his postwar aims in liberated areas. With considerable justification, the new president acted to counter the perceived threat of Soviet expansionism, despite the obvious limitations on the power of the United States.[18] Many of Roosevelt's advisors welcomed Truman's decisive and confrontational style. These men had become dissatisfied with Roosevelt's continued faith in Moscow's willingness to cooperate with the United States and encouraged the new president to adopt a tougher stance on negotiations with the Russians. Ambassador Harriman informed Truman during private discussions that Stalin was imposing his will on the nations of Eastern Europe in utter disregard of all wartime agreements. Admiral Leahy and Secretary Forrestal joined Harriman in asserting that Soviet behavior represented a serious political and strategic threat to American security. In response, Truman assured his advisors that he intended to be firm in his dealings with Stalin and to insist upon the fulfillment of Allied agreements.[19]

Truman embraced without hesitation the hard-line attitude toward Stalin that many of Roosevelt's advisors recommended. "To a man of Truman's blunt, contentious personality," John Lewis Gaddis has observed, "this tough policy must have seemed particularly congenial."[20] Almost immediately, Truman came to rely on those advisors most dedicated to a policy of toughness toward the Soviet Union.[21] On April 23, 1945, the president told his advisors that when he met Molotov that day, he would assume a firm stand on Poland and demand Soviet compliance with the Yalta agreements.[22] Although Truman had not abandoned completely the possibility of a reconciliation with the Soviet Union,[23] his uncompromising rhetoric indicated that he did not fully share his predecessor's confidence in the probability of Soviet-American cooperation for the resolution of postwar international problems.

Leahy applauded the change in American policy. With the imminent defeat of Germany, he noted, "no particular harm can now be done to our war prospects even if Russia should slow down or even stop its war effort in Europe and Asia."[24] Thus the Truman administration began at an early date to question the wisdom of continuing to encourage Soviet involvement in the war against Japan. While harsh words would not induce the Soviet Union to retreat from Eastern Europe, the situation in Asia was different. The United States could prevent a repetition of this unhappy series of events in East Asia because the Red Army was not in occupation of the area. American leaders recognized that if American forces liberated the nations under Japanese domination, Soviet expansion in Asia would not emerge as an international headache in the postwar world.

Harriman believed that the United States should resist Soviet expansionism not only in Europe but in Asia as well. He explained to Truman that the United States could expect the same pattern of Soviet conduct in Manchuria and Korea that existed in Poland and Rumania. On May 12, 1945, Harriman reminded the president that Russian intervention in the Pacific war would entail Soviet participation in the occupation and reconstruction of Japan. In regard to Korea, Harriman alleged that during discussions at Yalta, Stalin had questioned the need for trusteeship should the Koreans prove able to create a "satisfactory government." American diplomatic records provide no evidence of such a statement, yet Harriman advanced the opinion that unless the United States acted to prevent it, there "would unquestionably be a Bolshevik or Soviet government" in Korea after World War II.[25]

That same day, Undersecretary of State Joseph C. Grew registered similar anxiety over the consequences of Soviet entry into the Pacific war. He urged Truman to obtain Stalin's assent to a number of conditions prior to the implementation of the Yalta agreement on the Far East. Grew desired Moscow's unqualified support for Chiang Kai-shek's regime in China, respect for the terms of the Cairo Declaration, and agreement to the establishment of a four-power trusteeship in Korea. Grew echoed Harriman's sentiments when he argued that the Soviet Union, in refusing to fulfill its promises in Europe, had sacrificed American trust. Thus, the United States had every right to deny Stalin a free hand in Asia.[26] Grew's recommendations, coupled with Harriman's remarks, apparently had a significant impact on the president. Their assessment, as subsequent events would reveal, appears to have convinced Truman that if Stalin occupied the Korean peninsula unilaterally, Korean self-government meant sovietization.

Korea's fate ultimately was tied to American military capabilities and Truman's strategy for the defeat of Japan. If Stalin refused to endorse a Korean trusteeship, only prior American occupation of the peninsula could guarantee independence for Korea. American military leaders never ceased emphasizing that defeating Japan was the highest priority. General MacArthur, for example, pressed Washington not to delay a frontal assault on the heartland of Japan. He also favored early Soviet participation in the Pacific war, remarking cynically that Moscow would inevitably seize Manchuria and Korea after World War II and might as well earn these territorial acquisitions.[27]

Grew disagreed strongly with MacArthur's reasoning. If Moscow entered the Pacific war, he predicted, the Soviet Union would become the dominant power in postwar Asia and constitute an even greater threat than Japan to American security. Grew offered the dire prophecy that once the Soviets entered the war, "Mongolia, Manchuria, and Korea will gradually slip into Russia's orbit, to be followed in due course by China and eventually Japan." To avert such a distasteful turn of events, the United States had to maintain its military power and control several strategic areas in the Pacific. It would be fatal to trust the Soviet Union, Grew warned, since Stalin would exploit any sign of American weakness. While Grew kept these visions of falling dominoes in Asia largely to himself, Harriman did not hesitate to convey similar apprehensions to Truman. On May 15, the ambassador exhorted the president to meet with Stalin and Churchill within a few weeks to terminate the developing split among the Allies. Harriman specifically mentioned the Korean trusteeship as an issue urgently in need of clarification.[28]

An apparently insoluble dilemma challenged Truman's foreign policy in Asia. Washington had to devise a military strategy for victory over Japan that would provide a strategic position from which the United States could react effectively in the face of anticipated Soviet duplicity. On May 21, the War Department presented its case in defense of MacArthur's two-phase plan for the defeat of Japan. It specifically rejected Grew's suggestion that the United States withhold the Yalta concessions until Stalin promised to respect the sovereignty of China and Korea. The War Department judged the entire issue to be of academic interest alone because "Russia is militarily capable of defeating the Japanese and occupying Karafuto, Manchuria, Korea and Northern China before it would be possible for the U.S. military forces to occupy these areas." On the positive side, Soviet intervention in the war against Japan would save American lives. Faced with conflicting advice, Truman rejected the State Department's position. The president had no choice. American options were few and far from promising. On May 25, Truman approved MacArthur's plan.[29]

Truman soon realized, as had Roosevelt, that if the United States could not use its military power in Asia to compel Soviet caution, diplomatic agreement was the only alternative. At the same time, his tough rhetoric had done little to alter Stalin's policies in Eastern Europe. Rather than arranging for an early meeting of Allied leaders, as Ambassador Harriman desired, the president decided instead to dispatch Harry Hopkins to Moscow in an effort to resolve outstanding differences and encourage Soviet compliance with Washington's definition of the Yalta agreements. State Department officials formulated a detailed set of instructions regarding Korea for the Hopkins mission. It was particularly important, they believed, for Hopkins to obtain Soviet support for a four-power trusteeship which guaranteed equal representation in the Allied civil administration of postwar Korea. Moreover, Hopkins was to gain Stalin's assurance that the international arrangement would concentrate on training reliable *local* Koreans for self-government. The State Department hoped that, through Allied cooperation, trusteeship would produce a Korean government that truly reflected the free will of the people. Both the War and Navy departments approved these recommendations, but both counseled delay regarding specific arrangements pertaining to military matters.[30]

Thus the Truman administration had resurrected Roosevelt's policy of seeking Allied agreement for a detailed trusteeship arrangement in postwar Korea. All this planning was superfluous, however. At Moscow, Hopkins completely ignored the State Department's instructions and failed to discuss in detail Korea's future. He merely reminded Stalin that at Yalta, he and Roosevelt had agreed only to a four-power trusteeship of unspecified duration. Hopkins then suggested that the period of international guidance might last as long as twenty-five years, but certainly a minimum of five years. Stalin avoided a discussion of specifics as well, but he reaffirmed his unqualified endorsement of a four-power trusteeship for Korea.[31]

Stalin's comments to Hopkins provided little evidence that the Soviet leader intended to undermine the Korean trusteeship agreement. Soviet conduct in Eastern Europe did suggest the possibility, however, of Stalinist ambitions in Asia. Chiang never doubted for a moment Moscow's sinister plans for Korea and continually pestered Washington about the existence of Soviet-trained Korean guerrillas in Siberia. Nevertheless, the United States closely adhered to its impartial stance. In June 1945, Grew announced publicly that the KPG did not have "at the present time the qualifications requisite for obtaining recognition." That same month, during discussions with T. V. Soong, Truman stated confidently that Stalin intended to endorse both Chiang's government in China and international control over postwar Korea.[32] The president apparently had made up his mind to trust Stalin to fulfill his promises. In the absence of a willingness to use military power, Truman had no other alternative.

Military strategy buttressed Truman's commitment to a trusteeship for Korea. In contrast to Grew and other officials in the State Department, American military leaders appeared far less troubled about Soviet aspirations in Asia. Following the collapse of Germany, Truman's military advisors continued to lobby for direct invasion and Soviet entry in the Pacific war as the best method for defeating Japan. Late in May 1945, the Joint Chiefs of Staff (JCS) discarded a proposal to land troops in Manchuria and Korea, because such an operation would prolong the war and have doubtful impact on the Japanese war machine. Since Washington's highest priority was the rapid subjugation of Japan, "the employment of substantial United States forces in Manchuria and Korea is not justified."[33] A military strategy of this sort precluded the achievement of a sufficiently powerful military position after the war from which the United States could block Soviet expansion on the northeast Asian mainland.

Truman gave final approval to MacArthur's invasion plan—codenamed "Olympic"—at a White House strategy meeting on June 18, 1945. At that time, Marshall managed to convince Navy Chief of Staff Admiral Ernest R. King that the United States had to occupy the island of Kyushu prior to a direct invasion of Japan. His strongest argument emphasized that operation Olympic was the least expensive strategy available, particularly in comparison with a potential landing on the Korean peninsula:

> An outstanding military point about attacking Korea is the difficult terrain and beach conditions which appear to make the only acceptable assault areas Fusan *(Pusan)* in the southeast corner and Keijo *(Seoul)*, well up the western side. To get to Fusan, which is a strongly fortified area, we must move large and vulnerable assault forces past heavily fortified Japanese areas. The operation appears more difficult and costly than assault on Kyushu. Keijo appears an equally difficult and costly operation. After we have undertaken either one of them we still will not be as far forward as going into Kyushu.

Marshall's strategy called for Soviet military movement into Manchuria and Korea in order to accept the surrender of Japan's forces.[34] Although Truman approved these recommendations, he decided to delay final authorization for the second phase of the plan—the actual invasion of Japan—since he was aware that the successful testing and use of the atomic bomb might make this costly operation unnecessary.[35]

American military planners already were preparing for the possible sudden collapse of Japan in the aftermath of an atomic attack. On June 14, the JCS instructed MacArthur and Pacific Fleet Commander Chester W. Nimitz to be ready for Japan's premature surrender and to formulate plans for the early occupation of Japan. On June 29, Truman approved this action and also authorized an intensification of bombing and blockade operations against Japan in order to reduce the enemy's ability to resist an American invasion. If a direct assault on Japan became necessary, Washington believed that operations could commence no earlier than November 1, 1945.[36]

While completing military plans, the Truman administration also prepared for the Potsdam Conference. Early in May 1945, Secretary Stimson requested a policy position paper on Korea from the State Department. The report pointed out that widespread unrest and demands for agrarian reform were likely in Korea after years of imperialist exploitation. The lack of an experienced and representative group of exiles to assume governmental responsibilities would compound Korea's problems. Alarmingly, the report predicted that Moscow would "probably occupy all or part of Korea" and insist upon establishing a friendly government composed of exiles trained in the

Soviet Union. The State Department reasoned that poor economic conditions in postwar Korea would encourage a favorable reception of Communist ideology; a Soviet-sponsored socialist regime "might easily receive popular support."[37]

For the State Department, Korea's future hinged upon the ability of the Allies to agree on a multinational invasion force for the liberation of the peninsula. Although American participation was important, it was vital that none "of the interested countries alone . . . invade Korea," particularly the Soviet Union. Final briefing papers for Potsdam urged that the Allies designate Korea a combined zone of military operations under a single command. A four-power international supervisory body would replace the military government as quickly as possible to shorten the duration of occupation and reduce the chance of tension within the Grand Alliance. At Potsdam, American planners hoped to obtain "agreement among the three powers that, with China's anticipated cooperation, they will jointly support whatever measures appear best adapted to develop in Korea a strong, democratic, independent nation." Finally, the State Department wanted Truman to elicit from Stalin specific assurances of his concurrence with the Cairo Declaration.[38]

Truman's Korea policy thus envisioned the achievement of independence in three stages consisting of Allied occupation and military government, international administrative supervision, and finally complete sovereignty.[39] Significantly, American military leaders approved the State Department plan but warned that the United States "should not attempt to back up the Cairo Declaration with armed force."[40] There appeared to be no cause for anxiety, however, since Moscow still advocated a trusteeship for Korea. In July 1945, Stalin raised the Korean issue during consultations with T. V. Soong for the development of a postwar Sino-Soviet treaty ratifying the Yalta agreement on the Far East. Molotov commented that the Korean trusteeship proposal was unusual and unprecedented, thus requiring a detailed understanding among the Allied nations most concerned about Korea's future. Soong was evasive. He later told Harriman that he was afraid Moscow intended to install Soviet-trained exiles in the postwar Korean government and thereby dominate the nation. Harriman fully shared Soong's apprehension. He implored Truman to have the State Department prepare "a detailed discussion of the character of the proposed four-power trusteeship for Korea" in anticipation of the Potsdam Conference. Evidently the president acted on this advice, since Leahy cabled instructions to Grew for the preparation of such a study while en route to Germany.[41]

News of the successful testing of the atomic bomb reached Truman on the day he arrived at Potsdam. Stimson recorded in his memoirs that at this point the president began "losing his interest" in Soviet entry into the Pacific war.[42] The atomic bomb soon would have a decisive impact on American policy toward Korea. As later developments would reveal, both Truman and his newly appointed Secretary of State James F. Byrnes hoped that employing the atomic bomb against Japan would end the war quickly. While their primary reason for using the bomb was to save American lives, Truman and Byrnes surely must have recognized the diplomatic and strategic benefits of an early Japanese surrender. If the Pacific war ended prior to Moscow's declaration of war on Japan, the United States could avoid the numerous anticipated complications entailed in Russian participation in the reconstruction of Japan. Furthermore, Japan's premature surrender would permit the United States to occupy Korea unilaterally and avoid the distasteful necessity for trusteeship.

Stimson sensed the danger associated with leaving anything to chance. He insisted that an agreement on the multinational occupation of Korea remained of vital importance:

> If an international trusteeship is not set up in Korea, and perhaps if it is, these Korean divisions [in Siberia] will probably gain control, and influence the setting up of a Soviet dominated local government, rather than an independent one. This is the Polish question transplanted to the Far East.[43]

Japan's rapid surrender, however, would preempt Soviet entrance into the Pacific war, thereby eliminating the possibility of a sovietized Korea. For Truman and Byrnes, the atomic bomb would offer an avenue of escape from the Korean dilemma.

Stalin's comments at Potsdam convinced Truman that such a strategy in Korea was feasible. On July 17, Stalin stated that he would not declare war on Japan until China ratified the terms of the Yalta agreement on the Far East. Truman countered that there existed certain misunderstandings about the provisions of the accord. For example, the United States believed that the Chinese port of Dairen ultimately was to become a free port under the supervision of China. On the following day, Stalin announced that the Soviet Union would not be prepared to wage war against Japan before August 15, 1945.[44] These initial exchanges confirmed that if the United States could compel Japan to surrender during the first two weeks of August, it could pre-empt Soviet entry into the Pacific war. Byrnes privately proposed that the Allies issue an ultimatum demanding Japan's capitulation within two weeks and threatening complete destruction after that deadline. If Soong stood firm in resisting Soviet demands for acceptance of the Yalta concessions and Stalin delayed military action in Asia, the atomic bomb would bring the prompt defeat of Japan, he reasoned, "and this will save China."[45] Concurrently, such a chain of events would preclude Soviet control over Dairen and Korea as well.

On July 22, the Allied leaders addressed the issue of international trusteeship. Stalin pointed to Molotov as the expert on the subject and suggested that the time had come to consider specific areas, such as the Italian colonies and the mandated islands. British Foreign Minister Anthony Eden's sharp rejoinder was "Do you want our mandates?" Stalin replied that there were other mandates deserving attention; the Allies could also exchange views on Korea. Churchill openly objected to further discussion of the matter, but Truman stated his willingness to refer the trusteeship issue to the Council of Foreign Ministers. An acrimonious and prolonged discussion then ensued regarding the fate of the Italian colonies, as Churchill displayed marked suspicion of Moscow's motives and intentions in the Mediterranean. Reluctantly, the prime minister agreed to allow the Council of Foreign Ministers to consider the Soviet proposal on trusteeship.[46] Unfortunately, the Allies had reached no firm agreement on Korea because the trusteeship question had become entangled in the unrelated issue of Anglo-Soviet competition in the Mediterranean. The last and best chance to settle the Korean problem amicably had been lost.[47]

Leahy later observed, accurately, that the long discussion of trusteeship had in fact revealed nothing definite about Stalin's postwar aspirations.[48] Britain's overreaction made the task of assessing Soviet intentions no easier. Moscow's proposal on trusteeship was inoffensive enough, while the Soviet Union possessed a clear right to lay claim to certain Axis mandates. Additionally, the Yalta agreements called for Allied negotiations to determine the specifics of an international trusteeship system.[49] Events in Eastern Europe, however, prevented Truman from trusting Stalin. On July 23, Harriman visited Stimson and painted a disturbing picture of Stalin's ambitions in colonial areas. The Soviet Union, Harriman avowed, was no longer acting like a continental power but was seeking "to branch in all directions." He speculated that Stalin favored an immediate trusteeship in Korea in order to demand a similar settlement on Hong Kong and Indochina. Aware that Britain and France would scoff at these proposals, Harriman believed Stalin and Molotov would "probably drop their proposal for trusteeship of Korea and ask for solitary control of it."[50]

Stimson conveyed Harriman's scenario to Truman during a conversation later that morning. The president agreed that Russia was demonstrating an expansionist intent, but he thought Stalin was bluffing. Stimson reported in his diary that Truman then assured him that "the United States was standing firm and he was apparently relying greatly upon the information as to S-1." Earlier that day, Truman had received word that the United States would be able to drop an atomic bomb (code-named "S-1") on Japan during the first week of August.[51] Truman and Byrnes undoubtedly reasoned that if they used the bomb on schedule and Japan surrendered, the Soviet Union would not enter the Pacific war and only China, Britain, and the United States would occupy Korea.

Marshall did not share Truman's certitude about this atomic strategy. On July 23, he explained to Stimson that Soviet troops already were massing in Siberia and the United States could do little to prevent the seizure of any territory Stalin desired. Marshall continued to favor early Soviet intervention into the Pacific war as the surest method for hastening Japan's subjugation. During the Allied military meeting the following day, the American position seemed to reflect Marshall's viewpoint. Soviet General Alexei E. Antonov stated that the Soviet army would enter the war in the latter part of August. He then requested a target date for American invasion of Korea. Marshall responded that the United States did not contemplate a landing in Korea in the near future. Since Korea was vulnerable to air attacks from Japan, Washington was concentrating instead upon the early occupation of Kyushu as its highest priority.[52]

Ignoring the planning papers, American military leaders thus agreed to nothing specific regarding the multinational occupation of Korea. The Allies did not establish clear lines for ground action because, as Truman explained in his memoirs, "it was not anticipated by our military leaders that we would carry our operations to Korea." On July 26, Allied military planners met again and settled upon zones of air and naval operations, resulting in the division of Korea

just below the 41st parallel. When Antonov asked for the exact date
of the American landing on Kyushu, Marshall replied that the
United States would begin its operations in late October. Antonov
expressed approval but openly voiced a preference for American
action at an earlier date.[53]

Meanwhile, American military experts apparently had altered their
position and now accepted Truman's argument that victory over
Japan no longer required Soviet participation in the Pacific war. On
July 25, Marshall requested MacArthur's plan for the occupation of
Japan in the event of sudden surrender, as well as information on
force requirements for landing in Korea. In response, MacArthur's
headquarters informed Washington that its plan, although incomplete, provided for the occupation of Japan twelve days after surrender and entry into Korea at a later date. Marshall immediately
ordered MacArthur to prepare to enter Japan on a moment's notice
and to establish the occupation of the Korean peninsula as his next
highest priority.[54] During discussions with Lieutenant General John
E. Hull, Marshall asserted that if the Soviets invaded Korea, the
United States had to gain control over at least two major ports. Therefore, Marshall and Hull settled upon a line near the 38th parallel as a
minimum policy objective, but they remained hopeful that Japan's
quick surrender would make Soviet military action in Korea unnecessary.[55]

Washington's Korea policy thus experienced a remarkable transformation during the Potsdam Conference. Truman and his advisors
decided to discard trusteeship in anticipation of a rapid end to the
Pacific war that would forestall Soviet occupation. At the Council of
Foreign Ministers meeting on July 23, Byrnes joined Eden in opposing detailed discussion of trusteeship. Molotov agreed to table his
proposal, but he asked that the final protocol provide specifically for
adding the trusteeship issue to the agenda at the foreign ministers
meeting scheduled for September in London. When Eden objected,
Molotov insisted that the protocol at least note Moscow's raising of
the issue. After some discussion, Byrnes said he would support this
request.[56]

But when the Allies drafted the final protocol, both Byrnes and
Eden opposed the inclusion of a general statement on trusteeship.
Byrnes claimed that Moscow's proposal was unacceptable because
"trusteeship as presented in the Soviet request was much broader and
it was not his understanding that the Big Three had agreed to refer it

to the Council of Foreign Ministers." Molotov relented, declaring that he did not intend to press the matter.[57] And so, the final protocol noted only that the Allies had examined the trusteeship issue but referred specifically to the Italian colonies alone. Stalin grudgingly acquiesced, commenting that "the Russians were given very little in this paper."[58] Despite Moscow's genuine desire for an accord at Potsdam, the Allies had reached no definite agreement on Korea.

Truman's strategy for preempting Soviet intervention in the Pacific war proceeded according to plan. On July 26, the United States and Britain issued the Potsdam Declaration threatening Japan with "prompt and utter destruction" if it did not surrender forthwith. Two days later, Byrnes confessed to Forrestal that "he was most anxious to get the Japanese affair over with before the Russians got in." If Moscow moved into Japanese-occupied areas, he warned, "it would not be easy to get them out."[59] In the absence of a response from Japan, the United States dropped atomic bombs on Hiroshima and Nagasaki on August 6 and 9 respectively. In the interim, the Soviet Union declared war on Japan and subscribed to the Potsdam Declaration, which included a reaffirmation of the pledge to strive for the eventual independence of Korea.[60] For Truman, Stalin's decision to enter the war earlier than American leaders expected was tragic because it spoiled his strategy for achieving unilateral American occupation of Korea. Yet one scarcely can fault the Soviet Union for trying to avert a *fait accompli* and to ensure participation in the determination of Japan's future. At the same time, Soviet entry into the Pacific war meant that the United States was not in any position to guarantee Korea's postwar independence.[61]

Byrnes observed in his memoirs that Japan's abrupt surrender was no surprise.[62] Soviet intervention in the war before August 15, however, certainly was unexpected. The SWNCC already was putting the finishing touches on plans for the occupation of Japan. On July 28, MacArthur had cabled his proposal—code-named "Blacklist"— which anticipated unified Allied occupation and administration of Japan, Korea, the China coast, and Formosa. Nimitz opposed MacArthur's plan and sent Admiral King his own proposal, which called for a more rapid occupation under the direction of the navy. This interservice feud forced the JCS to defer action until after the Potsdam Conference. While MacArthur and Nimitz searched for a compromise, Marshall considered including Korea in the Chinese zone of operations and cabled Lieutenant General Albert C. Wedemeyer,

American advisor to Chiang in Chungking, requesting comments on the idea.[63]

Moscow's declaration of war against Japan meant that the United States could not afford the luxury of further delay. On August 10, Washington ordered Wedemeyer to assist China in occupying Formosa and Korea, while American forces would concentrate on Japan. That same day, Japan asked for surrender terms and the administration made one final stab at preventing unilateral Soviet occupation of Korea. Byrnes instructed the SWNCC to prepare a plan for Soviet-American occupation of Korea, a plan which would divide the peninsula into two zones with the line as far north as possible.[64] American military leaders cautioned against such action, pointing out that the United States had limited men and material in that area whereas the Soviet army was poised on the Korean frontier. Nevertheless, late in the evening on August 10, the SWNCC instructed Colonels C. H. Bonesteel III and Dean Rusk to find a line in Korea that would harmonize the political desire to have American forces receive the surrender as far north as possible with the obvious restrictions on the ability of the United States to reach the area. Bonesteel and Rusk decided upon the 38th parallel as a suitable dividing line, and the SWNCC incorporated this provision into a preliminary draft of "General Order Number One."[65]

Truman, recognizing the need to act quickly, informed the other Allies immediately of the general terms for accepting Japan's surrender. He still hoped that the United States could occupy most of Korea. On August 11, the president ordered Marshall to arrange for the occupation of Dairen and a port in Korea as soon as possible.[66] In all probability, Truman was acting on the advice of Edwin W. Pauley, the American representative on the Allied Reparations Commission, who sent an urgent cable from Moscow on the same day recommending quick and drastic measures:

Conclusions I have reached through discussion on reparations and otherwise . . . lead me to the belief that our forces should occupy quickly as much of the industrial areas of Korea and Manchuria as we can, starting at the southerly tip and progressively northward. I am assuming all of this will be done at no risk of American lives . . . and occupancy to continue only until satisfactory agreements have been reached between the nations concerned with respect to reparations and territorial rights and other concessions.[67]

The following day, Harriman strongly endorsed this call for vigorous action:

> Considering the way Stalin is behaving in increasing his demands on Soong, I recommend that these landings be made to accept surrender of the Japanese troops at least on the Kwantung Peninsula and in Korea. I cannot see that we are under any obligation to the Soviets to respect any zone of Soviet military occupation.

The ambassador urged that the United States establish a position in Korea and at Dairen as soon as practicable.[68]

At the SWNCC meeting of August 12, Admiral M. B. Gardner outlined Truman's desires. He proposed a revision of General Order Number One to include the 39th parallel, thus providing for American occupation of Dairen and a larger portion of the Korean peninsula. After referral of the proposal to the JCS, the SWNCC reaffirmed the 38th parallel, probably because the Red Army already had entered Korea. Brigadier General George A. Lincoln explained that the Soviet Union certainly would not accept the new line, nor could the United States hope to reach a point further north.[69] Thus the final draft of General Order Number One possessed only minor changes with respect to Korea; on August 15 Truman dispatched it to the other Allies for approval. The JCS was satisfied that the 38th parallel provided both for American control over the capital of Korea and for sufficient land to apportion zones of occupation to China and Britain. Yet American leaders did recognize that the Allies had not agreed on administrative and governmental control in Korea after occupation. The JCS advised Truman to obtain a detailed agreement, while at the same time formulating a policy directive for the eventual American occupation commander.[70]

Years later, Truman tried to portray the 38th parallel decision as the product of military expediency and convenience. "Of course," the president remarked in his memoirs, "there was no thought at the time other than to provide a convenient allocation of responsibility for the acceptance of the Japanese surrender."[71] In reality, political and strategic considerations were primarily responsible for American actions.[72] Truman and his advisors believed that if Stalin dominated the Korean peninsula, the Soviet Union could undermine Chiang's position in China and put the security of Japan in jeopardy. Consequently, at the time of Japan's surrender, the occupation of some portion of Korea was Washington's second priority in Asia. But after Truman jettisoned trusteeship, the United States lacked sufficient power to block Soviet military occupation of the entire peninsula once Moscow had entered the Pacific war. Many American leaders therefore doubted whether Stalin would accept the 38th parallel, and a "short period of suspense" followed Washington's transmission of General Order Number One to Moscow. The JCS, anticipating a rejection, was prepared to order the immediate occupation of Pusan.[73] Just as Stalin maintained good faith on trusteeship, however, he also cooperated in approving expeditiously the terms for accepting Japan's surrender.[74]

Scholars have criticized the decision to divide Korea into two zones of occupation and have advanced a variety of reasons to buttress their position. Certainly the line was ill advised as a permanent boundary since it cut across natural areas of geographic, cultural, and climatic continuity. On the west coast, for example, a small peninsula was part of the American zone, yet the United States possessed no land connection to the area.[75] Given the alternative of complete Soviet control, however, Truman thought he had registered a major success. Stalin's decision to intervene prematurely in the Pacific war had ruined Truman's strategy for excluding the Soviet Union entirely from participation in Korea's reconstruction. As a result, the United States had to settle for half a loaf since its troops were more than six hundred miles away. The Red Army could have occupied the entire peninsula before American forces reached Korea, and Truman discerned the political importance of avoiding such an event. If he had not, the United States would never have pressed for a zone of occupation in that area.[76] Only Stalin's willingness to accept the surrender agreement made possible the subsequent American occupation of southern Korea. Under these circumstances, control over half the Korean peninsula was the most that Truman or anyone else could have expected.[77]

Stalin's decision to approve the American proposal for a division of Korea at the 38th parallel was not the product of altruism. In all probability, Stalin sought to maintain good relations with Truman in order to gain an equal voice in determining Japan's future development.[78] At the same time, the Soviet leader undoubtedly viewed the 38th parallel as a suitable division of Korea into spheres of influence. Furthermore, the line possessed some basis in history while constituting a rough halving of the peninsula.[79] Stalin would have preferred a unified and "friendly" Korea, but he opted for temporary division in the interests of Allied harmony. If Soviet-American relations deteriorated, he could always retain control in the north and preserve Soviet national security interests in northeast Asia. An attempt to seize the entire peninsula, on the other hand, would only alarm Washington and thereby negate possible concessions in more important areas.[80]

A concern for the future of Japan also dominated Truman's thinking with respect to Korea. The president believed that American occupation of southern Korea would make it infinitely easier for the United States to maintain its command over the postwar reconstruction of Japan. When Stalin requested a Soviet zone of occupation in Japan, Truman refused to comply. Harriman, suspecting that Moscow sought to dominate Japan and Korea, enthusiastically applauded this decision. On August 27, the ambassador met with Stalin and apparently won his consent for the American occupation policy in Japan. Significantly, Stalin chose to respect the Korean arrangement despite Truman's obduracy regarding Japan and subsequently instructed the Red Army to remain north of the 38th parallel.[81] Yet Truman's refusal to grant Stalin an equal voice in determining policies for Japanese reconstruction meant that a successful resolution of the Korean problem would be far more difficult. Nevertheless, Truman remained outwardly optimistic. At a news conference less than a week after Japan's surrender, the president confidently declared that Korea eventually would emerge as a free and united nation.[82] In view of the absence of firm Allied agreement on Korea, wishful thinking alone could justify Truman's cheerful outlook.

Perhaps worse, the administration never seemed to understand that the United States would face the formidable task of implementing change in postwar Korea in a chaotic atmosphere. The impact of Japanese colonial policies had been particularly traumatic on Korea's traditions and social institutions.[83] Anti-imperialist agitation and revolutionary nationalism soon would complicate the formulation and implementation of American policy in Korea.[84] Most underground leaders inside Korea favored rapid and sweeping reforms, but few had developed specific programs for postwar reconstruction. None could claim experience in government, while factional disputes prevented united and purposeful action.[85] The only major group that enjoyed some semblance of cohesion was the Communist party, which had operated as the leading element in the resistance move-

ment. The undisputed leader of the Korean underground was Pak
Hŏn-yŏng, a Communist who had organized cells and published a
radical newspaper before and during World War II.[86] On the eve of
Soviet-American occupation of Korea, the Communist party, according to Gregory Henderson, was extremely popular, particularly
among young Koreans, and "unquestionably the country's most
important single political force."[87]

Not surprisingly, the Japanese fretted more about Pak's underground than the feeble exile movement and therefore suppressed
news of Allied military victories. In the aftermath of Japan's surrender, Japanese leaders in Korea understandably feared retaliation from
their former servants. When the Koreans staged a spontaneous holi-
day to celebrate Japan's defeat, replete with wild parties and mass
demonstrations, these anxieties were if anything heightened. Consequently, Japan's governor, Noboyuki Abe, approached local Korean
leaders and proposed the formation of a transition government capable of maintaining law and order and protecting Japanese lives and
property. Prominent leftist leader Yŏ Un-hyŏng agreed to cooperate,
but only on the condition that Abe release all political prisoners,
guarantee freedom of speech, and forswear interference in Yŏ's political activities. Abe consented and on August 15 Yŏ formed the "Committee for the Preparation of Korean Independence."[88]

Yŏ promptly set about creating local "people's committees" (an
unfortunate designation) to assume administrative responsibilities.
Most Koreans accepted Yŏ's authority, including landlords, intellec-
tuals, students, and professional people. Moreover, Yŏ's 135 committees were able to exploit the Japanese communication, transportation, and administration network, rapidly achieving a measurable
amount of centralized power. These people's committees quickly
expropriated the land of the Japanese and their Korean collaborators,
while simultaneously releasing all political prisoners. By the end
of August, Yŏ had emerged as the unchallenged de facto leader
throughout Korea.[89]

Soviet entry into Korea enhanced this leftward drift. Yŏ realistically
recognized that he had to respect the desires of the Communists if he
expected Soviet backing. Predictably, wealthy Koreans were the subject of ever increasing political repression, as Yŏ's collaborators denied
conservatives any influence in political affairs. When news arrived in
late August that the United States would occupy southern Korea, Yŏ
decided to convene a national congress in Seoul to provide his regime

with the stamp of legitimacy. Although Yŏ tried to attract a broad cross section of Korea's political leadership, the Communists managed the proceedings from the outset and engineered the adoption of a platform advocating the expropriation of all Japanese property and recommending a number of other specific social and economic reforms. On September 6, 1945, in the presence of six hundred delegates, Yŏ proclaimed the establishment of the "Korean People's Republic" (KPR) and promised elections before March 31, 1946.[90]

Meanwhile, the Truman administration was involved in a frantic scramble to achieve military occupation of Korea without delay. Washington initially had instructed Stilwell's Tenth Army to land on the Korean peninsula. After Truman ordered American military leaders to occupy the peninsula ahead of schedule, the JCS contemplated relying on Chinese forces to enter Korea but then turned to the Twenty-Fourth Corps stationed on Okinawa and under the command of Lieutenant General John R. Hodge. As in other areas, availability and a need to act fast dictated the choice of the occupation force.[91] Obviously, Truman and his advisors had not anticipated that the United States would have to occupy only a portion of Korea on such short notice. In fact, on the eve of American entry into Korea, Washington had not completed a definitive set of directives for the commander of the occupation force.

Shortly after Japan's surrender, MacArthur began to formulate detailed instructions for Hodge. On August 22, he requested information from the JCS pertaining to Allied agreements on Korea, explaining that he intended to operate on the assumption of quadripartite occupation. In reply, the JCS informed MacArthur that the State Department had no knowledge of any specific agreement regarding the occupation; the Allies had only settled upon a trusteeship for Korea after Japan's defeat. Accordingly, the JCS ordered MacArthur to administer Korea's civil affairs in a way that would facilitate the implementation of the trusteeship arrangement. Moreover, the commander of the United States Armed Forces in Korea (USAFIK) should strive to create an Allied control council in Korea for the coordination of occupation policy.[92]

Early in September, Washington cabled a directive to MacArthur clarifying these instructions. As soon as practicable after arrival, the USAFIK commander was to contact the Soviet occupation commander and propose the formation of an administrative body capable of formulating unified policies for all Korea. In accordance with established policy, the JCS authorized Hodge to utilize Japanese officials and Korean collaborators temporarily where security permitted and technical expertise was in short supply. On September 7, 1945, MacArthur formally established American control in Korea south of the 38th parallel. The next day, General Hodge and his Twenty-Fourth Corps finally landed in Korea.[93] At that time, Washington had not finished detailed guidelines for the occupation. It would be nine months before Washington would send Hodge a final directive on Korea. Forced to rely on expediency and common sense, rather than on long-range plans, American officials in Korea manifested uncertainty and vacillation from the start. One member of the American Military Government (AMG) later dubbed the United States occupation of Korea as "operation trial and error."[94]

An atmosphere of anarchy developed in southern Korea soon after American troops arrived on the peninsula. Korean exile groups encouraged internal instability by distributing copies of the Cairo Declaration that purposely mistranslated "in due course" as "immediately" or "in a few days." In his initial report to Washington, H. Merrell Benninghoff, Hodge's political advisor, observed that "southern Korea can best be described as a powder keg ready to explode at the application of a spark."[95] Hodge wisely sought assistance from local Korean leaders to deal with the threat of domestic violence. Upon requesting a meeting with two representatives from each party, 1,200 Koreans responded to the startled American general's invitation. While these politicians universally condemned any delay in the restoration of Korean self-government, there was agreement on little else. Given the revolutionary climate, it was hardly surprising that Hodge, from the outset, placed a premium on the maintenance of law and order in southern Korea. He judged even the most remote threats to the security of his command intolerable. Less than two weeks after the start of American occupation, Hodge began to send a steady stream of cables pleading for removal of the partition at the 38th parallel and military withdrawal at the earliest possible date.[96]

Early reports of Soviet behavior in northern Korea made a bad situation seem dangerously worse. After visiting the Soviet zone, an Australian journalist informed MacArthur that the Russian army was treating the people with "barbarous cruelty" and striving to replace the existing order with a "Bolshevik philosophy." Moscow's ultimate purpose, he speculated, was the establishment here not of a democratic but a Communist type of government. Their concept . . . embodies the complete reduction of the social structure to chaos, absolute integration and mass destruction. . . . I believe that you can anticipate aggressive action in support of their fundamental purpose which is not so much the establishment of a sound peace and its preservation as it is the imposition of their own philosophy of life in Japan and Korea.[97]

Many wealthy Koreans, who had fled southward following Soviet entry into the north, were relating stories to American occupation officials of looting, confiscation, and even sexual assaults. Still more disturbing, the Communists reportedly were usurping political power and organizing "people's committees."[98] For Truman and his advisors, the similarities between events in northern Korea and Eastern Europe must have been painfully obvious.

Within one month after Japan's surrender, the United States thus confronted agonizing problems in Korea. Despite Truman's desperate attempts to eliminate any possible chance for Stalinist expansion in Korea, sovietization north of the 38th parallel already seemed well under way. By contrast, the future of American occupation in southern Korea appeared fraught with dangerous complications. Yet Truman's predicament was largely of his own creation. On several occasions, Stalin had indicated a desire for an Allied agreement on trusteeship for Korea, but Truman's consistent lack of enthusiasm for a firm settlement had prevented the achievement of an accord. As a result, we shall never know whether trusteeship would have reconciled Soviet-American differences in Korea. Instead, the Soviet Union and the United States each occupied half of the peninsula, thereby requiring a diplomatic agreement to end the artificial division of Korea. Since Soviet-American relations in Europe had recently experienced a steady and serious deterioration, it was highly improbable that either Stalin or Truman would acquiesce in any agreement appreciably strengthening his adversary.[99] Thus, Korea emerged at the end of World War II as a divided nation that was not independent but a captive of the Cold War.

CHAPTER 3

In Search of a Settlement

Joint Soviet-American occupation of Korea in 1945 was among the most unfortunate legacies of World War II. From the outset, Korea's future would depend on the ability of the United States and the Soviet Union to maintain friendly relations in the postwar world. Contemporary observers immediately acknowledged the symbolic importance of the Soviet-American confrontation across the 38th parallel. If the major powers agreed to end the artificial division of the peninsula and grant Korea its independence, the world could expect future cooperation in other areas.[1] Any reason for optimism vanished, however, as Washington and Moscow began to implement unilateral policies of zonal reconstruction that totally disregarded the interests of their adversary.[2] Each nation's approach reflected its own political, economic, and social system, since both American and Soviet leaders wanted Korea to emulate their model for national development.[3] The result was the emergence of two Koreas and the peninsula became a major battleground in the Cold War. Tragically for Korea, the price of liberation from Japanese domination was dismemberment.[4]

Korea's partition was particularly undesirable because the 38th parallel separated two areas that were traditionally dissimilar. The north was rich in industry, hydroelectric power, and such minerals as coal, iron ore, and a variety of chemicals. The south, on the other hand, was much more agricultural and produced large amounts of rice and fish. More important, the two zones possessed basic social and religious differences and even were separated politically during ancient times.[5] Divergent systems of land tenure represented yet another major contrast. South Korea suffered from serious agrarian overpopulation and Japanese absentee landownership. Moreover, the American zone contained an inordinate share of rich and conservative landlords, destitute farmer-tenants, and dissatisfied workers.[6] Land-lordism was much less prevalent in the north, where plots were smaller and less productive. Finally, Japanese colonialism had shattered traditional patterns in Korea, but the process of development and modernization was incomplete as World War II came to an end. Severe dislocation, uncertainty, and tension in Korean society further complicated an already difficult situation.[7]

John R. Hodge, the USAFIK commander, lacked the necessary training and experience to deal effectively with the complex challenges he faced in Korea. A tough, gristly combat soldier who had served with distinction at Leyte, Bougainville, and Okinawa, he could boast little understanding of politics or administration.[8] Upon arrival, Hodge hardly endeared himself to the local populace when he commented tactlessly that "Koreans are the same breed of cats as the Japanese."[9] He promptly turned for information and advice to those Koreans who could speak English and had ties to American missionaries. Consequently, the AMG soon earned the derisive sobriquet "government by interpreter."[10] Declining morale within the USAFIK was another persistent problem that Hodge never managed to resolve. Inadequate housing, irregular delivery of supplies, and inferior post exchange facilities only stirred greater discontent among American soldiers already anxious to return home after the surrender of Japan.[11]

Koreans assailed the AMG almost from the moment of its creation. At his first press conference, Hodge announced that the limitations on American manpower would require the temporary utilization of Japanese administrative personnel. Protests from the Korean people were immediate and violent, producing far more confusion than the policy sought to prevent. Criticism of Hodge's action was harsh in the United States as well.[12] On September 12, Truman publicly defended the decision as a matter of practical necessity but promised to remove the Japanese officials as soon as possible. The SWNCC now saw that it would be a mistake to use Japanese officials during the occupation and ordered Hodge to abandon the policy. In Korea, Hodge had deposed Governor Abe even before receiving these instructions from Washington.[13]

Nevertheless, the administration's Korea policy was a target of continuing adverse publicity. Undersecretary of State Dean G. Acheson therefore advocated the formulation of a detailed public clarification. Such a policy statement, he suggested, should emphasize that the use of Japanese technicians was only temporary while reminding observers that the achievement of Korean independence would require "time and patience." On September 18, Truman issued a statement on Korea summarizing Acheson's arguments. It included a pledge that any Japanese officials retained in positions of importance would act wholly as "servants of the Korean people." By October 18, Hodge had removed virtually all Japanese nationals from the American zone.[14] While the incident seemed somewhat trivial, it held great significance for the future. By reacting so quickly in order to silence popular dissent, the United States had established a dangerous precedent. Korean leaders now concluded that Washington would alter policy in the face of political protests and mass demonstrations.[15]

American occupation officials never really learned how to respond to the chaotic atmosphere in Korea. Increasingly, they perceived most Koreans as impetuous children unaware of the magnitude of the Soviet threat facing their nation.[16] To foster stability, Hodge and the AMG turned to the most educated and wealthy members of Korean society for advice and support. For Benninghoff, Hodge's political advisor, the attitude of the upper class was the most encouraging aspect of Korean politics. Consequently, American representatives in Korea developed a close relationship with conservative Korean landowners and businessmen from the outset of the occupation. Not surprisingly, Hodge began at an early date to urge Washington to facilitate the return of the KPG to Korea. Acting as a figurehead government, he argued, Kim Ku's regime would stabilize the situation.[17]

Under the circumstances, Hodge's refusal to cooperate with the KPR was a foregone conclusion. Equating events in Korea with those in Eastern Europe, he easily accepted the argument that Yŏ's government was under Soviet domination and therefore subversive. Hodge summarily dismissed Yŏ's claim to legitimacy, declaring that the KPR represented only a minority of the Korean populace. He then outlawed the people's committees and created new local councils under conservative control.[18] Although the Communists did in fact dominate Yŏ's government, the KPR had demonstrated efficiency and popularity during its short period of ascendance. Genuine impartiality and a desire for national self-determination seemed to require that the United States at least cooperate with Yŏ. Yet Hodge's preference for stability and his dread of Soviet ambitions in southern Korea precluded an evenhanded approach. While officially sponsoring neither the conservatives nor the radicals, Hodge pursued policies designed to bolster rightist political power.[19]

Virtually every attempt Hodge made to fashion a political coalition around the conservatives culminated in frustration and disillusionment. Factional disagreements were so intense that unity was out of the question. "Every time two Koreans sit down to dinner," one American official lamented at the time, "they form a new political party." Benninghoff sadly admitted that the KPR was far better organized than the "democratic conservatives."[20] Undaunted, Hodge remained determined to forge a political alliance in Korea that excluded the extreme left. Early in October, Major General Archibald V. Arnold, the American military governor, announced the appointment of an "Advisory Council" comprised of eleven prominent Koreans under the chairmanship of Kim Sŏng-su, a leading conservative. Most Koreans considered the Advisory Council unrepresentative, since Kim, a wealthy prewar landlord and businessman, typified its membership. Foolishly, Hodge appointed a well-known collaborator to the body, ensuring that it would be "universally hated and distrusted throughout Korea."[21] Nevertheless, Hodge anticipated that the Advisory Council would undermine Yŏ's popularity and foster Korean self-government under conservative direction. Despite American efforts, these Korean leaders exhibited far more concern with achieving special privileges and advancing their own political status than with democratic principles.[22]

Soviet actions in northern Korea during the autumn of 1945 suggested that Moscow was much better prepared than the United States to deal with the problems of Korean occupation. Soviet officials at once established a close working relationship with local Korean Communists. Moreover, many Koreans who had accompanied the Soviet occupation force were Russian citizens or members of the Red Army.[23] Yet Stalin probably was not following a preconceived "blueprint for sovietization." It is more likely that Moscow instructed its occupation commander, Colonel General Ivan Chistiakov, to use any local Koreans who were friendly toward the Soviet Union in fashioning a provisional government.[24] On August 25, Chistiakov sanctioned the authority of the KPR, but he also consulted with other well-known leaders such as Cho Man-sik. In its initial phase, Russian occupation policy manifested notable caution, as Chistiakov permitted local Koreans to organize people's committees. In contrast to Eastern Europe, Stalin allowed the Koreans to exercise a degree of real authority. Conceivably, the Soviet leader did not believe that national self-determination necessarily would result in an anti-Soviet government.[25]

Benninghoff never doubted for a moment that the Soviet Union intended to impose a puppet regime on northern Korea as a prelude to extending its imperialist hold over the entire peninsula. Comparing Korea to Rumania, he predicted that the Soviet Union "will sovietize northern Korea as they sovietized eastern Europe." Hodge fully shared Benninghoff's certainty regarding Moscow's hostile intent. The Soviet commander in the north, he complained to Washington in an early cable, had not responded to his communications, thereby preventing any progress toward Korean independence and self-government. For Hodge, continued partition was part of the Soviet expansionist strategy in Korea, since the south's inability to obtain coal and electric power in the north was causing economic distress in the American zone. The artificial division of Korea, Hodge concluded, has "created a situation impossible of peaceful correction with credit to the United States unless immediate action on an international level is forthcoming to establish an overall provisional government which will be fully supported by occupation forces under a common policy."[26]

In China, Chiang Kai-shek already had decided that it was pointless even to attempt cooperation with the Soviets. Only active promotion of the KPG would forestall a Communist takeover throughout Korea. Chiang urged American representatives in Chungking to use members of the KPG in the military government of Korea. He even suggested formal recognition of the Kim Ku regime.[27] Administration officials in Washington understood that acting along these lines would reinforce Stalin's determination to retain his hold on the north. As early as September 3, 1945, the Soviet Union had assailed the KPG and rejected its claim to legitimacy. Writers in the Soviet press insisted that Korea had to rely on its closest neighbors for postwar economic, social, and political development. These articles mentioned Syngman Rhee by name and warned that Moscow could never be certain of Korea's friendship if individuals hostile to the Soviet Union gained political power.[28]

Consequently, the United States maintained its nonrecognition policy toward the KPG. Washington informed Chiang that it would welcome the participation of all qualified Koreans in the AMG but would withhold official status for any individual or group. On October 16, Acheson formally announced that the United States would provide transportation to Korea for all exiles. Significantly, Byrnes cabled Patrick J. Hurley, who replaced Gauss as U.S. ambassador to China, that the administration was especially interested in facilitating the return of Kim Ku and another prominent exile named Kim Kyusik. At the same time, the State Department wanted to avoid any ties with Rhee. On September 5, it had delayed the approval of Rhee's return because his passport bore the title "High Commissioner."[29] Undoubtedly, Truman's diplomatic advisors were cautious because they realized that Rhee's anti-Soviet convictions would hamper American efforts to establish contacts with the Soviet occupation commander. At this point, Preston Goodfellow interceded on behalf of his old friend and persuaded Ruth B. Shipley, chief of the State Department's Passport Division, to issue the necessary papers. Without consulting anyone, Shipley granted the passport after deciding that Rhee was "a nice patriotic old gentleman."[30]

While en route to Seoul aboard an American military transport, Rhee stopped in Tokyo for a meeting with MacArthur. During discussions, MacArthur confirmed that Rhee would receive no special considerations from the United States. Yet, in a cable to Washington, political advisor George Atcheson spoke strongly against an impartial stance:

> I believe the time has come when positive American action, in the political field in Korea, should be taken. I realize that to give open official approval or support to any one leader, group or combination, is contrary to past American thinking. But situation in Korea fully warrants such a step and there is reason to believe that unless positive action is taken to give the Koreans a start in governmental participation and organization, our difficulties will increase rather than diminish, and the Communistic group set up and encouraged by the Soviets in northern Korea will manage to extend its influence into southern Korea with results which can readily be envisaged.[31]

Apparently, MacArthur agreed with Atcheson's assessment, since Rhee returned to Korea aboard MacArthur's private plane.[32]

Upon his arrival, Hodge greeted Rhee with great fanfare, praying that this ostentatious welcome would contribute to political stability. He even provided Rhee with a room in the AMG's hotel, gas coupons, and a personal bodyguard. On October 21, Rhee appeared as an unscheduled speaker at a celebration in honor of the American occupation forces. Hodge introduced Rhee personally to a crowd of more than fifty thousand Koreans, praising him as "a great man who has given his entire life to the freedom of Korea." According to the USAFIK commander, Rhee was "a man driven from his home by oppressors who . . . has worked without personal ambition to get Korea into the family of free nations and he has lived to see this being accomplished." There can be little doubt that such favoritism engendered Soviet distrust of American motives and intentions in Korea. Rhee, in his remarks at the celebration, not only chastised the Soviet Union but also denounced partition at the 38th parallel. He declared that the people of Korea would fight to achieve reunification and would demonstrate that "we are quite able to run our affairs." Subsequently, Rhee moved expeditiously to create a political coalition under his own direction.[33]

Meanwhile, Rhee's friends in Washington were prodding the administration to sponsor Rhee. On November 5, Jay Jerome Williams, one of Rhee's wartime boosters, wrote Truman asking him to appoint Goodfellow as his personal representative in Korea. Not only had Hodge requested Preston Goodfellow's services, but Goodfellow's familiarity with Korean exile leaders would be useful in ending political factionalism in postwar Korea. John Carter Vincent, director of the Office of Far Eastern Affairs, vigorously opposed the plan, pointing out that Williams, Rhee, and Goodfellow had criticized the State Department's wartime policy on Korea.[34] Responding to Truman's request for advice, Byrnes recommended that the president permit Goodfellow to join the AMG if Hodge desired it but without any official status. Truman instructed his secretary of state to "handle the matter as you see fit." Shortly thereafter, Goodfellow traveled to Korea and became Hodge's special advisor.[35] This was an incredible blunder, but the administration innocently allowed it to happen without fully understanding its political implications. Few actions could have done more to undermine Washington's efforts to avoid being linked with Syngman Rhee.

By now, Truman's advisors had concluded that unless the United States and the Soviet Union agreed to a settlement in the near future, Korea would never achieve either reunification or independence. Further delay instead would increase the likelihood that Korea's partition would become permanent. To solve the Korean problem, the SWNCC had revived the trusteeship formula during mid-September and had begun work on a specific proposal. Washington remained hopeful as well that the Soviet occupation commander would agree to coordinate with Hodge in the implementation of uniform occupation policies. Significantly, the SWNCC instructed Hodge to create an administrative structure suitable for use throughout Korea should the final trusteeship agreement conform to American plans for reconstruction.[36] By early October, however, Hodge had informed Washington that Chistiakov still was spurning substantive negotiations. Faced with Moscow's intransigence, the administration decided to approach the Soviet government with a formal request for local coordination.[37]

Truman's diplomatic advisors worked on a draft proposal for breaking the Korean deadlock during the second week of October. To obtain firsthand information from Korea, the State Department instructed Benninghoff to return at once to the United States. During subsequent discussions, Benninghoff stated frankly that the United States could expect an improved situation in Korea only if Washington provided more civilian advisors and economic aid, created a "figurehead government," and eliminated the artificial division at the 38th parallel. Decisive steps were imperative, he warned, since popular support for the American occupation was beginning to erode.[38] Military leaders in the United States also were anxious for some sort of settlement because withdrawal from Korea was a basic element in the overall plan for American demobilization. For Secretary of War Robert P. Patterson, it was absolutely essential to reduce the number of troops in Korea at the earliest possible date. The War Department favored the creation of a Korean "constabulary army" capable of preserving law and order with help from a small detachment of American troops.[39]

By October 18, the State Department had completed work on its proposal and had obtained approval from the JCS. Four days later, the SWNCC forwarded the final recommendations to Byrnes. The plan provided that Washington would open negotiations with Moscow as soon as possible for the coordination of occupation policy in Korea, the removal of the 38th parallel partition, and the establishment of an international trusteeship.[40] To prepare the American people for the planned *démarche,* Vincent announced publicly on October 21 that the United States endorsed the principle of Allied cooperation in the supervision and guidance of dependent peoples. The United States and China already had agreed to a period of preparation for self-government in Korea, and Vincent was optimistic

about the prospects for Soviet-American cooperation in the reconstruction of that nation.[41] Alarming news from Tokyo then suddenly
brought forth a sense of great urgency. MacArthur reported that the
Soviet Union was stripping factories and industrial installations in
northern Korea and shipping these materials to Russia. He alerted
Edwin A. Locke, Jr., Truman's personal representative, that unless
the United States acted swiftly, Korea's partition would become permanent.[42]

On November 3, Byrnes informed Harriman in Moscow of the
administration's new policy decision on Korea, instructing him to
approach the Soviets with a request to end the 38th parallel as "a
closed barrier." The United States also desired adequate and regular
delivery of coal and electric power to the south, uniform fiscal policies, coastwide shipping, orderly resettlement of displaced persons,
and the resumption of interzonal trade and communications. Harriman was to ask the Soviet government to grant its occupation commander the power to negotiate locally for the realization of Korean
independence. Four days later, Byrnes further instructed Harriman to
raise with Molotov the issue of alleged Soviet removals of power sta-
tion equipment from the area along the Yalu River.[43]

Harriman immediately complied with Byrnes's directive, but he
was pessimistic about the chances for success. Stalin would not loosen
his grip over northern Korea because the area could then become a
springboard for an attack on Russia. From the Soviet viewpoint, Harriman reasoned, Korea was no different than Finland, Poland, or
Rumania. Forrestal echoed Harriman's skepticism about the prospects of Moscow's accepting the American proposal. Byrnes, he
thought, did not comprehend Soviet ideology.[44] The War Department was somewhat more sanguine. Yet it did not foresee a quick
settlement and therefore urged the implementation of a public information program to counter criticism of continued American occupation of Korea. If Soviet-American negotiations failed, however, the
War Department favored prompt withdrawal from the peninsula.[45]

Members of the State Department, by contrast, attached special
significance to the achievement of a trusteeship agreement for Korea.
The preliminary draft for such an arrangement contained no fewer
than thirty-eight articles. Alger Hiss and other State Department
officials defended the length and detail of the document. The
Korean accord, they argued, "will be the first of several trusteeship
agreements and should be a model for them."[46] Vincent confidently

assured the War Department that Soviet-American negotiations would result in the termination of the Korean partition, the creation of a trusteeship, and the withdrawal of American troops. Vincent added, however, that Stalin's willingness to accept the American proposal would depend to a large extent on the ability of the USAFIK commander to be impartial toward the various political factions in southern Korea. Recognition of a particular group, he cautioned, might "encourage the Soviet commander to sponsor a similar group in his zone and thus postpone establishment of a unified Korea." Vincent's advice was unnecessary, since the War Department already had dispatched a warning to Hodge. Noting Soviet hostility toward Rhee, it had reminded the USAFIK commander that close relations with Rhee would tend "to jeopardize success of United States negotiations . . . regarding 38°."[47]

Truman's Korea policy thus had come full circle during 1945, as the administration returned to the trusteeship formula as the only way short of war to achieve Korean independence and self-government.[48] The chances for success now were rather slim, however, since both the United States and the Soviet Union were entrenched firmly in a divided Korea. Nevertheless, Truman managed to enlist British and Canadian support for convening a meeting of the Council of Foreign Ministers at the earliest possible date to discuss Korea and a number of other issues. During these negotiations, the United States would propose "establishing an international control of Korea for a period of five or more years in preparation for self-government" and recommend that "assent of China and the Soviet Republics should be obtained through diplomatic channels."[49] On November 16, 1945, the State Department announced that the United States intended to approach the Soviet Union again in an effort to reestablish "communications, trade, and free passage of individuals" between northern and southern Korea. A positive response from the Russian government, the administration hoped, would open the way to Korea's reunification and independence.[50]

If Truman and his advisors thought that the Koreans had changed their minds regarding trusteeship, they were sadly mistaken. Rhee seized the initiative and attempted to unify all political elements around a demand for immediate self-government. His associates became the most outspoken critics of the 38th parallel partition and mobilized opposition both to trusteeship and to cooperation with the Soviet Union. Early in November, Rhee convened a conference of forty-five political parties and issued a demand for Korea's immediate independence. If the United States would recognize the KPG, Rhee and his followers promised elections within one year. The conference adjourned after adopting a resolution expressing "shock and consternation" over Vincent's proposal for a joint trusteeship in Korea.[51]

Rhee's activities constituted an intentional threat to the administration's strategy for negotiating a settlement with the Soviet Union. Yet Hodge believed that the United States should bolster the conservatives rather than restricting their activities. Economic distress in the American zone was providing the KPR with a powerful weapon for discrediting the United States, and the conservatives were eager to assist occupation officials in countering leftist agitation. The USAFIK commander appealed for American recognition of Kim Ku's government, while MacArthur offered to transport the KPG from Chungking to southern Korea.[52]

Assistant Secretary of War John J. McCloy favored approval of Hodge's recommendations. Syngman Rhee was not only reliable, he advised Acheson, but also self-confident and clear-headed in purpose. Since the Soviet Union probably would refuse to negotiate, McCloy suggested that the AMG maximize the use of Korean exiles to prepare them for the rapid assumption of governmental responsibilities.[53] Acheson would not go much beyond fostering the return of officials in the KPG to Korea without special status. Kim Ku and other members of his regime thus arrived in Korea on November 23 as nothing more than private citizens. Acheson's caution was justified. Prior to the KPG's departure from China, Chiang had provided it with a large amount of money and several Chinese advisors.[54] Although the exact nature of China's influence in Kim Ku's regime was unclear, Stalin certainly could not have been pleased about the KPG's close contacts with Chiang.

William R. Langdon, who had joined Benninghoff as a political advisor to Hodge, rejected the logic of the administration's persistent devotion to impartiality. Ironically, the man who had fathered the idea of trusteeship for Korea now advised Byrnes to jettison the policy and actively support Kim Ku's regime. Not only did "all elements and parties" consider the KPG to be "quasi-legitimate," but popular hostility to trusteeship meant that it would be foolish for the United States to continue to advocate international control. Langdon submitted a detailed plan for transferring power in Korea to Kim Ku with or without Moscow's approval. Hodge, noting the steady rise in Yŏ's popularity among the uneducated, working masses, concurred. Since Yŏ refused to renounce his claim to legitimacy, Hodge informed MacArthur that he would issue a "declaration of war" on the KPR to halt its activities.[55]

But Langdon and Hodge were overreacting. Not all the leftists were under Soviet direction, and many were simply demanding major reforms. Langdon himself admitted that it was not clear which political group enjoyed the widest popular support. Still, the political chaos in southern Korea had convinced Langdon and Hodge that the safest course was recognition of the KPG. Yet embracing the conservatives would not resolve the American dilemma; it would merely increase leftist animosity and make the chances of a settlement with the Soviet Union more remote. Perhaps worse, rising inflation, economic deterioration, and the steady influx of northern refugees into the south added to the already mounting unrest in the American zone.[56] Byrnes was aware of the precarious situation in Korea, but he apparently thought that only a Soviet-American agreement offered an answer to Washington's predicament. Stalin, he reminded Langdon, would not accept an American *fait accompli*. Langdon retorted that the Korean desire for immediate self-government was so strong that any effort to implement a trusteeship would ignite civil strife. As an alternative, he suggested Soviet-American negotiations at the governmental level for the creation of separate governments in each zone.[57]

Despite Langdon's warnings, the administration maintained its firm commitment to a Korean trusteeship, although it decided to delay the announcement of the policy until Hodge had time "to make necessary arrangements to prepare to counteract the expected unfavorable reception by the Koreans of the trusteeship plan." By late November, the SWNCC had formulated a detailed position paper on American policy in Asia for the upcoming Council of Foreign Ministers meeting in Moscow. After acknowledging that the Soviets assigned special strategic significance to Korea, the SWNCC report offered the following realistic observation:

In this regard, we must recognize that the United States occupies an exposed and untenable position in Korea from both a military and political standpoint. A prolonged occupation of Korea on our part cannot but create suspicion by the USSR that we have advanced our mili-

tary strength in East Asia to points beyond those which are necessary
and requisite for the security of the United States. . . .

Washington therefore should anticipate and accept the Soviet desire
for inordinate influence in Korea. The paper recommended trusteeship as a means of lessening the likelihood of Russian domination,
reducing tensions in northeast Asia, and permitting American withdrawal. If Stalin insisted upon exclusive control, however, the United
States should terminate any further consideration of trusteeship and
grant Korean self-government.[58]

Secretary Byrnes thus traveled to Moscow in December 1945 determined to negotiate a trusteeship arrangement for Korea. Upon his
arrival, however, he received an alarming report from Seoul that conditions in southern Korea had reached crisis proportions. Popular
resentment over the denial of self-government had become so widespread, Hodge exclaimed, that a favorable atmosphere now existed in
the American zone for "radical leftism if not raw Communism." The
general public was manifesting an increasing tendency "to look to
Russia for the future" because of "the usual oriental slant" of "doing
homage to the man with the largest weapon." The USAFIK commander warned against any attempt at trusteeship and labeled outside
supervision a "sword of Damocles" hanging over the Korean people.
Although he admitted that the Koreans were not prepared for independence, Hodge was convinced that the lesser evil was a quick restoration of self-government. In the absence of a suitable agreement, he
recommended dramatically that the United States and the Soviet
Union withdraw and leave Korea to its "own devices and an inevitable upheaval for its self-purification."[59]

Not surprisingly, Byrnes acted immediately at Moscow to place the
Korean matter on the agenda. Subsequently, he proposed that the
occupation commanders engage in local negotiations to resolve the
issues Harriman had raised in November. The creation of a unified
administration represented the indispensable first step, he claimed,
for Korean reunification, trusteeship, and eventual independence.
Molotov countered that a general agreement for a Korean trusteeship
was a prerequisite for any discussion of specific issues relating to
reunification. He requested a copy of the American proposal and
time to study its provisions. British Foreign Minister Ernest Bevin
wanted to see the original Soviet-American agreement, but Molotov
explained correctly that there had been only "an exchange of views."

The foreign ministers agreed to defer consideration of the matter until Molotov had studied the American proposal.[60]

In the final American paper, Byrnes merely summarized his lengthy trusteeship proposal. He focused instead on the Harriman recommendations and the vital necessity for local coordination to lift the barrier at the 38th parallel. His proposal also included provisions for the possible extension of trusteeship to ten years. On December 17, Bevin spoke strongly in favor of the American position. He suggested referring the proposal to committee to work out the details. Molotov explained that he had not had sufficient time to consider the plan and requested a delay then and again at the meeting the following day. Finally, on December 20, Molotov accepted the American argument that local discussion of "urgent" questions was needed, but he wanted prior agreement on a long-term trusteeship plan as well. Bevin inquired whether Moscow found the American proposal acceptable. Molotov replied that he would distribute a counterproposal that evening. Byrnes expressed his desire for cooperation but, for some unexplained reason, alleged that the American plan corresponded to "what Stalin had in mind four months ago in Berlin." Bevin then stated that further consideration of the Korean issue would await receipt of the Soviet paper.[61]

As promised, Molotov later circulated the Soviet proposal on Korea. It contained four specific provisions. First, the major powers would create a "provisional, democratic Korean government" to undertake all necessary measures for the development of Korean industry, transportation, agriculture, and culture. Second, representatives from Soviet and American occupation forces would form a "Joint Commission" to consult with local Korean parties and social organizations to formulate procedures for the creation of a provisional government. Third, the Soviet-American Joint Commission would "work out measures of help and assistance (trusteeship) in the political, economic, and social progress" of Korea toward democratic self-government and independence. It also would formulate a five-year trusteeship plan and submit it for approval to the four major powers. Finally, the Soviet and American occupation commanders would convene a "Joint Conference" within two weeks to answer "urgent questions" and begin permanent coordination of administration.[62]

Byrnes approved Molotov's proposal on December 21 with only minor alterations. Initially, the Soviet Union and the United States both judged the Moscow agreement on Korea entirely satisfactory. Moscow agreed to a trusteeship because it still desired a united Korea under a government friendly toward the Soviet Union. Opposition to such a plan would mean unilateral American control in the south, while at the same time reducing the likelihood of compromise and concession on other issues.[63] Yet Moscow would not risk the emergence of an anti-Soviet regime in Korea and therefore refused to end the partition of the peninsula prior to the successful implementation of a specific plan for a provisional government and trusteeship. Byrnes too negotiated in good faith, patiently searching for a compromise that was satisfactory to both nations. He accepted the Soviet proposal in the interests of Soviet-American cooperation and because it was only marginally different from the American plan. More important, Byrnes intended to utilize the Korean accord as a bargaining counter during later negotiations. On the day after the adoption of Moscow's proposal on trusteeship, Byrnes indeed reminded Molotov of American concessions on Korea and requested similiar Soviet consideration with respect to Washington's position on Rumania and Bulgaria.[64]

Truman's advisors certainly realized that the Moscow agreement would please few Koreans. Administration officials were convinced, however, that Korea's political immaturity justified a denial of immediate independence. The temporary continuation of outside control seemed the only way to secure Soviet cooperation for the achievement of reunification. To follow the advice of Langdon and Hodge and undertake unilateral action in southern Korea would merely guarantee the permanent division of the peninsula. As expected, news of the trusteeship plan sparked a storm of protest in the American zone that bordered on mass hysteria. Extremists held street demonstrations, closed stores and schools, and staged work stoppages. Rowdy youth groups roamed the streets of Seoul intimidating AMG personnel and distributing leaflets and posters decrying trusteeship.[65]

Predictably, Hodge instantly appealed to Washington for a reconsideration of its position on Korea's future. The United States, he believed, should "kill the trusteeship idea." The JCS responded with the optimistic prediction that once Hodge had explained the decision fully, the Koreans would accept the Moscow agreement. Instead, the situation in southern Korea deteriorated further. Kim Ku ordered his followers not to cooperate with American occupation officials and even threatened to seize power. Subsequently, all Korean employees of the AMG went on strike. Hodge now informed Washington that it should avoid even using the word "trusteeship," since any mention of it "immediately precludes any normal process of reasoning of the Koreans."[66]

Initially, the Communists and members of the extreme left joined all Koreans in denouncing trusteeship, but suddenly they reversed themselves and became the most outspoken defenders of the Moscow agreement. During a demonstration on January 3, 1946, they hastily substituted the word "up" for "down" on their signs, which then read "Up with Trusteeship!" In all probability, Soviet officials had ordered the switch, but the Communists could hardly have expected the United States to adopt a more favorable attitude toward their political aspirations if they had opposed trusteeship. More important, members of the extreme left manifested laudable realism in recognizing that Korea could not achieve reunification and independence except through fulfillment of the Moscow agreement.[67]

Byrnes reacted to these Korean protests against trusteeship in an unexpected and extremely unfortunate fashion. Upon his return from Moscow, he delivered a radio address summarizing the results of the conference. After expressing displeasure over the lack of progress toward Korea's reunification, Byrnes voiced satisfaction that the United States and the Soviet Union had agreed to open discussions for the resolution of pressing administrative and economic problems. He then mentioned the trusteeship agreement, but he included the suggestion that the Joint Commission members "may find it possible to dispense with a trusteeship" because the ultimate goal in Korea was to hasten the restoration of full sovereignty. Evidently in response to Korean complaints and without Moscow's approval, Byrnes had added a qualification to the recently negotiated Soviet-American accord on Korea.[68] Curiously, Acheson later told the Chinese that Moscow favored this abandonment of a basic provision in the Korean settlement. Since the trusteeship arrangement would only complicate Korea's future, he argued, it was unnecessary.[69] In reality, the Soviet Union must have concluded that the United States did not intend to respect the terms of the Moscow agreement.

Truman's reaction to the Moscow Conference was partially responsible for the equivocation on trusteeship contained in Byrnes's speech. On December 26, the president told Leahy that his secretary of state was guilty of appeasement at Moscow. The appearance of compromise, he suggested, actually masked a complete Soviet victory. In his memoirs, Truman charged that "Byrnes lost his nerve in Moscow" and granted unnecessary concessions without the president's knowledge or consent.[70] At an evening meeting three days later, Truman conveyed his displeasure to Byrnes. Thus, when the secretary of state qualified American policy on Korea the next day, he undoubtedly was acting in accordance with Truman's wishes. By early 1946, there can be no doubt that the president had ruled out any further compromises with Stalin. In a now famous unsent letter dated January 5, Truman explained to Byrnes that at Moscow he should have demanded the creation in Korea of a strong central government and positive measures for economic reconstruction. In his concluding sentence, Truman stated defiantly, "I'm tired babying the Soviets."[71]

In Korea, Hodge eagerly grasped Byrnes's statement to reassure the KPG that the United States did not intend to implement a trusteeship. Despite clear evidence to the contrary, he privately told Kim Ku and Syngman Rhee that trusteeship was not an indispensable aspect of the Moscow agreement. Hodge even issued a public statement pledging that independence would follow rapidly after reunification and the creation of a provisional government.[72] These assurances had the desired effect. Kim Ku ordered AMG employees back to work, thus ending four days of near pandemonium. A relieved Hodge cabled Washington that the crisis had passed. The KPG had been able to retreat with only a minimal loss of prestige, the USAFIK commander observed, because Byrnes had provided "a very small hole for saving Korean face." If Washington refrained from future references to trusteeship, Hodge predicted, the issue would disappear.[73]

Hodge's actions after the Moscow Conference contributed to an increasingly polarized political situation in southern Korea. He considered anyone who favored trusteeship to be a Communist sympathizer, while strengthening his ties to the conservatives who depended on opposition to trusteeship for popular appeal. This approach entailed great risks, since the United States ultimately would confront an inescapable dilemma. The Moscow agreement demanded that Washington advocate some form of trusteeship for Korea. If Truman expected to resolve the Korean predicament, he either would have to persuade the conservatives to accept trusteeship or abandon the extreme right entirely.[74] Failure to implement the Moscow agreement, on the other hand, would guarantee the permanent partition of the Korean peninsula.

In preparation for the opening of Soviet-American negotiations on

Korea, Secretary of War Patterson visited the American zone of occupation during January 1946. Shortly after his arrival, Patterson conferred with Hodge and privately recorded his confidence in the ability of the USAFIK commander. He also spoke to several Korean leaders "dressed in black coats, swallow-tails, with striped trousers." At a press conference, the secretary of war explained that Hodge was doing "a constructive job" because he was relying on the best talent in Korea for advice. Although he declined to specify when the major powers would grant Korea complete independence, Patterson exhorted the Korean people to "maintain a united political front so that the world may know exactly what you want."[75]

Significantly, Patterson chose not to comment on a number of questions that newsmen had submitted prior to the press conference. He refused to respond to any inquiries about the nature of the trusteeship agreement, for example, or to explain how the foreign ministers had broached the issue during the Moscow Conference. Nor would Patterson outline the troop strength of the American army during the remainder of the occupation. This evasiveness angered the American soldiers in Korea. They had met on January 9, prior to the arrival of the secretary of war, to organize protests against further delays in demobilization. Patterson discussed these grievances with six soldiers and expressed sympathy for their plight. He then informed them of Washington's intention to replace half of the occupation force with volunteers and draftees during the next five months. Since Korea's transition from military occupation to self-government and independence would be swift, the United States could reduce significantly the number of troops stationed on the peninsula. After observing conditions in southern Korea, however, Patterson concluded that the American occupation forces enjoyed warm and comfortable barracks, good food, and adequate health facilities.[76]

Upon his return to Washington, Patterson held another press conference. American policy in Korea, he explained, sought to assist "the Koreans in getting an independent stable government in order that the Japanese may not renew their designs there . . . for further aggressive warfare." The Soviet Union shared this objective but disagreed on the leaders most able to create a friendly and peaceful Korea. Patterson then voiced hope that subsequent negotiations between the United States and the Soviet Union would resolve such outstanding differences.[77] Comments in the Soviet press seemed to justify a degree of optimism, as Russian writers confidently antici-

pated that Soviet-American cooperation would produce reunification
and a rapid restoration of economic recovery and political stability. In
the United States, commentators looked to the successful implementation of Korean trusteeship as an indication of rising confidence and
mutual trust among the great powers.[78]

Soviet-American negotiations at the local level to answer "urgent
questions" represented an early test of whether the Moscow agreement would resolve the Korean predicament. Hodge and Chistiakov
promptly agreed to convene a joint conference in Seoul sometime
during the third week of January 1946. The JCS instructed the
USAFIK commander to rely on Harriman's letter as the foundation
for negotiations. His primary objective was to remove the 38th parallel as a fortified barrier in Korea and establish a liaison with the
Soviet commander to facilitate economic and administrative coordination. Domestic reforms, however, would have to await the achievement of reunification.[79]

On January 16, the Soviet delegation arrived in Seoul and met
immediately with American representatives to discuss ending the
38th parallel partition. After fifteen sessions, it was quite apparent
that the two delegations interpreted the Moscow agreement dif-
ferently. The Soviets sought coordination of policy and the exchange
of goods alone; the Americans favored complete administrative and
economic integration.[80] Moscow declined, for example, to discuss
either the free circulation of newspapers in the north or uniform fiscal
policies. Moreover, the Soviets would agree to offset fertilizer and
power deficiencies in the south only in return for rice shipments to
the northern zone. The American delegates desired more extensive
coordination, while insisting that there was no rice surplus in the
south. The Soviet delegation refused to alter its position and suggested a temporary adjournment.[81] Plainly, Moscow had no intention
of weakening its control in northern Korea.

Soviet unwillingness to accept American proposals for dealing with
"urgent questions" irritated Hodge, who complained to Washington
that point four of the Moscow agreement consisted of "weasel
words." Hodge's frustration was understandable, since he blamed the
partition for food and electricity shortages in southern Korea. Certainly, Moscow could have acted to ease Hodge's problems, but rising
suspicion of Washington's insincerity, coupled with a desire to
weaken the American hold south of the 38th parallel, precluded any
magnanimous gestures.[82] Furthermore, the Soviet position was legal-

ly correct, since the Moscow formula did not envision complete zonal integration.

Despite Hodge's unhappiness, the final Soviet-American agreement on economic and administrative coordination constituted an encouraging sign. Rail, truck, and coastwide shipping trade between zones was resumed, as was nationwide mail service. The negotiators also agreed to create a permanent liaison between commands and to begin coordination at checkpoints along the 38th parallel. While the Soviet delegation approved the use of uniform radio frequencies, it refused to permit free distribution of newspapers in the north or to allow unified fiscal policies. The Russians flatly rejected joint control over transportation, electric power, and communications, arguing that a definitive national arrangement for economic and administrative unity had to await the creation of a provisional government for all Korea.[83]

For Hodge, the behavior of the Soviet delegation confirmed his worst suspicions. The USAFIK commander warned Washington that it could expect a similar divergence of interpretation when negotiations began for the creation of a provisional government. He urgently requested a detailed directive for the forthcoming political conference. As an essential precondition for negotiations, Hodge believed that the United States should insist upon the immediate establishment of complete freedom of speech, press, and movement throughout Korea. If Moscow refused to open the northern zone, the USAFIK commander recommended that Washington permit him to "discreetly let the Korean people know that the Soviets are failing to cooperate with the U.S. in breaking down the 38° barrier."[84] The State Department rejected Hodge's plan, no doubt recognizing that it would hardly facilitate Soviet-American negotiations. Washington would authorize only the issuance of a press release stating that the American delegation had favored a wider agreement for zonal integration.[85]

American occupation officials saw that the fate of Korea hinged on the outcome of the Joint Commission deliberations. Unless the United States acted swiftly to bolster conservative elements in southern Korea, they believed, the extreme left and the Communists would dominate the provisional government. Hodge placed special importance on maximizing the popularity and prestige of Kim Ku and his followers. He even wanted Washington to sponsor the KPG's participation in United Nations activities. Benninghoff undoubtedly had the Joint Commission negotiations in mind when he suggested that the administration refer to the Korean representative body working under the Joint Commission as an "interim government," rather than a "provisional government," since the Kim Ku regime already held the latter designation.[86] Acheson spurned both proposals and instructed the American command to treat the KPG as a political party alone and without any special status. The War Department, while approving this action, noted that "this confusion might conceivably give the US members of the Joint Commission some bargaining advantage in discussions with the Soviets establishing a 'Provisional Government'."[87]

Washington had good reason to withhold any hint of public support for the KPG. Kim Ku and his backers had made plain their determination to block implementation of the Soviet-American agreement on Korea. During January 1946, Kim Ku had organized all conservative groups into an "Anti-Trusteeship Committee" dedicated to the restoration of Korea's sovereignty at the earliest possible date.[88] Even Hodge could see that such blatant opposition to the Moscow agreement was counterproductive. As a result, Archer L. Lerch, Arnold's replacement as military governor, publicly warned the Korean people that violent protests and political unrest would in fact guarantee the imposition of a trusteeship. In addition, Hodge outlawed several rightist youth groups that had been in large part responsible for the political agitation and violence in southern Korea during the occupation.[89] Despite these actions, American occupation officials still considered Yŏ's KPR the primary threat to law and order.[90]

For the Soviet Union, Hodge's efforts to prevent criticism of the Moscow agreement were thoroughly inadequate. On January 19, *Tass* denounced the AMG for permitting verbal attacks not only on trusteeship but on the Soviet Union as well. Three days later, it charged Hodge with inspiring public opposition to the Moscow agreement.[91] The USAFIK commander summarily dismissed these accusations as groundless. In response to Moscow's indictment, Hodge explained in a public statement that there was nothing reprehensible about advocating freedom of expression. While Hodge's defense of a basic democratic principle may have been laudable, it did not contribute to a successful resolution of the Korean problem. In fact, Hodge privately heaped scorn on the Moscow agreement, arguing that Soviet and Korean views on trusteeship were incompatible.[92]

Faced with Hodge's obduracy, the Soviet Union decided to publicize the text of the American proposal on Korea at the Moscow Conference in an effort to embarrass the United States. In its original form, Byrnes's plan had not included measures for a provisional government and would have postponed independence for ten years. In a deliberate fabrication, *Tass* then claimed that the Soviet Union had opposed trusteeship from the start but American resistance to immediate self-government had forced Molotov to accept the trusteeship arrangement. George F. Kennan, the American chargé in Moscow, speculated that the Soviets sought to portray all nonleftist political leaders as collaborators and reactionaries and thereby insist upon their exclusion from participation in the provisional government. If successful, this strategy would eventuate in Communist control over a reunited Korea.[93]

Acheson acted at once to counter these Soviet claims. The United States, he publicly declared, was committed to the rapid achievement of a united and independent Korea. Byrnes had proposed lifting the barrier at the 38th parallel, rather than the creation of a provisional government, because reunification was the necessary first step for the promotion of Korea's welfare. Acheson then falsely alleged that, at Moscow, Byrnes and Molotov had discussed the possibility that trusteeship might not be necessary, but, if it was, the arrangement would last at least five years and perhaps longer.[94] Meanwhile, Harriman met with Stalin and tried to reassure the Soviet leader of American good faith. Stalin, in reply, pointed angrily to reports from Korea that the American military governor was encouraging criticism of the Moscow agreement. Harriman insisted that the rumors were without foundation and inconsistent with American policy. Stalin remained skeptical. Washington, he thought, should issue a public disavowal of any actions that had contributed to anti-Soviet sentiment in southern Korea.[95]

At the outset of 1946, then, Washington's search for a settlement in Korea had resulted in a renewed commitment to the achievement of a trusteeship. The prospects for successful implementation seemed questionable at best, however, given the rapidly developing pattern of mutual distrust between the United States and the Soviet Union. Nevertheless, there was reason for optimism. Initial Soviet-American negotiations at the local level had experienced significant progress, and the overall Moscow agreement provided a workable framework for permanently resolving the Korean problem. "Only persons soaked in mistrust," Herbert Feis has observed, "could have resisted the cheerful conclusion that the Soviet Government was going to abstain from using its advantageous position in Korea to thwart [American objectives] in Japan or China."[96] Yet Truman had concluded in the aftermath of the Moscow Conference that the agreement on Korea was tantamount to appeasement. This attitude suggested that the administration was prepared to assume a tough stance during subsequent negotiations with Moscow and demand Soviet acceptance of the American vision of Korea's future.

If Truman had decided to adopt an inflexible posture on Korea, such an approach would involve distinct limitations. Soviet interests on the Korean peninsula were unquestionably greater than those of the United States. At the time, Truman had not formulated a concrete plan to produce the requisite military and economic power to force a settlement on American terms. Perhaps more important, Stalin undoubtedly believed that since Korea was of secondary importance to American national security, Washington would not risk involvement in a major war to impose its will. The absence of any vital interests in Korea, coupled with the lack of sufficient power to alter the course of events significantly, meant that an American decision to assume a hard line on the Korean issue would result in little more than rhetorical bombast.[97] If Truman wanted to be tough with Stalin, Korea was surely the wrong place for a test of strength.

CHAPTER 4

Patience with Firmness

Truman's policy toward the Soviet Union experienced a fundamental reorientation during the first months of 1946. Previously, the administration had been willing to compromise with Moscow. After the Moscow Conference, however, Truman decided to "get tough with Russia." For both political and diplomatic reasons, the president had concluded that granting further concessions to the Soviet Union would be unwise and dangerous. Secretary Byrnes accepted the change and labeled the new approach "patience with firmness."[1] In Korea, the new policy meant that Washington would demand Soviet acceptance of the American interpretation of the Moscow agreement. If Stalin failed to acquiesce, the United States would remain in occupation of southern Korea presumably until the Soviets agreed to a settlement on American terms.

Events in Korea during 1946 illustrated well the distinct limitations of Washington's new policy. An equitable solution to the Korean problem was possible only if the United States and the Soviet Union were willing to compromise. In the absence of serious negotiations, Korea never would achieve reunification and independence peacefully. Yet the administration apparently believed that it could outwait Stalin and compel the Soviet Union to relinquish its grip on northern Korea. Truman confidently expected that his new posture of verbal toughness would force Moscow "to play the game the American way."[2] But rather than encouraging a settlement, Washington's policy of "patience with firmness" guaranteed that Korea would be a permanently divided nation.

Soviet actions in northern Korea early in 1946 suggested that Moscow did not intend to retreat. During the autumn of 1945, the Soviets had permitted the northern Koreans to elect representatives to local people's committees. But when the United States yielded to southern Korean protests against the Moscow agreement, the Soviet Union quickly reappraised its policy. To ensure Russian mastery over a friendly northern Korea, Moscow proceeded to install its trusted clients into positions of authority. Symbolic of this shift in policy was Chistiakov's decision to place Cho Man-sik under house arrest for opposing trusteeship.[3] The most important of the new leaders in northern Korea was an obscure exile named Kim Il Sung (Kim Ilsŏng) who had not even arrived in the Soviet zone of occupation until September 1945. At a conference in the northern capital of Pyongyang during February 1946, representatives elected Kim chairman of the "Provisional People's Committee."[4] From this point onward, only Korean leaders unquestionably loyal to the Soviet Union occupied the higher administrative and political offices in the northern zone.[5]

At the same time, Moscow recognized that most Koreans wanted sweeping social and economic change. In March 1946, the Soviet Union implemented a major reform program expropriating land held by Japanese collaborators, large landlords, and the church. The northern Korean regime distributed this land without requiring cash payment. The following June, Kim Il Sung's government nationalized all large-scale industry, transportation, communications, and banking, while mandating the eight-hour day and proclaiming sexual equality.[6] These Soviet-sponsored actions had a significant if indirect impact on southern Korea. As Langdon, Hodge's political advisor, observed at the time, reforms in the north "have fallen heavily on the unfortunate conservative and propertied classes, many of whom have taken refuge in our zone."[7] While it is impossible to be absolutely certain about events in northern Korea, the Soviet Union appears to have satisfied the popular desire for significant reforms while simultaneously building a sound foundation for a Korean socialist state. Possession of land was of particular importance, since it gave the average citizen a stake in the new government. With the exception of endorsing trusteeship, Moscow definitely had a better understanding of Korean political and social affairs than did the United States.[8]

American occupation of southern Korea demonstrated far less organization and more division in purpose than Soviet policy in the north. Hodge was in large part responsible for American problems because of his preoccupation with the perceived threat of a Communist seizure of power in the south. An obsessive fear of Soviet expansionism dictated virtually all of Hodge's actions as occupation commander; invariably his highest priority was the maintenance of law and order. As a result, during October 1945, he organized a Korean "National Civil Police Force" to assist the USAFIK in preserving internal stability. Occupation officials chose individuals with prior police experience, however, resulting in the selection of a preponderant number of Koreans who had obtained training from the Japanese. This Korean police force at once established close ties with the extreme right and openly directed hostility toward the left. Since many members of the Korean police force had helped the Japanese to suppress the wartime underground, they naturally feared retaliation if leftist elements assumed political power.[9] Nevertheless, Hodge viewed the Korean police force as a partial answer to American manpower shortages.[10] Late in November 1945, he happily predicted that a group of twenty-five thousand trained Koreans would be able to relieve the USAFIK of normal police functions by January 1, 1946.[11]

Declining morale within the American occupation force was an even more urgent reason causing Hodge to plead for drastic steps toward Korean self-government. Not only should the United States provide the local police force with large amounts of surplus arms and equipment, but Hodge wanted the administration to authorize the creation of a "National Defense Force" as well. Such a "constabulary army," he reasoned, would attract members of the scattered paramilitary forces in southern Korea and therefore end the dangerous competition between these private armies. Secretary of War Patterson enthusiastically endorsed Hodge's suggestion. If the United States organized and equipped a constabulary army, no further increases in strength would be necessary for the USAFIK.[12] The State Department, afraid that such action might imperil negotiations with the Soviet Union, registered its vigorous dissent. Consequently, the administration deferred a decision on the National Defense Force until after the opening of discussions at the Joint Commission.[13]

Apparently, Hodge had expected Washington to approve his plan for a National Defense Force. During February 1946, he opened a training school in Seoul and solicited candidates from a number of quasi-military groups operating in southern Korea since liberation. Hodge was so pleased with the results that he then organized a "National Youth Association" to provide the manpower for a genuine Korean army at some future date. An Ho-sang, a graduate of the University of Jena in Germany and an avowed admirer of Hitler's Nazi Youth, became the director of this new organization. While the United States provided the equipment and advice, An Ho-sang

developed a program of anti-Communist political indoctrination and
strict discipline that readily lent itself to rightist exploitation. Far
from contributing to internal stability, Hodge's actions encouraged
domestic violence and unrest. By the summer of 1946, youth groups
representing both the right and the left were engaged in guerrilla
warfare and terrorism on a major scale throughout the American zone
of occupation.[14]

To his credit, Hodge was not entirely insensitive to the popular
desire in southern Korea for change. In fact, he favored extensive
social and economic reforms.[15] However, Truman's diplomatic advisors adamantly refused to approve any major reforms prior to the formation of a provisional government. Hodge believed that the steady
deterioration of conditions south of the 38th parallel precluded further delay. Increasingly, he came to blame his difficulties on the State
Department's refusal to follow any of his policy recommendations. In
one particularly bitter cable, Hodge demanded to know who was
responsible for advising against a decision to abandon trusteeship and
grant Korea its immediate independence. Warning that the Korean
people were losing confidence in the United States, he appealed for
positive steps to counter rising Soviet influence in the south. The
USAFIK commander even volunteered to serve as "a sacrificial goat,"
leaving Korea and assuming all blame for Washington's failure to
achieve a bilateral settlement with the Soviet Union. If Washington
persisted in its present course of delay, Hodge believed Stalin eventually would dominate the entire peninsula. Korea "will never be really
united," he pessimistically concluded, "until the Russians are sure
that the whole will be soundly communistic."[16]

For Hodge, conservative political elements in the American zone
represented the only certain barrier to Stalin's expansionist ambitions. During January 1946, Hodge implored Washington to delay
the convening of the Joint Commission until the right had an opportunity to form a broader and more unified political coalition.[17] To
that end, he prevailed upon Kim Ku and Rhee to liquidate the KPG
in return for the creation of a new "Representative Democratic Council." None other than Preston Goodfellow, having recently arrived in
Korea as Hodge's advisor, became the principal architect of this new
advisory body. Not surprisingly, conservatives dominated the Representative Democratic Council and Rhee served as its chairman.
Hodge publicly avowed that the body did not constitute a provisional
government but was merely a device to increase the Korean role in

the formulation of American occupation policies.[18] In reality, Hodge was trying to mobilize unity among the conservatives in anticipation of the Joint Commission's deliberations. Benninghoff even recommended that Washington grant $50 million in aid to the new advisory body in order to bolster its prestige and offset rising Soviet popularity in the south.[19]

During early 1946, the Korean conservatives experienced a steady rise in popularity because of American sponsorship and popular opposition to trusteeship. Yet Hodge's maneuvers to strengthen the right, while successful, had unfortunate consequences. "By throwing United States support only to the right in a country which demanded and needed radical reform," Glenn Paige has observed, American occupation officials "alienated a healthy segment of the left which could have been wooed and perhaps even won by a living exposition of American democracy." Far worse, once excluded from access to political power, many militant Korean radicals opted for a closer alliance with the Communists.[20] Moreover, Hodge's actions further reduced the likelihood of a Soviet-American settlement. Moscow admittedly would have sought extensive leftist and Communist representation in the provisional government regardless of events in the south. However, American preferential treatment for the conservatives caused the Soviet Union to become even more inflexible in its demands for a friendly Korea.

Early in 1946, the State Department had begun to prepare for the Joint Commission negotiations. It had not completed its work, however, when Hodge requested instructions. Thus, the USAFIK commander received an SWNCC policy paper on February 11 that dealt only with point one of the Moscow agreement. Washington instructed Hodge to take no action beyond the formation of a provisional government, while encouraging "the various Korean political factions to reach fundamental agreements on the political, economic and social policies to be applied by the new government, including essential democratic reforms." Significantly, the SWNCC paper also authorized Hodge to civilianize the military government rapidly and provide local Koreans with the experience necessary to allow swift assumption of governmental responsibilities. In the event of a breakdown at the Joint Commission, the administration intended to implement a program of "Koreanization" in the southern zone alone.[21]

Hodge still thought that the United States had to obtain Soviet

consent for freedom of speech, press, and movement throughout
Korea prior to the opening of negotiations at the Joint Commission.
If Moscow demurred, it would not be possible to acquire an accurate
cross section of Korean opinion. During February 1946, Harriman
visited Korea. Hodge evidently persuaded the ambassador that unless
the United States guaranteed unrestricted freedom of expression in
Korea, the Soviet Union would install a puppet regime on the peninsula. Upon his return to Washington, Harriman conveyed to Truman
his conviction that Stalin sought to extend Soviet ideology and territorial hegemony throughout East Asia. Since "the Russians . . . were
going to take advantage of" Hodge's vulnerable position, an American posture of firmness in Korea was essential.[22] Presumably in
response to Harriman's advice, Washington approved Hodge's recommendation to insist upon the right of free expression in consultations
at the Joint Commission. If Moscow spurned this proposal, Hodge
would announce that the Soviet Union was barring free speech and
elementary civil liberties. American leaders were confident that popular criticism of Moscow would then force Stalin to retreat and accept
Washington's position.[23]

Simultaneously, news arrived in Seoul of the creation of the "Provisional People's Committee" in the north. For Hodge, these events in
the Soviet zone suggested that the Communists would attempt to
seize power in the south in the very near future. To counter this serious challenge, Hodge informed Washington of his intention "to
keep up prestige of the Korean Representative Democratic Council,
make every effort to gain full backing of the Korean people, and discredit the Communists. This will probably get liberal and pink press
of US on my back, but feel any other local action now would be
fatal." Truman's advisors were similarly alarmed. One State Department memorandum warned that the Soviets "are applying the same
tactics they have applied in Eastern Europe in order to gain control
. . . through military minority groups controlled by the Soviet Government."[24] But Washington did not believe that an effective response to the Soviet threat required an exclusive reliance on Rhee and
Kim Ku. The War Department instructed Hodge to broaden his base
of support and to insist on open conservative advocacy for social and
fiscal reform. If the conservatives declined to adopt such a program,
the cable concluded, "it should be made clear to them that they can
receive no further U.S. backing."[25]

Soviet and American representatives finally met in Seoul on March

20, 1946, for the start of the Joint Commission negotiations. Even before hard bargaining began, both sides had drawn clear lines of disagreement. In his opening statement, Colonel General Terenty F. Shtikov declared that the Soviet government was committed to the realization in Korea of "a true democratic and independent country, friendly to the Soviet Union, so that in the future it will not become a base for an attack on the Soviet Union." Therefore, the Korean provisional government had to reflect not only wide representation but also unqualified support for the terms of the Moscow agreement. In response, Hodge emphasized that the United States was determined to see that "a government that corresponds to the views of the majority is established." Only national self-determination, he argued, could produce "the political, economic, and social progress of the Korean people, the development of democratic self-government and the establishment of the national independence of Korea."[26] As in Eastern Europe, Korea's fate hinged upon the ability of the great powers to resolve divergent interpretations of an international agreement.[27]

Shtikov, during the early sessions, resisted the American desire for nationwide consultations; he favored discussions within each individual zone instead. The American delegation, in its private cables, dismissed the Soviet position as arbitrary. Strangely, American representatives in Seoul were surprised at Moscow's determination to implement the trusteeship agreement.[28] During later sessions, Shtikov favored consultation only with parties that backed the Moscow agreement. The American proposal for a national "Consultative Union," he insisted, was contrary to the Moscow agreement and therefore unacceptable. Shtikov also opposed treating Korea as a unit. Administrative or economic integration, he explained, had to await the creation of a provisional government.[29]

Despite these differences, the negotiators ultimately reached agreement on the first phase of action at the Joint Commission. This stage would include consultation with local parties, consideration of a political platform, recommendation of a charter, and the choice of personnel for the provisional government. The Joint Commission organized three subcommittees to formulate specific measures for attaining each objective. Moscow thus had demonstrated an unmistakable willingness to implement the Moscow agreement, but only if the United States agreed to a provisional government and trusteeship prior to reunification. Soviet political advisor G. M. Balasanov told his American counterpart Langdon that Moscow expected a workable settlement in Korea before the end of May 1946.[30]

Although there was ample reason for mild optimism, Hodge continued to issue pessimistic forecasts from Seoul. He chided Washington in particular for its devotion to negotiations and its failure to consult him before adopting the trusteeship policy. Byrnes's patience finally wore thin. In a letter to Patterson, he denied that the administration had failed to keep Hodge informed on the terms of the Moscow agreement. Byrnes confessed himself "somewhat perturbed by the attitude taken by General Hodge" in view of the relatively promising start in the Joint Commission negotiations. The secretary of state reminded Patterson that the United States was committed to the fulfillment of the Moscow agreement. Thus, Hodge's job was to cooperate with the Soviets, not to debate the wisdom of a Korean trusteeship.[31]

Patterson replied immediately. In his letter to Byrnes he emphasized that interdepartmental coordination was crucial to the successful formulation and implementation of American foreign policy. His recent visit to Korea had convinced him of Hodge's earnest desire for cooperation. Even Harriman, the secretary of war explained, had been "so favorably impressed by General Hodge's ability and diplomacy that he now believes that there is a possibility for reaching a solution in Korea which will be satisfactory to the United States." The JCS too categorically stated its confidence in Hodge, commenting that the State Department probably had not kept the USAFIK commander adequately informed.[32]

An emerging deadlock at the Joint Commission soon overshadowed this dispute between the State and War departments. Shtikov had made it quite plain that both commands had to agree on the parties for consultation and all had to support the Moscow agreement fully. Soviet suspicion of American intent naturally increased when the American delegation announced that there were five hundred legitimate parties and social organizations in southern Korea eligible for consultation compared to only forty in the north. When Shtikov objected to consultation with groups hostile to trusteeship, Langdon retorted that Korean hostility to the Moscow agreement did not constitute an acceptable criterion for determining legitimacy. Byrnes instantly approved the American delegation's decision to resist Moscow's attempt to exclude those parties opposing trusteeship from consultation.[33]

Many observers surmised that the absence of published reports from the Joint Commission probably indicated a lack of progress in negotiations. Rumors of armed clashes at the 38th parallel did nothing to allay popular apprehension.[34] The Soviet Union, quite obviously, was using the trusteeship issue as a device to prevent a sizable group of anti-Soviet Korean leaders from obtaining access to political power. Yet the United States was in the unenviable position of insisting upon consultation with those very individuals who sought to undermine the work of the Joint Commission. Nevertheless, State Department official Vincent endorsed the actions of the American delegation, arguing that to disenfranchise an "overwhelming majority of southern Koreans because they disagree with us as to their readiness for independence would be unreasonable and undemocratic."[35] In reality, as Langdon admitted, fears of sovietization dictated the behavior of the American delegation. The United States believed that the exclusion of the conservatives would ensure a Communist seizure of power. Rather than bowing to Soviet demands, Washington assumed a posture of inflexible opposition. "If we can hold this fort all along the line from Korea to Timbuktoo," one American official remarked at the time, "we may start to get somewhere."[36]

Washington's resort to a patient but firm approach in Korea paid immediate dividends. On April 18, the Soviet-American negotiators appeared to have broken the deadlock with the publication of a joint communiqué on consultation. The Joint Commission agreed to consult all "democratic parties and social organizations which are truly democratic in their aims" and would sign a declaration pledging to uphold Soviet-American decisions on the creation of a provisional government. More important, the communiqué included as well a provision requiring all signatories to accept the trusteeship section of the Moscow agreement.[37] Hodge recorded his satisfaction with the compromise, since it seemed to permit consultation with the extreme right. Despite the agreement, however, the USAFIK commander still worried that the Communists would dominate the provisional government. Since "the southern political structure includes almost equally left . . . and moderate-rightists," Hodge apprised the War Department, "we would either have to nominate an unrepresentative slate for the south or expect its being outnumbered by combined strength of North and South Moscow controlled groups."[38]

Moscow's stand on consultation after the compromise also irked Hodge. Shtikov wanted to exclude many prominent conservative leaders because they were affiliated with no specific organized groups. The American delegation insisted upon consultation with "all schools of political thought irrespective of our estimate of their popular backing." Hodge exhorted Washington to hold firmly to the principle of wide consultation until the Soviet Union accepted the American position. In the meantime,

> we shall build up evidence of exclusions of all but Leftist parties in north and south and lack of facilities for US to observe in the north. We will then demand either immediate lifting of 38 barrier and complete freedom in north for the political activities of moderate parties or else acceptance of our views in matter of composition of government, structure, etc.

If Moscow objected, Hodge postulated that the "threat of full publicity . . . to which the Russians have already shown their sensitivity" would force Soviet compliance. Washington approved Hodge's recommendations.[39] The stage was now set for a complete breakdown in negotiations at the Joint Commission.

In contrast to Hodge, Syngman Rhee and Kim Ku greeted the Soviet-American compromise with dismay, since it required them to sign a pledge of support for trusteeship. The Representative Democratic Council had declared its opposition to perpetuation of outside control, but now it would have to reverse itself or risk exclusion from the Joint Commission negotiations. Hodge endeavored to resolve the dilemma. The Korean people still enjoyed unfettered freedom of expression, he declared, and former military governor Arnold, now head of the American delegation at the Joint Commission, seconded his assessment. The Soviet Union certainly did not share Hodge's interpretation of the compromise agreement. In fact, Moscow's representatives at the Joint Commission had already begun to argue with considerable justification that a mere signature on a pledge provided no guarantee of support for the Moscow agreement. Shtikov stated frankly that he would not sanction consultation with those groups most critical of trusteeship. When the American delegation adamantly upheld the principle of absolute freedom of expression, negotiations reached an impasse.[40]

On May 7, Hodge informed Washington that he would propose an adjournment of the Joint Commission the following day *sine die*. He offered several reasons for his decision. First, the American stand against Soviet demands for the exclusion of parties not under its domination would bolster the morale of anti-Communist Korean nationalists. Second, advocacy of free speech was a sound position internationally, since no nation would favor penalizing individuals for resisting outside control. Third, Hodge reasoned that if the United States forced the Soviet Union to back down, popular pressure in the north would weaken the foundations of Moscow's puppet regime. Finally, the USAFIK commander stated boldly that if "Korea is to be truly independent, the time for a showdown on Soviet pretensions is now." The only way to achieve Korea's reunification, Hodge advised, "is by standing firm on the position we have taken and letting the Soviets make the next move."[41]

For some observers at the time, the adjournment of the Joint Commission on May 8 constituted the first step toward civil war. Indeed, by the spring of 1946, scattered acts of violence and the discovery of assassination plots were everyday occurrences in the American zone.[42] Langdon appealed to the administration to approach Moscow at the government level with a request for adoption of a timetable to achieve mutual military withdrawal by February 1947.[43] While Washington appreciated the gravity of the situation in southern Korea, it was bent on showing its resolve. Acheson informed Seoul on May 18 that the administration would not reopen negotiations at the Joint Commission until Moscow recognized the principle of freedom of expression. Ultimately, Soviet resistance to consultations with critics of trusteeship would discredit Moscow inside Korea and compel Stalin to accept the American position.[44]

Late in May and in accordance with prior plans, the SWNCC authorized an election in southern Korea for the creation of a limited degree of representative government. The facade of self-rule in the north, Truman's advisors believed, had placed American governance in the south in an unfavorable light. Responding to advice from Walter Bedell Smith, the new American ambassador to the Soviet Union, Washington instructed Hodge to maximize Korean participation in the formulation of occupation policy and obtain a truly representative provisional government.[45] Langdon welcomed this new policy directive. The Soviet strategy, he asserted, depended upon American frustration and eventual withdrawal opening the way to a Communist seizure of power. Through unity, patience, and resolve, however, the United States could foster the emergence of a strong, independent, democratic coalition and thereby thwart Moscow's plan.[46] Even

Preston Goodfellow was pleased. Upon his departure from Korea, he proclaimed that the Koreans were ready for self-government. If Moscow refused to permit the Joint Commission to reconvene, he favored holding elections without delay for a separate southern Korean government.[47]

Moscow quickly indicated that the success of Washington's strategy was unlikely. Both *Izvestia* and *Pravda* castigated the United States for violating the Moscow agreement and then adjourning the Joint Commission without justification. The Soviets charged that Hodge was encouraging reactionaries to oppose the Moscow agreement while refusing to consult a number of truly democratic parties. The United States was determined to install reactionaries in the Korean provisional government at all costs, they insisted, in order to prevent democracy and subordinate Korea to American political and economic influence. As a result, Moscow was demanding "precise and undeviating observation of the obligations undertaken . . . at the Moscow Conference." There could be no reunification of Korea prior to the formation of a provisional government. Furthermore, Moscow would never consult with Korean leaders hostile to the Soviet Union. Under no circumstances, one Soviet writer declared, would the Soviet Union permit "imperialist forces" to use Korea "as a base and jumping-off place for an attack on our country."[48]

Moscow's verbal toughness did not weaken the administration's commitment to "patience with firmness" in Korea. In fact, Edwin Pauley's trip to northern Korea during the early summer of 1946 strengthened Washington's confidence in its hard-line approach. Pauley was Truman's representative on the Allied Reparations Commission and had expressed concern in December 1945 about the reports of Soviet removal of equipment from northern Korea. On December 7, Pauley had announced that a final assessment of reparations for Korea would have to await an analysis of the needs of the entire nation. In view of the temporary division of Korea, he suggested that a survey team inspect both the American and Soviet zones. Two weeks later, Truman approved Pauley's proposal. On March 22, 1946, Pauley further advised that the United States should request Soviet permission to enter northern Korea for the purpose of verifying reports of large-scale removals of industrial equipment from that area.[49]

At a press conference on May 2, Truman endorsed Pauley's recommendations. Only full knowledge of the resources and productive capacity of northern Korea, the president remarked, would permit a proper formulation of a reparations program for Japan and "any long-range plan for the peaceful economy of East Asia." Eleven days later, Byrnes formally requested that Moscow allow Pauley to enter northern Korea. To everyone's surprise, Chistiakov granted permission for the inspection.[50] Subsequently, Pauley compiled a detailed account of his trip to the Soviet zone. Upon his arrival in northern Korea on May 29, Chistiakov assured him that the rumors of Soviet removals were without foundation. Pauley inspected a large number of pig iron, fertilizer, aluminum, and textile factories. The Soviets denied entrance only to a small area on the northeast coast around Hungnam, arguing that the train ride to that location would require far too much time. While he did notice some generators crated for shipment, Pauley attributed looting to the illegal acts of the Koreans themselves. Upon inquiry, many of those people who had reported Soviet removals told Pauley that they had not witnessed personally such activities.[51]

After his return to Seoul, Pauley reported that there were "no substantial industrial removals from the Russian-administered territory of Northern Korea." In marked contrast to Manchuria, the Soviets were striving to rehabilitate and restore northern Korea's industrial activity, rather than cripple economic recovery. In his formal report to Truman, Pauley noted that Soviet policies in northern Korea indicated Moscow's intention to stay in occupation until its puppets achieved complete control. Since Korea's economy was conducive to the development of communism, the Soviet strategy was experiencing success. Pauley then complained that Korea was "not receiving the attention and consideration it should." The confrontation of democracy and communism across the 38th parallel, he stated bluntly, meant that Korea was "an ideological battleground upon which our entire success in Asia may depend." Pauley warned against any American concessions to the Soviet Union because the loss of Korea would endanger the security of Japan.[52]

Pauley also proposed a series of specific policy actions. First, the United States should inaugurate a propaganda campaign highlighting Soviet violations of existing agreements dealing with Korea's future. Second, the AMG should educate Koreans on the advantages of the democratic system. Third, American economic aid to Korea for recovery was advisable. Finally, the United States should transfer to Korea a number of teachers and technicians to foster industrial growth. Unless the United States met popular needs and desires, Pauley concluded, the Soviet Union eventually would dominate the entire peninsula. Pauley's report impressed Truman greatly. The president immediately arranged a meeting with Byrnes for a thorough reassessment of American policy in Korea.[53]

Earlier in June 1946, Assistant Secretary of State for Occupied Areas John H. Hilldring had arrived at similar conclusions. He drafted a memorandum stressing the need to broaden the base of Korean participation in governmental affairs. According to Hilldring, the deadlock at the Joint Commission was

> the result of a clash between United States insistence upon respect for the principle of freedom of speech and Soviet determination to prevent certain avowedly anti-Soviet Korean leaders from participation in the Provisional Korean Government. These leaders constitute a group of older *"emigre"* Koreans who have returned to Korea since the capitulation of Japan. They are not thought to be completely representative of Korean political opinion, nor are they felt to be essential to the establishment of Korean democracy or the attainment of United States objectives in Korea. On the other hand, their presence on the political scene greatly increases the difficulty of reaching an agreement with the Soviet Union. For these reasons, it can be concluded that attainment of United States objectives in Korea is on the whole hampered rather than aided by their participation in Korean politics.

Hilldring also wanted the AMG to continue to pursue coordination with the Soviets and an early resumption of negotiations at the Joint Commission. Perhaps American observance of the Moscow agreement in combination with growing Korean enthusiasm for participation in southern political affairs would force Moscow to recognize the principle of freedom of expression.[54]

Following the advice of the State Department, Truman approved the policy recommendations of Pauley and Hilldring. In a letter to Pauley, the president outlined his intention to institute a series of reforms in the American zone, including land distribution and even the nationalization of certain industries.[55] On July 17, the War Department instructed Hodge to forsake his exclusive attachment to the Korean conservatives in favor of a broad coalition embracing liberals and moderates as well. Wide Korean support for American occupation policies would add substance to the administration's position and place pressure on Moscow to resume negotiations at the Joint

Commission. Washington would not consider a direct approach to the Soviet Union at the governmental level, the War Department concluded, unless political unrest in southern Korea reached crisis proportions.[56] In a letter to Hodge, Joint Commission delegate Charles W. Thayer explained that the administration wanted to permit the Russians "to come back gracefully and without loss of face."[57] But these new instructions again had ignored Hodge's recommendations, and the USAFIK commander made no effort to hide his displeasure. Without stronger action for the resumption of negotiations, he protested, the Koreans would become more restive and the occupation force less popular. Direct contact at the government level was imperative.[58]

Still, the State Department adamantly refused to alter its stand. Hilldring professed that "the United States has more to gain by pursuing a positive constructive program in Korea than by demonstrating to the Soviets . . . our anxiety to dispose of the Korean problem quickly." The War Department, endorsing Hodge's assessment, disagreed and therefore referred the matter to the SWNCC for review. Early in August, the SWNCC informed the JCS that for "tactical reasons" the United States had "to indicate to Soviets in every way possible that U.S. is determined to remain in Korea until U.S. objectives have been achieved." Thus, it was reasoned, the State Department's policy was the correct approach at that time and deserved an opportunity to demonstrate its success.[59] On August 3, the War Department cabled Hodge that the position of the State Department had prevailed. There would be no American *démarche* at the government level and Hodge was to implement Washington's most recent policy directives. Additionally, occupation officials were now to impress upon the Koreans that trusteeship was a fundamental aspect of the Moscow agreement; they could not expect immediate independence. Under no circumstances was the AMG to convey a sense of impatience, because the administration was determined to "stick it out" and force Moscow "to make the first step towards a resumption of negotiations."[60]

Despite the SWNCC's decision, the Truman administration remained badly divided on the issue of Korea. American military experts were dubious about the prospects for successful implementation of the Pauley and Hilldring proposals. More important, an improvement in southern Korea's economic situation would require considerable financial support and the War Department judged its resources inadequate for the task.[61] Probably in response to persistent prodding from his military advisors for withdrawal, Truman intervened. In a letter to Patterson dated August 12, the president frankly observed that the United States would have to continue to occupy Korea for "a considerable length of time." Successful implementation of Pauley's recommendations would require the War Department to cooperate fully in the acquisition of adequate funds and experienced personnel. Truman informed Patterson that he expected his cooperation and was instructing the Navy Department to provide every assistance necessary for the achievement of American objectives in Korea. Two days later, Secretary of the Navy Forrestal joined the State Department in pledging total support for Truman's new policy in Korea. He promised to cooperate with Patterson and the War Department in carrying out Pauley's proposals.[62]

Meanwhile, Hodge had begun reluctantly to implement the administration's directives. During the summer of 1946, he attempted to build a moderate coalition around the leadership of Kim Kyu-sik, former foreign minister in the KPG. Kim was well suited for the role, since the elderly scholar-statesman had been the symbolic leader of Korean liberals after World War I and was regarded as one of the few selfless leaders in postwar Korea.[63] Everyone recognized that Washington's new policy sought to increase mass support for the United States in the south and thereby outflank growing Soviet influence. Rumors quickly circulated that the AMG was preparing to organize an interim council excluding all extreme conservatives. On July 1, 1946, Military Governor Lerch announced that the AMG soon would sponsor the formation of a South Korean Interim Legislative Assembly (SKILA) that would be half-elected and half-appointed. Lerch emphasized, however, that the SKILA would constitute merely a step toward democracy and not the creation of a permanent separate government.[64]

This new policy, if implemented in September 1945, might have contributed to the emergence of a united, democratic, and independent Korea. Now, however, the fortunes of the moderate coalition would depend on whether the United States and the Soviet Union resolved their differences in Korea and arranged a settlement acceptable to both sides.[65] While the chances for success seemed slim, the wisdom and realism of the new American approach represented a welcome change from past policy. Almost immediately, Langdon reported progress toward the achievement of political unity. Much to the chagrin of Syngman Rhee and Kim Ku, Kim Kyu-sik easily managed to join forces with Yŏ and form a "Coalition Committee" to build support for American policy.[66]

Elections for an interim legislative assembly alone would not resolve southern Korea's political problems since the nation had no familiarity with democracy. The traditional reliance on community government meant that individual freedom of choice had little chance of prevailing. Widespread illiteracy meant that it would be possible to use the secret ballot only at the final stage of an indirect election process. And then there was the disturbing problem of Syngman Rhee, who maintained considerable popularity because of Hodge's initial backing and his reputation as a patriotic leader. During discussions in Washington, Thayer recommended that Rhee "be gently eased out of the Korean political picture" since he "had outlived his period of usefulness." Subsequent events showed that this was more easily said than done. Nevertheless, Hodge, in approving the SKILA plan, publicly reaffirmed American advocacy of the Moscow agreement.[67]

Conservative Korean leaders began at once to mobilize in an effort to control the forthcoming SKILA elections. The Communist party, on the other hand, denounced American policy as premature and in violation of the Moscow agreement. Pak Hŏn-yŏng, Communist leader of the wartime underground, instituted an organized campaign to disrupt the Kim–Yŏ coalition. Yŏ held out against Communist pressure and labored diligently to moderate leftist demands for immediate and sweeping reforms.[68] Washington's professed willingness to reopen talks with the Soviet Union also hampered Communist operations. On August 13, 1946, Acheson reiterated the administration's position that it was ready to resume Soviet-American negotiations at any time. Kim and Yŏ therefore experienced marked progress in reducing Communist political appeal and in increasing popular enthusiasm regarding the SKILA elections.[69]

American occupation officials, while preparing for the selection of delegates to the interim legislature, also took steps to provide certain Koreans with experience in government and administration. Hodge appointed several local leaders to work with various AMG bureaus as a prelude to the creation of a South Korean Interim Government (SKIG). The USAFIK commander even began to transfer operational control to the Koreans on August 31, 1946. Most southern Koreans acclaimed this new opportunity to participate in governing their own affairs. While many Koreans joined the Kim–Yŏ coalition in anticipation of eventual self-government, a desire for major reforms caused several moderate leaders of the right to split with the extreme conservatives. At the same time, Hodge acted to regularize fiscal and economic policies in the American zone. He also formally established a "constabulary army," supplying it with American equipment and allowing it to participate in the military maneuvers and antiguerrilla operations of the USAFIK. By early 1947, the constabulary army had elevated its prestige and effectiveness to the point where it could check the police force, which frequently abused its power.[70]

For Langdon, the success of Washington's policy in southern Korea was more apparent than real. On August 23, he assailed the administration's strategy of delay, arguing that the "law of diminishing returns has set in." Since leftists in the American zone were bent upon an obstructionist course, any progress toward genuine democracy was impossible. Only reunification, Langdon insisted, would satisfy all Koreans and end domestic political unrest. Consequently, a resumption of the Joint Commission negotiations was essential. Significantly, Arthur C. Bunce, Hodge's economic advisor, disagreed with Langdon's dire assessment. In a cable to Byrnes, Bunce admitted that the situation was difficult but voiced unqualified agreement with Pauley's recommendations. If Washington spent enough money, he predicted, the United States would be able to "outsit the Russians and sell democracy." Bunce's comments reinforced the administration's determination to persevere. While postponing "an approach to the Soviets on the governmental level," Washington instructed the AMG to encourage local support for land reform, equal economic opportunity, trade unionism, and freedom of political expression.[71]

American optimism appeared justified after Langdon visited the Soviet zone on October 9, 1946. While in the north, Hodge's political advisor enjoyed not only freedom of movement but also cordial treatment. During discussions, Soviet political advisor Balasanov confided to Langdon that his government was anxious to reconvene the Joint Commission. However, Moscow would never agree to consult with Rhee and Kim Ku because these two leaders were hostile to the Soviet Union. He also disdained the American notion that opposition to trusteeship was compatible with support for the Moscow agreement. Langdon argued that eventually Rhee and Kim Ku would favor trusteeship and therefore should participate in the consultation process. Balasanov vehemently disagreed, but he accepted a compromise nonetheless. Langdon and Balasanov decided that a pledge not to undermine the work of the Joint Commission was sufficient to warrant consultation.[72]

Langdon returned from Pyongyang in a buoyant mood. In his report to Washington, he explained that the Langdon–Balasanov compromise would require all Korean parties to promise not to "foment or instigate mass opposition" either to the Joint Commission or the Moscow agreement. More important, Balasanov demonstrated a genuine desire for cooperation, while commenting hopefully that a Soviet-American settlement in Korea would foster a relaxation of tension in other areas. But on October 26, Chistiakov communicated to Hodge his willingness to resume talks based only on the "exact fulfillment" of the Moscow agreement. With some justification, the Soviet occupation commander observed that it would be counterproductive to discuss the implementation of the Moscow agreement with those Koreans whose pledge of support was "an empty declaration." Chistiakov reminded Hodge that it was the United States, not the Soviet Union, that had suspended the Joint Commission. Only the creation of a provisional government, however, would open the door to Korea's reunification and economic recovery.[73]

On November 1, Hodge proposed the resumption of the Joint Commission negotiations based on the Langdon–Balasanov compromise. The United States remained committed to the principle of freedom of expression, but Hodge agreed that instigation of mass opposition to the Moscow agreement was improper and an abuse of free speech. Then the USAFIK commander attempted to defend his previous actions. The Moscow agreement, Hodge argued lamely, was not specific on the exact nature of the trusteeship envisioned for Korea. Chistiakov replied on November 26 that it was imperative to exclude from consultation all Koreans who previously had opposed trusteeship. The Langdon–Balasanov compromise provided no guarantee that these "reactionary parties and groups" would "retreat from their hostile position towards the Moscow Decision, but merely curtail temporarily their activities . . . so that they may have an opportunity to take part in the consultation with the Joint Commission." While Moscow was a champion of free speech, it also believed that consultation with such groups would hamper efforts to implement the Moscow agreement.[74]

Hodge quickly grasped at Soviet support for freedom of expression. The two nations, he suggested, were close to arriving at a basis for the resumption of negotiations at the Joint Commission. Although exclusion of those opposed to a trusteeship violated the principle of freedom of speech, Hodge offered to accept the Soviet proposal of October 26 as the basis for discussion. The absence of any Soviet reply, coupled with the rigidity of Chistiakov's prior communications, convinced Bunce that Moscow had spurned the latest American proposal.[75] As 1946 came to a close, it appeared that negotiations between the United States and the Soviet Union never would resume, leaving Korea a divided nation.

Moscow's reluctance to reconvene the Joint Commission demonstrated that the administration's policy of "patience with firmness" would not induce the Soviets to retreat. Ironically, further delay instead had undermined the American position south of the 38th parallel as Hodge's efforts to build political unity and stability failed miserably. The Communist party understood that Washington's "Koreanization" policy soon would rob them of any influence in southern affairs. Late in September, Pak Hŏn-yŏng organized a campaign of strikes and disturbances to protest the creation of a separate government. The Communists resorted to threats and bribes; they even kidnapped Yŏ in an effort to destroy the Coalition Committee. Initially, Hodge resisted pressure from the right to retaliate, following a course of inaction. If the United States opted for repression, the general could foresee Communists becoming martyrs, while American occupation officials would appear to resemble the Japanese. After a serious riot at Taegu in October, however, Hodge issued a warrant for Pak's arrest and permitted the police and rightist youth groups to punish the Communists. A vicious circle of violence then emerged as rightist brutality provoked leftist retaliation, setting off a new round of savage excesses.[76]

Hodge easily accepted the simple explanation that political turmoil in the American zone was part of a Soviet plot to seize power. In fact, many Koreans were expressing frustration with rising inflation and persistent shortages. Worse still was the onerous rice collection program. Chaotic postwar economic conditions and the influx of refugees from the north had created a severe food deficiency, compelling Hodge to institute a program of forced requisitions. For most Koreans, the quotas were excessive. As the general public resisted collection, Hodge increasingly turned to the Korean police to enforce the system. Unfortunately, the police exploited far-reaching powers for investigation and punishment to eliminate leftist opposition, frequently resorting to terrorism and torture. To a group of visiting American congressmen, the United States appeared to be following an "uncertain, fumbling, confused policy" in Korea.[77]

Rising violence and disruption in the American zone jeopardized the upcoming SKILA elections. Simultaneously, Kim and Yŏ were finding it more difficult to promote political unity in the prevailing atmosphere of murder, sabotage, and destruction. When the Coalition Committee complained that domestic instability would make truly free elections impossible, Hodge convened a "Joint American-Korean Conference" to investigate the reasons for popular discontent.[78] Kim and Yŏ were not, however, entirely satisfied. When the Coalition Committee announced on October 4 that it favored the early creation of an interim legislative assembly, it attached certain conditions. Kim and Yŏ demanded the elimination of any American veto over legislation, exclusion of collaborators as candidates for election, recognition of the national authority of the body, and provisions for close observation and supervision of the voting process to ensure fairness.[79] This conditional endorsement permitted American occupation officials to proceed with plans for the creation of the SKILA.

Cooperation between the United States and the Coalition Committee was exceedingly short-lived, primarily because Hodge thoroughly mishandled the SKILA elections. Ignoring the demands of the Kim–Yŏ group, Military Governor Lerch announced on October 13 that the AMG would conduct elections within five days. Yŏ immediately protested that recent disturbances provided a poor atmosphere for free choice. Moreover, many Korean leaders were in hiding and would be unprepared for participation.[80] Despite such cogent arguments, the AMG held elections from October 17 through 22 without serious disorders. Kim and Yŏ boycotted the voting process, however, because of Hodge's unnecessary haste. As a result, and because followers of Rhee and Kim Ku controlled the administrative facilities, the conservatives scored a sweeping victory. Many collaborators gained election, and only fourteen of forty-five representatives to the SKILA were not extreme rightists. Nevertheless, Hodge was elated. Lerch announced that the SKILA would convene to begin its deliberations no later than November 3, 1946.[81]

Few knowledgeable observers accepted the outcome of the SKILA elections as a product of the popular will. Even Bunce, in one private letter, admitted that the elections were "a rubber stamp affair."[82]

Fearful of a leftist victory, the AMG election law guaranteed a rightist triumph. Indirect elections permitted the village "hetman" to dictate the selection of electors, while the taxpayer qualification meant overrepresentation for Korean landlords, businessmen, and professional people. The Coalition Committee also charged police interference, misrepresentation, and falsification of returns. In view of the intimidation, beatings, and mob action of the prior month, no reasonable person could have expected truly free elections.[83] Perhaps worse, according to former AMG official E. Grant Meade, "the majority of the people were in favor of the left, but were too apathetic, cynical, and poorly organized to make a real contest of the election."[84]

American blunders during and after the SKILA elections showed once again that the administration's policy toward Korea suffered from illogic and inconsistency. After striving diligently to fashion a moderate alternative in Korean politics, the AMG proceeded to undermine the Kim–Yŏ group. American occupation officials were preoccupied with limiting leftist political power in the south. Communist dominance in the north meant that maximum rightist representation in the American zone was crucial to the maintenance of some sort of balance.[85] To placate Kim, Hodge promised to appoint more moderate delegates to the remaining forty-five seats. He even asked Kim to supply him with a list of prospective candidates and from it Hodge selected what one observer considered a fair cross section of Korean political thought. Hodge also approved new elections in two districts where evidence of fraud was particularly apparent. Early in December, the American occupation commander proudly announced that the SKILA would convene on schedule with Kim serving as president of the interim legislative body.[86]

Hodge's efforts to appease Kim and the moderates infuriated the extreme right. On December 12, twenty conservative delegates boycotted the opening session of the new legislature in protest over Hodge's appointments. Rhee already had met with the USAFIK commander and had condemned his actions. Hodge, in response, warned Rhee that he would not permit the extreme conservatives either to intimidate him or to seize power illegally.[87] Unable to influence Hodge, Rhee traveled to the United States and tried to arrange a meeting with Byrnes. After the State Department rejected his request, Rhee publicly scolded the Truman administration for appeasement, blaming Washington's advocacy of trusteeship for producing a divided Korea.[88]

Rhee's activities chagrined American leaders both in Washington and in Seoul. If the extreme conservatives remained loyal to Rhee, the United States would have no choice under the Langdon–Balasanov compromise but to insist upon their exclusion from consultation.[89] To counter Rhee's disruptive tactics, the State Department instructed the AMG to strengthen the Coalition Committee and the SKILA. The rising popularity of moderate forces in southern Korea would persuade Rhee that his cause was hopelesss. On December 21, Hodge recommended to Rhee that he dissolve the Representative Democratic Council, since "it no longer has any official status as an advisory body connected with the military government."[90]

Washington's attempt to undermine Rhee's political position caused the rightist leader to implement a bold and aggressive new strategy. Recognizing that the popular desire for self-government was gathering strength, he issued a proclamation demanding immediate independence and national self-determination for southern Korea alone. If the United States failed to comply, Rhee ordered his followers to stage acts of violence and sitdown strikes to demonstrate that Washington was "helpless without cooperation of his group." These were not idle threats. Aside from Rhee's substantial popularity, Hodge had appointed many extreme conservatives to positions in the South Korean Interim Government who were now Rhee's operatives. Faced with this sharp challenge to his authority, Hodge begged Washington for help, warning that "we cannot and must not overlook his potential to do irreparable damage unless carefully handled." Perhaps Goodfellow or Arnold, he pleaded, could approach Rhee and persuade him to forsake his demands for a separate southern Korean government.[91]

By the end of 1946, it was painfully clear that Truman's policy of "patience with firmness" in Korea had failed. Not only had Moscow refused to reconvene the Joint Commission, but events in the American zone were not likely to force the Soviet Union to retreat as the administration had anticipated. Washington's decision to sponsor the creation of a moderate coalition in southern Korea had alienated Rhee thoroughly. Hodge was guilty of utter incompetence in attempting to bolster the Kim–Yŏ group. Even worse, rapid deterioration continued to characterize economic and social conditions south of the 38th parallel. Drastic steps to improve the situation were imperative, yet the military and diplomatic capabilities of the United States with respect to Korea were extremely limited. Hodge was barely able to maintain the security of his military command in southern Korea, let alone apply enough pressure on the Soviet Union to moderate its position. Understandably, many administration officials were advocating the redeployment of American occupation forces from Korea to Japan, where the United States had far more vital strategic interests.[92]

Yet Truman's predicament in Korea was predictable. Once the president had chosen not to entertain any more proposals for compromise with Moscow, a Soviet-American deadlock was certain. Significantly, the administration remained wedded to its policy of verbal toughness even after the breakdown in negotiations at the Joint Commission.[93] Truman's harsh words, however, did not produce the desired change in Moscow's behavior; nor did holding firmly to principle raise the odds favoring a settlement on American terms.[94] The gap between ends and means in Washington's Korea policy was both obvious and dangerous. If Truman failed to bring the administration's objectives in line with American capabilities, the United States would have no choice but to withdraw from southern Korea forthwith under humiliating circumstances. Far from resolving American problems, by the end of 1946 "patience with firmness" in Korea had resulted in a deeper crisis gravely threatening the credibility and prestige of the United States throughout East Asia.

CHAPTER 5

An Avenue for Escape

American experiences in Korea during 1946 left little doubt that an attempt to outwait the Russians was foolish. Not only had Moscow refused to negotiate, but Washington's position in southern Korea was rapidly becoming untenable. By early 1947, American leaders knew that further indecision would invite disaster, but domestic pressure for demobilization and a balanced budget seriously limited the administration's policy options. Significantly, Truman shared the popular desire to restrict the extent and duration of the United States commitment to preserve world peace and stability. In Korea, however, a decision to withdraw would involve grave dangers. The departure of American occupation forces, one group of military planners noted in October 1946, would "leave Korea's politically immature people open to control through highly-organized Communist minorities." Yet this JCS study predicted pessimistically that Moscow probably would obtain at least indirect sway throughout Korea by 1956 regardless of American actions.[1] Faced with this distasteful dilemma, Truman began to search for an avenue for escape in Korea that would permit the administration to maintain its credibility in Asia without an unqualified commitment of American power.[2]

After more than a year of military occupation, reports from Seoul afforded scant room for optimism. During October 1946, Hodge informed Washington that he expected a Soviet-sponsored invasion of southern Korea within six months and doubted the ability of the USAFIK to deter a northern Korean attempt at forcible reunification. He urgently requested additional troops and permission to strengthen the rightist youth groups. In a personal letter to Secretary of War Patterson, the occupation commander sadly explained that "things are far from smooth" because

the Koreans want their own country to themselves and . . . the Russians are constantly infiltrating their highly trained and indoctrinated agitators into our zone to take full advantage of every possible point in the low level economic situation that can cause discontent. . . . The international flavor is becoming heavy and there can be no question but as to the worldwide push of Communism with the main all-out effort now directed against the United States. I hope our nation wakes up before we become too saturated with the Soviet brand of "democracy."

Early in 1947, Hodge cabled the War Department that inflation, power shortages, and insufficient food were contributing to a major economic crisis which was discrediting the AMG and spawning domestic violence. Hodge appealed to the administration to forsake its persistent devotion to negotiations with Moscow. This policy, he observed, only encouraged further dismay, discouragement, and declining Korean morale.[3]

Once again, Washington ignored Hodge's advice. Both Vincent and MacArthur considered the utilization of youth groups for defense to be "entirely inappropriate." Furthermore, the State Department still hoped for an early resumption of negotiations at the Joint Commission and wanted to avoid any indication that Washington favored a sharper confrontation. As one administration official explained at the time:

Our position in Korea is clearly hopeless unless cooperation with the Russians can eventually be achieved. Unilateral action must be presented as a short-run course which has been forced upon us. Our program, it should be emphasized, is a means of demonstrating to the USSR that cooperation is desirable.

If Washington demonstrated its firm intention to fulfill its commitments and its willingness to cooperate with the Soviet Union, Truman's diplomatic advisors believed that Korea would gain a democratic government and national independence.[4]

War Department officials were determined nevertheless to force a thorough reconsideration of American policy in southern Korea. During January 1947, manpower and material shortages were so acute that a continued occupation seemed impossible. Truman's military advisors complained that the War Department lacked sufficient resources to finance American operations in Korea—which now cost more than $1 million daily. Patterson decided that the State Department had to ask Congress for additional funds or accept the necessity for military withdrawal. Simultaneously, MacArthur submitted a series of proposals for breaking the Soviet-American deadlock. On January 22, Washington began to consider his recommendations, which included the submission of the Korean issue to the United Nations, the formation of an international commission of disinterested nations to devise a plan for fulfilling the Cairo Declaration, a four-power conference to clarify the Moscow agreement, and, finally, a high-level Soviet-American conference to resolve basic issues preventing reunification and independence. Further delay, MacArthur warned, would be calamitous for the Korean people, Allied wartime commitments, and American prestige and influence in Asia.[5]

On January 23, Assistant Secretary of War Howard C. Peterson received detailed comments on MacArthur's proposal from experts in the War Department. This memorandum rejected as premature both MacArthur's recommendations and the alternative course of granting southern Korea immediate independence. These military officials proposed instead that the United States redouble its efforts for an agreement with the Soviet Union while transferring administrative responsibility from Hodge to the State Department. After reading the memorandum, Vincent concurred that MacArthur's recommendations were impractical because all of them required Soviet cooperation for success. A new approach to Moscow, on the other hand, probably would be useless and merely indicate Washington's impatience. Vincent endorsed Patterson's proposal to request $50 million from Congress to continue American occupation. The State Department apparently retained confidence that if the United States stood firm the Soviet Union eventually would retreat.[6]

Patterson spoke strongly in favor of adopting the War Department's proposal at an SWNCC meeting on January 29. At that time, he labeled Korea the "single most urgent problem now facing the War Department." After noting significant shortages of transportation, electric power, and fertilizer, the secretary of war emphasized that a paucity of able Korean political leaders only magnified the AMG's problems. Further negotiations with the Soviet Union also seemed pointless. Despite Patterson's arguments, the SWNCC decided that continued occupation of Korea was essential. To relieve pressure on the War Department, Truman's advisors agreed to approach Congress with a request for financial assistance to prevent economic and political collapse in the American zone of military occupation. The SWNCC also created a "Special Inter-Departmental Committee" composed of Arnold, James K. Penfield, and J. Weldon Jones (representing the War Department, State Department, and Bureau of the Budget, respectively) to formulate a positive program for aid to Korea.[7]

Soviet policy in northern Korea early in 1947 further encouraged the administration to abandon its patient and firm approach. Having completed its reform program the Provisional People's Committee held elections from November 1946 to March 1947 for representatives who would create a permanent government. As anticipated, there was only one candidate for each office who sought either approval or rejection from the voters. In February, a "Congress of People's Committees" convened and approved retroactively all previous reforms. It also adopted a national economic plan for the completion of nationalization and the consummation of agrarian collectivization. The congress then created a permanent "People's Assembly," which in turn elected a presidium and organized a supreme court.[8] Moscow's actions had hardly taken place in a vacuum. Much as the United States was building the foundation for self-government in southern Korea, the Soviet Union was fashioning a separate regime north of the 38th parallel.

While Moscow consolidated its position in northern Korea, Rhee accelerated his public attack on American occupation policies in the south. Langdon reported early in 1947 that Rhee's "henchmen" were organizing a campaign of violence and obstruction aimed at embarrassing the United States. He urged Washington to issue a statement warning those involved in disruptive activities that opposition to the Moscow agreement would preclude participation in any provisional government. The administration complied at once, publishing Hodge's public order calling on all Koreans to cease instigating opposition to the AMG. Significantly, the USAFIK commander freely admitted in his statement that the Korean dissidents, through "ill-advised political activity," were hampering and delaying a settlement at the Joint Commission.[9]

Words alone would not deter Rhee. Because of early American backing, the extreme conservatives dominated not only the Korean police force but the National Youth Movement as well. In fact, the USAFIK had provided training and equipment for both groups. The National Youth Movement now numbered approximately 30,000 and was under the command of a former officer in the Chinese army named Yi Pŏm-sŏk, who retained close ties with Chiang Kai-shek.

Ultranationalism and strict discipline were the prime characteristics of the movement. Unfortunately, most members were sons of wealthy landlords and businessmen, who, as Langdon lamented in one cable, invariably belonged to "those political parties which, by their agitation of the 'trusteeship' issue, . . . have caused US-USSR relations in the country to become even more strained." Another official observed cynically that "the Kuomintang youth groups were hardly ones to emulate in the quest of establishing a sound basis for a democratic society in Korea." Nevertheless, the National Youth Movement was a major source of political agitation and the police represented an unreliable check on its activities.[10]

American attempts to reduce criticism from the extreme right made Rhee angry and even more determined to force the United States to alter its policies. The old patriot now began a personal assault on Hodge, charging that the USAFIK commander was responsible for the delay in granting independence to Korea. In a personal letter to MacArthur, Rhee appealed for help in persuading Washington to forsake further negotiations with Moscow. He urged instead separate elections for a provisional government in southern Korea alone.[11] At the SKILA, the conservatives obtained passage of a resolution denouncing trusteeship and rejecting any compromise on the principle of freedom of expression. Hodge grumbled that although the great majority of Koreans opposed trusteeship, a few rightist leaders were exploiting the issue to further "their own ends and rebuild a waning personal power." If the Joint Commission reconvened, he confessed, the United States would have to accept the exclusion of these groups from consultation.[12]

Rhee's strategy had placed the United States in a nearly impossible position. If Moscow agreed to resume negotiations, the absence of the conservatives would guarantee that a reunited Korea would have a leftist-dominated provisional government. Nor would the formation of a separate government in southern Korea necessarily improve the situation, since Korean leaders seemed incapable of cooperation. Hodge was unable to suggest any alternative courses of action worthy of consideration, offering instead an extremely dire prognosis:

> Korea has developed into a real hot-spot of the Orient, now ripe for a full-fledged civil war of unsurpassed savagery unless positive and cooperative international action is taken immediately. It is my carefully considered opinion that unless the Joint Commission should successfully

reconvene or positive action be taken in Korean situation on a national
level within the next two months, we may lose the opportunity of
accomplishing our avowed mission in Korea and will have lost the confidence of the Koreans.[13]

Few American leaders familiar with the Korean predicament could
have quibbled with Hodge's assessment. The administration had to
alter its policy in Korea or risk a catastrophe.

Late in February 1947, the Special Inter-Departmental Committee
completed its reconsideration of the Korean problem. Its report concluded that the USAFIK's position soon would become untenable if
the United States maintained its present policy. Granting independence to a separate South Korea, on the other hand, would stimulate
further economic deterioration and lead eventually to Soviet domination. The United States could refer the entire Korean matter to the
United Nations, but this measure would constitute an admission of
failure and draw charges of bad faith from the Soviet Union. Since
Washington's biggest problems in southern Korea were lack of money
and an uncooperative populace, the Special Inter-Departmental
Committee recommended instead the adoption of a plan for $600
million in economic aid over three years. Implementation of the assistance program in conjunction with an approach at the Council of Foreign Ministers would demonstrate to Congress Truman's determination to fulfill American commitments in Korea and convey to
Moscow the extent of Washington's resolve. Without such positive
action, the administration would have no choice but to withdraw militarily and thereby "seriously impair the U.S. world position."[14]

Truman's advisors thus had devised an aggressive program that
offered some hope of receiving wide popular backing in southern
Korea. Once the Korean people began to enjoy the benefits of self-
government and economic recovery, American leaders believed that
democracy and private enterprise would provide a stable basis for
Korea's independence. Yet the committee's recommendations also
constituted in essence a decision to create a separate government
south of the 38th parallel. These administration officials assumed
that if the United States spent enough money, Stalin would be unable to match the effort and would have to accept a settlement on
American terms. Obviously, the United States could not betray any
sign of weakness or the policy was doomed to fail. Washington's
defeat in a clear test of strength with Moscow, the committee's report

emphasized, could have disastrous worldwide ramifications. The State Department endorsed the program enthusiastically, although it reiterated its opposition to approaching the Soviet government for the resumption of negotiations at the Joint Commission.[15]

In Korea, Langdon had arrived at conclusions resembling those of the Special Inter-Departmental Committee. He favored the building of a strong constitutional, representative, democratic government in southern Korea under the leadership of Kim Kyu-sik. A constructive program of economic assistance coupled with Koreanization would foster the emergence of a genuinely moderate political majority. The American policy, if successful, would prevent Rhee from seizing power and induce the Soviets to cooperate at the Joint Commission. Bunce echoed Langdon's faith in the plan.[16] To muster support for this activist program in Korea, Hodge returned to Washington early in 1947. Patterson pressed Truman to meet with the USAFIK commander and discuss the critical nature of the situation in Korea. Hodge was "a splendid soldier," the secretary of war told the president, with a "brilliant fighting record" during World War II.[17]

Shortly after his arrival in the United States, Hodge conferred with Truman at the White House. The USAFIK commander commented in detail on the economic distress and political chaos in the American occupation zone, stating emphatically that only a Soviet-American agreement would provide for the resolution of Korea's difficulties. Evidently Hodge's remarks impressed the president, for Truman authorized one final overture to the Soviet Union. In his public comments after the conference, Hodge chastised Moscow for creating a powerful army in northern Korea in direct violation of the Moscow agreement. He speculated that the military force included at least 500,000 troops. This establishment placed southern Korea at the mercy of its militarily superior northern neighbor. If Soviet recalcitrance continued, Hodge explained that the United States would have no choice but to sponsor a separate government in southern Korea.[18]

While in Washington, Hodge also appeared before the Senate Armed Services Committee on February 25. In his recollections of the testimony, Senator Harry Byrd of Virginia remembered the USAFIK commander's warning that if the United States withdrew, the northern regime would seize control over the entire peninsula. Undoubtedly, Hodge did not recommend continued occupation but probably emphasized instead the necessity for a negotiated settlement.[19] In any event, at a press conference that same day, newly appointed Secretary of State George C. Marshall announced that he had ordered a new study of American policy in Korea. The *New York Times* lauded Washington's apparent determination to prevent Korea from becoming a "new Poland" in Asia. It also predicted that Marshall would raise the issue at the upcoming Council of Foreign Ministers meeting scheduled for April in Moscow.[20]

Truman's reconsideration of his policy in Korea came at a particularly troublesome moment in his administration. Adoption of the recommendations of the Special Inter-Departmental Committee would require congressional approval. In 1946, however, the Republican party had registered significant gains in the midterm elections. For the first time since 1930, the Democrats were in a minority in both houses of Congress. Accordingly, Truman and his advisors expected staunch congressional opposition to foreign aid and military expenditures. Congress provided early justification for the administration's apprehension when it cut $6 billion from the budget to allow for a reduction in taxes. Simultaneously, the crisis in Greece and Turkey forced Washington to reassess its overall strategy in the Cold War.[21] The outcome of this reappraisal would have a decisive impact on American policy in Korea.

On March 10, 1947, Hilldring signaled the administration's new interest in resolving the Korean impasse when he addressed the Economic Club of Detroit. In his speech, the assistant secretary of state declared that an American failure to fulfill its moral obligations to Korea would bring "discouragement and disappointment to democratic peoples everywhere . . . , and the damage to real democracy throughout the world would be incalculable." Consequently, Washington intended to fortify its position in southern Korea while waiting for the Joint Commission to reconvene.[22] Two days later, Truman used similar arguments when he delivered his famous address to Congress requesting economic and military assistance for Greece and Turkey. As the president explained in his "Truman Doctrine" speech, "I believe that we must assist free peoples to work out their own destinies in their own way."[23]

Scholars generally agree that in 1947 the United States rejected with finality the prewar policy of isolationism and assumed complete responsibility for the preservation of international stability against the challenge of Soviet ideology and power.[24] Yet one must question whether the Truman Doctrine speech actually represented a major turning point in postwar American diplomacy. The United States already had registered opposition to totalitarianism during World War II and had implemented certain measures after 1945 to counter the Soviet threat. The failure of "patience with firmness" had compelled the administration to alter its tactics, but the basic strategy had not changed. Truman now sought to contain the Soviet Union through the use of economic assistance, and this policy required congressional approval. The crisis in Greece and Turkey was then merely the first occasion obliging Truman to request an appropriation of funds.[25]

Truman's actions regarding Greece and Turkey reveal his preference for limited means in combating the Soviet threat. In the Truman Doctrine speech, the president himself asserted that "our help should be primarily through economic and financial aid which is essential to economic stability and orderly political processes." At relatively low cost, and without the loss of American lives, Truman expected to halt Soviet expansion through encouraging the development of local self-defense.[26] The administration suspected, however, that Congress and the American people would not accept the financial burdens involved in adopting the containment policy. The Republican party had made plain its determination to reduce government spending, and its emphasis on economy threatened to circumvent Truman's strategy. The president was aware that it would be impossible to implement containment unless he educated the general public to the necessity for accepting the responsibilities of world leadership. Consequently, his speech appealed directly to emotion and portrayed the Soviet threat to American security as immediate, dire, and global in proportions.[27]

But Truman's elaboration of the containment policy actually implied a much wider commitment of American power and prestige than the president intended. Truman, in reality, envisioned a plan of "rational interventionism" relying wholly on economic aid and technical advice. Far from being revolutionary, containment sought to preserve American security through a measured increase in an already reluctant commitment to act decisively for the achievement of international peace and stability.[28] Containment was, at the same time, a logical and somewhat realistic response to the perceived Soviet strategy of political intimidation and subversion. Conscious of the severe restrictions on American manpower, the Truman administration never contemplated using combat troops. Nor did most American leaders believe that an outbreak of hostilities would be probable if the United States provided southern Korea with limited military assistance. According to the SWNCC defense program, southern Korea would receive small arms and enough radios, vehicles, and spare parts to equip a "police-style constabulary army" consisting of about 25,000 individuals.[29]

Korea thus provides an excellent example of containment in Asia. In 1947, the United States embarked on a long and difficult road leading toward the creation of a stable government in southern Korea capable of defending itself. Dean Acheson, during the Senate Foreign Relations Committee hearings on aid to Greece, confirmed that the administration was contemplating a $200 million program in economic and technical assistance for Korea spread over three years. This plan, if successful, would permit the United States to withdraw from Korea, but not at the price of surrendering the peninsula to Soviet domination.[30] Rather, the emergence of a viable government south of the 38th parallel would induce Moscow to compromise and permit reunification on terms acceptable to the United States. At least that was the hope.

American leaders had found what appeared to be a promising avenue for escape from the Korean predicament at a time when the pressure for military withdrawal was acute. During early 1947, disgruntled members of the American occupation force instigated a publicity campaign to dramatize the desperate plight confronting the United States in Korea. Several servicemen wrote letters to newspapers and relatives complaining about insufficient food, inferior medical care, inadequate housing, deficient clothing, and preferential treatment for the officers. Perhaps worse, some berated the AMG for inefficiency and corruption, charging occupation officials with brutality and illegal search and seizure.[31] Hodge received word of these accusations while in Washington and promptly ordered an investigation. Subsequent reports dismissed these grievances as either exaggerated or groundless, attributing them to the loneliness of newly arrived soldiers.[32] Nevertheless, the administration undoubtedly discerned that a decision to delay withdrawal much longer involved significant political risks.

Simultaneously, the State Department was refining its aid program for southern Korea. In its final form, the plan envisioned $540 million in assistance to the new provisional government. Within three months after securing congressional approval, civilian advisors would replace military officials, while Korean participation in governmental affairs would expand greatly. In addition, the president would appoint a new political advisor in Korea with much wider administrative and decision-making powers. On March 28, Acheson forwarded the proposal to Patterson. The State Department, he explained, intended to implement the program during fiscal 1948 even if negotiations resumed at the Joint Commission.[33] In response, Patterson expressed doubts that an aid program would improve conditions in southern Korea because the situation was "potentially explosive." In a letter to Assistant Secretary of War Peterson, Patterson faulted the State Department's plan for prolonging the occupation and advocated instead "a course of action whereby we get out of Korea at an early date and . . . all our measures should have early withdrawal as their overriding objective."[34]

While agreeing on the necessity for military withdrawal, Hodge did not favor an abrupt end to American occupation. Upon his return to southern Korea, he publicly endorsed a program for economic and political assistance. "If we can't get Russian cooperation," Hodge remarked at a press conference, "we must carry out our commitments alone." The USAFIK commander emphasized that the United States was not creating a separate government, but only attempting to foster freedom, democracy, and sound government in southern Korea. Some observers in the United States and Korea speculated that once Moscow understood the scope of the American plan, it would move to reconvene the Joint Commission. For these optimists, news that Lieutenant General G. P. Korotkov had replaced Chistiakov as occupation commander suggested that the Soviets had opted for a more conciliatory approach.[35]

Truman was not as eager as Hodge to publicize American plans for Korea. On two occasions during the spring of 1947, the president denied having reached a decision on extending aid to the divided nation.[36] In all likelihood, Truman did not want to alarm Stalin on the eve of Marshall's final overture at the upcoming meeting in Moscow. The administration had made an irrevocable decision, however, to break the Korean deadlock. If the Soviets refused to reopen negotiations, the United States intended to implement its aid program for southern Korea and, as a last resort, submit the entire issue to the United Nations for consideration. Washington was determined to withdraw as well, since it believed that the United States could not afford to match Soviet military power on the peninsula. Vincent summarized the administration's attitude when he stated succinctly that "our program seems to us to be the only feasible way of accomplishing [the reduction of our commitments] once we rule out the alternative of abandonment of Korea to USSR domination."[37]

For Truman and his advisors, then, the fourth Council of Foreign Ministers meeting in April 1947 represented the last chance for the Soviet Union to choose cooperation rather than confrontation with respect to Korea. Shortly after his arrival in Moscow, Marshall cabled to Washington, for comment, a draft letter to Molotov requesting resumption of the negotiations at the Joint Commission. Acheson's reply advised that any American overture should emphasize total Soviet responsibility for the Korean impasse. Moscow had sought to exclude a majority of the Korean leaders; until it reversed its position and recognized the principle of freedom of expression, any further negotiations would be futile. Acheson obviously had dismissed Marshall's final overture on Korea as a gratuitous formality. Once Moscow reaffirmed its intransigent position, the United States, with the appearance of legitimacy, would implement the Moscow agreement in the southern zone alone.[38]

Soviet-American negotiations at Moscow were a dismal failure. Following the meeting's adjournment, Truman decided that it would be unwise to conduct further bilateral talks with Moscow at the government level. Instead, Washington would concentrate in the future on building "situations of strength" in local areas to halt the Soviet advance. At the same time, Soviet-American differences now were receiving wide comment in the American press as the existence of a "Cold War" became common knowledge among the general public.[39] Strangely, the Moscow Conference of 1947 also witnessed a Soviet-American reconciliation, albeit temporarily, on the issue of Korea. Stalin surely was aware that a separate government in southern Korea would be anti-Soviet and probably decided to make one final stab at a negotiated settlement.[40]

Marshall's letter to Molotov at Moscow adhered to Acheson's recommendations. It blamed the Soviet Union for blocking the economic reunification of Korea and thereby preventing the realization of the Cairo Declaration. The American occupation commander had attempted to reopen the Joint Commission negotiations, but the Soviet commander had not responded favorably. The deadlock, Marshall insisted, was the product of the Soviet Union's desire to exclude a majority of southern Korea's leaders from consultation because of a

unilateral definition of the word "democratic." He then recommended that, in the interests of Korea's well-being, the Joint Commission
reconvene on a basis of respect for the principle of freedom of expression. In the meantime, Washington intended to implement the Moscow agreement in its own zone of occupation.[41] Marshall's letter was
tantamount to an ultimatum. If the Soviets did not agree to reconvene the Joint Commission on American terms, there would be no
more negotiations.

Not surprisingly, Molotov's response charged that the United States
had violated the terms of the Moscow agreement and therefore was
responsible for the absence of progress at the Joint Commission. Economic and political reunification was a prerequisite for Korean independence and prosperity, Molotov agreed, but possible only after the
formation of a provisional government. Unfortunately, he went on,
the American delegation had insisted upon consultation with individuals avowedly opposed to the basic provisions in the Moscow
agreement and the Soviet delegation had correctly resisted this demand. After summarizing Soviet-sponsored reforms in the north,
Molotov then cleverly pointed to the absence of similar progress in
the south. Since Moscow was dedicated to Korea's eventual independence, however, the Soviet Union would agree to reconvene the Joint
Commission on May 20 "on a basis of an exact execution of the Moscow Agreement on Korea."[42]

Marshall quickly recognized that Moscow planned to use the
phrase "exact execution" to exclude Korean leaders opposed to trusteeship. To avoid any further misunderstandings, he again wrote
Molotov and recited the American interpretation of the Moscow
agreement. The United States believed that the Joint Commission
should not deny any Korean representative the right of consultation
simply because of previously expressed views on the future government of Korea—provided each individual was willing to cooperate
with the major powers. The United States welcomed the suggestion
in Molotov's letter, Marshall continued, that the Soviet Union favored free elections after reunification. If Molotov found the contents
of his letter acceptable, Marshall concluded, the United States would
participate in a resumption of negotiations at the Joint Commission
on May 20, 1947.[43]

In his reply, Molotov referred specifically to the exchange of views
between the occupation commanders on the "conditions for consultation" at the Joint Commission. He then accepted Hodge's amend-

ments to the Soviet proposal of November 26, 1946, which provided for consultation only with those groups fully in accord with the provisions of the Moscow agreement. Signing the communiqué agreed to on April 18, 1946, was sufficient for consideration, he explained, but the negotiators were obliged to exclude from consultation any party or group that "fomented or instigated" active opposition to the work of the Joint Commission. On May 12, Marshall approved Molotov's proposal. It was clear, however, that the extreme conservatives would continue to criticize trusteeship. As Langdon explained, unless the Soviet Union approved unrestricted freedom of expression, the right would not participate.[44]

Administration officials were certain that the threat of a program of economic assistance in southern Korea had forced Moscow to compromise. A confident Truman stated publicly that Secretary Marshall's actions represented a major step toward the realization of a unified and democratic government for all Korea. Few observers in the United States resisted the temptation to repeat Truman's optimism, since the Soviet Union seemingly had backed down in the face of American economic superiority.[45] Rather than producing a settlement, however, Truman's strategy could lead only to a more intractable Soviet-American stalemate in Korea. As Patterson cautioned at the time, a Soviet retreat was unlikely; Moscow occupied a stronger geographic position with regard to Korea, while the United States had few important strategic or economic interests directly involved in the peninsula. Yet both Truman and Marshall discounted Patterson's argument that the benefits of continued occupation were not worth the expense. They still expected to obtain a settlement on acceptable terms and without an unqualified commitment of American power.[46]

Meanwhile, in Korea, Syngman Rhee had received word of the Truman Doctrine speech with undisguised delight. In a personal letter to the president, he congratulated Truman for his "courageous stand against communism" and urged him to "instruct the American military authorities in Korea to follow your policy and abandon their efforts to bring about coalition and cooperation between nationalists and communists." Rhee insisted that Washington should consider Korea as much a "bulwark against communist expansion" as Greece.[47] News of the Marshall–Molotov compromise suddenly transformed rightist euphoria into utter consternation and despair. Kim Ku announced his intention to recreate the KPG and attempt a seizure of power. When Military Governor Lerch barred the KPG from staging political meetings, the Representative Democratic Council demanded immediate American withdrawal and the transfer of political authority to an interim government. It also declared defiantly that it would accept neither trusteeship nor the conditions for consultation. Langdon, in a cable to Washington, ridiculed Rhee and Kim Ku as diehards whose "fate is bound up in the *status quo*." They obviously wanted to embarrass the United States and sabotage the Joint Commission. Since most southern Koreans were jubilant about the resumption of negotiations, Langdon advised the administration to ignore rightist protests.[48]

Rhee's displeasure was understandable. He and Kim Ku cringed at the thought of exclusion from participation in the new provisional government. Although the popular desire for self-government was genuine, the extreme conservatives were in fact exploiting the issue of trusteeship to advance their own political ambitions. Major General Albert E. Brown, Arnold's replacement as head of the American delegation at the Joint Commission, attempted to placate Rhee during several private conferences but experienced little success. Finally, Brown had to warn Rhee and Kim Ku directly that continued criticism of the Soviet Union and trusteeship would result in exclusion from consultation.[49] Rhee replied bitterly that American participation in the Joint Commission guaranteed the emergence of a coalition government in Korea and an eventual Communist takeover. Unless the United States clarified the exact nature of the trusteeship contemplated for Korea, Rhee ominously predicted the outbreak of violent rebellion throughout southern Korea.[50] Hilldring quickly instructed Hodge firmly to resist Rhee's demands. The United States was determined to fulfill the provisions of the Moscow agreement and would advocate the creation of a separate southern Korean government only if negotiations with Moscow failed.[51]

Soviet-American deliberations at the Joint Commission resumed in a cordial atmosphere of informality and ease. But almost immediately the negotiators began to disagree on the conditions for consultation. The Soviets proposed sending invitations for participation in a "consultative body" only to the thirty largest parties, while all other groups would merely submit completed questionnaires. The United States, on the other hand, opposed this proposal and sought discussions with all parties claiming a minimum of a thousand members in two or more provinces. The Joint Commission then could choose a representative body of individuals to form a provisional government.

Shtikov, as head of the Soviet delegation, requested a recess to study the American proposal. A press report that the negotiations had adjourned indefinitely illustrated well the extent of pessimism surrounding the Joint Commission talks.[52]

Nonetheless, the Joint Commission enjoyed steady progress during subsequent sessions, despite certain differences of opinion. On June 7, it completed an agreement on consultation. The Soviets accepted consultation with all parties that signed the communiqué pledging support for the Joint Commission. The Americans, in return, agreed to Moscow's proposal to include a provision in the questionnaires regarding mandatory exclusion of Japanese collaborators from participation in the provisional government because of "the soundness of the principle it represents." Washington's representatives also approved the formation of a "consultative body." Submission of the applications for consultation were due no later than June 23, 1947. After subcommittee 1 had studied the applications, it would compose a list of eligible parties and extend invitations for consultations in Seoul on June 25 and in Pyongyang five days later. Any party or social group could submit a completed questionnaire expressing its preferences with respect to the nature of Korea's future government. On July 5, the Joint Commission and the Koreans would begin work on the creation not only of a provisional government but also a program outlining the structure, principles, and platform of the final Korean government. Marshall publicly acclaimed the agreement as "especially gratifying," voicing hope that the Joint Commission would create a provisional government at an early date.[53]

American leaders easily concluded that the Truman Doctrine speech was responsible for the progress at the Joint Commission. One War Department official speculated that Stalin expected his new attitude of conciliation would

> cause the US Government, or at least Congress, to be so optimistic as to abandon, in expectation of early agreement by the Joint Commission, the proposed program of economic, political and educational rehabilitation in our zone, mentioned by General Marshall. The Soviets would then have reason to hope that delay and obstruction in the Joint Commission will so discourage the US people, and the Korean people, as to assure eventual accomplishment of Soviet aims. . . .[54]

Although this scenario may have been accurate, Stalin certainly would not maintain his conciliatory approach if it appeared that action at the Joint Commission would not produce a provisional government friendly to the Soviet Union. Nevertheless, the administration's confidence in the power of containment as a coercive force now was complete. Truman ordered the formulation of an economic aid program for Korea regardless of events at the Joint Commission. If the threat of economic assistance had induced Soviets to compromise, he reasoned, similar tactics eventually would force Moscow to agree to reunification as well.

Administration planners, however, did not judge American interests in Korea sufficient to warrant an unqualified commitment of power. In fact, one JCS study concluded that Korea was second only to the Philippines in its strategic *unimportance* to the national security of the United States. On the other hand, Greece, Italy, and Iran alone needed American assistance more than Korea. Significantly, the JCS strongly advocated the adoption of an aid program for Korea because

> this is the one country within which we alone have for almost two years carried on ideological warfare in direct contact with our opponents, so that to lose this battle would be gravely detrimental to United States prestige, and therefore security, throughout the world. To abandon this struggle would tend to confirm the suspicion that the United States is not really determined to accept the responsibilities and obligations of world leadership, with consequent detriment to our efforts to bolster those countries of Western Europe which are of primary and vital importance to our national security.

Containment in Korea was essential, then, for ideological and diplomatic reasons rather than military and strategic factors. The JCS indirectly referred to Korea's limited worth when it advised that "current assistance should be given Korea only if the means exist after sufficient assistance has been given the countries of primary importance . . . for the United States."[55]

Truman's military advisors obviously classified Korea as a peripheral issue in their postwar strategic calculations. Nevertheless, they agreed with the State Department that the United States had to make a genuine effort to build economic strength and political stability in southern Korea prior to withdrawal. By contrast, Truman's diplomatic advisors were more sanguine that a positive approach would compel the Soviets to accept a settlement on American terms. On

June 3, 1947, Acting Budget Director Frederick J. Lawton approved the $215 million Korean assistance program for fiscal 1948. In forwarding the plan to Truman, Lawton noted that the State Department "feels that economic improvement in South Korea will help to overcome Soviet reluctance to reunite the two zones." Moreover, reunification would facilitate the achievement of economic self-sufficiency, thereby reducing the cost and duration of American assistance. State Department officials also had prepared for the president a message to Congress requesting approval for the Korean aid program. Truman's diplomatic advisors were confident that the strategy of containment would achieve American objectives in Korea at relatively low cost.[56]

Circumstances prevented the administration from implementing its containment policy in Korea during 1947. First, Chiang Kai-shek was badgering Washington for more economic and military assistance. But the president was hesitant to sponsor Chiang because of Communist military victories over the Nationalists.[57] If Truman denied aid to the Kuomintang, he would have far more difficulty securing an appropriation for Korea. Second, Truman saw that Congress would be parsimonious irrespective of the nation involved. If the administration submitted too many requests in Asia, it would imperil the program for European economic recovery. Congressional reluctance to approve aid for Greece expeditiously during the spring of 1947 caused Truman to consider postponing the appropriation request for Korea. Then, on June 27, Senator Arthur H. Vandenberg took the decision out of the administration's hands. The influential Republican leader notified Acheson that he would oppose any new authorizations for foreign assistance during the remainder of that congressional session.[58]

While Congress was frustrating the application of containment in Korea, events at the Joint Commission experienced a fatal deterioration. The ability of the United States and the Soviet Union to cooperate had surprised Rhee and Kim Ku. Originally the two leaders had disdained to work with the Joint Commission, but now they announced their willingness to participate in consultations. Similarly, when Rhee saw that his strategy of confrontation merely reinforced Washington's determination to implement the Moscow agreement, he toned down his criticism of Hodge and the AMG.[59] Yet both Rhee and Kim Ku still vigorously opposed trusteeship. Once again Brown lectured the extreme right that such an attitude would preclude participation in the consultative process and the new provisional government.[60]

Rhee now resumed his pugnacious posture, rebuking the United States for violating the principle of freedom of expression and intending to betray Korea. Kim Ku organized a series of demonstrations against trusteeship and, on June 24, one group of extreme rightists even pelted members of the Soviet delegation with stones and dirt. Shtikov protested immediately, but Hodge did nothing.[61] These activities substantiated Soviet charges that the pledges of the extreme conservatives to cooperate with the Joint Commission were insincere. Shtikov's demand for the exclusion of rightists opposed to trusteeship was a virtual certainty. Hodge now faced an unpleasant choice. He could not tolerate open defiance of American authority, yet repression of the conservative critics would spawn more violence. Rather than punishing the demonstrators, the USAFIK commander decided merely to chide Kim Ku publicly for his behavior. As expected, the extreme conservatives chose not to apply for consultation and did not even fill out questionnaires. Hodge cabled Washington that Kim Ku now was planning a number of rail and power strikes to demonstrate public hatred of trusteeship.[62]

On June 25, the Joint Commission resumed its deliberations in an "extremely cordial" atmosphere. A preliminary Consultative Body composed of 425 Korean leaders was present. The negotiators had registered the results of the questionnaires, which revealed the delicate nature of the American predicament in Korea. While the leftist respondents manifested considerable unity, organization, and purpose, the rightist element was thoroughly divided. In the north, three parties and thirty-five social organizations, representing approximately thirteen million individuals, filed for consultation. In the south, on the other hand, more than four hundred parties registered with the Joint Commission and claimed an incredible combined membership of sixty-two million people (three times larger than southern Korea's entire population). Slightly more than fifty percent of the respondents were rightist, but even Hodge admitted that the results "obviously indicated duplication and padding." Rhee frankly confessed that he had submitted a questionnaire simply to gain participation in consultation.[63]

Moscow's representatives naturally viewed the number of parties seeking consultation in the south as inordinately high. The right was primarily responsible for the exaggerated figures, since two-thirds of those groups registered were members of the conservative element.[64] If the Joint Commission disqualified only a small number of rightist parties, a leftist majority was certain. Shtikov lost no time insisting on the exclusion of those eight parties belonging to the "Anti-Trustee-ship Committee," which he blamed for the assault on the Soviet dele-gation.[65] Agreeing with the American delegation that the disqualifi-cation of the rightist parties in question would ensure a leftist dominated provisional government, Marshall approved without hesi-tation Brown's request to oppose firmly the exclusion of these par-ties.[66] Soviet-American negotiations thus returned to the same point of impasse confronted in the spring of 1946.

Washington's options at the Joint Commission were now painfully obvious. If the United States inflexibly demanded full rightist partic-ipation in the consultative process, reunification was impossible. On the other hand, a decision to compromise and exclude the most extreme conservatives would guarantee a leftist majority in the new provisional government. The situation seemed even more bleak after the American delegation visited Pyongyang early in July. Joseph E. Jacobs, Hodge's new political advisor, was a member of the group and cabled his observations to Washington. Since Jacobs previously had served in Albania, administration officials undoubtedly read his assessment with keen interest. In his report, Jacobs observed that an authentic Communist satellite regime similar to the Soviet puppet governments in Eastern Europe now controlled affairs in northern Korea. The added presence of a strong army and police force meant that even if the Joint Commission managed to form a representative provisional government, the northern Communists could easily ex-ploit political divisions in the south to obtain total control. For Jacobs, the strategy of the extreme conservatives was both logical and realistic, since the survival of the Korean right depended on the fail-ure of the Joint Commission and American sponsorship of a separate government in southern Korea.[67]

American officials in Seoul now concluded that a negotiated agree-ment acceptable to the United States was no longer attainable.[68] Dur-ing the second week of July, the attitude of the American delegation at the Joint Commission stiffened noticeably, as it firmly rejected the Soviet position on consultations. Hodge asserted that Shtikov's de-mand for the exclusion of conservative parties refusing to renounce membership in the Anti-Trusteeship Committee was a "leftist ruse" designed to prevent all rightist participation in the provisional government. He informed Washington of his intention to insist upon complete freedom of speech for all groups, even at the risk of permanent adjournment. Hodge then lifted the ban on public demonstrations against the Moscow agreement. The conservatives hailed this action as signaling an end to appeasement of the Soviet Union. Few observers failed to discern Washington's apparent willingness to accept an inevitable and final breakdown in negotiations at the Joint Commission.[69]

Rhee's campaign against trusteeship and cooperation with the Soviet Union then reached a climax. During discussions with Hodge, Rhee explained that he and his followers might not participate in a new provisional government or even support it if the Joint Commission was responsible for its creation. Then, on July 19, a rightist fanatic assassinated Yŏ who had been working hard to attract rightist backing for the Coalition Committee. Yŏ's death demonstrated dramatically the price of pursuing a moderate political course. Few Korean leaders in the future could oppose Rhee and advocate cooperation with the Joint Commission without placing their lives in grave danger.[70] Jacobs cabled Washington that a partnership with Rhee was the only remaining option if the United States expected to counter mounting violence and unrest south of the 38th parallel. Ironically, however, Washington's quixotic search for a political alternative to the extreme right had alienated Rhee thoroughly and the conservatives no longer were responsive to American advice and influence.[71]

State Department officials by this time had acknowledged that the creation of a separate government probably was unavoidable. On July 25, Jacobs received word that Washington was giving urgent consideration to a number of alternatives for breaking the deadlock over Korea. The administration promised a specific policy directive within one week. In the meantime, the American delegation at the Joint Commission was "to use all appropriate measures to insure continuance of negotiations."[72] But Washington still winced at the thought of victory for "Rhee's corrupt minority." Realizing that democracy never could flourish in the prevailing atmosphere of terror, extortion, and destruction, the administration ordered Hodge to take steps for the elimination of police corruption and youth group violence. These actions, while admirable, would come too late to undermine the predominance of the extreme right in southern politics.[73] Occupation officials simply lacked enough time to alter political conditions. On July 29, Shtikov spurned the final series of American proposals at the

Joint Commission and negotiations reached the point of complete collapse. Jacobs informed Washington that the Soviet representatives had resorted to a strategy of stall and delay; the American delegation urgently needed new instructions.[74]

That same day, John M. Allison, assistant chief of the Division of Northeast Asian Affairs, finished work on a draft proposal aimed at breaking the Korean deadlock permanently. Allison's plan outlined specific measures to meet three different contingencies. First, if the Soviet Union broke off negotiations at the Joint Commission prior to August 5, the United States would request a special meeting of the Council of Foreign Ministers. At this conference, Marshall would propose free elections under United Nations supervision to select delegates for a legislature in each zone of occupation. These Korean leaders then would choose representatives to serve in a provisional government that would speak for the entire nation. After consultation with the four major powers, the new Korean government would arrange for withdrawal of foreign troops and the acquisition of aid for economic recovery. If Moscow refused to accept the American proposal, the United States would submit the issue to the United Nations and implement the same plan in southern Korea alone.[75]

Allison's second contingency provided that if the Soviet Union persisted in its intransigence at the Joint Commission beyond August 5, Marshall would suggest that the two delegations formulate a joint report summarizing the extent of progress toward Korean self-government. Simultaneously, the United States would implement the program outlined in the first contingency in southern Korea and submit the Korean issue to the United Nations for resolution. Finally, Allison's proposal provided for the possibility that Moscow might not respond to any American *démarche*. In that case, the United States would create a separate government in the American zone and refer the issue of Korean reunification to the United Nations on September 10, 1947. Early in August, an Ad Hoc Committee of the SWNCC advised approval of Allison's plan. In its report, the committee warned that without positive action, rising violence in southern Korea would force the United States to withdraw. To abandon Korea under such circumstances would guarantee Soviet dominance over the entire peninsula and "discourage those small nations now relying upon the U.S. to support them in resisting internal or external Communist pressure."[76]

Patterson and Forrestal eagerly embraced Allison's proposal, presumably in the belief that it would speed withdrawal. Hilldring added his support as well. In preparation for the new American initiative, the State Department released a series of statistics pertaining to negotiations at the Joint Commission in a transparent attempt to portray the Soviet Union as the champion of minority rule in Korea.[77] Then, in accordance with Allison's second contingency, Ambassador Smith, on August 12, presented Molotov with a letter from Marshall proposing that the Joint Commission formulate a report on the progress of Korean independence. Since previous efforts to realize Korea's sovereignty had experienced little success, Marshall recommended a Soviet-American conference on August 21 to discuss the course of negotiations at the Joint Commission.[78]

Washington also took steps to bolster Hodge's position in southern Korea. The State Department issued a press release stating categorically that the United States had one policy in Korea and Hodge had "faithfully and consistently acted in conformance therewith under difficult and complex circumstances."[79] Yet after the American initiative of August 12, the AMG would have no trouble with the conservatives. Now the left alone would assail American policy, since a separate government served rightist purposes. Thus, Hodge instructed the police to conduct a series of raids against the extreme left, seizing subversive documents and imprisoning several Communist leaders. For Jacobs, a viable southern regime closely allied with the United States required drastic measures. He believed Washington should abandon its "provisional" policies and create a separate governmental structure in southern Korea. Hodge agreed and requested permission to close all remaining leftist newspapers. "The time for politeness, accepted as weakness by the Communists and by the Russians," the USAFIK commander boldly proclaimed, "is ended."[80]

Meanwhile, Brown had proposed that the two delegations at the Joint Commission begin work on a summary report. Shtikov replied that he had no authority to discuss the matter. American occupation officials in Seoul suspected another Soviet attempt to stall the negotiations and exhorted Washington to implement the remainder of its contingency plan aggressively. Brown informed Shtikov that the United States planned to formulate a unilateral response subject to change if Moscow decided to participate. On August 20, the American delegation completed a separate report and forwarded it at once to Washington.[81] Three days later, the administration received Molotov's answer to Marshall's proposal. The Soviet leader reiterated Moscow's position that those parties belonging to the Anti-Trusteeship Committee had to renounce opposition to the Moscow agreement in order to qualify for consultation. He then decried the recent arrests and imprisonments in southern Korea as "abnormal and inadmissable." Nevertheless, Molotov accepted the American proposal for the formulation of a joint report in the interests of achieving Korea's independence.[82]

In Korea, Shtikov now indicated that he was prepared to begin consideration of a summary report, but the American delegation obviously had registered a *fait accompli*. Brown, in reply, delivered a blistering denunciation of the Soviet delegation for its protests against the recent arrests in the American zone. He reproached Shtikov for exploiting a false issue to mask Moscow's resistance to broad consultation with all legitimate Korean groups. More important, it was Soviet-sponsored infiltration of subversives into southern Korea that had made these defensive operations necessary. Brown gratuitously offered to release these people, however, if the Soviets would free political prisoners in the north and agree to a formula for wider consultations at the Joint Commission. Jacobs observed privately that American attendance at future sessions was pointless in view of Shtikov's "uncompromising, untenable, and intransigeant" attitude.[83]

Administration officials were determined to maintain the initiative and therefore decided to abandon all future efforts to work through the Joint Commission. On August 26, Robert A. Lovett, Acheson's replacement as undersecretary of state, wrote a letter to Molotov charging the Soviet Union with violating the Marshall–Molotov compromise. Members of the Anti-Trusteeship Committee had signed the required pledge of cooperation and had not agitated against the Moscow agreement, yet the Soviet delegation had demanded unjustifiably the exclusion of these parties from consultation. Rather than being guilty of "oppression and persecution," he continued, Hodge was trying to maintain law and order in the American zone. Since future discussions in Korea would be useless, Lovett recommended a four-power conference in Washington to convene on September 9, 1947, for consideration of the joint report. At that time, the United States would propose the adoption of a plan for achieving Korea's reunification and economic recovery.[84]

In Moscow, Ambassador Smith predicted that the Soviets would not accept Washington's latest *démarche,* arguing that Korea occupied a vital strategic location for the Russians. Lovett cabled Smith's assessment to Seoul and instructed Jacobs to prepare for the likely submission of the Korean matter to the United Nations for consideration.[85] On September 4, Washington received the anticipated Soviet rejection of Lovett's proposal. In his letter, Molotov condemned the United States for hampering the emergence of a democratic government in Korea. The Soviet leader rejected both British and Chinese participation in future Soviet-American deliberations, insisting that negotiations at the Joint Commission alone could resolve the Korean problem. After receiving Molotov's letter, Truman, following Allison's third contingency plan, instructed Marshall to address the United Nations General Assembly on September 17, 1947, and place the Korean issue on its agenda.[86]

Truman resorted to action at the United Nations not merely to break the Korean stalemate but also to facilitate American withdrawal at the earliest possible date. Given the monumental problems facing the administration in its struggle with the Soviet Union, Washington's desire to leave this strategically unimportant area was scarcely surprising.[87] Congressional hesitancy to provide southern Korea with financial aid, coupled with the limitations on American manpower and material, had in fact eliminated the other alternatives. As Jacobs noted in September 1947, unless the administration found an answer to the Korean predicament soon, "we may have to abandon the country willy nilly."[88] But without Soviet cooperation, successful withdrawal would require the creation of a separate southern Korean government. The extreme right now dominated southern politics, however, a fact that few in Washington fully appreciated. Consequently, after the United States disengaged, the emergence of a truly open and democratic society in southern Korea would be a virtual impossibility.[89]

For many scholars, Truman's decision to submit the Korean issue to the United Nations revealed his desire to cast aside an unwanted burden. The administration, critics charge, was attempting to exploit the international organization and withdraw from Korea without appearing to abandon an American commitment.[90] But this interpretation does not provide an acceptable explanation for American behavior. International involvement actually was another essential element in Truman's strategy of containment in Korea. Although American leaders expected Soviet refusal to cooperate, they hoped the United Nations would agree to sponsor elections in the American zone alone.

A separate government south of the 38th parallel would then enjoy moral and material support from the world community, contributing to its internal economic strength and political stability. Similarly, United Nations sponsorship might persuade Congress to authorize an appropriation for economic assistance.[91] International action seemed to provide the means to bridge the gap between the administration's objectives in Korea and its reluctance to commit unlimited American power to achieve success.[92] For Truman and his advisors, the United Nations offered an avenue for escape from Korea that would lead to the fulfillment rather than the abdication of American obligations to this small Asian nation.

CHAPTER 6

A House Divided

Congressional reluctance to finance new international commitments during the summer of 1947 forced the administration to postpone temporarily the application of its containment policy in Korea. Nevertheless, Truman and his advisors were willing to be patient because they anticipated a marked improvement in the Korean situation once the United Nations began to consider the reunification issue. Certain State Department officials emphasized that relying on the United Nations would produce some indirect benefits. Washington could demonstrate, for example, its good faith, its desire to fulfill its commitments, and its devotion to international cooperation. Moreover, the Korean issue provided an excellent opportunity to assume an unequivocal stance in defense of national self-determination before the world community.[1] Some American leaders even predicted that if the United Nations showed unity and resolve, Stalin might agree to a settlement in Korea on the administration's terms. After all, during the Iranian crisis early in 1946, world opinion had seemed to play a significant role in Moscow's decision to withdraw.[2]

Predictably, Truman's United Nations gambit in Korea was destined to fail. Stalin was certain to reject Lovett's proposal of August 26 because the Soviet Union would be in a minority at any four-power conference. Similarly, Moscow would resist action at the United Nations. Since a large majority of member nations were aligned closely with the United States, however, Stalin could not prevent the General Assembly from endorsing American policy. Yet without Soviet cooperation, the United Nations would be unable to achieve Korean reunification. To his credit, Truman expected the Soviet Union to be uncooperative, but he still held out hope that adverse world opinion would induce Stalin to retreat. In fact, political and psychological pressure of this sort would merely harden Moscow's resolve. Ultimately, Truman's attempt to legislate an agreement on Korea, rather than reaching a settlement through diplomacy, would eliminate any fleeting chance for a genuine resolution. Far from achieving peaceful reunification, the United Nations would contribute to the emergence of two Koreas both dedicated to ending the artificial division of the peninsula regardless of cost.[3]

After receiving Molotov's rejection of the latest American initiative on September 4, the administration moved quickly to prepare for action at the United Nations. Undersecretary Lovett informed Molotov on September 16 that the United States would place the Korean issue on the agenda of the international organization the following day. In his speech before the General Assembly, Secretary of State Marshall professed that the primary reason for the Soviet-American impasse over Korea was Moscow's adamant stand against the principle of unfettered freedom of expression. Since the United States and the Soviet Union had been unable to fulfill past agreements on Korea, Marshall asked for international action to remove this threat to world peace.[4] The State Department already had in hand a proposal to break the Korean deadlock, a plan which provided for free elections under United Nations supervision within six months after adoption. This legislature, reflecting the two-to-one population superiority of southern Korea, would formulate a constitution and appoint officials for a provisional government. Perhaps the most important provision called for the creation of a "United Nations Temporary Commission on Korea" (UNTCOK) comprised of eleven nations to supervise the elections, foster freedom of choice, and report its findings to the General Assembly.[5]

Communist military victories in China during the summer of 1947 added urgency to the task of obtaining approval for the American proposal. Political instability in China represented yet another serious threat to the security of the American occupation force in southern Korea. Truman, acknowledging both the strategic and political relationship between events in China and Korea, dispatched Lieutenant General Albert C. Wedemeyer on a fact-finding mission to the two nations during September 1947 pursuant to an overall reappraisal of American policy in Asia.[6] Wedemeyer, shortly after his arrival in China, cabled Marshall that the Soviet Union was implementing a masterful plan for dominance throughout Asia. His warning confirmed Washington's suspicion that Stalin would spread Russian influence into any area where conditions seemed conducive to conquest.[7]

In his report from Korea, Wedemeyer declared ominously that the

"same sinister forces that militate against a program of democratiza-
tion and rehabilitation in other areas of the world are present in
Korea." Although outright invasion was improbable, Wedemeyer
believed that Korea had to develop sufficient military strength to
combat the threat of Soviet-sponsored infiltration and subversion.
Any further attempts to cooperate with Moscow would not only be
useless but would advance the Soviet strategy of political expansion and economic enslavement. By contrast, premature withdrawal
would guarantee a complete Soviet victory, while limited financial
assistance would not result in economic self-sufficiency. For Wedemeyer, any "ideological retreat" in Korea was unacceptable because
it would enhance Soviet prestige in Asia, thereby weakening the
American position in Japan.[8]

Wedemeyer admitted, however, that the creation of genuine democracy in southern Korea would not be easy. Both the local police
and the National Youth Movement, he reported, had committed
countless acts of torture, extortion, brutality, and arbitrary arrest,
earning the universal hatred and distrust of the general public. Yet
the AMG had to rely on these very elements to maintain law and
order. Under present circumstances, truly free elections would be
impossible because the extreme right would control the outcome.
Nevertheless, Wedemeyer thought southern Korea could emerge as a
vital "bulwark of freedom" in Asia if the United States provided
extensive economic assistance and formed an American-officered
"Korean Scout Force." With exaggerated optimism, he predicted
that positive American measures of this kind would compel the
Soviet Union eventually to accept a "neutralized Korea" as a buffer
zone in northeast Asia.[9]

While mulling over Wedemeyer's report, Washington asked Jacobs
for his ideas on future policy in Korea. Hodge's political advisor
pointedly replied that consideration of any specific plan would be a
waste of energy prior to the administration's determination of whether Korea was crucial to American security interests. If Washington
decided not to apply a policy of containment in Korea, he recommended a quick and graceful withdrawal. This option would eventuate in anarchy and considerable bloodshed, Jacobs admitted, but he
then philosophically offered justification for such action:

> In any event we cannot give democracy, as we know it, to any people or
> cram it down their throats. History cries loudly that the fruits of

democracy come forth only after long evolutionary and revolutionary processes involving the expenditure of treasure, blood and tears. Money cannot buy it; outside force and presure [*sic*] cannot nurture it.

Regardless of the ultimate outcome of the policy reassessment, Jacobs appealed for an early decision, warning that delay would make the entire Korean question of academic interest alone.[10]

Some administration officials shared Wedemeyer's judgment that the United States could ill afford to abandon Korea. Francis B. Stevens of the Division of East European Affairs asserted that certain ideological imponderables outweighed Korea's strategic value. He opposed withdrawal on political grounds, arguing that Korea

> is a symbol to the watching world both of the East-West struggle for influence and power and of American security in sponsoring the nationalistic aims of Asian peoples. If we allow Korea to go by default and to fall within the Soviet orbit, the world will feel that we have lost another round in our match with the Soviet Union, and our prestige and the hopes of those who place faith in us will suffer accordingly. In the Far East, the reliance of national movements on American support would be seriously shaken, and the consequences might be far reaching.

In conclusion, Stevens claimed that a complete Communist victory in Korea would reinforce Stalin's devotion to his expansionist strategy of subversion and indirect aggression.[11]

Despite Stevens's assessment, strategic considerations dominated the outlook of most of Truman's advisors with respect to Korea. Both the Policy Planning Staff and the Division of Northeast Asian Affairs agreed that the global commitments of the United States were so extensive that the administration might have to withdraw prematurely from the peninsula. On September 15, the SWNCC requested comments from the JCS on the relationship of Korea to American national security.[12] In a now famous memorandum, the JCS responded categorically that "from the standpoint of military security, the United States has little strategic interest in maintaining present troops and bases in Korea." While any American offensive on the Asian mainland would bypass Korea, Truman's military experts believed that an enemy position on the peninsula would be vulnerable to air attack. Thus, the United States could contribute more effectively to its national security by deploying the Korean occupation forces in areas of greater strategic importance. The JCS warned that in the absence of a major program for social, political, and economic rehabilitation, disorder and unrest in Korea would undermine Washington's position thoroughly. Forced withdrawal, rather than voluntary disengagement, would be humiliating and inflict infinitely greater damage on the international prestige of the United States.[13]

For many American leaders, the JCS report demanded precipitate withdrawal from Korea. George F. Kennan, head of the Policy Planning Staff, was particularly impressed. In a letter to the State Department, Kennan explained that if the JCS assessment was correct, "we feel that our policy should be to cut our losses and get out of there as gracefully but promptly as possible." The JCS report merely added weight to the War Department's argument that the United States could not afford to implement a positive program in Korea. Other administration officials, however, were more sensitive to the warnings of Wedemeyer and Stevens. The State Department in particular assigned great importance to achieving a settlement "which would enable the U.S. to withdraw from Korea as soon as possible with the minimum of bad effects." Rather than make a hasty decision, Truman elected to wait until the United Nations had acted on the American proposal. If the international organization managed to create a Korean provisional government, Congress might consider approving an economic aid program. Even then, as Leahy noted at the time, the "feasibility of [Wedemeyer's] recommendations will . . . have to be considered . . . in relation to U.S. commitments and possible future commitments elsewhere in the world."[14]

Surprisingly, Hodge emerged as a vocal proponent of the State Department's position. Late in September, the USAFIK commander urged implementation of Wedemeyer's recommendations during discussions with Kenneth C. Royall, the new secretary of the army who was visiting southern Korea on a fact-finding mission. Although he shared the JCS assessment of Korea's limited strategic value, Hodge believed that the United States could not tolerate further Soviet expansion without irreparable damage to American prestige. He favored only staged withdrawal over a nine-month period. Prior to departure, the United States would have to train and equip a strong local army. Since economic self-sufficiency was the key to southern Korea's survival, Hodge also advocated a five-year rehabilitation program. Apparently, Hodge's advice persuaded the War Department that outright abandonment of Korea would be ill advised. It now

decided to press for implementation of a billion-dollar aid plan for
Korea over five years, a program which would permit the United
States to withdraw safely. Through interdepartmental coordination
and congressional cooperation, the United States might be able to
build an "ideological bridgehead on the Asian mainland."[15]

Moscow evidently concluded that Washington's *démarche* at the
United Nations represented a potential threat to the Soviet position
in northern Korea. At the Joint Commission, Shtikov recommended
mutual Soviet-American military withdrawal from the peninsula,
arguing that then the Korean people could organize a provisional
government independently. Brown replied that an American response was impossible now that Korea's fate was in the hands of the
United Nations. Almost certainly, Stalin was trying to force American
disengagement from Korea prior to the application of containment.
Without American military protection, southern Korea could not
compete with its economically and militarily superior northern neighbor. United Nations consideration of the Korean issue would damage
Moscow's international image as well. An anticipated American
refusal to withdraw, on the other hand, would shift blame for the
absence of Korea's independence from the Soviet Union to the
United States.[16]

Moscow's proposal for mutual military withdrawal strengthened
the position of those American leaders favoring an early departure
from Korea. Lovett and Charles E. Saltzman, who had replaced
Hilldring, already had suggested that the JCS and the Policy Planning Staff develop plans for withdrawal should the United Nations
fail to resolve the Korean problem. Administration officials now had
to devote immediate attention to the matter. During a cabinet meeting on September 29, Marshall observed that the Soviet proposal
provided an opportunity for "getting out of Korea." In response,
Harriman questioned whether the United States could leave Korea
"without loss of face." Subsequently, the Policy Planning Staff and
the State Department advised that the administration could not
"scuttle and run" in Korea without damaging American prestige. Yet
the creation of a viable southern Korea would require considerable
money and effort. If the administration attempted to develop a
capacity for self-defense south of the 38th parallel, however, Moscow's proposal would provide justification for an eventual disengagement and blunt harsh criticism of the United States for appearing to
shirk its responsibilities. Thus, the administration decided to incor-

porate the Soviet idea on withdrawl into its proposal at the United Nations.[17]

As expected, the Soviet Union attempted to affix blame to the United States for the Korean impasse and thereby undermine American policy at the United Nations. In a letter to Marshall dated October 10, Molotov alleged that Washington, through its insistence on consultations with reactionary Korean parties, had prevented implementation of the Moscow agreement at the Joint Commission. Now the Soviet delegation had proposed mutual military withdrawal and the United States refused to respond, once again prolonging the achievement of Korea's independence. Finally, Molotov reiterated that the Soviet government opposed United Nations consideration of the Korean issue. One week later, Undersecretary Lovett sent a reply to Molotov. Since military withdrawal was linked to the question of independence for Korea, he avowed, any decision on the issue required action at the United Nations. Lovett emphasized that the United States believed international consideration of the Korean problem was the only alternative because Soviet-American negotiations had reached a stalemate.[18]

At the United Nations, Warren R. Austin, in his capacity as permanent representative, presented a draft resolution on Korea on October 17, 1947, and urged rapid international approval. This plan differed from the State Department's draft of September 18 in only two respects: It specifically called for elections no later than March 31, 1948, and provided for Soviet-American military withdrawal after the formation of a provisional government.[19] The following day, Brown, as head of the American delegation, suggested a recess of the Joint Commission in anticipation of international action. During the next session, Shtikov announced that the Soviet delegation would withdraw from the negotiations permanently because the United States had blocked implementation of the Moscow agreement. On October 23, the Soviet representatives left Seoul and the Joint Commission negotiations officially ended.[20] Less than one week later, Moscow submitted a formal proposal to the United Nations for joint Soviet-American withdrawal from Korea.[21] Now the future of a divided Korea was fully in the hands of the international organization, if it chose to act.

Washington's efforts to break the Korean deadlock had a profound impact on domestic politics in the American zone. At first, the Korean people reacted as administration officials expected. Molotov's rejection of a four-power conference to revise the Moscow agreement brought a wave of unfavorable, anti-Soviet comment. Rhee, Kim Ku, and leading prewar conservative Kim Sŏng-su recognized at once the significance of the breakdown in Soviet-American negotiations. The extreme right initiated a high-powered publicity campaign to force the United States to grant immediate elections for a separate government, although it appealed to Washington to delay military withdrawal.[22] During October, relations between Rhee and the AMG quickly deteriorated. On one occasion, a large group of conservatives staged a demonstration outside Hodge's headquarters. Hodge responded the following day with a public announcement that the United States could not set a specific date for elections until after international consideration of the Korean matter.[23] A furious Rhee now charged Hodge with trying to foster the revival of communism in southern Korea. The AMG could expect work stoppages and "a great deal of trouble," he threatened, if elections did not occur in the very near future.[24]

Not only did the prospect of renewed internal violence and disorder confront a disturbed Hodge, but the Soviet proposal for mutual military withdrawal made him even more nervous. Beginning in May 1947, the USAFIK commander viewed with growing anxiety the imminent Soviet military disengagement from northern Korea. In the aftermath of a Russian withdrawal, Hodge believed that the northern Korean puppet army might mount an invasion against the south. In response, Washington instructed Hodge to rely on "the means available in case of operations across the border by Korean groups from the north."[25] After Moscow formally proposed withdrawal, Hodge again urged the administration to reassess the implications of a unilateral Soviet withdrawal from northern Korea. In particular, the occupation commander requested an increase in the number of civilian advisors in southern Korea and permission to create a large constabulary army.[26] Washington refused to comply. Once representatives of the United Nations were present in Korea, the administration believed that the threat of armed invasion southward across the 38th parallel virtually would disappear.[27]

This expectation rested on the key assumption that Soviet intentions in Asia essentially were limited. Marshall indicated as much during a cabinet meeting on November 7, when he presented a Policy Planning Staff report on the world situation. The secretary of state speculated that the Soviet Union did not want war but sought to use tactics of indirect aggression and subversion to extend its influence into areas of instability. Asia was particularly susceptible to Moscow's strategy because the area suffered from persistent uncertainty. Then Marshall directed his remarks specifically to conditions in Korea, observing glumly that there was

> no longer any real hope of a genuinely peaceful and free democratic development in that country. Its political life in the coming period is bound to be dominated by political immaturity, intolerance and violence. Where such conditions prevail, the Communists are in their element. Therefore, we cannot count on native Korean forces to help us hold the line against Soviet expansion. Since the territory is not of decisive strategic importance to us, our main task is to extricate ourselves without too great a loss of prestige.

Marshall proposed that the administration carefully formulate plans for countering the Soviet challenge based upon a realistic assessment of American capabilities. Since the Soviet Union's military and economic power in Asia was limited, the United States still could counter the threat effectively.[28]

Marshall's assessment fortified the determination of many American military planners to leave Korea at the earliest possible moment. On November 10, Wedemeyer, now director of planning and operations, informed Hodge and MacArthur that the Department of the Army was considering a proposal for disengagement during the autumn of 1948 regardless of events at the United Nations. He requested comments on the logic of this option should Moscow reject simultaneous withdrawal. Hodge responded that, in his opinion, the Soviet Union would never cooperate with the United Nations or permit reunification. He therefore recommended, as he had during his conversations with Royall two months earlier, that the United States supervise the formation of a separate government in southern Korea to include the creation of a large constabulary army and the implementation of an economic aid program. Rhee and his cohorts would score a landslide victory in separate elections, he admitted, not least because of a probable leftist boycott. Nevertheless, Hodge was hopeful that several moderate leaders would gain office and temper Rhee's reactionary extremism.[29]

For Hodge, American military withdrawal from Korea would be disastrous unless the United States fulfilled certain conditions. He thought Washington should adopt the five-year rehabilitation program that the AMG had formulated the previous September. If it were implemented, a well-staffed American embassy then could provide supervision and periodic reports to Washington on the progress of recovery. Once the southern Korean government developed economic strength and political stability, Hodge predicted that "national feeling among the north Koreans may be aroused and sufficient pressure brought to bear upon the Soviets to compel them to permit . . . an amalgamation of the two areas." Hodge's recommendations provided an unmistakable blueprint for the application of containment in southern Korea. Yet his expectations were much grander. If successful, containment in Korea would act as a liberating force and ultimately produce reunification of the peninsula under a government acceptable to the United States.[30]

Reports from Seoul during the autumn of 1947 suggested that the emergence of a liberal democracy in southern Korea was highly unlikely with or without American assistance. Jacobs informed the State Department that Rhee's activities and the response of the extreme conservatives to the Joint Commission questionnaires indicated how even the most educated Koreans possessed no conception of basic democratic principles. Worse still, Rhee was afraid that he might lose truly free elections and intended to rely on the police and rightist youth groups to manufacture an electoral victory. Moderate Korean leaders appealed to occupation officials to check rightist political intimidation, but the AMG could do little to restrain the extreme conservatives. By late October, arbitrary arrest and prolonged imprisonment had obviated any possible leftist challenge. Although Hodge still detested Rhee, he prodded Washington to authorize separate elections without further delay, arguing that the Communists were then at a low point in terms of popularity and activism.[31]

While the prospects for American success in Korea appeared slight, Washington's policy at the United Nations experienced rapid progress. On November 4, the organization's political committee approved the American proposal on Korea, which now provided for Soviet-American withdrawal from the peninsula within ninety days after the creation of a provisional government. Some administration officials were troubled about appearing unduly hasty, but the Soviet proposal on withdrawal gave the United States no choice. Much to the satisfaction of Truman and his advisors, the General Assembly passed the American-sponsored resolution on November 14 by a wide margin.[32] American leaders were also happy with the composition of the UNTCOK. Of the nine members, Canada, Australia, China, France, El Salvador, and the Philippines all had close economic, political, and military ties to the United States. Only Syria and India were likely to hamper the pursuit of American policy objectives, while the final member, the Ukraine, probably would decline to serve.[33] Marshall was jubilant. He immediately instructed Hodge to prepare for elections and contact the UNTCOK to determine a specific date for the balloting.[34]

Thus, the United Nations had chosen to follow the path that reflected the political and diplomatic imperatives of the United States, but one possessing little realistic chance of leading to Korea's peaceful reunification. After all, Moscow already had announced its refusal to cooperate with the United Nations.[35] Furthermore, many nations worried about the violence and political instability in southern Korea and cautioned against international involvement in the Korean affair. H. V. Evatt of Australia, for instance, insisted during discussions with administration officials that Korea was a question for Soviet-American resolution or, as a last resort, a Japanese peace conference. Marshall strongly disagreed, arguing that only international action could break the Korean deadlock. He assured Evatt, however, that the United States did not intend to desert Korea and was determined to fulfill its commitments. John Foster Dulles, a member of the American delegation at the United Nations, then expressed optimism that the international organization would induce the Soviet Union to cooperate in the achievement of Korean reunification and independence. These arguments failed to convince Evatt, who remained skeptical about the wisdom of Australia becoming involved in the complicated Korean dispute.[36]

Events in southern Korea made it much harder for American leaders to reassure wavering members of the United Nations. After the General Assembly approved the American resolution, Rhee accelerated his campaign for early elections south of the 38th parallel. Jacobs cabled Washington that the extreme right wanted "rigged" elections and therefore opposed international supervision. Conservative reliance on terror and intimidation, he concluded sadly, "readily lends itself to Soviet charges that Rhee is reactionary, pro-Japanese and Fascist." To silence Rhee, Major General William F. Dean, Lerch's replacement as military governor, announced that any further steps toward self-government in Korea had to await the arrival of the

UNTCOK. Rhee now denounced the United States for breaking its pledges to Korea and playing into the hands of the Communists. Other Korean leaders also had begun to express fears that the United Nations would not authorize elections without Soviet consent. Finally, on December 7, Hodge publicly reassured the southern Korean people that there would be elections in the near future, but only under the supervision of the United Nations.[37]

For many of Truman's diplomatic advisors, Hodge now represented a significant barrier to the future success of American policy in Korea, since he could neither restrain Rhee nor maintain law and order in southern Korea. The JCS disagreed and staunchly resisted a proposal for Hodge's relief. General Dwight D. Eisenhower, army chief of staff, argued that Hodge's knowledge and experience were invaluable, while Assistant Secretary of State Saltzman pointed out that removal of the USAFIK commander would constitute a major triumph for Rhee and the extreme right.[38] Several State Department officials remained dissatisfied with Hodge's performance, however. W. Walton Butterworth, director of the Office of Far Eastern Affairs, believed that Hodge's tolerance of "police state tactics" in southern Korea would alienate members of the UNTCOK and thereby damage the image of the United States at the United Nations. American military leaders were not sympathetic to such arguments. In fact, one Army Department official suspected that Butterworth was "laying the necessary groundwork to place the blame for ultimate US failure in Korea at the doorstep of the Army."[39]

State Department officials had good reason for concern. On December 3, an alleged supporter of Kim Ku assassinated rightist leader Chang Tŏk-su, who recently had emerged as an advocate of supervised elections. For State Department official Penfield, recurrent political violence in southern Korea was intolerable in view of the imminent arrival of the UNTCOK. He demanded that the AMG act decisively for the prompt restoration of internal stability. Lovett also instructed Hodge to prevent the police from engaging in any further abuses of power.[40] Langdon attempted to assure Washington that occupation officials already had adopted strong measures to control domestic unrest. He promised to investigate Chang's assassination personally and press the Korean police to release all purely political prisoners. But Langdon reminded Lovett that Korea was "politically excited, restive, and frustrated, and economically on a subsistence margin." Washington had to take these disruptive factors into consideration if it expected to evaluate the AMG's performance accurately.[41]

Langdon blamed Rhee and the extreme right for the chaotic atmosphere in southern Korea. But occupation officials sadly were coming to realize that without Rhee's cooperation, an acceptable solution to the Korean problem would not be possible. Even Lovett admitted in one cable that nothing could "prevent Rhee from running away with the election." A realistic assessment seemed to suggest that the United States should begin to cultivate good relations with Rhee and the extreme right as soon as possible. Washington then could hope that Rhee would become less strident and intolerant when he had to depend on American aid for his regime's survival. Meanwhile, Truman's advisors were fearful that Rhee's actions would alienate the UNTCOK. Accordingly, Washington ordered the AMG to concentrate on creating an atmosphere in which the Korean people at least appeared to enjoy freedom of choice, thereby ensuring international supervision of the electoral process.[42]

American trepidation over a possible erosion of support at the United Nations was thoroughly justified. Canada was not at all enthusiastic about participating in the UNTCOK mission. Prime Minister MacKenzie King strenuously opposed any involvement in the Korean affair during December 1947, precipitating a cabinet crisis in Canada. Truman delivered a personal appeal to King not to withdraw from the UNTCOK. In reply, King asserted that only nations directly concerned should be involved in the determination of Korea's destiny. For King, the UNTCOK was embarking on a "fool's errand," since Soviet cooperation was extremely improbable. In the end, the price of international intervention would be too high, as the United Nations would experience frustration and embarrassment, thereby weakening its ability to influence events in more important areas such as Europe. If the major powers could not agree, King questioned whether the smaller nations could find an answer to the Korean impasse.[43]

Canadian obduracy came as a complete surprise to the United States. One State Department official speculated that "King was making this issue a declaration of independence to show that Canada reached its decision independently of the United States." Since a Canadian boycott of the UNTCOK would damage American prestige seriously, he suggested that the administration permit King simply to avoid appointing a representative. If Washington did not press the Canadian government, the issue might disappear quietly. Apparently Truman rejected such an approach, since he instructed Lovett to address another direct appeal for cooperation to King. In his letter, Lovett stressed that a "calculated policy of boycott" would defeat the entire program of the United Nations and serve to advance Soviet interests while hampering the realization of Korea's independence. Most important, the United States and Canada had to avoid even the appearance of discord in their mutual relations because enemy nations would exploit any disagreement to undermine the security of both countries.[44]

King now decided to dispatch his foreign minister, Lester B. Pearson, to Washington to discuss the matter in detail. During conversations with American leaders, Pearson explained that King feared the consequences of United Nations involvement in such a volatile issue. Even Britain agreed that Korea was of secondary importance and would hinder cooperation in the United Nations Security Council. Canada opposed as well Washington's apparent desire to exclude the northern Koreans from the United Nations debate. Lovett responded that without at least token Canadian participation in the UNTCOK mission, adverse publicity would destroy the temporary commission's credibility. After expressing sympathy for the American stand, Pearson suggested that Truman make one final plea for a reversal of Canada's position.[45]

On January 5, 1948, Truman again wrote Prime Minister King appealing for Canadian cooperation with the United Nations resolution on Korea. The president emphasized that international involvement was aimed at producing a settlement, not at increasing Soviet-American tensions. Without Canadian participation, the UNTCOK would be unable to achieve Korean independence. More important, the world community would misinterpret a Canadian boycott and begin to question the viability of the United Nations. Truman asked King to consider the "larger picture" and avoid any speculation about Canada's commitment to the international organization. Although Truman admitted the probability of a Soviet boycott of the UNTCOK, he predicted that the presence of the temporary commission on the peninsula would lead eventually to Korea's reunification and independence.[46]

Evidently, Truman's resort to pressure diplomacy brought the desired result, since King agreed to appoint a representative to the

UNTCOK. But King notified the United States that if Soviet cooperation should "not be forthcoming, and the Commission not return its mandate to the United Nations in view of the impossibility of carrying out that mandate in the whole of Korea, our representative will be told to withdraw from the Commission."[47] Even King's conditional support satisfied Truman, who quickly conveyed his gratitude to the prime minister for Canada's change of heart. International encouragement for the UNTCOK's mission was vital, he explained, because it might compel the Soviets to permit entry into northern Korea. In his subsequent comments, however, Truman revealed the actual nature of his expectations. If the Soviet Union refused to cooperate, the president pointed out that the UNTCOK, since it would enjoy complete freedom of action, then could observe elections in southern Korea alone. Even a strong government south of the 38th parallel, Truman reminded King, would constitute a major step toward democracy for the entire nation.[48]

Despite the misgivings of several members, the UNTCOK traveled to Korea in January 1948 in search of a solution to the Korean problem. Upon its arrival, Hodge greeted the temporary commission along with an extremely large crowd that one observer described as "a rightist show." Predictably, the extreme left boycotted the welcoming ceremonies and declared its unwillingness to cooperate with the UNTCOK. The Communist party demanded instead prompt Soviet-American withdrawal and tried to organize a general strike and a campaign of sabotage to protest international involvement. To preserve law and order, Hodge invoked a curfew and warned against any acts of violence.[49] Simultaneously, Hodge provided the UNTCOK with office space, housing, transportation, and food. Thus, while leftist leaders were either in hiding or in jail, the right controlled government services upon which the temporary commission would depend for its daily needs. Given these circumstances, the UNTCOK would have great difficulty maintaining its impartiality.[50]

Moscow's attitude was central to the prospects for the UNTCOK's success. Many observers thought that the Soviets would not defy overwhelming pressure from the world community for international action and would permit reunification during 1948. Any reason for optimism vanished, however, when the Ukraine announced its refusal to participate in the activities of the UNTCOK. Marshall had anticipated Soviet intransigence. He sent instructions to Langdon to impress upon the temporary commission that it had the power to hold elections in southern Korea alone.[51] In its first meeting, the UNTCOK expressed regret over the Ukrainian decision. Despite the late arrival of the delegate from El Salvador, the temporary commission rapidly agreed to approach each occupation commander with a request for cooperation and the release of all political prisoners. Also, the UNTCOK organized two committees; one was to ensure the existence of a free atmosphere in Korea, while the other would determine who would participate in consultations with the temporary commission.[52]

Hodge answered the UNTCOK with a pledge of full cooperation in the holding of free and unfettered elections in the American zone. The Korean people were ready, he asserted, to assume the responsibilities of self-government. To no one's surprise, Soviet occupation commander Korotkov ignored the temporary commission's communication. United Nations Secretary General Trygve Lie then approached the Soviet delegation directly with a plea for cooperation. In reply, Andrei Gromyko reminded Lie that the Soviet Union already had indicated its "negative attitude" toward the UNTCOK's activities. Austin now pressed Lie to declare his advocacy of supervised elections in southern Korea alone.[53] Rhee also moved to exploit Moscow's uncooperative stand, publicly demanding separate elections and the creation of a security force in southern Korea.[54] For the first time, the objectives of Rhee and the United States were identical.

For Kim Kyu-sik, internationally supervised elections in the American zone alone would be disastrous. On the eve of the temporary commission's arrival, the moderate Korean leader had formed a "National Independence Federation" to build support for the convening of a "North-South Conference" to eliminate the partition of Korea. Only the Koreans themselves, Kim insisted, could end partisan strife and achieve the political unity necessary for reunification. He predicted that the arrival of the UNTCOK would not bring reunification but would instead guarantee the permanent division of Korea.[55] Significantly, Kim managed to enlist the backing of Kim Ku, who split with Rhee and announced his opposition to anything less than nationwide elections.[56] He also experienced success during consultations with the UNTCOK, impressing members of the temporary commission with the strength of his arguments. If the UNTCOK desired truly free and democratic elections, Kim advised, "it will take considerable time to make necessary preparations." Should Moscow bar entry to the northern zone, the moderate leader strongly urged the UNTCOK to refer the entire matter back to the United Nations Interim Committee for reconsideration. Several temporary commission members were receptive to Kim's viewpoint. Consequently, a number of the UNTCOK delegates favored a delay until the temporary commission could confer with the United Nations Interim Committee.[57]

Rising violence and disruption in the American zone contributed to this hesitancy. In January 1948, the extreme left organized a "General Strike Committee" to instigate work stoppages and acts of sabotage throughout southern Korea. Within four months, political unrest produced almost three hundred deaths and more than ten thousand imprisonments. Hodge's efforts to counter political turmoil south of the 38th parallel greatly disturbed certain members of the UNTCOK. Delegates George Patterson of Canada and S. H. Jackson of Australia began to exert strong pressure on their colleagues to investigate Hodge's "police tactics." For Jacobs, criticism of the AMG and bickering among the UNTCOK members was delaying the formation of a separate government in the south. Only Liu Yu-wan of China and Jean-Louis Paul-Boncour of France were realistic enough to accept the fact that the elections would be imperfect and would exclude the northern Koreans. If the UNTCOK fully endorsed American policy, Jacobs reasoned, such dissidents as Kim Kyu-sik and Kim Ku would bow to the inevitable and advocate separate elections as well.[58]

Rhee, having failed to prevent internationally supervised elections, now feared that the temporary commission might delay the creation of a separate government indefinitely. He therefore threatened to stage widespread demonstrations and spark acts of political violence unless elections occurred in the very near future. Jacobs alerted the administration that it could not ignore Rhee because the conservative leader boasted a sizable following. Yet Rhee's popularity, he remarked disdainfully, "has nothing to do with love or veneration for the man. . . . It is . . . the result of a wide belief that Rhee is the source of all present and future political power in South Korea, the supreme protector of vested interests and the existing order of things, and that he is the man on whom to stake all one's fortunes." Both Jacobs and Hodge agreed that referral of the Korean issue back to the United Nations would be calamitous. Occupation officials appealed to Washington to persuade the Interim Committee not to delay elections any longer.[59] Hodge also informed the administration of his desperate need for more troops to maintain law and order. Unable to supply additional forces, Washington approved MacArthur's suggestion to authorize an expansion of the Korean constabulary army to 50,000.[60]

Events in northern Korea confirmed that the formation of a separate southern Korean government was an urgent necessity. American liaison officers in Pyongyang reported that the northern Korean regime was on the verge of promulgating a new constitution. On February 16, 1948, the People's Committee proclaimed its intention to form a government representing all Korea within the next few months.[61] In subsequent statements, the northern Koreans condemned the UNTCOK as a tool of the United States and called upon all southern Koreans to resist the creation of a separate government. In addition, the People's Committee demanded immediate American military withdrawal from the peninsula.[62] Leahy's private reaction undoubtedly mirrored that of most administration leaders when he piously denounced these northern Korean actions as blatant defiance of the United Nations and an example of Soviet "satellization." Since the northern Koreans possessed a strong army, Moscow's puppet regime could conquer the entire peninsula easily if the United States failed to create a strong government in the south.[63]

Northern Korea's actions, by contrast, reinforced the reticence of the UNTCOK. The temporary commission already had concluded that separate elections would harden the division of Korea and open the way to a bloody civil war. On February 6, it decided to refer the Korean matter to the Interim Committee for reconsideration in view of the Soviet Union's uncooperative attitude. In its report, the UNTCOK recommended that the United Nations authorize the election of consultants alone to assist in determining Korea's destiny. S. H. Jackson, the Australian delegate, suspected that the Interim Committee would ignore the UNTCOK's advice. He therefore prevailed upon his colleagues to include in the report the suggestion that any government emerging from separate elections would represent only the southern zone and not all Korea. Jackson also wanted to attach an assessment of conditions in southern Korea emphasizing Hodge's penchant for political repression, but his colleagues rejected this proposal. Indian delegate K. P. S. Menon thus traveled to New York carrying a report that contained few specific recommendations from the UNTCOK on how to resolve the Korean predicament.[64]

Jacobs harshly criticized the UNTCOK's actions as hasty, unfair, and based "almost solely on testimony given by immature Korean leaders who are . . . completely overlooking the need for unity on a sensible, coherent plan for salvaging what may yet be salvaged for their country." He blamed the temporary commission's uncooperative attitude on a "British bloc" that allegedly was conspiring to retain American troops in Korea presumably forever. By delaying free elections and major reforms, India, Australia, and Canada, with the assistance of Syria, were playing "into Soviet hands." Jacobs singled out Jackson as a Communist sympathizer who was using the civil rights issue to frustrate the United States, thereby repaying Washington for excluding Australia from participation in the occupation of Japan. Syria, on the other hand, was opposing separate elections to gain leverage regarding American policy toward Palestine. Only China and the Philippines understood that Moscow would never allow Korea's reunification except through an invasion from the north.[65]

World leaders had not failed to notice the marked increase of violence and disruption in southern Korea. In the interests of peace and stability, the Interim Committee thus decided to consider the UNTCOK report earlier than it originally had intended. The United Nations now confronted the distasteful choice either to reject positive action in the face of Soviet intransigence or to sponsor separate elections and solidify the Korean partition. Most members of the Interim Committee believed, however, that supervised elections would allow most Koreans to experience democracy and might even spur popular demands in the north for reunification. Withdrawal and inaction, on the other hand, would open the way to Communist control throughout the peninsula.[66] Marshall instructed the American ambassador in the capital of each UNTCOK member to press for acceptance of separate elections as the lesser evil. The British reaction was typical of those nations who opposed American policy recommendations. London believed that separate elections would reinforce the division of Korea and questioned the logic of antagonizing the Soviet Union on what appeared to be an issue of secondary importance. Nevertheless, the British agreed to approve the formation of a separate southern Korean government as a last resort.[67]

Washington was acutely aware of widespread resistance in the United Nations to supervised elections in southern Korea alone. Yet the administration ruled out any further delays. Marshall instructed

Austin to acquiesce only in a brief adjournment for the examination of the UNTCOK report. During later deliberations, the American delegation was to insist upon fulfillment of the November 14 resolution in those areas open to observation. When Menon presented the UNTCOK report, American delegate Philip C. Jessup urged the Interim Committee to authorize elections for a separate southern Korean government.[68] Menon's response was noncommittal, although he did state that Korea would be ready for independence only after reunification. The Interim Committee now declared a ten-day recess to consider both the UNTCOK report and Jessup's proposal.[69]

While the Interim Committee studied Menon's recommendations, the administration inaugurated a high-powered campaign to mobilize support for the American position. In cables to Britain and India, Marshall emphasized that the Koreans would not accept mere consultation with the United Nations because the vast majority of the people favored quick elections and immediate independence. While he admitted that conditions in the American zone were less than ideal, the secretary of state vigorously denied that the situation bordered on utter chaos. Marshall's tactics worked. On February 23, London informed Washington that it would accept Jessup's proposal, disavowing any desire to hinder the accomplishment of American objectives. India concurred as well, in large part because the United States promised that elections would produce a government for all Korea and not just the south. Once a legislature emerged representing two-thirds of Korea, Marshall insisted in one cable to New Delhi, Moscow would have no choice but to recognize its legitimacy. Thus, the United States managed to convince two of the Interim Committee's most influential members that separate elections would promote, rather than prevent, the implementation of the November 14 resolution on Korea.[70]

On February 24, Jessup formally recommended that the UNTCOK observe elections for representatives to a national assembly in those areas of Korea accessible to the temporary commission. He confidently predicted that this measure would bring democracy to the majority of the Korean people and open the way to Soviet-American military withdrawal. Two days later, the Interim Committee approved Jessup's proposal without amendment. Significantly, Canada and Australia voted against the resolution, while eleven other nations abstained.[71] Jessup's presentation greatly impressed advocates of the American proposal, but Washington's diplomatic maneuvers and the recent coup in Czechoslovakia were the key factors producing the administration's triumph.[72] Now the stage was set for the creation of a separate government as a prelude to American military withdrawal.

In Korea, Hodge eagerly approached the temporary commission asking for the early establishment of a specific date for the elections. After consultations between Menon and the USAFIK commander, the UNTCOK convened to consider the matter. Despite Patterson's absence from this meeting, the temporary commission informally approved Hodge's recommendation for elections on May 9 under international supervision.[73] On the anniversary of the March First Rebellion of 1919, Hodge apprised the southern Koreans of the UNTCOK's decision.[74] Patterson, on his return from Japan, was irate. The Interim Committee, he protested, had not ordered but only "recommended" that the UNTCOK supervise elections. His main concern was that Korean moderates and leftists would boycott the elections and thereby guarantee a sweeping victory for the extreme right. Far worse, the temporary commission had acted without his consent. When his colleagues refused to issue a clarification of the decision, Patterson walked out in a huff.[75]

Menon immediately relented and agreed to reconsider the whole matter. When the UNTCOK reconvened on March 12, Jackson suggested that the temporary commission revoke its original decision in view of the probability of an electoral boycott. Instead, the UNTCOK should sponsor a national conference for the holding of nationwide elections under international supervision and then withdraw from Korea. Jackson spoke vehemently against any action that would bar northern participation in elections because this would reinforce Korea's partition at the 38th parallel. French delegate Paul-Boncour disagreed. He urged instead the rapid implementation of the initial decision to supervise separate elections. Syria's representative then offered a compromise: The temporary commission would observe elections in southern Korea alone on May 9, 1948, but only if an atmosphere conducive to freedom of choice existed. In a crucial vote, the UNTCOK approved the Syrian compromise, although Canada and Australia dissented. Thus, the temporary commission discarded the aim of reunification before or through a nationwide election. This decision meant that the United Nations would have a moral obligation to defend the government emerging from separate elections in the south.[76]

Washington now became virtually obsessed with preventing any

further delays. Several Korean religious groups, for example, requested a one-day postponement of the elections (May 9 was a Sunday),
but the United States refused. When Langdon attributed this suggestion to American missionaries, Marshall asked several churches in the
United States to instruct their representatives to advocate holding
elections on schedule.[77] Ultimately, the administration grudgingly
agreed to postpone the elections to May 10. Jacobs reported that a
solar eclipse was expected on May 9 and Koreans would construe it as
a bad omen. For Niles Bond of the Division of Northeast Asian
Affairs, the Soviet Union had conspired to force the postponement.
In a marginal note on the cable, he confessed his amazement at "the
lengths to which the Commies will go!"[78] His comment illustrates
well the mood in Washington early in 1948.

American occupation officials were preparing for separate elections
even before the UNTCOK agreed to supervise the balloting. For
example, the AMG initiated a publicity campaign chastising Korean
leaders threatening to boycott the elections.[79] Hodge recognized that
without a large voter turnout, the southern Korean government
would not enjoy enthusiastic international approval. He was determined, therefore, to maximize the participation of the Korean people in the election, implementing an extraordinary program to educate the southern populace on the democratic process. The AMG
used radio broadcasts, classroom sessions, pamphlets, handbills,
loudspeakers, and train exhibits to inform the people "better than
they have ever been informed of anything in their history."[80] The
campaign was a huge success. On April 14, the AMG could report
that more than ninety percent of all eligible voters or approximately
eight million people had registered. For Hodge, these statistics
proved that despite Communist threats of violence, there existed a
strong desire among the people for elections. One AMG official was
far more candid when he observed that without the American propo-
ganda drive, force would have been necessary to register voters.[81]

Moscow hardly looked with favor on events in southern Korea. To
offset Washington's successes, the Soviet Union attempted to force
the United States to recognize the legitimacy of the northern regime.
On March 17, Russian occupation commander Korotkov informed
Hodge that he no longer would act as mediator between the United
States and the northern Koreans. He forwarded a letter from Kim Il
Sung as well, indicating that the northern Korean government in-
tended to halt the flow of electricity to the American zone on April

15 because the United States had not paid its bills.[82] One week later, Hodge confronted a more immediate crisis when the northern Democratic Coalition Front proposed a "North-South Conference" to arrange nationwide elections and obtain withdrawal of all foreign troops. This conference would convene in Pyongyang on April 14, and the northerners invited a group of thirteen southern Korean leaders to attend, including Kim Kyu-sik and Kim Ku. Kim Kyu-sik responded favorably and asked Hodge to provide credentials and transportation. Not surprisingly, the USAFIK commander refused either to help or to hinder southern Koreans choosing to participate in the conference.[83]

Jackson and Patterson encouraged Kim Kyu-sik and Kim Ku to attend the North-South Conference and even promised to postpone separate elections in the event of success. Prior to departure, Kim Kyu-sik requested that the northern Koreans accept certain conditions, including pledges that the conference would not advocate a dictatorship, nationalization of all industries, foreign military bases, or less than free elections. When the northern Koreans consented, Kim Kyu-sik and Kim Ku traveled to Pyongyang, arriving in the northern capital on April 21.[84] After a week of discussions, however, it was clear that the conference was indeed a sham. The constitution and governmental structure it outlined paralleled closely the Soviet system. Delegates also issued a proclamation blaming the United States entirely for the partition at the 38th parallel and calling on all true Korean nationalists to demand the immediate withdrawal of American forces and the UNTCOK. Although Kim Kyu-sik was disappointed with the results, he returned to Seoul with a promise from Kim Il Sung that the northern government would accept truly free elections and not cut off electric power. In return, Kim Kyu-sik agreed to boycott elections in the south.[85]

Immediately following the North-South Conference, Communist leaders in southern Korea intensified their program of violence and subversion. They utilized threats of rioting and assassination to convince the UNTCOK it should not supervise the elections. If this strategy failed, the chaos at least would discourage voter turnout. The local police retaliated with accelerated antileftist repression, while Hodge placed the constabulary army on permanent alert. The SKIG also organized a series of "Community Protective Associations" to assist in the maintenance of local law and order. These bodies soon degenerated into unruly youth gangs armed with clubs and axes roaming the countryside terrorizing anyone suspected of being a Communist.[86] During the first four months of 1948, police and political extremists killed more than 250 people. There were another 200 victims of indiscriminate violence in April including eight election officials and two candidates.[87]

Domestic instability peaked during the week just prior to the May 10 election, when more than 300 people died, of whom only 32 were policemen. The local police could influence and intimidate voters in more subtle ways. The AMG, for example, required the southern Koreans to register for the election at the same place where they obtained food ration cards, a situation tailor-made for blackmail. At the same time, threats, beatings, robbery, and imprisonment were the order of the day. Occupation officials naturally were troubled about the Korean extremists exerting excessive and improper political pressure on the average citizen. But the AMG was either unable or unwilling to restrict in any way the activities of the police and the youth groups.[88] To argue that an atmosphere conducive to freedom of choice existed in southern Korea during early 1948 would have been ridiculous.

Predictably, the extreme conservatives dominated the list of candidates for the May 10 elections. The subsequent legislature therefore would not reflect a representative cross section of southern Korean political opinion. Of the nearly one thousand candidates, the AMG estimated that more than three-fourths were allied closely either with Rhee or with Kim Sŏng-su.[89] Twelve candidates, including Rhee, ran without opposition. In a blatant demonstration of Rhee's inordinate influence over the electoral process, the National Election Committee rejected the application for candidacy of Daniel Choi, who wanted to run against Rhee.[90] Despite obvious unfairness and tampering, the UNTCOK nevertheless agreed to a compromise that permitted international supervision of the elections. On April 28, five members voted that a "reasonable degree of free expression" existed in southern Korea. The representatives from Australia, Canada, and Syria chose not to participate in this shameful charade and abstained.[91]

Once it had decided to supervise elections in southern Korea, the UNTCOK confronted an impossible task. Before and during the balloting, observation teams had scarely enough time to make even cursory investigations. As Leon Gordenker explains, members of the UNTCOK "could hardly do more than show themselves and hope to attract complaints and significant information."[92] When the southern

Korean people cast votes on May 10, the elections produced the resounding victory for the extreme right that everyone expected. David E. Mark, the American vice-consul in Seoul, reported that voting occurred in a calm, quiet, and orderly atmosphere. More than ninety percent of all registered voters cast ballots and, in a number of areas, all voting was completed within the first four hours the polling places were open. One editorial in the *New York Times* praised the outcome, commenting that the results surpassed the records of long-established democracies in the realm of voter participation. The elections, it concluded, were indicative of Korea's readiness for independence and self-government.[93]

Jacobs, in his private communications, was far more reserved in his assessment. He noted that the organization and efficiency of the elections were unprecedented and therefore "should give rise to a certain degree of caution . . . in our appraisal of that efficiency." Certainly, the number of ballots cast in an election provided a poor yardstick for measuring the health of a democratic political system. After all, the United States constantly pointed to such high voter turnout in the Soviet Union as proof of the undemocratic nature of its elections. By any reasonable standard, the southern Korean elections of May 1948 failed to produce results that accurately reflected the popular will. Koreans cast ballots in many cases for independence, rather than for any particular candidate. Moreover, the average citizen, after being ignored for so long, now enthusiastically welcomed communication and contact with political leaders, experiencing an enjoyable new "sense of participation." Finally, the police force and the youth groups either persuaded or compelled wavering Koreans to vote. On election day alone, political violence resulted in forty-five deaths.[94]

For many observers in the United States, the southern Korean elections were extremely discouraging. One writer commented disparagingly that police terrorism and a leftist boycott constituted "a perverted application of democratic principles of free elections."[95] Nevertheless, Marshall was elated with the outcome and immediately congratulated the southern Korean people. According to the secretary of state, "the fact that some 90 percent of the registered voters cast their ballots, despite the lawless efforts of a Communist-dominated minority to prevent or sabotage the election, is a clear revelation that the Korean people are determined to form their own government by democratic means."[96] More important, the southern Korean elections permitted Washington to proceed with its schedule for military disengagement. Less than two weeks after the election, the JCS ordered MacArthur to implement the preparatory phase of the withdrawal operation—code-named "Crabapple." American dependents promptly began to leave Korea, while Hodge transferred surplus military equipment to the constabulary army.[97]

For Truman, the southern Korean elections surely represented a major foreign policy success, particularly after more than two years of frustration and failure. Not only had the United Nations fully supported American aims, but the new southern Korean government now could expect to receive international diplomatic approval and encouragement as well. The administration undoubtedly would have sponsored separate elections in any case, but international supervision provided the United States with a crucial propaganda victory. Moscow's refusal to cooperate with the United Nations had damaged Soviet prestige in the world community, while Washington had demonstrated its devotion to the principles of democracy and national self-determination. But the United Nations also had helped to create a situation fraught with danger. "In both north and south Korea," one American official observed later, "the drive for national unification was to be a primary political force: neither area could be expected to be satisfied with the status quo."[98] Rather than resolving the Korean problem, international involvement resulted in the formal emergence of Korea as a house divided and inviting an attempt at forcible reunification.

CHAPTER 7

The Dilemma of Withdrawal

Scholars long have accepted the easy interpretation that the Truman administration was unwilling to adopt a firm stand against Soviet expansionist ambitions in Korea. Far worse, with the benefit of hindsight, writers have charged that Truman and his advisors created an anti-Communist government south of the 38th parallel and then failed to provide sufficient moral and material support to ensure its survival.[1] Such an appraisal does not provide an accurate picture of the extent of Washington's commitments in Korea after May 1948. Rather than staging a quick withdrawal after the formation of the new South Korean government, for example, the administration postponed disengagement for more than a year, defying the advice of American military experts. Simply stated, Truman did not intend to shirk American responsibilities in Korea. His strategy envisioned instead the emergence of an economically strong and politically stable South Korea that would permit the United States to withdraw safely and without surrendering the entire peninsula to Soviet domination.[2]

Once the United Nations intervened in the Soviet-American dispute over Korea, the administration began to devote serious attention to developing a schedule for military withdrawal. From the outset, State Department officials worried that if the United States ignored its commitments in Korea, the United Nations would not continue to play an active role in Korean affairs. Early in January 1948, the State–Army–Navy–Air Force Coordinating Committee (SANACC) received a report from its subcommittee on the Far East discussing the issue of withdrawal. The paper stressed that the United States could not disengage militarily before the Korean elections because this step would constitute a sign of bad faith while jeopardizing local law and order. The subcommittee therefore recommended the development of a program for the creation of a strong constabulary army and the implementation of a multiyear plan for economic development prior to departure. Still, the report acknowledged that manpower shortages demanded early withdrawal from Korea. After reading this paper, staff members of the newly created National Security Council (NSC) decided to instruct the SANACC to "prepare, as a matter of priority, a report on Korea for Council consideration" and submission to the president.[3]

Simultaneously, American military planners completed a tentative timetable for withdrawal, providing for a series of troop reductions over a period of three months. This Army Department study speculated that Korean elections would occur no later than March 31, 1948. If the National Assembly convened by May 15, the report continued, Korea would have a provisional government no later than August 15. In accordance with the United Nations resolution, the United States would complete military withdrawal from the peninsula ninety days later on November 15, 1948. In the interim, the administration would present a financial aid request to Congress for occupied areas, a proposal which would include funds for Korea. Such limited assistance, the Army Department hoped, would place Korea on the road to economic self-sufficiency.[4]

Beginning in January 1948, Army Department officials pressed the State Department to finish a detailed financial assistance program for Korea. If Congress did not receive the aid request by March 1, they cautioned, military withdrawal could not proceed on schedule.[5] Truman's diplomatic advisors were suspicious of the Army Department's apparent desire to disengage from Korea regardless of conditions at the time of departure. W. Walton Butterworth, office chief for Far Eastern Affairs, observed that the United States had a moral commitment to Korea and had to avoid the slightest hint of attempting to "scuttle and run." Although it was willing to support withdrawal by November 15, the State Department was convinced that flexibility was essential. South Korea's survival was doubtful if it did not have an adequate security force prior to American departure. Secretary Marshall privately confessed his misgivings about whether the Army Department would permit enough time to train a constabulary army sufficiently powerful and disciplined to prevent a North Korean invasion.[6] During a cabinet meeting on March 12, he advised that there was surplus military equipment available in South Korea and the USAFIK should use it to train more Koreans for service in the constabulary army.[7]

Undersecretary of the Army William H. Draper was utterly dissatisfied with the State Department's attitude. Marshall and his colleagues, he complained, seemed to consider the adoption of a firm date for withdrawal as synonymous with appeasement. During his testimony before the House Committee on Foreign Affairs, Draper stated bluntly that the United States could not occupy South Korea forever. Sooner or later, the Koreans would have to resolve their own problems.[8] Draper's consternation was understandable. In February 1948, the JCS concluded that the United States could not block a Soviet thrust into Europe without congressional approval for a $9 billion supplement to the defense budget. Truman refused to approve the request. The United States could not counter Soviet expansion everywhere, he explained, and still maintain its domestic financial and economic strength.[9] Restrictions on defense meant that withdrawal from areas not vital to American national security was inevitable. Accordingly, the JCS reported on February 21 that since the troops "now deployed in Korea are sorely needed elsewhere . . . , it would be highly desirable to withdraw our forces . . . and to utilize them for essential and pressing needs." Truman therefore decided to authorize the JCS to begin preparations for disengagement from Korea before the end of 1948.[10]

On March 25, 1948, Truman received the final SANACC report on American policy in Korea. The proposal, NSC-8, outlined steps for the creation of a separate and independent South Korea. It noted that the American zone suffered from economic weakness and the threat of military invasion from a Soviet-sponsored regime in the north. To abandon South Korea to Communist domination would improve the Soviet political and strategic position with respect to China and Japan. As a result, NSC-8 recommended that the United States provide $185 million in economic aid to South Korea for fiscal 1949 and create "so far as practicable" a small constabulary army capable of self-defense "against any but an overt act of aggression by north Korea or other forces." The paper projected American military withdrawal no later than December 31, 1948. NSC-8 ended with a warning that the United States should "not become so irrevocably involved in the Korean situation that any action taken by any faction in Korea or by any other power in Korea could be considered a *casus belli* for the U.S."[11]

After discussions at the NSC meeting of April 2, Truman approved NSC-8. His decision reflected a desire to pursue a middle road in responding to the Soviet challenge in Korea. The United States could not cut and run because this act would constitute a betrayal of its commitments. Washington's allies and enemies alike would condemn the administration for exploiting the United Nations as a cover for the abandonment of Korea. Nor was Truman willing to guarantee South Korea's political independence and territorial integrity against open military aggression. The Soviet military advantage on the Asian mainland would make such an operation foolhardy at best. Instead, the Truman administration would attempt to foster indigenous economic strength, political stability, and military power so that South Korea could protect itself. Truman was operating on the central assumption that the Soviet Union would not permit North Korea to attempt military conquest of the peninsula. As Leahy remarked at the time, "the U.S.S.R. does not intend to accomplish its political purposes by the use of armed force but will continue its efforts by infiltration and underground activities."[12]

That same month, Royall and Draper traveled to South Korea in the company of four American economic experts to gather the necessary information for a specific assistance program. After three days of discussions with prominent local businessmen and political leaders, Truman's advisors concluded that the Koreans were eager to assume control over their own affairs. In its report, the Army Committee offered this assessment:

> For a time after withdrawal . . . the new independent Korean Government will require continuing American aid, advice, food and raw materials in order to maintain at least the present ration level and to achieve necessary rehabilitation and governmental effectiveness. This assistance we feel should be provided for an interim period, with steps taken to assure that it is properly utilized. The Committee believes that firm support by the United States and the United Nations to the new Korean Government will inestimably help to develop participation in future Far Eastern trade on a basis valuable to the Korean people and to their neighbors.

Financial assistance alone, the committee reasoned, would provide Korea with sufficient means to train technicians and exploit its own resources. Eventually, South Korea would obtain the capacity for self-sufficient economic growth.[13]

State Department officials were enthusiastic about the Army Committee's recommendations. The Truman administration therefore decided to continue financial aid through fiscal 1949. If the new South Korean government "shows more vitality than they expect it will," American planners then would consider implementation of a major recovery program during fiscal 1950.[14] Meanwhile, the Army Department had authorized the expansion of South Korea's security force to fifty thousand troops, the formation of an American advisory team, and the transfer of all necessary military equipment before withdrawal. Truman's military advisors visualized the creation of a well-equipped constabulary army having enough strength "to impose martial law, to combat military or guerrilla forces . . . , or to repel minor invasions from the north." Despite reservations about the prospects for economic recovery, the administration had no intention of leaving South Korea "defenseless" at the time of American withdrawal.[15] With American aid and advice, the Koreans ultimately would achieve the political and economic stability requisite for self-defense, thereby frustrating the Soviet strategy of expansion.

But when South Korea's newly elected legislature assumed power in the spring of 1948, it confronted a host of vexing problems. American occupation policy had brought severe limitations on civil liberties, for instance, among them press censorship, arbitrary arrest, and restrictions on freedom of speech. At the same time, thuggery and political violence precluded the maintenance of genuine law and order. Even worse, South Korea's economy was on the verge of collapse. By early 1948, industrial productivity was still eighty percent below wartime levels. Furthermore, South Korea suffered from food shortages, rampant inflation, high unemployment, profiteering, and a thriving black market. Lacking trained technicians, raw materials, power resources, and replacement parts, the prospects for future economic growth were bleak.[16] On the eve of elections in South Korea, Hodge had made an attempt to remedy the unsuccessful policies of the past. The AMG announced new land reform measures that permitted individuals to purchase farms with gradual payments over a fifteen-year period. But the situation required more drastic action if the Republic of Korea (ROK) was to become a genuine "bulwark of democracy." The steady exodus of people fleeing from the north to the American zone after 1946 compounded South Korea's difficulties.[17]

Not surprisingly, the North Korean government sought to exploit and accelerate the economic deterioration in the south. On May 14,

North Korea shut off electric power across the 38th parallel. Hodge protested, appealing to the Soviet occupation commander to restore power and participate in new negotiations to resolve the dispute permanently. The Soviets replied that Hodge would have to deal directly with the North Korean government.[18] When the Soviet occupation commander announced that he would not act even as a mediator, Marshall decided to approach Moscow. In a letter to Molotov, the secretary of state requested a reversal of the decision, explaining that the loss of electricity had produced great hardship for the South Korean people. Soviet official Andrei Vyshinsky's curt response blamed the United States for the power shutoff because it had not fulfilled its financial obligations. Even so, he said, the North Koreans were willing to negotiate a settlement; only Washington's refusal to recognize the legitimacy of the People's Committee prevented the resumption of electric power.[19] During July, Hodge made one final stab at resolving the dispute, but he insisted upon Soviet participation. When the Soviet occupation commander again refused to mediate, the administration abandoned further discussion of the matter.[20]

Rhee and the extreme right may very well have welcomed the power shutoff. Now the average South Korean citizen would find it difficult to trust either Moscow or the government of North Korea. Perhaps more important, Kim Kyu-sik and Kim Ku had accepted as sincere Kim Il Sung's promise to maintain electric power, and the decision to terminate it destroyed the credibility of Rhee's two main adversaries.[21] Even before the power shutoff, however, it was obvious that the new South Korean government would be decidedly anti-Soviet. Just prior to the elections, the SKIG had issued a statement denouncing Soviet obstructionism and domination over the north. The most vocal sponsors of this resolution subsequently gained election to the new legislature.[22] Then, on May 29, the legislative assembly met secretly and overwhelmingly elected Rhee as chairman of the body. Two days later, the new legislature formally convened in its opening session. Hodge delivered an address appealing to the North Koreans to hold democratic elections and join the south. He suggested that the legislature leave one hundred seats vacant for the northern representatives, while establishing a liaison with the UNTCOK.[23]

Hodge's speech reflected Washington's desire to maintain international involvement in the Korean affair. Indeed, in a letter to Army Undersecretary Draper, Lovett registered the State Department's opposition to a restrictive role for the UNTCOK. The United States instead should encourage the temporary commission to fulfill its consultative function as a positive element in American withdrawal operations.[24] MacArthur evidently opposed a cooperative approach, since he prevented the UNTCOK from entering Japan for the purpose of drawing up its report on the Korean elections. When Marshall objected to this decision, MacArthur relented, but the UNTCOK already had chosen to travel to Shanghai instead. On June 7, the temporary commission returned to Seoul and three days later voted to make itself available for consultation with the new government of South Korea.[25] Yet chronic disunity within the UNTCOK still precluded the adoption of a firm position on the most controversial issues. Since vigorous action would reveal its deep divisions, the temporary commission had no choice but to perform an essentially passive role. A consensus did exist, however, that the new South Korean government was not national in character. Ignoring protests from the legislative assembly, the UNTCOK recognized its authority as legitimate in South Korea alone. On the other hand, the temporary commission voted to attend the next session of the legislative assembly and pledged its support for the new South Korean regime.[26]

On June 25, the UNTCOK approved a preliminary report on the recent elections in the American zone. A majority of the temporary commission's members agreed that high voter turnout and an atmosphere of freedom proved the elections were "a valid expression of the free will of the electorate in those parts of Korea which were accessible to the Commission . . . which . . . constituted approximately two-thirds of the people in Korea."[27] Canada, Australia, and Syria sharply disagreed with this statement, and Australian delegate Jackson even walked out of the meeting in protest. Despite such discord, Salvadoran delegate Miguel Valle addressed the new Korean legislature on June 30. He announced that the temporary commission considered the South Korean government to be legitimate and was prepared to open consultations. In reply, Rhee thanked the UNTCOK for its approval and support. If the temporary commission now could supervise elections in the north, he declared, the elected representatives then could occupy their seats in the "National Assembly."[28]

After receiving international sanction, the new legislature turned its attention to formulating a governmental structure. On July 12, the South Korean leaders completed work on the constitution. Superficially, the ROK was a traditional democracy based on the popular election of representatives to a unicameral legislature for a two-year term. The legislative assembly elected a president to serve for four years, who in turn appointed a prime minister and cabinet members subject to the approval of the legislature. Several peculiarities in the scheme contradicted democratic traditions, however. The assembly could not alter the provisions of presidential budget proposals, for example; it only could approve or reject. The president also possessed great powers over the formulation and implementation of policies that did not require legislative coordination. After declaring a state of national emergency, the chief executive could rule by decree, appropriating money and passing laws without the consent of the assembly. Yet the president could not dissolve the legislature if it opposed his policies. In the likely event of a disagreement, therefore, prolonged deadlock and eventual executive dictatorship were almost inevitable.[29]

Nevertheless, Korea's progress toward democracy was a matter of great satisfaction to Truman and his advisors. As the administration prepared for the formal transfer of political power to the new South Korean government, it also decided on a major change in American personnel. On April 27, Marshall had recommended that Truman appoint John J. Muccio of Rhode Island as the first ambassador to the ROK. A career foreign service officer, Muccio had obtained his experience in Latin America, Asia, and finally in Berlin. Muccio speculated later that Truman chose him because of his familiarity with the problems of military occupation in a divided nation—Germany.[30] Shortly thereafter, American military leaders decided to replace Hodge as soon as possible. Obviously, the USAFIK commander's ability to cooperate with Rhee would be essential for successful withdrawal. Hodge's continued presence in South Korea would only encourage tension and disagreement. Thus, the JCS selected Major General John B. Coulter (Hodge's executive officer) because he had avoided involvement in internal political affairs. Yet Washington did not want to give the impression that it was reacting to pressure from Rhee. The JCS therefore instructed MacArthur to delay announcing the change of command until the eve of Hodge's departure from South Korea.[31]

Army Department officials now were determined to withdraw from Korea on schedule, regardless of conditions in the ROK at the time of departure. Early in June, Secretary Royall authorized the shipment of a six-month supply of ammunition, assorted military equipment, and replacement parts. He then proposed to Marshall that logistical and administrative preparations for tactical withdrawal begin on July 1, 1948. Since Hodge would be ready to transfer the direct administration of American responsibilities in South Korea to the State Department on September 2, Royall wanted the secretary of state to organize a diplomatic mission capable of effective operation at the earliest possible date. By the end of July, the Army Department had evacuated the last military dependents from South Korea.[32] But the State Department was not prepared to move with such haste. On July 8, Lovett reminded Royall that NSC-8 called for a flexible policy on withdrawal and coordination with the United Nations. While disengagement could begin as scheduled on August 15, the State Department insisted that the Army Department had to be ready to suspend, adjust, or delay the withdrawal operation on a moment's notice.[33]

Reports from Seoul seemed to justify the State Department's caution. Hodge moaned that South Korea's new legislators were less concerned with the general welfare of the nation than with obtaining "personal and individual power, by fair means or foul." For Jacobs, political competition in the legislature, coupled with the UNTCOK's qualified endorsement for the ROK, demanded a delay of American disengagement. Moreover, the legislative assembly would not finish the formation of a government until July 30, but the withdrawal schedule required completion of this process thirty days earlier. Thus, Jacobs urged Marshall to

> bring this fact strongly to attention Department of Army so that its operational plans based on that date will be delayed accordingly [until September 15] and thus prevent this phase of our planning and operations from getting our [*sic*] of line with political phases. By all means no action to implement William Day [withdrawal day] should be taken as resulting publicity will complicate if not jeopardize our hope that UNTCOK will give formal approval to new government.

Marshall acted swiftly on this recommendation and began to press the UNTCOK members' home governments to extend some form of recognition to the ROK. If the international organization did not acknowledge the national character of the Rhee government, Marshall reasoned, the Soviets would create a separate regime in the north and make Korea's partition permanent.[34]

In Moscow, Ambassador Smith pragmatically observed that the

United Nations could not prevent the creation of a puppet government north of the 38th parallel. Following American withdrawal, he speculated, Communist North Korea would "enforce its claim of united government for all Korea, preferred method to be usual infiltration and carrying off political coup when time [is] ripe."[35] Indeed, on July 10, Kim Il Sung announced that work on a constitution was near completion. This document provided for a national government with its capital at Seoul. He explained that the People's Committee would sponsor elections throughout Korea on August 25, while displaying a new national flag sporting a hammer and sickle. Kim Il Sung also rebuked the United States for creating a police state in the south and demanded immediate American military withdrawal.[36]

To counter North Korea's claim to legitimacy, the administration decided to permit the South Korean government to send representatives to the United Nations.[37] This decision involved major risks, since Syngman Rhee was emerging as an even greater source of embarrassment for the United States. Early in April, Hodge advised Washington to retain a tight grip over all aid to South Korea. "Already Rhee is passing word around," he reported, "that economic aid from United States 'is in the bag,' meaning his bag, and that no US official will be able to tell Koreans how they shall use it." Hodge later alerted the administration that it could expect "all sorts of shenanigans" from Rhee after he had brought "in his gang of carpetbaggers."[38] Since Rhee's election as the first president of the ROK was certain, many American officials despaired that he would exploit his position of power to establish a personal dictatorship. Perhaps worse, Jacobs predicted that Rhee's "loose bombastic utterances" against the Soviet Union and communism eventually would have a disastrous impact on American policy at the United Nations.[39]

Unfortunately for the administration, there was nothing the United States now could do to deny Rhee a position of predominance in the South Korean government. On July 17, the legislative assembly promulgated the constitution and three days later it elected Rhee as the ROK's first president, thereby satisfying his lifelong ambition.[40] Subsequent scholars, as John Lewis Gaddis has pointed out, have debated whether Syngman Rhee's rise to preeminence in postwar Korean political affairs was the product of "inadvertence or design."[41] For some, Truman's policy in Korea from its inception was inconsistent, inept, and irresolute. Washington thereby became increasingly committed, unintentionally, to a group of individuals wedded to a philosophy at variance with American ideals.[42] Writers at the other extreme dismiss American professions of support for democracy in Korea as insincere. They contend that from the very beginning, Truman favored and actively encouraged the political triumph of Syngman Rhee. For the United States, Rhee's obvious dictatorial proclivities were less worrisome than his willingness to cooperate for the achievement of American political, economic, and strategic objectives in the postwar world.[43]

Both interpretations overestimate the power of the United States to determine events in Korea after World War II. In reality, Rhee's victory was the outgrowth of forces largely beyond Truman's control. For example, the Soviet Union was thoroughly unwilling to permit conservative political leaders in Korea to participate in the process of reconstruction. Moscow's apparent determination to impose an undemocratic Communist system on Korea caused American officials to look upon the extreme right as the lesser of two evils. Beyond that, Rhee had earned his victory. During World War II and after, Syngman Rhee consistently demonstrated that he was politically astute and opportunistic, even ruthless, in his pursuit of power. Administration officials, at least in Washington, honestly attempted to prevent a political triumph for Rhee during the first two years of the occupation. In the end, Truman deserted his goal of democracy in Korea only after the Soviet Union and Rhee had removed any chance for the early achievement of this objective. The final outcome hardly corresponded with the original desires and expectations of most American leaders.

Having attained political dominance, Rhee had no intention of permitting anyone to challenge his authority. He appointed only his closest political associates and trusted functionaries to government office.[44] Despite criticism from rival politicians, on August 4 the legislature approved Rhee's cabinet selections, including Yi Pŏm-sŏk, leader of the National Youth Movement, the compromise candidate for prime minister. Two days later, Rhee informed Hodge that the newly formed government was prepared to assume full administrative authority in South Korea. While stating his desire to continue "felicitous" relations with the United Nations, the new president also urged Washington to delay withdrawal. The United States could not leave, he insisted, until the ROK had achieved the military capability requisite for self-defense.[45]

Hodge and Jacobs agreed with Rhee's assessment. In separate cables, they informed Washington that the announcement of imminent withdrawal would destroy morale in South Korea and with it all previous progress toward the creation of a strong government. The Communist party unquestionably would renew its strategy of subversion and attempt to seize political power after American disengagement. Hodge advanced the opinion that "we should stand firm everywhere on Soviet perimeter, including Korea, until we know more clearly what actions will be taken in General Assembly and what will be outcome of our present negotiations with respect to . . . Germany." Washington's top representatives in Seoul concurred that while the United States should start to transfer authority to the ROK, a delay of complete military withdrawal was imperative.[46]

Such advice confirmed the growing conviction of officials in the State Department that it was necessary to postpone disengagement. Not surprisingly, the Army Department manifested greater confidence than Truman's diplomatic advisors in South Korea's ability to defend itself. During the orientation of Muccio as the new American ambassador to the ROK, military officials avowed that containment in Korea did not require the presence of combat forces from the United States. Stalin would not order an invasion across the 38th parallel, they claimed, because his strategy relied instead on indirect aggression. Furthermore, Syngman Rhee "was, as a result of the Army's substantial effort in training and equipping the South Korean forces, in a strong bargaining position to talk with the North Koreans on unification." Positive American action therefore had placed the Soviet Union on the defensive and provided sound reasons for optimism. In response, Muccio agreed to advocate a wider role for the State Department in supervising Korea's economic recovery.[47]

Muccio then attempted to justify the dilatory attitude of the State Department. Truman's diplomatic advisors were hesitant to assume full responsibility for South Korea's economic rehabilitation "owing to a feeling that Congress did not want State to handle programs of this nature." Draper brushed aside this explanation. Marshall and his colleagues, he argued, were trying to shirk their responsibilities. If the State Department's indifference persisted, Draper suggested that the Army Department might order the removal of all military equipment from Korea intended for transfer to the constabulary army. Since the State Department did not consider South Korea sufficiently important to generate interest in its survival, it would be foolish to leave a substantial military investment in an area destined for Soviet domination.[48]

To end this interdepartmental dispute, Truman intervened. On August 16, the president ordered the departments involved to decide which agency was best able to manage the Korean rehabilitation program. During subsequent discussions, the Army Department insisted upon the rapid termination of its obligations in Korea. By contrast, Lovett professed that the State Department did not have enough trained personnel to supervise the program, while Congress had shown a desire to exclude the diplomatic branch from any involvement in foreign aid. Paul G. Hoffman, director of the Economic Cooperation Administration (ECA), voiced sympathy for Lovett's position, but he strongly agreed with the Army Department's contention that the military should not administer the foreign assistance programs of the United States.[49]

Hoffman soon recognized that the ECA was the only logical candidate to supervise the aid program for South Korea. A consensus also existed that a small-scale operation would be a waste of time and money. Yet Hoffman doubted whether Congress would "continue to pour money into Korea, which was a rather questionable investment." Despite these reservations, he agreed to formulate a specific assistance plan in cooperation with the State Department for inclusion in the budget proposal for fiscal 1950. Significantly, as one State Department memorandum revealed, the ECA director was far from satisfied. In fact, he was skeptical about the logic of the entire venture:

> The whole problem is one of State Department foreign policy. It has no economic justification. [Hoffman] would hold out hope that Korea would offer any kind of economic bulwark. He gathers that it has no strategic importance from a military point of view. ECA will look to the State Department for leadership in the program to be carried out. He regards the operation as a holding one—making good on pledges to Korea.

On August 25, Truman instructed the Army Department to transfer its responsibilities to the ECA on January 1, 1949. Hoffman began at once to gather personnel and organize an aid mission to South Korea.[50]

Saltzman, as assistant secretary of state for occupied areas, supervised completion of a draft proposal for aid to Korea early in September. His memorandum rejected as unwise continued reliance on annual relief appropriations and emphasized instead the advantages of a multiyear program for the development of economic self-sufficiency. The proposed plan called for American aid to begin in 1949 and envisioned congressional approval for $180 million in economic assistance to South Korea during fiscal 1950. Hoffman eagerly advocated adoption. Draper was happy with the proposal as well, largely because the State Department finally had taken a direct role in Korean affairs. Even so, he expressed skepticism whether Congress would authorize an appropriation of funds. Lovett agreed, stating flatly that the program was "too rich for my blood at the moment." Coupled with similar requests, aid to Korea would place an excessive strain on the American economy. Nevertheless, Lovett admitted that the United States could not abandon South Korea. He therefore approved Saltzman's draft proposal and promised to work for congressional consent.[51]

Meanwhile, the administration finished preparations for the official transfer of governmental power from the AMG to the South Korean government. At the United Nations, the American delegation drafted a letter from Hodge to the UNTCOK informing the temporary commission of the successful formation of a Korean government. The United States scheduled an inauguration ceremony for August 15, the anniversary of Japan's surrender. Hodge's subsequent departure from Korea in conjunction with the arrival of Muccio would symbolize the end of American occupation and the restoration of Korea's sovereignty.[52] To avoid losing international backing for the ROK as a result of these actions, on August 12 the State Department announced the appointment of Muccio as "special representative" to South Korea, rather than ambassador. While the United States intended to await final action at the United Nations, the statement continued, Washington believed that the Rhee government was the political authority envisioned in the November 14 resolution. It also expressed the hope that the North Korean people, whom the Soviet Union had denied freedom of choice, would join the ROK "in due course."[53]

American military government officially ended as planned on August 15 with the formal establishment of the Republic of Korea. MacArthur attended the inauguration ceremony and delivered a speech declaring that the 38th parallel "barrier must and will be torn down. Nothing shall prevent the ultimate unity of your people as free men of a free nation." Observers in the United States commented positively on events in South Korea, since the administration's policy appeared to have given birth to a broadly based government that enjoyed international approval.[54] Truman was thrilled. In a letter to Hodge, he credited the USAFIK commander with producing the "outstanding success" of creating a constitutional government in Korea and thereby bringing freedom to a downtrodden people. "By your skill, initiative and diplomacy," the president enthused, "you have overcome seemingly insurmountable obstacles and you have earned the gratitude of the people, both of the United States and of Korea." For Truman, national self-determination had triumphed in South Korea, at least on the surface.[55]

American military experts too were pleased in the wake of the formal inauguration of the ROK, because the United States now could withdraw on September 15 as scheduled. In preparation for disengagement, the Army Department organized the Provisional Korean Military Advisory Group (PKMAG) on August 15. Composed of 240 men, the PKMAG's mission was to create, train, and equip a constabulary army of sufficient strength to deter an invasion from the north.[56] While welcoming this action, the State Department withheld approval for withdrawal on September 15. In a memorandum to the Army Department, Butterworth emphasized that NSC-8 did not preclude further delay. More important, the American public now favored firm resistance to further Soviet expansion in Korea, rather than precipitate withdrawal. Butterworth concluded with a reminder that both Hodge and Jacobs had advised postponement of disengagement until the United Nations acted on the UNTCOK report.[57]

Army Department officials remained adamantly opposed to an indefinite prolongation of military occupation in Korea. Ultimately, American leaders arrived at a compromise. The USAFIK would commence withdrawal on September 15 but would be prepared to halt the operation on a moment's notice. Furthermore, the JCS instructed Hodge not to refer to the imminence of disengagement upon his own departure from Korea. The Army Department approved these instructions with reluctance because the Chinese Communists had just overrun all of Manchuria; the United States now seemingly occupied an untenable position in Korea.[58] Nevertheless, when Hodge left

Korea he exuded optimism, predicting that a working democracy in South Korea would weaken Soviet dominance in the north and open the way to peaceful reunification.[59]

Simultaneously, the administration struggled to retain active international involvement in the Korean affair. The UNTCOK had completed its final report on July 25. Much to the satisfaction of the United States, the temporary commission informed the United Nations that "a reasonably free atmosphere" existed in Korea during the May elections. The UNTCOK's report recommended, however, that the international organization not extend its presence or expand its role in Korea. While it approved Washington's creation of a constabulary army, the temporary commission strongly urged the United Nations to terminate its involvement in the Korean matter after the United States withdrew. In Korea, Jacobs was afraid that the temporary commission might leave the peninsula prior to international consideration of its report. Only the presence of the UNTCOK, he urgently cabled Washington, could restrain the Soviet "stooges" inside South Korea and north of the 38th parallel. Marshall ordered Austin to campaign actively at the United Nations for an extension of international involvement in Korean affairs. The UNTCOK would contribute not just to the ROK's prestige, the administration believed, but also to the stabilization of relations with the north and the development of political and social stability throughout the peninsula.[60]

South Korea's new government experienced a sadly inauspicious beginning. During August, several of the nations with representatives on the UNTCOK informed Washington of their unwillingness to extend unqualified recognition to the ROK.[61] Still worse, almost from the outset, disagreement and friction surfaced between the South Koreans and the United States. The agreement on the transfer of governmental authority, for example, provided that the United States would retain command over the constabulary army and the police force until the completion of withdrawal. Both the prime minister and the foreign minister threatened to resign in protest over this infringement on Korea's sovereignty.[62] Fearing that the dispute would prevent his departure, Hodge pressed Washington to permit the arrival of Muccio as scheduled on August 23 even if the agreement remained unsigned. Once in Seoul, Muccio could tell Rhee that there would be no economic or military assistance until the ROK approved the terms of the transfer agreement. The administration summarily dispatched Muccio to South Korea to assume primary responsibility for American policy.[63]

Two days after his arrival in Seoul, Muccio cabled Washington that Rhee had signed the transfer agreement. In all probability, Muccio had utilized economic aid as a diplomatic weapon to induce the South Koreans to accept a compromise. The United States agreed to permit the ROK to assume control over the police as of September 3, but it would retain authority over the constabulary army until military withdrawal. The transfer agreement stated as well that the United States would begin its departure at "the earliest practicable time."[64] Early in September, Rhee formally asked the United States for economic and military aid. While Muccio advocated approval of the request, he insisted that any technicians or advisors serving in Korea possess total freedom of action to ensure the efficient utilization of American assistance. It was doubtful, however, whether the Korean legislature would accept such conditions. Several legislators already had recorded their opposition to the Korean-American Financial and Property Settlement because it required the ROK to repay the United States for the costs of the occupation.[65]

Events in North Korea represented a more dire threat to the survival of the ROK than discord with the United States. On August 25, the People's Committee sponsored elections, allegedly nationwide, for delegates to a "Supreme Korean People's Assembly." During the first week in September, this body met in Pyongyang and promulgated a constitution. The legislature also elected a "Supreme People's Council" and chose Kim Tu-bong as chairman. Kim Tu-bong then selected Kim Il Sung as premier and called upon him to form a cabinet, thereby providing the ruling authority for the "Democratic People's Republic of Korea" (DPRK). The new North Korean government claimed to represent the entire nation, stating its intention to send delegates to the United Nations.[66] As his first act, Kim Il Sung addressed letters to both Truman and Stalin requesting recognition and the removal of occupation troops. On September 19, Stalin formally recognized the DPRK as Korea's legitimate government and pledged Soviet support. In compliance with Kim's request, he also announced that the Soviet Union would withdraw its forces from North Korea before the end of 1948. The Soviet leader then invited the United States to follow suit.[67]

These developments apparently caught Truman and his advisors completely off guard. Stalin's maneuver had placed the administra-

tion in an embarrassing and dangerous position. North Korea unquestionably was stronger than South Korea militarily, economically,
and politically, and Moscow could disengage without hesitation. Truman could not act with such alacrity, however, since American withdrawal would place the existence of the ROK in jeopardy. On the
other hand, South Korea's continued dependence on American military protection virtually would preclude widespread international recognition of the ROK as the legitimate national government of Korea.
Far more ominous, two Korean governments soon would control their
own affairs, each committed to the destruction of its rival. In the
aftermath of Soviet-American withdrawal, civil war for the purpose of
forcible reunification was a near certainty. Knowledgeable Americans
saw that South Korea had little chance of surviving such a struggle.[68]

Aware that North Korea constituted a grave threat to the survival of
South Korea, the Army Department instructed John B. Coulter, the
new USAFIK commander, to minimize all equipment removals from
Korea during withdrawal. Although it was still desirable to "button
it up as soon as practical," American military leaders did not want to
leave the ROK defenseless at the time of disengagement.[69] For Rhee,
the formation of a rival government in the north demanded an indefinite postponement of American withdrawal. He sent Cho Pyŏng-ok
to Washington as his personal representative to press the Truman
administration not to desert Korea "when the battle was only half
won." While in the United States, Cho tried to persuade American
leaders that disengagement would only invite a Communist invasion
from the north. During September, Chang Myŏn, the new Korean
ambassador to the United States, joined Cho in Washington and he
too implored the administration to delay withdrawal. At the same
time, he voiced fears that representatives from the north would
attend the next session of the United Nations, thus endangering the
ROK's chances for obtaining recognition and subsequent admission
to the international organization.[70]

American problems in South Korea reached a dramatic climax in
October when a major rebellion erupted in Chŏlla namdo, a county
in the southernmost portion of the peninsula. Near the town of Yŏsu,
a small group of Communists, who had managed to infiltrate the
constabulary army, staged the original uprising on the night of October 19. Some two hundred soldiers soon joined the rebellion in protest over alleged officer abuse. Peasants and workers then added their
support to the uprising because of growing dissatisfaction with eco-

nomic deterioration and police corruption. The rebel force quickly swelled to more than three thousand people and proceeded to occupy the town of Yŏsu, establishing "people's courts" to try and execute policemen, army officers, and government officials.[71] The "Yŏsu Rebellion" rapidly spread to Sunch'ŏn, as rebels seized ammunition centers and burned police stations. Many people joined the uprising in anticipation of an imminent North Korean invasion. The rebels even raised the North Korean flag in Sunch'ŏn and pledged loyalty to the DPRK. While expanding their area of control, the Communist leaders punished anyone suspected of supporting the Rhee regime. Americans in Seoul thought the ROK was on the brink of total collapse.[72]

Coulter was determined to avoid direct involvement in the Yŏsu Rebellion. The PKMAG, however, promptly mobilized loyal constabulary forces to move against insurgent strongholds. The uneven terrain, and the fact that rebels wore American uniforms and used American equipment, made the task of the constabulary army extremely difficult. On October 27, ROK forces began to counterattack and the result was a bloodbath. Fighting in the streets of Yŏsu spared few citizens, and the constabulary army's retaliation against the rebels was merciless. Government forces either beat to death or summarily executed anyone suspected of sympathizing with the insurgency.[73] Meanwhile, Rhee implemented strong measures to purge any remaining leftists in the ROK's security forces. The legislature passed the National Security Act, which imposed, in essence, martial law in South Korea. The government proceeded to dismiss schoolteachers and civil administrators suspected of disloyalty, while censoring newspapers and imprisoning dissident editors. The constabulary army eventually reestablished control in the south, but the Yŏsu Rebellion significantly weakened popular confidence in the young and inexperienced government of South Korea.[74]

Administration officials in Washington received news of the Yŏsu Rebellion with shock, not least because of the widespread public support for the uprising. Most of the rebels were not Communists or fellow travelers but average citizens with legitimate grievances. More distressing, the incident revealed the ease with which the Communists could infiltrate the constabulary army and exploit popular discontent. Although the loyal ROK military units operated effectively, it would be some time before real stability prevailed in South Korea. For Muccio, the new government faced a clear challenge:

If the government and nation arose to the occasion, the Rebellion
would become the spark which drew all but the Communist elements
in the nation together. . . . If, on the other hand, no firm stand were
taken for reform, if efforts at change were virtually branded "treason,"
if a new spirit of patriotism were not infused into the people, the situation could rapidly deteriorate into mass uncertainty, discontent and
anarchy.

Most informed observers perceived that the Rhee government had
reached an early crossroads. Only political unity and serious reform
could elicit popular confidence in the ROK and counteract adverse
propaganda from the north.[75]

North Korea's ability to exploit such disturbances as the Yŏsu
Rebellion increased the likelihood of an overt military assault across
the 38th parallel. As Muccio noted in one cable, it was "more than
probable that if the internal South Korean situation worsens to the
extent likely under continuous North Korean-inspired disturbances,
the North Korean Army would intervene under the banner of restoring order and aiding 'democratic' elements of the population." Confronted with invasion from the north, Muccio argued, the ROK's
chances for survival were not good. Popular opposition to Rhee's
heavy-handed leadership was on the rise. The domestic situation presented a "grave picture," and Muccio expected an invasion from the
north in the spring of 1949. Only continued American military protection, he advised Washington, could forestall the demise of the
ROK. The United States had to delay withdrawal and provide South
Korea with a "period of grace" for the development of economic and
political stability.[76]

One outside event that had a distinct influence on the administration's deliberations on withdrawal was the Communist triumph in
China. The Chinese Nationalists never missed an opportunity to
warn the South Koreans that the United States eventually would
abandon the ROK to Soviet domination.[77] In November, Rhee
moved vigorously to obtain a postponement of American withdrawal.
Muccio cabled Washington that the ROK's president was planning to
appeal to the United Nations for passage of a resolution permitting
the United States to occupy South Korea until it developed the capacity for self-defense.[78] Subsequently, Rhee addressed a personal letter
to Truman requesting formally that the United States delay military
withdrawal. He mentioned, moreover, that an unequivocal statement

of Washington's commitment to defend the ROK would reassure the South Korean people and prevent the loss of hope. Rhee also wrote to MacArthur pleading for tanks, patrol ships, combat aircraft, and machine guns to assist South Korea in its fight against communism. He claimed that "the mere appearance of their existence at our disposal will give the people assurance of their security."[79]

Truman and his advisors thus faced an annoying dilemma. There were compelling reasons for withdrawal, but the administration feared that the South Korean government would collapse shortly after disengagement. Such an eventuality would inflict serious damage on the credibility and prestige of the United States. Consequently, the Truman administration, although determined to end American occupation, would not ignore its political commitment to the survival of South Korea. In the wake of the Yŏsu Rebellion, Marshall, Lovett, and Saltzman all went on record against fixing a specific date for the completion of withdrawal because of the prevailing atmosphere of chaos in South Korea. Complete disengagement at that time would be premature and prejudicial to American security interests in Asia. Since the United Nations had not acted on Korea, the January 15 deadline for total withdrawal also was unrealistic. Accepting these arguments, Washington instructed MacArthur to halt disengagement and maintain one regimental combat team in South Korea until the United Nations requested withdrawal.[80]

Army Department officials were still anxious to implement the withdrawal operation—now code-named "Twinborn." They accepted the latest postponement grudgingly because Korea continued to drain the Army Department's shrinking financial resources. Early in December 1948, the administration decided to reduce the defense budget for fiscal 1950 and lower the ceiling on military expenditures for the following year. Despite warnings from the JCS that such restrictions would undermine its ability to preserve American national security, Truman approved these decisions. The administration's approach was the direct outgrowth of the president's persistent desire to limit the postwar commitments of the United States in international affairs. Even the crisis over Berlin failed to shake Truman's conviction that the world situation in 1948 did not rule out further reductions in the size of the American military establishment and the defense budget. Spurning advice from Forrestal and others, the president placed a higher priority on financial aid to American allies than on building the military power of the United States.[81]

Truman's strategy for halting Soviet expansionism therefore emphasized the capacity for local self-defense. The administration hoped to achieve this objective in areas outside of Western Europe and Japan without providing an unqualified guarantee of military protection. South Korea represents a prime example of Truman's preference for economic rather than military means to counter the Soviet challenge in those nations that were important but not vital to American national security.[82] In formulating an economic assistance agreement, American leaders studiously sought to avoid making an unlimited commitment to the survival of South Korea. The Army Department strenuously opposed a categorical statement that aid to the ROK was vital to American security: "An Oriental mind would literally interpret and readily misconstrue this statement as an unconditional guarantee of continued full support. Future circumstances may not warrant such a construction. It would be difficult then to repudiate." Worse still, a pledge of open-ended support would have serious "psychological implications" because it would retard the development of a spirit of self-reliance among the South Koreans.[83]

Some of Truman's diplomatic advisors also thought that the United States should not exaggerate the anticipated benefits of American economic aid. Since the United States was "using economic assistance as a political prop," one State Department official advised, "we should have language that will enable us to play by ear without embarrassment." On the other hand, if the administration was not optimistic about the prospects for success, congressional approval for the Korean aid program was unlikely.[84] Until June 30, 1949, it could draw funds for the ROK from congressional appropriations under the program for Government Aid and Relief in Occupied Areas (GARIOA). After that date, the administration would be unable to finance its operations in South Korea. Presumably, American military withdrawal could eliminate GARIOA as a financial option even earlier. Despite certain reservations, Truman's advisors agreed nonetheless that congressional approval for a Korean aid program was vital not only for prompt disengagement but also for the long-term survival of the ROK.[85]

On December 11, the Truman administration announced that it had concluded negotiations with the ROK on an economic assistance package. It provided in part that the United States could terminate all aid without notice if the South Koreans abused the program. Thus, Truman's advisors ensured that future assistance was contingent upon the ROK's performance. That same month, Hoffman and his ECA team arrived in Korea to determine the extent of South Korea's needs. Press reports speculated that the administration intended to request congressional approval for $300 million in economic aid over three years. In his comments to newsmen, Hoffman predicted that Congress would authorize assistance for the ROK. Significantly, he also hinted that Washington might expand the program in the event of reunification.[86] American leaders therefore anticipated that the promise of economic benefits would spur popular demands in North Korea for amalgamation with the south.

Washington's commitment to provide economic assistance to South Korea had an alarming impact on the ROK. Officials in the Rhee government manifested a new sense of self-confidence, resulting in the issuance of a number of belligerent public statements. On December 18, for example, Foreign Minister Chang T'aek-sang announced that North Korea constituted "lost territory" and the ROK planned to recover it at the earliest possible moment regardless of cost. If the Communists prevented the North Korean people from fulfilling their desire for reunification, Chang declared, South Korea would resort to military conquest and eliminate the artificial division at the 38th parallel.[87] Muccio and Coulter received news of this statement with surprise and consternation. During immediate consultations with Rhee, the American ambassador assailed Chang's comments as bellicose and unduly provocative. Such pronouncements, Muccio admonished, were not only ill advised, but contrary to the United States policy of pursuing reunification through peaceful means alone.[88]

But verbal protests would not deter Rhee from attempting forcible reunification as soon as the ROK possessed sufficient power to launch an invasion into North Korea. Coulter was aware of this danger and wanted to limit the offensive military capabilities of the ROK, thereby minimizing the chances for an assault northward across the 38th parallel. For Rhee and his supporters, however, North Korea's military superiority was intolerable. In December, Rhee requested a large number of combat planes and coast guard ships with maintenance supplies for six months. Without hesitation, Coulter cabled Washington recommending disapproval of the aircraft provision.[89] Rhee soon recognized that an aggressive posture would jeopardize all American aid to the ROK and diminish the opportunities for eventually achieving his objective of reunification. To reassure the United

States, he dismissed his foreign minister. Nevertheless, the incident left an indelible imprint on the Truman administration. Under no circumstances would the United States provide the ROK with enough military power to stage an offensive into North Korea.[90]

By the end of 1948, the Truman administration was still wrestling with the dangerous Korean predicament. The new South Korean government had demonstrated scant political unity, making decisive progress toward economic recovery virtually impossible. Moreover, the Soviet Union had trained and equipped a powerful army in North Korea capable of conquering the entire peninsula following American withdrawal. As a result, the administration manifested an embarrassing reluctance to end American occupation of South Korea. And now another factor had emerged to complicate further the dilemma of withdrawal. Washington wanted to provide the ROK with enough military equipment to guarantee its survival. Yet once the United States removed its troops from the peninsula, nothing could stop Syngman Rhee from attempting forcible reunification.[91]

Nevertheless, the Truman administration remained committed to military disengagement at the earliest possible date. If the United States continued to occupy South Korea, the ROK never would develop the confidence necessary for the maintenance of self-defense, let alone the achievement of widespread international diplomatic and moral support. With American assistance and advice, on the other hand, there was reason to expect the eventual realization of economic recovery and political stability south of the 38th parallel. Despite serious weaknesses, American leaders still were hopeful that the Rhee government, in the absence of an unqualified commitment of American power, ultimately could compete on equal terms with the Communist regime in the north. But Truman's strategy for countering the threat of Soviet expansionism in Korea could produce neither success nor failure until after American military withdrawal.

CHAPTER 8

Test Case of Containment

Washington's decision to postpone withdrawal from Korea during the autumn of 1948 demonstrated the administration's commitment to South Korea's survival. If Truman actually sought to abandon the ROK, his refusal to order military disengagement made little sense. On the other hand, American leaders had not acted with notable vigor in attempting to formulate and implement an aid program for South Korea. Without extensive American help, the ROK never could attain the level of economic self-sufficiency requisite for genuine political independence. The Truman administration's hesitancy was partially the outgrowth of domestic politics in the United States. After all, few people thought Truman would be president in 1949. Following his surprising reelection, however, Truman appeared determined to adopt a more positive approach in both domestic and foreign affairs. This fresh sense of confidence in the administration had a significant impact on American policy in Korea.

In his inaugural address, Truman outlined an important new element in his foreign policy. The United States, he explained, would begin to utilize economic aid and technical advice for the improvement of internal conditions in underdeveloped countries. Commentators subsequently labeled this new strategy "Point Four." Although Truman later denied that the policy was anti-Communist, Point Four obviously sought to dissuade recipient nations from adopting the Soviet model for political, economic, and social development.[1] The success of the Marshall Plan in Europe encouraged administration officials to believe that a similar approach would produce economic recovery elsewhere in the world.[2] Dean Acheson, Truman's new secretary of state, unquestionably shared this opinion. Through a reliance on limited means, Acheson was confident that the United States could foster the emergence of "situations of strength" in strategic locations around the globe and thereby prevent further Soviet expansionism.[3] To an extent, the United States had followed the Point Four strategy in South Korea before 1949. Not surprisingly, at the start of Truman's second term the ROK occupied a central place in his policy toward the underdeveloped nations of Asia.

Events in China enhanced South Korea's importance for the administration. Truman and his advisors believed that Chiang Kai-shek himself was primarily responsible for the imminent triumph of communism in China. Despite considerable American assistance, Chiang had lost the support of the Chinese people because he had ignored popular grievances and failed to implement reforms. In South Korea, however, the United States had a second chance to build a popular and democratic government worthy of emulation in Asia. If Washington could promote economic strength and political stability south of the 38th parallel, it would prove that other nations could resist Soviet domination without an unlimited commitment of American power. As Truman explained in his memoirs, the United States wanted the Rhee government "to bring a measure of prosperity to the peasants that would make them turn their backs on the Communist agitators."[4] During 1949, Truman and his major advisors increasingly came to view South Korea as not just a bulwark against further Soviet expansionism but also the test case of containment in Asia.

International action on the Korean issue late in 1948 contributed to the administration's confidence in the wisdom of its strategy. Originally, Washington had planned to ask the United Nations to recognize the ROK as the government it had envisaged in its resolution of November 14, 1947. Britain and Canada had notified the administration, however, that it could not support this position.[5] Rather than risking public opposition from two close allies, Washington altered its proposal. The United States now would recommend that the United Nations recognize the ROK as the only legitimate government on the Korean peninsula and allow representatives from South Korea to participate in its future deliberations. North Korea, by contrast, would not have a chance to present its case, although the administration would not insist upon this provision. Washington's revised proposal also provided for a new "United Nations Commission on Korea" (UNCOK) to supervise the dissolution of all non-ROK military and administrative organizations in Korea and to report to the General Assembly on the progress of reunification. Since the administration believed that Canada, Syria, and India had lacked a strong interest in

Korea's future, it intended to encourage the exclusion of these nations from membership on the new international commission.[6]

On October 30, the Political and Security Committee of the United Nations began to consider the UNTCOK report. The temporary commission, while noting American cooperation and Soviet obduracy, concluded that both nations and "the tension prevailing in the international system" were responsible for the Korean impasse. Only reunification would permit all of Korea to experience political, economic, and social progress, but the UNTCOK offered no plan for achieving this result. The findings of the temporary commission included the ominous prediction that in the absence of a negotiated settlement, a civil war and forcible reunification would follow Soviet-American withdrawal. The United Nations again faced a painful choice. A decision to terminate its involvement in the Korean affair meant that the United Nations would abandon its moral obligation to the ROK. Adoption of the American proposal, however, would alienate the Soviet Union and in all probability lead to involvement in a civil war.[7]

In its final form, the draft resolution provided that within ninety days after adoption the UNCOK would observe and verify Soviet-American withdrawal from the peninsula. Washington's decision to forsake its claim that the ROK was the national government of Korea now produced its biggest diplomatic reward. On November 21, the Political and Security Committee voted unanimously against a Soviet proposal to invite representatives from the DPRK to participate in the debate.[8] Some commentators in the United States did not appreciate the extent of the American victory and demanded United Nations recognition of the national character of the ROK as well. Administration officials realized, however, that if the United States assumed an extreme and inflexible position, a number of nations would refuse to cooperate, thus barring further progress toward the achievement of American objectives. Conditional recognition from the United Nations definitely was preferable to impartiality.[9]

Truman's policy on Korea at the United Nations experienced total success during the last month of 1948. On December 6, the Political and Security Committee voted by a large margin to reject the DPRK's claim to legitimacy and instead to invite the ROK to send representatives to the United Nations.[10] It then turned its attention to Washington's proposal calling for continued international involvement in Korean affairs. John Foster Dulles delivered a strong speech appealing for United Nations approval of the resolution. He stressed that it would be "unthinkable that the United Nations should in any way disown the consequences of its own creative program."[11] Once again, American diplomatic pressure was effective. On December 8, the Political and Security Committee overwhelmingly voted to recommend that the General Assembly adopt the American resolution. It amended the proposal to provide for withdrawal of foreign troops from Korea "as soon as practicable," rather than ninety days, after adoption. At the same time, the committee refused to recognize the ROK as Korea's national government, observing that it controlled only half the peninsula.[12]

Four days later, the General Assembly easily approved the American-sponsored resolution despite sharp criticism from the Soviet delegation. After rejecting Moscow's proposal to disband the planned commission on Korea by a wide margin, the General Assembly voted to create a new commission that would be smaller than its predecessor, excluding both Canada and the Ukraine. Within thirty days, the UNCOK would arrive in Korea and begin to cooperate with the ROK for the achievement of reunification.[13] Dulles spoke for the administration when he publicly applauded the General Assembly's stand. The United Nations, he explained, had not surrendered to the North Korean strategy of political intimidation. Privately, Dulles suggested that international acceptance of Washington's policy in Korea might possess even broader significance: "Overwhelming Assembly vote on Korea starts South Korea off with as much political and moral backing as can be mobilized through UN. Apart from Korea, . . . Korean case in Assembly has contributed to more friendly relations between Far Eastern peoples and the US."[14] For Truman and his advisors, the United Nations resolution of December 12 represented a stunning victory for the United States over the Soviet Union in the Cold War.

Soviet officials hardly welcomed Washington's triumph at the United Nations. Nevertheless, Moscow had prepared for such an eventuality. The Soviet Union now accelerated its propaganda campaign stressing the significance of its military withdrawal from Korea before the end of 1948. Both *Pravda* and *Izvestia* called on the United States to terminate its occupation of South Korea as well. Soviet commentators casually dismissed references to the probability of civil war following withdrawal as ridiculous and insulting to the Korean people.[15] The administration saw that it had to take positive steps in the direction of disengagement in order to counter Moscow's efforts to discredit the ROK. Washington therefore instructed MacArthur to withdraw all military forces from South Korea with the exception of one regimental combat team. By early 1949, the United States could announce that all remaining American troops in Korea were under the command of Brigadier General William G. Roberts, head of the PKMAG.[16]

But partial withdrawal did not satisfy Truman's military advisors who wanted a specific date for complete disengagement. Less than two weeks after the United Nations called for the removal of all foreign troops from Korea "as soon as practicable," Undersecretary Draper asked the State Department to approve the withdrawal of all remaining troops from the ROK no later than March 31, 1949. Since the protection of South Korea was not worth a major war, he argued, the American occupation force would be a liability in the event of military conflict in Asia.[17] Political and diplomatic factors reinforced military justification for withdrawal. On December 30, the Soviet Union announced that it had completed military disengagement and asked the United States to comply with the United Nations resolution as well. Moscow charged that American occupation and plans for economic assistance constituted imperialism and proved the United States was seeking to exploit Korea. The administration could not ignore the risks involved in a decision to delay complete withdrawal. The Soviet Union would use Washington's continued presence in Korea as a propaganda weapon to undermine international backing for the ROK.[18]

Communist successes in China convinced other American leaders that the United States had to postpone disengagement from Korea indefinitely. Max Bishop, chief of the Division of Northeast Asian Affairs, believed that with the loss of China, American abandonment of the ROK would destroy the confidence and morale of all nations in Asia. Perhaps worse, Communist conquest of South Korea would advance greatly the Soviet drive to dominate Japan—"a target of prime importance to world communism." Bishop opposed early withdrawal because it might contribute "to the expansion of a hostile communist politico-military power system in Northeast Asia." The United States should strive instead to create a ring of strong states in Asia capable of halting further Soviet expansion. J. Leighton Stuart, the American ambassador in China, even urged Washington to seize the military and diplomatic initiative in Korea. Decisive action through "the United Nations framework," he speculated, "might catch the Soviets off balance" and counter the loss of prestige the United States would suffer following the anticipated fall of Chiang's regime.[19]

MacArthur's judgment played a major role in the Truman administration's decision to reevaluate its policy toward Korea. Late in December, he informed Washington that although he would maintain one regimental combat team on the peninsula, he did not think it was a requirement of his assigned mission "to secure or to make plans to secure southern Korea." In the absence of Soviet intervention, the ROK would have to depend on its own military forces for protection. For Butterworth, director of the Office of Far Eastern Affairs, MacArthur's attitude was disturbing, especially in light of reports from Seoul that the ROK was not receiving sufficient military assistance. USAFIK Commander Coulter cabled Washington that South Korea did not have enough equipment to maintain a viable constabulary army. He appealed for an early decision on the extent of the administration's commitment to provide the ROK with the ability to defend itself. These reports, combined with the warnings from Bishop and Stuart, convinced Butterworth that the United States had to reconsider its Korea policy. In a memorandum to Lovett dated January 10, he proposed an immediate redefinition of American aims in Korea under NSC-8. Subsequently, the State Department decided to request comments both from Muccio and MacArthur on the broad military, political, and psychological issues related to the withdrawal question.[20]

Washington received a prompt response from Muccio. The ambassador stated frankly that South Korea had not attained the stability necessary for survival in the wake of early American withdrawal. He strongly recommended that the United States delay disengagement for "several months" until it was certain an invasion from the north would not follow its departure. Only continued American occupation would provide the "breathing space" that the ROK needed to develop political stability and economic recovery. After South Korea resolved its manifold problems, the United States could withdraw safely and without fear of Communist conquest of the entire peninsula. Rhee's request for a delay of military withdrawal, Muccio argued, would provide justification before the international community for a postponement of American departure. While he shared the desire to disengage, Muccio asserted that the National Security Council had to consider the consequences of premature withdrawal. In response to Muccio's assessment, Lovett, on January 17, formally referred the Korean matter to the NSC and requested a thorough reexamination.[21]

Two days later, Washington received MacArthur's appraisal. In his cable, MacArthur recommended American withdrawal from Korea no later than May 10, 1949—the anniversary of Korea's first election. Long-range stability in South Korea, he observed, was not likely because of the ROK's "penchant for dictatorship" and total inability to improve economic conditions. MacArthur emphatically opposed a guarantee of military protection for the ROK, noting that in the "event of any serious threat to the security of Korea, strategic and military considerations will force abandonment of any pretense of active military support." While the people of Japan would accept withdrawal if Washington announced its intentions in advance, MacArthur warned the administration that a policy of delay invited disaster: "The longer US forces remain in Korea the greater the risk of being placed in position of effecting withdrawal under conditions amounting to direct pressure rather than as a voluntary act. Damage to US prestige in such event would be irreparable." Not only could the United States not guarantee the ROK's survival, but it was improbable that it could train and equip an indigenous army strong enough to protect South Korea from either subversion or invasion. Finally, MacArthur mentioned that the UNCOK, by encouraging disengagement, could provide a valuable "psychological cover for withdrawal."[22]

Although the Truman administration ultimately would delay disengagement despite the general's recommendations, it agreed with MacArthur's judgment that the United States should supply only "economic aid and military assistance" to those friendly governments on the mainland still resisting Russian domination. MacArthur further emphasized that Washington's primary objective should be to establish defensive positions on major islands circling the Asian continent. In March 1949, the general even made his views public, possibly in an effort to influence the administration's policy. During an interview with British journalist G. Ward Price, MacArthur traced a "line of defense" for the United States in the Pacific excluding both the ROK and Taiwan:

It starts from the Philippines and continues through the Ryukyu Archipelago, which includes its main bastion, Okinawa. Then it bends back through Japan and the Aleutian Island chain to Alaska. Though the advance of the Red Armies in China places them on the flank of that position, this does not alter the fact that our only possible adversary on the Asiatic continent does not possess an industrial base near enough to supply an amphibious attacking force.

While MacArthur apparently accepted the inevitability of Communist control throughout Korea, he was confident that the United States could preserve its security interests in Asia.[23]

Understandably, the South Koreans wanted the United States to expand rather than reduce its commitments to the ROK. During discussions in Washington, Cho Pyŏng-ok spoke fearfully about how, with the fall of China, hostile Communist forces would surround the ROK. Rash leaders in South Korea, he told Butterworth and Bond, now might advocate a deal "with north Korea on terms laid down by the latter." In reply, Butterworth advised that South Korea had to pursue a dynamic policy of progressive reform and thereby promote the popular loyalty necessary for internal political unity and strength. If the ROK ignored popular demands, it would make the same fatal mistake that Chiang had made in China. Cho responded that an "enlightened and progressive program . . . might well be a luxury which could not be afforded by a government fighting for its very existence." Butterworth countered that if the ROK satisfied the desires of the people, it might not have to worry about its survival.[24] These comments provided a concise summary of the State Department's position on Korea. While opposing early withdrawal, Truman's diplomatic advisors viewed the ROK's ability to develop popular support as the key to successful self-defense against the threat of Communist expansion.

To reassure the South Koreans, Truman dispatched Royall and Wedemeyer to the peninsula early in February on a fact-finding mission. Just prior to their arrival, North Korea intensified its campaign of border violence and guerrilla action. Rhee quickly appealed to Washington for an increase in military assistance. In their conversations with Royall and Wedemeyer, the South Korean officials harped on the importance of military power for the protection of the ROK and the eventual achievement of reunification. Yi Pŏm-sŏk predicted that the Soviet Union was about to start a third world war. Thus, as the situation in China deteriorated, "Korea should be increasingly important as a stepping stone for offensive action." He thought the

United States should delay withdrawal while providing the ROK with more military aid to overcome the temporary superiority of the northern regime. In response, Wedemeyer reiterated the State Department's argument that "the greatest contribution that the Koreans could make to the overall world situation would be to establish stability in their homeland, to develop a happy, industrious people; a strong government along democratic lines." Korea's highest priority, he said, was to create economic strength, not a large military force that "would make a disproportionate drain on the country's economy."[25]

Rhee dismissed these arguments. Only superior military power, he insisted, would achieve Korea's reunification. Once South Korea invaded the north, Rhee predicted that because of low morale, "a large proportion of the North Korean army would desert." The reunification of Korea was within easy grasp because the people in the north were hostile to the Communist regime. Success, however, would require the State Department to jettison its policy of vacillation that already had "played a strong part in the loss of China." Rather than accepting a similar "sellout," Rhee threatened not to approve American withdrawal unless the United States enlarged its military advisory group and the amount of military aid to the ROK.[26]

This exchange with Rhee convinced Royall that an early American withdrawal was imperative. During talks with Muccio and Roberts, he asserted that the United States could use Soviet disengagement from the north to justify its own departure. Muccio disagreed; the United States could not disengage until it had persuaded South Korea that it did not intend to desert the infant regime. If the South Koreans felt secure and confident, the ROK would achieve economic self-sufficiency and the political support of the masses. Roberts seconded Muccio's assessment. The ROK, he argued, warranted American assistance because its soldiers were loyal to the government and would fight to protect the nation. Although he did not think South Korea needed tanks or a navy, Roberts advocated extensive military assistance. Obviously, Royall had failed to alter the opinions of Washington's two most important officials in Seoul on the issue of withdrawal. In fact, Muccio returned to the United States with Royall to argue his case against any reduction in the American commitment to South Korea.[27] It thus would be amid conflicting advice that Truman would decide the extent of future American involvement in Korea.

On March 22, top administration officials reconsidered American policy in Korea at the thirty-sixth meeting of the National Security Council. The State Department began its reappraisal with a review of events in Korea during the previous year. Despite American aid and advice, the new South Korean government had not developed sufficient military and economic strength to defend itself against the challenge of the Soviet puppet regime in North Korea. If the United States withdrew abruptly from Korea at that time, the report declared, this "disengagement would be interpreted as a betrayal by the U.S. of its friends and allies in the Far East and might contribute substantially to a fundamental realignment of forces in favor of the USSR throughout that part of the world." Moreover, premature American withdrawal would shatter the confidence of South Korea and thus guarantee the rapid demise of the ROK. Such a dramatic Communist victory would damage American interests because it would destroy the viability of the United Nations and force smaller countries to seek an accommodation with Moscow. The study—NSC-8/1—therefore concluded that despite the uncertain prospects for success, Washington had to provide the ROK with continued diplomatic support and economic, technical, and military assistance.[28]

At the same time, NSC-8/1 acknowledged that American military disengagement was essential because the United Nations had asked for the removal of all foreign troops. Both Muccio and MacArthur had advised, however, that the United States could withdraw safely if the administration satisfied certain conditions. First, Washington had to train, equip, and supply a security force in Korea sufficiently powerful to maintain internal order and deter an open attack from the north. Second, the ECA had to implement a three-year program of technical and economic aid for recovery and self-sufficient growth. Finally, the United Nations had to continue its policy of diplomatic and political support as a boost to South Korea's morale. NSC-8/1 closed with the ominous prediction that if the United States delayed departure the "occupation forces remaining in Korea might be either destroyed or obliged to abandon Korea in the event of a major hostile attack, with serious damage to U.S. prestige."[29]

Truman approved NSC-8/1 on March 23 with certain significant revisions. In its final form, the paper—NSC-8/2—represented a compromise that sought to accommodate the conflicting desires of both diplomatic and military leaders. The administration now resolved to gain approval from Congress for a three-year program of economic aid to the ROK and military security prior to American withdrawal. Furthermore, the United States would provide enough equipment and arms to maintain a security force of more than 100,000 men. For Royall, NSC-8/2 had provided "an excellent solution to a tough problem." Yet Muccio admitted that "while there had been improvement [in South Korea] since the October uprising, there were still many questions marks which constituted a calculated risk that had to be taken."[30]

NSC-8/2 also established June 30, 1949, as a firm date for the complete withdrawal of American combat forces. The modifications made in NSC-8/1 reflected the determination of Truman's military advisors to prevent any chance for further postponement. The State Department, for example, favored withdrawal only after the United States had transferred all necessary military equipment to the constabulary army and consulted with the United Nations and the ROK. In its final form, however, NSC-8/2 provided for departure by June 30 without regard for any other contingency. It also set specific limits on the size of the army (65,000), coast guard (4,000), and police (35,000). These forces would receive light weapons alone, and the paper explicitly ruled out the creation of a Korean navy. Obviously, American military experts wanted to eliminate any potential for South Korea to attempt forcible reunification and thereby ignite a major war. At the same time, NSC-8/2 emphasized that American military withdrawal should in no way imply any lessening of the administration's interest in the ROK's future survival.[31]

Truman's new strategy in Korea depended for success on South Korea's ability to maintain moral and material support from the international community. On January 1, 1949, the United States had extended formal recognition to the ROK as the legitimate government of all Korea and pledged full support for the UNCOK's efforts to achieve reunification. Truman also promised that the United States would not withdraw until the ROK was capable of self-defense.[32] Even so, several members of the UNCOK were hesitant to become actively involved in Korean affairs. Upon his arrival in Korea, Egon Ranshofen-Wertheimer, the UNCOK's principal secretary, created a major headache for the United States when he stated publicly that in view of Moscow's intransigent attitude, the UNCOK should withdraw entirely from Korea. Muccio instantly appealed to the UNCOK to cooperate with the ROK and attempt to gain access to North Korea. The mere presence of the commission in Korea, the ambassador emphasized, bolstered the morale of the Rhee government and deterred an invasion from the north. During subsequent discussions, other American officials claimed that if the UNCOK simply appeared at the 38th parallel, the North Koreans would grant entrance rather than risk international condemnation.[33]

Evidently, the efforts of Washington's diplomatic representatives in Seoul were not in vain. After several meetings, the UNCOK recognized the ROK as legitimate and declared its commitment to the achievement of Korean reunification. Rhee, however, responded with a public announcement stating his complete opposition to any UNCOK attempt to contact the northern regime, arguing that this effort would constitute tacit recognition of the Communist government and an affront to the ROK.[34] Even before the arrival of the UNCOK in Korea, Rhee had stated publicly that UNCOK's mission, he believed, was to provide unqualified support for the ROK and investigate the undemocratic and illegal nature of the North Korean regime alone. Rhee's demand that the commission ignore criticism of his government and evidence of political repression in the south ensured that friction would emerge in relations between the UNCOK and the ROK. Nevertheless, the UNCOK attempted to cooperate. Rather than approaching the DPRK, it addressed an appeal directly to the Soviet Union, requesting assistance for the settlement of the Korean dispute. The commission also announced that it would stay in South Korea to observe and verify American military withdrawal.[35]

While Muccio was in Washington, Everett F. Drumright, the embassy chargé, pressed Rhee to cooperate with the UNCOK and avoid any disagreement. He privately implored the president of the ROK neither to criticize nor to restrict the activities of the commission in South Korea.[36] Drumright's efforts were for naught. Rhee prohibited all Korean citizens not affiliated with his government from contacting the UNCOK and stationed police outside the commission's headquarters to monitor visitors. Predictably, Ranshofen-Wertheimer vigorously protested Rhee's interference in the commission's operations. He reminded Drumright that the UNCOK's job was not only to foster reunification but to observe the development of democracy throughout Korea as well. Broad consultations were especially important in South Korea because the ROK resembled a "fascist police state." In reply, one American official pointed to "the tradition of misrule in Asia" to explain Rhee's behavior. He then told the UNCOK's principal secretary that the ROK's survival depended on international support and therefore justified overlooking its short-comings.[37]

While American officials in Seoul struggled to maintain friendly relations between the ROK and the UNCOK, the administration had it much easier at the United Nations. In February 1949, both Korean governments applied for admission to the international organization. During subsequent debate, Soviet representative Jacob Malik alleged that the United States had employed terror and intimidation to manipulate the elections in South Korea. The American delegation countered that commissioners from the United Nations had observed the voting process and verified the legitimacy of the results. Washington again scored a major diplomatic victory when the Security Council decided to refer the ROK's application to the United Nations Membership Committee. Malik decried the action as an outgrowth of Anglo-American dictation. Despite Moscow's protests, the Membership Committee recommended approval of the ROK's application.[38] To no one's surprise, the Soviet Union cast a veto on April 8 to prevent the ROK's admission. American delegate Warren Austin promptly condemned Moscow for again violating the will of the United Nations and blocking progress toward achieving Korea's reunification and independence.[39]

Drumright not only expected but even welcomed the Soviet veto. He observed happily that it would have the "advantageous effect of further alienating Korean people from Soviets and rendering more difficult Soviet attempts [to] attain hegemony" over the entire peninsula. Popular hostility toward the Soviet Union was especially desirable because of Rhee's inability to foster political unity in South Korea. A powerful coalition in the legislative assembly had surfaced early in 1949 to challenge Rhee's authority. Drumright informed Washington that the members of this "Young Group" were intensely nationalistic and therefore hostile to any trace of foreign dictation. The Young Group demanded immediate American military withdrawal and opposed the ECA program, favoring instead the achievement of reunification through negotiations with the North Korean regime. To Drumright, the leaders of this coalition were hopelessly naive and unrealistic because "they do not clearly recognize the nature of Sovietism . . . the world over, and the impossibility of compromise with the Soviets, without complete loss of independence, democracy, and, perhaps, life itself."[40]

American officials in Seoul endeavored to convince members of the Young Group that the magnitude of the Soviet threat demanded cooperation with Rhee. During private conversations, Vice-Consuls David Mark and Gregory Henderson reminded leaders of the coalition that the Soviets had stifled democracy in North Korea. Logically, the Korean assemblymen retorted that if a negotiated reunification was impossible, then civil war was inevitable. The American diplomats insisted to the contrary that eventual amalgamation was possible without violence or surrender:

> Korea was a miniature of the world. As Korea was split, so was the world. However, it was not certain at all that war between Russia and America was the inevitable outcome of this. Many Americans felt that after a number of years of tension, the Soviet Union might come to its senses, compromise, and change towards peaceful paths. That was the hope on which American foreign policy was based. Similarly, in Korea, the division might be a line of tension, as now, for a number of years without erupting into war. Then, if, finally, the United States and Soviet relations improved, so would North and South unify.

Although peaceful reunification might never occur, Mark and Henderson exhorted these South Korean leaders to work through the United Nations for internal political unity and thereby "provide a shining example for North Korea, and at the same time, be strong enough to discourage attack."[41]

Rhee disagreed with both the Young Group and the United States on the best method for accomplishing reunification. On February 18, the ROK's president appointed governors for five provinces in the north, causing speculation that an invasion of North Korea was imminent.[42] Then, the following month, Rhee sent Cho Pyŏng-ok to Washington again to plead for more military aid. South Korean Ambassador Chang presented Acheson with a memorandum prior to Cho's arrival outlining the objectives of his mission. Rhee's representative would request sufficient military assistance to attain "parity" with North Korea, thus providing South Korea with the "psychology of safety" requisite for social stability. The memorandum went on to explain that the ROK needed additional military power to achieve its two historic goals—unification, without which true economic and political independence was impossible, and strength to "contribute our due share as a bastion of democracy in the Far East in combatting the overexpanding communistic forces." The Rhee government believed that the United States should implement in South Korea a comprehensive program of extensive military aid just as it had done in Greece.[43]

Drumright vehemently opposed any expansion of the ROK's military capabilities, warning that Rhee was bent on forcible reunification. Moreover, Washington had to persuade the South Korean government to forsake its obsession with military power or significant progress toward economic and political strength would be impossible.[44] Drumright's comments probably contributed to the administration's decision to impress upon Rhee the limited nature of the military aid program contemplated for the ROK and the imminence of American withdrawal. Washington also worried that unless it notified Rhee, administrative and logistical preparations for departure would frighten the South Koreans. Acheson therefore instructed Muccio to inform both Rhee and the UNCOK of American intentions to withdraw within the "next few months." This message would avert any embarrassment likely to result from rumors prior to the official withdrawal announcement, while encouraging the Koreans to accept the decision.[45]

Muccio already had started to prepare Rhee for American disengagement during meetings immediately after his return to South Korea. He promised the ROK's president that the United States would provide substantial military aid both before and after withdrawal. On April 5, the ambassador outlined Washington's plans in more detail. Once Rhee grasped the limited scope of the military assistance program, he registered his dissatisfaction. Reunification, Rhee protested, would require a more extensive American commitment. The ROK needed airplanes and combat ships, not words, to achieve success. The majority of northerners, Rhee continued, despised Communist rule and favored unity with the south. Even the army would join a revolt when he "gave the signal." After further discussions, Muccio convinced Rhee, at least temporarily, that the United States would not alter its plans. He then asked the ROK's president to state publicly that American military assistance was sufficient for the preservation of South Korea's security. Rhee agreed that such an announcement would have psychological and political value. He promised to comply with Muccio's request in a few days.[46]

Following conversations with Rhee, Muccio met with the UNCOK to brief its members on American plans for withdrawal. The ROK, he observed, had experienced a recent improvement in economic and political conditions making it possible for the United States to remove its occupation forces. Muccio said he hoped the commission would observe and verify American compliance with the withdrawal provision of the United Nations resolution of December 12, 1948. French delegate Henri Costilhes spoke against American plans for military disengagement. The United States, he believed, should remain in occupation of South Korea for five additional years.[47] Muccio soon confronted an even bigger aggravation than the possibility of the UNCOK's resisting American policy. Rhee now announced that without a more "concrete commitment" for American military assistance, he would not sanction withdrawal. On April 14, Rhee sent a letter to Muccio formally requesting that the United States reaffirm the Korean-American treaty of 1882. Acting on instructions from Acheson, the American ambassador informed Rhee that while time had rendered the earlier agreement inoperative, Washington was willing to negotiate a new treaty. He again appealed for an official South Korean endorsement for American withdrawal.[48]

Apparently, Muccio managed to persuade Rhee to alter his position. At a press conference on April 18, the ROK's president announced that the United States would withdraw in the near future, but it would continue to provide military aid and advice. Rhee also stated confidently that the constabulary army could repel any attack from the north.[49] After a trip to the southern provinces, however, Rhee changed his mind and revived his demands for more military assistance. The ROK required enough equipment to arm an additional 100,000 troops plus 500 more American military advisors. Events in China only made the situation worse. When the Communist armies crossed the Yangtze River that month, Rhee declared that unless Washington provided greater military aid, he would oppose American disengagement. Muccio recommended that the administration satisfy Rhee's desires, since this was the price tag for obtaining the ROK's support for withdrawal. South Korea also appeared to need more military equipment, especially for its coast guard. The United States, Muccio advised, "cannot risk being penny wise and pound foolish."[50]

Acheson would not knuckle under to Rhee's demands. He instructed Muccio to announce instead the formal establishment of the Korean Military Advisory Group (KMAG), hoping that this measure would placate Rhee and bolster South Korean morale. On May 2,

Muccio presented Rhee with the official announcement of the KMAG. In response to Rhee's request, PKMAG Commander Roberts outlined his plans for the future of the military advisory group.[51] Rhee's minister of defense then pointed to events in China, suggesting that Washington's policy toward Korea now required revision. Muccio replied that while he deplored the situation in China, it further reduced the possibility of invasion from the north and might provide the ROK with "breathing space." When the defense minister complained that the United States had deserted Korea on two prior occasions in its history, Muccio countered that if the ROK "set up a sound, strong and good . . . Government that will satisfy the aspirations of the Korean people . . . , little trouble should be anticipated from North Korea." Rhee then spoke at length about the uncertainty surrounding Washington's willingness to defend South Korea. Muccio pointed to the economic and military assistance programs as proof of the American commitment to the ROK. At the close of the meeting, however, Rhee said he hoped Truman would "clarify this situation."[52]

Rhee now was determined to force the United States to alter its policy. On May 7, his Office of Public Information released a statement challenging Washington to define the extent of its commitment to the ROK. President Rhee wanted to know whether South Korea was in the first line of American defense. Did the United States consider an attack on the ROK equivalent to an attack on itself? The announcement also blamed Washington for permitting the Soviets to occupy the north, encouraging a revival of communism in the south, and preventing the ROK from developing the capacity for self-defense. This statement infuriated Acheson. He angrily instructed Muccio to inform Rhee that the United States considered such public pressure "not only a grave breach [of] ordinary diplomatic courtesy but also as sharply inconsistent with [the] spirit [of] mutual friendliness and good faith." These "unfortunate utterances," Acheson warned, "may well have serious adverse consequences in terms [of] pending requests [for] economic and military aid for Korea." If Rhee persisted in making "ill-considered" statements and "unrealistic" aid requests, the United States might decide to reduce rather than expand the size of its assistance program for South Korea.[53]

Muccio had already told Rhee that he was "disturbed and even shocked" at the "tone and content" of the recent government statement.[54] Yet the ambassador believed that the administration should provide the ROK with more military equipment, even combat ships and airplanes. These recommendations dismayed American military planners, who complained that Muccio was allowing Rhee to use additional military assistance as a condition for withdrawal. Louis A. Johnson, the new secretary of defense, addressed a letter to Acheson stressing the importance of avoiding "the unwarranted expense which will result from further delay and indecision in this matter." Previous postponements of Operation Twinborn, he noted, "have already created serious logistical and budgetary problems."⁵⁵ Acheson promised to consult Muccio regarding the issue of withdrawal, but he reminded Johnson that the State Department never had agreed to a specific date for departure. The United States had to be patient or risk losing any chance to achieve its aims in Korea. Simultaneously, Muccio sent another cable to Washington urging an increase in military aid for South Korea. If the administration complied with the ROK's request, he argued, "I still . . . may be able to sell Rhee on our target date thereby avoiding inevitable world censure should we appear to be withdrawing unilaterally."⁵⁶

Rhee's coercive tactics had a decidedly negative impact on Acheson. On May 9, he advised Muccio that additional military aid to the ROK was "absolutely out of [the] question." Not only did the United States lack the desired equipment, but it would not permit Rhee to extract a higher price for an endorsement of withdrawal. After receiving Muccio's consent, Acheson also approved the Army Department's request to downgrade the security classification of the withdrawal operation from secret to restricted. Now nothing could stop American disengagement on June 30.⁵⁷ Muccio subsequently informed Rhee that the United States would complete military withdrawal within the "next few weeks." Although there would be no reduction in American aid to South Korea, Washington did not intend to strengthen the ROK's military capabilities. Rhee explained that while he accepted these decisions, South Korea still needed a strong statement of American support to convince the people that withdrawal was not a "catastrophe." He also suggested that the United States create a "Pacific Pact" similar to NATO. Muccio cabled Acheson that Rhee, despite his disappointment, probably would not attempt to impede the completion of disengagement.⁵⁸

While Muccio's assessment of Rhee's attitude may have been correct, South Korea's ministers of foreign affairs and defense still were bent on forcing the United States to expand its commitment to defend the ROK. On May 19, they issued a joint statement demanding that Washington provide for "the adequate defense of the Republic of Korea before they withdraw their forces." Since the United States had "created the 38th parallel," it had a "moral obligation" to ensure South Korea's military parity with the Soviet puppet regime in the north. Muccio lost little time complaining to Rhee that this statement had created speculation in the press about a Korean-American rift on the issue of withdrawal. When Rhee called in his foreign minister for an explanation, Ben C. Limb (Yim Pyŏng-jik), "in a shrill voice," scolded the United States for "selling China down the river." South Korea's leaders had the right, he exclaimed, to publicize Washington's decision to repeat the same mistakes in Korea. Muccio calmly observed that if Rhee shared these views, then perhaps he should close the American embassy and leave South Korea. Recognizing that Limb had gone too far, Rhee prevailed upon his defense minister to apologize to Muccio both for the statement and for the behavior of his fellow cabinet member.[59]

Washington was determined to complete withdrawal on schedule even without the cooperation of the ROK. By the end of May, the United States had transferred the remaining arms, ammunition, communications equipment, vehicles, and spare parts of the USAFIK to the constabulary army. Faced with the inevitable, Foreign Minister Limb held a press conference and, in a remarkable reversal of opinion, declared that the ROK possessed enough military power "to conquer North Korea within three days." For Muccio, Limb's remarks represented "a refreshing contrast to the steady stream of official comment of late" focusing on South Korea's military weakness.[60] Privately, however, the Rhee government was desperately trying to persuade the United States to delay its departure. Two cabinet members visited Muccio and appealed for a six-month postponement of withdrawal. Rhee sent a frantic letter to MacArthur predicting an invasion from the north following American disengagement in the absence of more military assistance. South Korea, he pleaded, was involved in a "fight for its life" and needed ships, airplanes, and ammunition to halt the spread of communism for the rest of the "free world." At the United Nations, Cho Pyŏng-ok approached the American delegation and begged for a one-year delay of withdrawal until the ROK was capable of self-defense.[61]

Muccio informed the administration that "a sense of crisis bordering on panic" now prevailed in South Korea. "Clamour and fear aroused by troop withdrawal," he sadly confessed, "have far exceeded my expectations." Unless Washington found a way to reassure the ROK, the United States could expect the next three weeks to be extremely unpleasant. For the administration, the antics of South Korea's leaders to force a postponement of withdrawal were intolerable. On June 2, Undersecretary of State James E. Webb handed Chang an *aide-mémoire* protesting the ROK's distribution of erroneous information deprecating the extent of American military support and the size of the constabulary army. Constant references to the ROK's military weakness, Webb warned, would destroy the will of the South Korean people to resist an invasion and therefore courted disaster. Washington would not change its plans for withdrawal. In conclusion, Webb lectured the ROK's ambassador that no amount of military assistance would guarantee the survival of South Korea if the general populace was not determined to prevent a Communist seizure of power.[62]

On June 6, Muccio met with Rhee and discussed Webb's protest. The ROK's president claimed that he now had abandoned further efforts to delay American withdrawal. The following day, however, Rhee formally asked the United States to create a "Pacific Pact" devoted to blocking Communist expansion in Asia. When it became clear that an unqualified guarantee of military protection from the United States was not forthcoming, the Rhee government resumed its campaign to delay the departure of the American occupation force. Throughout the month of June, the ROK sponsored mass demonstrations protesting Washington's decision to withdraw. South Korean leaders emphasized that the United States had an obligation to ensure the survival of the ROK as a crucial bastion of democracy in Asia. Refugees from North Korea were particularly vocal in demanding additional military assistance and a firm pledge of American protection. The Communist regime in North Korea, they feared, had marked them for immediate execution after the invasion and conquest of South Korea.[63]

Despite these appeals, the administration refused to alter its plans for withdrawal before June 30. While acknowledging the possibility of armed invasion from the north, American leaders believed that the United States could ensure the survival of the ROK without having to rely on its military power. Just prior to withdrawal, Truman's military advisors prepared a detailed study discussing American alternatives in the face of an open assault across the 38th parallel. The paper began with a consideration of three immediate courses of possible future action in Korea. The United States could "encourage the Rhee Government to attempt the peaceful unification of Korea by direct negotiations with the North Korean regime." While possessing obvious propaganda value, neither government was likely to accept this alternative. If the negotiation option was "tested, tried and unsuccessful," the United States might consider organizing a Korean underground task force to operate in the north, taking advantage of popular hostility to the Communist regime and instigating a rebellion. North Korea could use this operation, the study cautioned, to justify not only continued subversion in the south but even an invasion. American military experts definitely preferred the third alternative, which provided only for American warships to make periodic visits to South Korea.[64]

The remainder of the report discussed a variety of options available to the United States after an open North Korean assault across the 38th parallel. Significantly, the study assumed that North Korea did not possess "the capability of sustained and comprehensive military operations without Chinese Communist and Soviet-Manchurian aid and support." If the United States chose not to counter an "all-out" invasion, Communist forces might destroy the ROK and conquer the entire peninsula. To avoid international "recrimination," the United States would have to take some positive action. The paper's first recommendation was that in the event of an invasion, Washington should evacuate all American citizens and military advisors from Korea. Then the United States should refer the matter promptly to the United Nations and request an emergency session of the Security Council. This measure would underline the "international character" of the situation and avoid "the onus of U.S. unilateral responsibility and action." Despite the likelihood of delay, inaction, and a Soviet veto, the administration could ignore the United Nations only at the risk of destroying the international organization. Far more important, this course of action would force Moscow to declare publicly its "cooperative or non-cooperative intentions."[65]

Since American military leaders had sought previously to limit United States commitments in Korea, it was not surprising that the authors of this paper opposed any further steps of a positive nature. The study dismissed, for example, the alternative of undertaking a "police action" with the sanction of the United Nations and multinational participation. Although this option would fortify the international organization and might even deter future acts of aggression, it also would require congressional approval and therefore entail disastrous delays. American participation would deplete the manpower and material resources of the United States at a dangerous moment in European affairs as well. Consequently, the paper recommended military participation in a "police action" as a last resort alone and only with "complete cooperation and full participation by other members."[66]

Predictably, the study advised against unilateral military intervention. An American "task force" would command universal respect and inspire anti-Communist movements in other countries. Furthermore, it "might have sufficient deterrent effect to cause North Korean withdrawal to the 38th parallel and obviate police action engagement." On the other hand, unilateral intervention would reestablish American responsibility for Korea after the United States had struggled for five years to extricate itself from the peninsula. Perhaps worse, if the United States intervened, the paper warned prophetically, this step might force China to align itself openly with North Korea and thus "lead to a long and costly involvement of U.S. forces in an undeclared war." A decision to send American combat troops back to Korea therefore would constitute unsound policy with adverse military implications. At the same time, if Washington resorted to unilateral military action, it would justify Soviet charges of American imperialism and might lead to a third world war.[67]

Finally, the study assessed the logic of extending to the ROK an unqualified guarantee of American military protection. While such a pledge might deter a North Korean invasion, it also would require a conversion from indirect economic aid to the direct supply of large amounts of military equipment to South Korea. It would be "militarily undesirable and strategically unsound," the paper stressed, to divert military aid to the ROK from areas with a higher priority. The United States would be sponsoring as well a government that appeared unable to maintain popular support. More important, in contrast to Greece,

> Korea is a liberated area which did not contribute to the victory and it is in the opinion of the Joint Chiefs of Staff of little strategic value. To apply the Truman Doctrine to Korea would require prodigious effort and vast expenditure far out of proportion to the benefits to be expected.

In summary, the study advised that if economic aid could not foster stability in the ROK, it was not worth the cost of military protection. After reviewing the paper, the JCS noted that the study's conclusions were consistent with its position on Korea's relationship to American security interests. The JCS emphasized that "any commitment to United States use of military force in Korea would be ill-advised and impractical in view of the potentialities of the overall world situation and of our heavy international obligations as compared with our current military strength."[68]

Washington's absolute refusal to extend an unqualified guarantee of military protection to South Korea gave the appearance that the United States would stand aside as the Communist empire absorbed the ROK. But while American leaders were determined to withdraw, they remained firmly committed to providing South Korea with extensive economic, military, and technical assistance. The administration's approach makes sense only in the context of a series of key policy assumptions. Truman and his advisors, for example, were convinced that the Soviet Union would not permit North Korea to stage an armed invasion. Accordingly, the containment of Communist expansion in Korea did not seem to require the direct application of American military power. Rather, the United States would help the ROK to achieve the economic strength and political unity necessary for the maintenance of self-defense. Domestic political pressure in the United States contributed to the administration's decision to rely on limited means. If Truman granted Rhee's request for an unqualified guarantee of military protection, Chiang Kai-shek's friends in Congress could argue with complete justification that similar action in China would have prevented the triumph of Communist forces over the Kuomintang.

Truman's strategy in Korea could not succeed unless Congress agreed to finance his aid program for the ROK. On June 7, 1949, the administration announced that it would ask for $150 million in economic and technical assistance for South Korea. The press release included the first official reference to the fact that the United States would withdraw its occupation forces from Korea in the very near future. The administration's decision to announce military disengagement simultaneously with its aid program for the ROK was not coincidental. The press release specifically pointed to American plans for assistance as proof that "this withdrawal in no way indicates a lessening of United States interest in the Republic of Korea, but rather another step toward the normalization of relations with that republic and a compliance on the part of the United States with the . . . December 12 resolution of the General Assembly." In conjunction with the UNCOK, the United States would continue to work for the achievement of a free and united Korea.[69]

Administration officials anticipated that Congress would not approve the Korean aid request without a fight, especially from the Republicans. Undersecretary Webb therefore advised Truman to send a special message to Congress emphasizing the vital importance of assistance for South Korea and the necessity for immediate passage of the bill. The State Department already had drafted such a statement and had secured the approval of the ECA and the Bureau of the Budget.[70] Truman acted on Webb's recommendation and transmitted a personal appeal to Congress for the continuation of assistance to the ROK past June 30, 1949. The United States, the president explained, was helping to build a military force in South Korea capable of self-defense "short of an aggressive war supported by a major power." But without sustained American assistance, Truman predicted, the ROK would collapse "inevitably and rapidly."[71]

Truman's message then focused on the Korean aid program itself. The United States, he promised would pursue genuine economic recovery and development, rather than mere relief. Modeled after the Marshall Plan, the program would cost only slightly more than maintaining the previous approach and would eventuate in economic self-sufficiency. Truman then revealed the wider significance of his Korean strategy in a remarkable statement that deserves quotation at length:

> Korea has become a testing ground in which the validity and practical value of the ideals and principles of democracy which the Republic [of Korea] is putting into practice are being matched against the practices of communism which have been imposed upon the people of north Korea. The survival and progress of the Republic toward a self-supporting, stable economy will have an immense and far-reaching influence on the people of Asia. Such progress by the young Republic will encourage the people of southern and southeastern Asia and the islands of the Pacific to resist and reject the Communist propaganda with which they are besieged. Moreover, the Korean Republic, by demonstrating the success and tenacity of democracy in resisting communism, will stand as a beacon to the people of northern Asia in resisting the control of the communist forces which have overrun them.

If Congress approved assistance for South Korea, Truman stated confidently, the United States would be able to take a major step toward achieving peace and democracy throughout Asia.[72]

On the eve of American military withdrawal, the future of South Korea no longer was a peripheral issue for Truman and his advisors; now it had come to assume great importance. To an extent, this change was an outgrowth of domestic political pressures in the United States. The failure of the Republican party to capture the presidency in 1948 had erased the last remnants of bipartisanship in foreign affairs. The Truman administration therefore recognized from the outset that it would obtain congressional approval for the Korean aid package only with considerable difficulty. Worse still, the supporters of Chiang Kai-shek would seize upon the Korean issue to focus public attention on the administration's responsibility for the Communist victory in China.[73]

In his message to Congress, Truman was attempting to prevent his critics from gaining enough backing to block passage of the Korean aid bill. Ultimately, if the assistance program was a success and the ROK survived, the administration could refute Republican charges that Truman's foreign policy invited disaster. Yet the president's message also showed that by the summer of 1949, Korea occupied a central position in Washington's overall approach in Asia. If South Korea were able to achieve political and economic progress with American assistance, it would prove that the United States could halt further Soviet expansion in Asia without an unqualified commitment of power. For Truman, the success of containment in Korea was therefore important for both political and diplomatic reasons, despite the obvious risks.

CHAPTER 9

Promise and Performance

On June 29, 1949, the United States withdrew the last of its combat forces from Korea, thus ending more than three years of military occupation. Embassy Chargé Everett F. Drumright noted in a cable to Washington that South Korea's leaders undoubtedly "shared the emotions of a second-string quarterback who suddenly finds himself carrying the ball after months of criticizing from the bench."[1] American leaders were confident, however, that the ROK could survive without American military protection. Indeed, during the first half of 1949, Washington had received a number of optimistic dispatches from Seoul reporting progress toward economic recovery and political stability. While the constabulary army had nearly eliminated guerrilla activity in South Korea, international diplomatic support had stimulated increasing self-confidence in the Rhee government.[2] But the administration's expectations were not entirely negative in nature, since many officials anticipated that containment in Korea would act as a liberating force. Eventually, the North Koreans would recognize the superiority of South Korea's political and economic system, overthrow the Communist regime in the north, and appeal for reunification under the ROK.

South Korea's performance after American withdrawal never seemed to justify the administration's confidence in the promise of containment through limited means. Rhee's penchant for political repression was particularly embarrassing in this regard. During May 1949, the ROK's president ordered the imprisonment of several newspaper editors who were vocal proponents of early American military withdrawal.[3] Dissidents in the South Korean legislative assembly, especially the Young Group, were determined to prevent Rhee from further expanding his political authority. Friction between the executive and the legislature had surfaced in the past, but now relations between the two branches experienced a complete breakdown. When

Rhee blocked an investigation of alleged corruption in his administration, the legislative assembly voted not to conduct any further
business until it obtained greater control over the members of Rhee's
cabinet.[4]

Rhee also was at odds with the Young Group over the role of the
UNCOK in achieving reunification. In June, members of the commission visited the 38th parallel and attempted to contact the North
Korean government. After warning the UNCOK to leave, North
Korean troops fired on the commission members. Ranshofen-Wertheimer now told John P. Gardiner, first secretary at the American
embassy, that the UNCOK would leave Korea as soon as it had verified Washington's military disengagement.[5] Kim Yak-su, a leader of
the Young Group, urged the UNCOK to stay, arguing that unless the
United Nations achieved reunification, a Korean civil war was inevitable. In response, the UNCOK agreed to make one final appeal to
North Korea for cooperation. Late in June, the commission formally
proposed internationally supervised elections throughout Korea for
representatives to a unified government.[6]

These efforts at achieving a reconciliation with the North Koreans
so angered Rhee that he decided to silence the Young Group permanently. On June 21, the ROK's president ordered the police to
arrest six of its members on charges of conspiring with North Korea to
overthrow the government. The following day, police imprisoned
Kim Yak-su.[7] Then, on June 26, an army officer assassinated Kim
Ku, who had been pushing for negotiations between the ROK and
North Korea. Rhee denied complicity in the killing, pointing out
that the assassin was a member of Kim Ku's own political party. Nevertheless, the incident combined with recent imprisonments indicated that disagreeing with the Rhee government could entail very
unpleasant consequences.[8]

During discussions with Rhee, Muccio complained that the latest
resort to political repression was damaging the ROK's image before
the world community. The ROK's president agreed that the arrests
were unfortunate, but he insisted that extreme measures were necessary because South Korea was "fighting for life against [the] Communist menace." For Drumright, Rhee's motives were patently political,
since Kim Yak-su had been his chief nemesis for some time. More
important, it was wrong to punish individuals who had contributed
greatly to strengthening democracy in South Korea. Although the
Young Group was not acting to prevent a Communist takeover,

Drumright observed, "their criticisms, if over-emotional, generally had a plausible basis; and their support of such popular measures as the local administration and land reform bills, against the conservatives, was instrumental in passing the legislation." American pleas for moderation had no effect on Rhee. In July, the police arrested seven more assemblymen in another blatant attempt to stifle criticism. Drumright reported that Rhee now could dictate to the legislative assembly.[9]

Events in North Korea were to some extent responsible for the increasing political repression in the ROK. In anticipation of American withdrawal, the DPRK accelerated its propaganda program for weakening the ROK. On June 28, 1949, North Korea announced the formation of a "United Korean Democratic Fatherland Front" dedicated to reunification under Communist rule through force if necessary. Communists in the north and south also joined forces in a new "Worker's Party" with Kim Il Sung as chairman and Pak Hŏn-yŏng as vice-chairman. On July 7, the DPRK demanded the immediate and total withdrawal of both the United States and the UNCOK from the peninsula. Furthermore, it appealed to the people of South Korea to revolt and oust the Rhee government from power as a necessary precursor to reunification. The North Korean government promised free elections throughout Korea no later than September 15, 1949.[10]

These disturbing events, coupled with Rhee's frantic, last-minute maneuvers to impede American military withdrawal, further complicated the administration's task of obtaining approval for economic assistance to South Korea. During hearings before the House Committee on Foreign Affairs, however, Truman's advisors consistently stressed that the Korean aid program offered the promise of ultimate success in Korea and elsewhere in Asia. On June 8, Undersecretary Webb referred to the wider significance of the ROK when he predicted that American assistance to South Korea would foster reunification on a democratic basis and thereby inspire millions of Asians. Although there were no guarantees of success, Communist dominance throughout Korea was a certainty without American help. ECA Director Hoffman then appeared before the House committee and outlined the administration's three-year program. He echoed Webb's comments on the importance of South Korea, labeling the ROK the "key outpost of democracy in the Far East today." The Korean aid plan, he avowed, would be cheaper than mere relief over the long haul. Hoffman then mentioned the promise of eventual liberation of

North Korea when he reasoned that reunification "of the country can be achieved on satisfactory terms only if the Government and economy of south Korea become so clearly vigorous and sound as to convince the people of north Korea that their best interests lie in union."[11]

Republican critics of the administration instantly grasped the Korean assistance program as a means to indict Truman's China policy. These congressmen argued that China was as much a symbol of democracy in Asia as Korea, yet the administration had done little to prevent a Communist victory in that nation. In reply to Webb's presentation, Walter Judd of Minnesota stated caustically that "Korea is the first of the rat holes that we will have to pour money into all around China if we do not plug the basic rat hole in China." Both Judd and Lawrence Smith of Wisconsin declared their opposition to the Korean aid request unless the State Department clarified its Asian policy.[12] One week later, Webb again appeared before the House committee to defend the administration's policy. The failure of democracy in China, he admitted, was regrettable but not the consequence of insufficient American aid. Chiang Kai-shek had chosen not to implement reforms and thus lost the confidence of the Chinese people. In Korea, on the other hand, the United States could contribute to the spread of democracy while strengthening the United Nations. The best weapon against Soviet expansionism, Webb concluded, was American assistance for the realization of prosperity and self-government in the underdeveloped nations of the world.[13]

Congressional opponents of the Korean aid bill then shifted their attack to the threat of invasion from the north after American military withdrawal. On June 17, John D. Lodge of Connecticut charged that it was meaningless to "talk simply about how economic aid will help them to resist communism and then make up our minds that we intend to diminish our forces." To substantiate his argument, Lodge pointed to a recent article in *Time* magazine discussing political instability in the ROK and the incredible size of the North Korean army. Major General Charles L. Bolte, director of Army Department planning and operations, insisted that the article exaggerated the dangerousness of the situation. The South Korean army had performed effectively in scattered military engagements at the 38th parallel and now was "far better equipped than the North Korean troops." Other American military officials advocated economic assistance to South Korea despite the absence of American troops. The

ROK's survival, they argued vaguely, possessed "indirect" importance for American military security. Truman's military experts agreed
that the Soviet Union could conquer the ROK "without any great
military difficulty," but they implied that an open invasion of South
Korea was unlikely.[14]

Truman could not permit a prolonged debate over the Korean aid
package because he would be unable to use GARIOA funds after
June 30, 1949. Consequently, the president met with congressional
leaders privately and attempted to convince them of the absolute
necessity for quick passage. Korea was the last "foothold of democracy" in northeast Asia, he remarked during discussions, and the
people of Asia would be less willing to resist Soviet expansionism if
the ROK collapsed. Although the Democratic leaders emerged from
the meeting with confident predictions about the chances for approval, Truman could not wait.[15] On June 23, Secretary of State Acheson
appeared before the House committee in a final effort to gain passage
before the deadline. Acheson testified that even without American
military protection, South Korea would be able to "hold [its] own
against the northern Koreans." The ROK's future survival depended
upon the achievement of economic self-sufficiency, however, and this
would require a continuation of American economic assistance. The
United States, Acheson told his listeners, could not abandon South
Korea because it "stands as a symbol of hope" for the rest of Asia.[16]

Despite the administration's appeals for rapid action, it was clear
that Congress would not approve the Korean aid bill prior to the June
30 deadline. Budget Director Lawton therefore proposed that Truman request supplemental assistance for two months "at the going
rate." In the meantime, Congress presumably would authorize the
entire package. On June 30, Congress passed a joint resolution providing for a one-month extension of American assistance to South
Korea under the 1949 Foreign Aid Appropriations Act. The following day, the administration registered an even more important victory
when the House Committee on Foreign Affairs recommended approval of the Korean aid bill.[17] The five Republican members of the
committee, however, issued a minority report opposing the assistance
program. Although their primary motives were blatantly partisan,
these congressmen nonetheless offered a valid and realistic critique of
the Truman administration's policy in Korea.

In their minority report, the Republicans claimed that political factionalism and domestic violence south of the 38th parallel meant the

economic assistance program would be "foredoomed to failure." Although the administration admitted that the ROK would not survive a major Communist military assault, it had withdrawn American troops "at the very instant when logic and common sense both demanded no retreat." Unless the United States "is prepared to meet force with comparable force," the report concluded, "economic assistance cannot of itself insure the safety or the integrity of South Korea." In fact, the administration's assistance program would "only enhance the prize to be taken by force of arms and internal intrigue." While South Korea would be the "logical 'showcase' for the wares of democracy in the Orient," the report predicted that the ROK would be unable to withstand the aggressive political tactics of Moscow because of the "surrounding climate of rampant Communism." The Truman administration's efforts to construct a "dike of sand" in Korea, the Republicans asserted dramatically, would not stem the "tides which threaten to wash away the foundations of every constitutional government in Asia."[18]

Administration officials had known all along that the Republicans would not permit authorization of aid to Korea without a fight. Rather than risk even greater opposition, they had not resisted passage of the Lodge amendment, providing for the termination of assistance if Communists joined the Rhee government. By July 8, Clark Clifford had notified the president that the Korean aid bill was a "rather urgent matter." Unless Truman exerted strong leadership, the Republican party would exploit the Korean issue to attack his China policy and thereby discredit the administration. Truman discussed the situation immediately with several Democratic congressmen. These leaders predicted that the floor debate in the House would be intense and the final vote extremely close. Thus they were leery of forcing the aid bill out of the Rules Committee "because of possibility of defeat on the floor." By the end of July, the administration had no choice but to request another extension of the interim aid program for Korea. In the end, Congress approved an appropriation of funds to provide temporary economic assistance to the ROK through February 15, 1950.[19]

In Korea, Syngman Rhee carefully watched these discussions and attempted to encourage favorable action. In his public statements, he pledged that South Korea would fight "to the last man" in defense of its liberty. When the House committee passed the Lodge amendment, Rhee was ecstatic. He quickly issued a public promise never to

appoint a Communist to his cabinet.[20] To the administration's chagrin, Rhee apparently concluded that he now could resume his
campaign of political repression in the name of anticommunism. In
July, police arrested several newsmen who had cooperated with the
UNCOK and allegedly had expressed opinions reflecting "the Communist line."[21] Acheson angrily instructed Muccio to inform Rhee
that the activities of these newsmen "cannot in our view be regarded
by any civilized standards as constituting offense, however, slight
against ROK." Furthermore, not only did "such arbitrary action" tar-
nish South Korea's international image, but it also strengthened the
hands of those who opposed the Korean aid bill and made passage of
the program "much more difficult." When Muccio conveyed Acheson's opinions to Rhee, the president of the ROK agreed to halt the
arrests. South Korean officials continued to insist, however, that
extreme measures were necessary for the preservation of internal security.[22]

For Rhee, North Korea's new propaganda campaign to discredit his
government justified an increase in military assistance for the ROK.
In Washington, Cho Pyŏng-ok requested sufficient equipment to
enlarge the constabulary army to 100,000. Moreover, the ROK still
wanted "a specific assurance that the United States would come to
the defense of the Republic of Korea in the event of an armed attack
against it." Acheson stated bluntly that such a commitment was "out
of the question."[23] Undaunted, Rhee kept up his pressure on the
administration, inviting Chiang Kai-shek and the president of the
Philippines to visit South Korea for discussions regarding the formation of a "Far East Security Pact." Early in August, Chiang arrived in
the ROK and conferred with Rhee. The two leaders emerged from
their meeting jointly urging the early creation of an anti-Communist
alliance in Asia.[24]

But the administration still would not alter its policy. On August
11, for example, Truman twice refused to comment on the logic of
Rhee's proposal for a Pacific Pact. On September 26, the president
sent a personal reply to Rhee's most recent request for more military
equipment. In his letter, Truman noted that the United States
already had given South Korea substantial military aid including a
large number of advisors. Far more important, Washington believed
that "the security of the Republic of Korea can best be served by the
development of an efficient, compact Korean force rather than by
amassing large military forces which would be an insupportable bur-

den on the economy of the country."[25] Certainly, South Korea could not charge that the administration was neglecting its defense establishment. On July 25, Truman had submitted the Mutual Defense Appropriations Program (MDAP) to Congress, a proposal which included military assistance for the ROK. In his message requesting prompt approval, the president pointed out that South Korea confronted a serious threat of invasion and needed enough equipment to deter an attack. If Congress passed his proposal, the ROK would be able to maintain "a small force to protect its internal security and defend itself against outside aggression short of full scale war."[26]

Some American officials endorsed additional military aid to South Korea only with deep misgivings. On July 19, the NSC staff received an intelligence report observing that the "predominant trend in Korea is toward complete Communist control" and this process "may be accelerated by the inefficiency and shortsighted authoritarianism which characterize the Republic's efforts to restrain Communism in its territory." Rather than launching an open invasion, however, Moscow probably would continue to rely on "psychological warfare, harassing border incidents and guerrilla operations throughout the Republic." As a result, there was a chance that the ROK could survive, particularly with American assistance and "the development of traditional Korean attitudes and standards that are incompatible with Communism." An Army Department study offered specific reasons for avoiding an open-ended commitment. First, if the United States limited the ROK's supply of reserve military equipment, Rhee would not be able to stage a sustained invasion into North Korea. Second, the constabulary army had been wasteful in its use of military supplies and now would have to exercise restraint. Finally, in the event of a North Korean assault the United States would lose less equipment to the Communist regime.[27]

In all probability, American military leaders based their recommendations to some extent on advice received from the commander of the KMAG. General Roberts opposed, for example, Rhee's request for large tanks because of the limited weight capacity of bridges in South Korea. At a press conference in June 1949, Roberts went into more detail:

Mechanization is unnecessary in this country as it is too hilly, too many mountains, and rice fields. Tanks could only be used on roads. . . . They can be stopped by obstacles, mines, bazookas, and [antitank]

guns. . . . Gadgets do not win wars. Good solid infantry training
under good officers will adequately defend [South Korea].[28]

Thus, the American military assistance program would seek to create
a relatively small and efficient force well schooled in military techniques. The administration intended to provide the ROK only with
essential military assistance for the maintenance of internal security
and an effective deterrent.[29]

Rhee's belligerence buttressed Washington's determination to limit military assistance to the ROK. During August, Roberts reported
that the South Korean army was responsible for recent border incidents because it had established salients north of the 38th parallel.
While opposing any expansion of the American military aid program, he also warned Rhee that if the ROK launched an offensive
into North Korea, "all advisors will pull out and the ECA spigot will
be turned off." Roberts had other complaints about the constabulary
army. Many of its officers were political appointees who lacked military expertise, loved ceremonies, and were preoccupied with rank and
status. Worse still, the South Koreans in general resisted American
advice. Rhee's high-powered recruitment program also had attracted
people of questionable ability and intentions for the constabulary
army. When the ROK requested tanks, heavy artillery, and more
ammunition in September, Roberts again registered a sharp dissent.
Approval of the proposal would not increase the ROK's security but
instead might "encourage an invasion of North Korea by South
Korean armed forces."[30]

Surprisingly, Muccio did not agree with Roberts that South Korea
had enough military equipment. Throughout the period following
American withdrawal, the ambassador prodded the administration to
provide additional military aid, including patrol boats and subma-
rine chasers, to the ROK. For Muccio, an expansion of assistance for
the constabulary army was especially important because of the necessity to control guerrilla operations in South Korea. If the United
States failed to provide more support, he warned, the Communists
would continue "to create terror and chaos in the south, the ultimate
objective of which is unmistakably to insure Soviet control of the
South Korean peninsula and thus wipe out non-Soviet influence
from the Asian mainland extending from the Arctic Circle to French
Indochina." When Moscow announced that it would provide North
Korea with an air force, Muccio implored Washington to send "high

performance aircraft" to the ROK as well. In any case, the United States had to fulfill the military assistance provisions outlined in NSC-8/2 with respect to the constabulary army and the coast guard.[31]

Truman's advisors in Washington were hesitant about authorizing additional military assistance. For one thing, they did not trust the South Koreans. Rhee constantly fueled American uneasiness, as on November 3 when he told Muccio that the ROK "would have to be prepared to fight and unify the country by force if necessary." More-over, Congress had not appropriated sufficient funds to accomplish previously established goals regarding the military capabilities of the ROK. Webb informed Muccio that fulfilling the provisions of NSC-8/2 would require diverting funds from more vital programs. "Deci-sions must be based on overall national interests," he explained, thus requiring an "evaluation [of] comparative risks." Webb asked Muccio whether South Korea could preserve its security without additional military aid. If it could not, it might be unwise for the United States to provide the ROK with any assistance.[32]

In response, Muccio stated that while the amount of military aid then contemplated for South Korea was "patently inadequate to cover all contingencies specifically an all-out attack from north sup-ported by Soviets and Chinese Communists, we are strongly of view [that] risks involved are not inacceptable [*sic*]." Although Moscow had greatly expanded the military capacity of the North Korean regime, Muccio still thought that the Soviets would not order an invasion of the ROK but would "instead continue present tactics of subversion and sabotage." The ambassador then reported "remark-able progress" toward controlling guerrilla activities, improving gov-ernment administration, and achieving economic recovery. Conse-quently, Muccio strongly advocated continued American assistance:

> Under no circumstances should MDAP for Korea be abandoned. Such a step would constitute utter reversal of a consistent policy toward ROK, would subject us [to] criticism and ridicule in UN and elsewhere, and would utterly destroy faith and confidence of Koreans and virtu-ally all other Far Eastern peoples in professed determination of US to combat Communist aggression and enormously facilitate Soviet pene-tration and conquest of all Far Eastern areas.

In conclusion, Muccio urged the administration to reconsider its pol-icy of limited military aid for the ROK, "since keeping South Korea free of Communist occupation can conceivably influence profoundly future course of Far Eastern developments."[33]

In December 1949, Rhee decided to make another formal request to the United States for more military equipment. In particular, the ROK's president wanted the administration to support the "development, supply, training and advising" of a South Korean air force. Muccio advised approval, arguing that the "request is a modest one." If Washington failed to increase military assistance, the ROK would attempt to purchase the equipment with its own funds, thereby hampering economic recovery.[34] Rather than approving Rhee's request, the administration sent an MDAP survey team to South Korea that same month to devise plans for future military assistance to the ROK. Washington's decision not to follow his advice angered Muccio. He cabled the administration that the "MDAP program for Korea, as presently constituted, is wholly inadequate." The success of the ECA program, Muccio reminded Washington, was "dependent on the maintenance of peace and order" in South Korea. He therefore suggested boldly that the United States double the size of the military aid program projected for the ROK.[35]

Despite endless appeals from Muccio during the autumn of 1949, the administration did not waver. Given the parsimonious mood of Congress and the anxiety surrounding Rhee's intentions, there was no alternative. Washington freely admitted that South Korea could not defend itself against a massive military assault from the north, but it believed the Soviet Union would not sponsor an invasion, particularly with a United Nations commission on the scene. For Truman and his advisors, maintaining international involvement in Korean affairs was therefore a high priority. Although several members of the commission had opposed Washington's decision to withdraw, the UNCOK had stayed in Korea to observe and verify the departure of American combat forces. The commission also had formally asked the Soviet Union at the United Nations for permission to inspect North Korea and determine whether Russian troops had withdrawn.[36] Naturally, the United States wanted the UNCOK to remain in South Korea permanently. Acheson even thought the United Nations should provide military observers to assist the commission.[37]

Political repression in South Korea made it much harder for the United States to induce the UNCOK to cooperate with its policy in Korea. When Rhee arrested the newsmen assigned to cover the commission's activities, the UNCOK suspended all press conferences to

"avoid any further repercussions." Although Rhee managed to persuade the commission to reverse its decision, the incident scarcely
encouraged a favorable assessment of the progress of democracy in
South Korea.[38] Muccio was especially jittery because the commission
was then in the process of formulating its report to the United
Nations. During the middle of August, rumors spread that the commission intended to recommend referral of the Korean dispute back
to the Soviet Union and the United States for settlement.[39] For Muccio, it was imperative for Washington to keep the United Nations
involved in the Korean affair. In a letter to State Department official
Niles Bond, the ambassador professed that the dispute in Korea was
an international rather than a bilateral issue. A new UNCOK was
indispensable for bolstering the ROK's morale and deterring an
attack from the north. In fact, the next commission, Muccio believed,
should have the specific duty of monitoring military activities on the
peninsula.[40]

In the end, the UNCOK report corresponded with neither Washington's desires nor its expectations. The commission informed the
United Nations that without a Soviet-American agreement, Korea
never would achieve reunification and probably would experience a
barbarous civil war. The UNCOK blamed both the Soviet Union and
the United States for posturing instead of working for a resolution of
the problem. Muccio was displeased with the report. In one cable,
the ambassador attempted to refute the document's other major conclusions. He strenuously denied, for example, the charge that Rhee
was an authoritarian leader. Although the South Korean police force
was guilty of political repression, the same conditions would exist in
Washington if the threat of an invasion were as great. Muccio agreed
that the administration was "inefficient and undisciplined," but he
predicted improvement with the passage of time. While the morale
of the constabulary army was high, the general public was loyal to
Rhee. Far more important, in contrast to North Korea the South
Koreans could criticize their government, as "the non-communist
opposition remains relatively free."[41]

Despite unhappiness over the commission's findings, administration officials recognized that the United States would have to endorse
the UNCOK report at the United Nations. Acheson even cleverly
devised a strategy to use the report for the creation of a new commission with expanded powers. Since there was a threat of war in Korea,
international respresentatives had to be on the scene to observe and

report any military activity leading to the outbreak of hostilities.[42] On September 26, the United States, China, Australia, and the Philippines jointly submitted a resolution to the Ad Hoc Political Committee of the United Nations providing for the maintenance of a commission in Korea to observe conditions and report any developments "which might lead to or otherwise involve military conflict." Rather than merely being available for consultations, the new UNCOK would offer its "good offices" formally to both the north and the south to achieve reunification. Moreover, the commission would be available to verify Soviet withdrawal.[43]

In his speech urging rapid passage of the resolution, American delegate Charles Fahy blamed the North Korean regime for the absence of reunification because it had "flouted" the desires of the United Nations. Still worse, North Korea had created the danger of a "brutal conflict," making a new commission necessary to act as a stabilizing force in Korea. In the event of conflict, Fahy concluded, the UNCOK would provide accurate information on its "nature and origin, and regarding the responsibility thereof."[44] Once again, American policy on Korea at the United Nations was a complete success. On October 3, the Ad Hoc Political Committee voted overwhelmingly to recommend the adoption of the resolution while rejecting a Soviet proposal to abolish the UNCOK and declare its previous activities an illegal interference in Korea's internal affairs.[45] Fahy subsequently addressed the General Assembly and appealed for passage of the resolution. Ignoring Soviet opposition, the General Assembly approved the American-sponsored proposal on October 21 by a wide margin. One month later, it also adopted a resolution asking the Security Council to reconsider the ROK's application for membership in the United Nations.[46]

Although the Truman administration seemingly had scored a major victory at the United Nations, the international action on Korea somehow lacked reality. The new commission was supposed to achieve a peaceful settlement in Korea, yet the United Nations resolution acknowledged the probability of armed conflict on the peninsula. "A miracle would be in order," Muccio candidly admitted, "to remove the 38th parallel and unify the country at the stroke of someone's pen."[47] Reactions in Korea to the United Nations resolution also suggested that the UNCOK's mission was foredoomed to failure. A summary of North Korea's attitude appeared in a letter to Trygve Lie, the secretary general of the United Nations, from Pak Hŏn-yŏng which denounced international consideration of the Korean issue in the absence of representatives from the DPRK. North Korea, Pak emphasized, remained committed to reunification by force if necessary. Rhee announced that he would cooperate with the new commission, but he staunchly opposed any consultation, negotiation, or contact with the North Korean regime. Not only would such action be useless, it would constitute appeasement. Rhee also said that he would not permit the commission to protect Communists in South Korea, stressing that the ROK's survival was at stake.[48]

During September 1949, the South Korean government stepped up its campaign of political repression. A bewildering group of agencies—including the police, the military, and various youth organizations—joined in punishing anyone suspected of subversive activity. Throughout October there was a steady rise in the number of investigations, arrests, indictments, and trials. To an extent, Rhee was able to utilize the judicial system to strengthen his autocratic rule. The South Korean police force systematically violated civil liberties to obtain evidence, often resorting to torture to obtain confessions.[49] These transgressions were most evident during the trials of arrested members of the legislative assembly. Judges prohibited defense witnesses, for instance, while permitting prosecutors to introduce a great deal of "irrelevant and immaterial" evidence. They even made prejudicial and subjective comments from the bench. Nevertheless, Vice-Consul Gregory Henderson informed Washington, the ROK still "failed to implicate the defendants in any subversive or communist plot against the Govt and failed to cast extraordinary suspicion of any kind over their activities."[50]

While the United States was distressed about the absence of political democracy in the ROK, South Korea's economic problems soon overshadowed all other difficulties. Rhee's obsession with achieving military security and political stability had placed a heavy strain on the ROK's financial resources. To an increasing degree, the government had resorted to heavy borrowing and an expansion of paper currency to finance its operations against domestic subversion. Deficit spending inevitably produced runaway inflation and financial instability.[51] Yet Rhee would not expand the government's tax base and permitted police, the military, and the youth groups to extract "voluntary contributions" from the general public. Some wealthy individuals escaped paying taxes altogether. By December 1949, the ROK's indebtedness to the Bank of Korea was more than sixty percent higher than the law allowed. Despite a significant increase in food production, South Korea's foreign trade remained seriously imbalanced. Insufficient electric power and inadequate managerial skill only magnified the ROK's economic crisis.[52]

Muccio notified the administration in November that South Korea's "unsound financial practices" had produced a dangerous deterioration of the economy. If the ROK did not correct these problems expeditiously, South Korea never would achieve recovery and economic stability. The ECA officials in Seoul, he went on, had formulated an eight-point reform program which stressed the need to improve tax collection procedures, raise the prices for public utilities, eliminate unnecessary government expenditures, adopt sound accounting procedures, and expedite the sale of vested property. During talks with Rhee, Muccio pushed for rapid implementation of these recommendations. The ambassador assured Washington that the ROK's president had grasped the extent of American "apprehension and urgency" and would devote immediate attention to the economic situation.[53]

For Butterworth, the deterioration of South Korea's economy was frightening. Muccio's reports from Seoul, he stated baldly, "read like China 1948!" Unless the United States induced the ROK to institute major fiscal reforms, economic disaster appeared inevitable. Butterworth therefore instructed Muccio to apply "firm, continuing and effective pressure" on Rhee to implement decisive reform measures in the area of taxation and public finance. Although the South Koreans probably would resent American advice, he was hopeful that Muccio could achieve some degree of success. Three days later, Butterworth provided Acheson with a summary of the economic crisis in South Korea. He emphasized in particular the ROK's failure to institute land reform, which was indispensable for maximum agricultural productivity. The legislative assembly had approved a bill to reduce farm tenancy in April 1949, but Rhee had not implemented the measure because of his dependence on large landowners as political allies.[54]

Acheson acted promptly to compel the South Korean government to institute reforms. The administration, he cabled Muccio, fully endorsed the ECA recommendations for a restoration of financial stability in the ROK. Acheson ordered Muccio to approach Rhee and demand rapid implementation of the ECA reform program with the advice of American officials. He was to impress upon the ROK's president that economic stability was as important to South Korea's survival as military security. "Unless President Rhee and his Government show the willingness and the ability to inaugurate measures designed to stabilize the internal economy of Korea," Acheson warned, "the United States Government will be forced to reexamine the character and extent of economic assistance which can be made available." Even before receiving Acheson's formal protest, Rhee apparently had decided to implement some of the ECA's recommendations. In late December, the ROK's president placed restrictions on government spending, increased the charges for public services, and tightened the tax collection system. But for American officials in Seoul, more extensive reforms were necessary to balance the budget and resolve the financial crisis.[55]

To spur the adoption of additional reform measures, Philip Jessup traveled to South Korea in January 1950 for talks with Rhee and other government leaders. When he visited the legislative assembly, its chairman remarked that the United States, "though sincere, seems rather scattered and weak" on the issue of foreign aid in comparison with "the definite and determined help of Soviet Russia" to North Korea. Jessup retorted that South Korea's future would depend on the ability of the ROK to be "successful in holding and maintaining the fundamental institutions of personal freedom." Then, during his speech before the Korean Chamber of Commerce, Jessup emphasized that the United States would provide assistance only for those nations willing to help themselves. Fundamental to the fight against Communist aggression, he continued, was the achievement of sound economic growth and political freedom. The ROK did not require greater military capabilities because "strength is not simply a matter of arms and force. It is a matter of economic growth and social health and vigorous institutions, public and private." Jessup then appealed for decisive steps to balance the budget and ensure political freedom.[56]

After listening to Jessup's address, Drumright judged it "the most candid speech made by an American official since the end of occupation." The South Koreans, however, certainly did not appreciate Washington's resort to public pressure. Immediately after the speech, Rhee issued a formal statement denying that the ROK faced an economic crisis or lacked popular support. During subsequent discussions, Rhee harped on the importance of additional military aid and promised victory in the struggle with the north. Jessup was impressed, believing the president had made a strong case for antiair-craft guns and some airplanes. Yet he admonished Rhee that the United States still expected the ROK to implement more measures for reform, particularly for the reduction of the high rate of inflation. Jessup then expressed the hope that upon his return to Washington, the administration "would have reports from Ambassador Muccio that . . . all of the major problems confronting Korea would have moved forward to a solution." He added that the United States was "sympathetic" toward the idea of a Pacific Pact but thought it "could not be imposed from outside." Rhee replied with a promise "to take active steps" to control inflation. Shortly thereafter, he announced his intention to sell government-owned land and facto-ries, while holding a bond issue and lottery to reduce the money supply.[57]

Muccio met with Rhee the day after Jessup's departure. He pre-sented the South Korean president with the ECA's program for finan-cial reform and Acheson's demand for its immediate implemen-tation. The United States was distressed, Muccio explained, that "President Rhee did not take a more serious view of the mounting inflation." Chinese officials too had claimed that they could halt inflation at any time. Their failure to institute financial reform, the ambassador pointedly observed, had contributed more to Chiang's downfall than Communist military victories. When Rhee attributed lack of progress to his ministers, Muccio disagreed, blaming instead "inordinate delay" caused by Rhee's refusal to delegate authority. In his summary cable to Washington, Muccio lamented that Rhee was simply unable "to grasp the thought that a Minister should be any more than a 'yes' man whose sole purpose was to carry out the Presi-dent's ideas." For the ambassador, Rhee's unwillingness to share lead-ership and responsibility was the main cause of the "unsatisfactory situation."[58]

At the outset of 1950, South Korea's political and economic per-formance during the previous six months provided scant justification for optimism regarding the promise of containment. Yet upon his return to Washington, Jessup reported that a consensus existed among American representatives in Seoul that South Korea was capa-ble of resisting Communist expansionist pressure. As a result, the administration continued to pursue the realization of a viable govern-ment south of the 38th parallel.[59] Events in China coincidentally pro-duced a sharp rise in the importance of the ROK to the administration's overall policy in Asia. By late 1949, Truman and his advisors had concluded that the mainland Chinese would invade Taiwan in the very near future and destroy the last remnants of the Kuomintang regime.[60] On January 5, 1950, the president announced his determination not to become embroiled in China's civil war. Although the United States would continue economic aid to Taiwan, American military assistance and advice would cease.[61]

Anticipating harsh criticism of the administration's stand on China, Acheson issued a public clarification. The secretary of state denied that Truman's statement signaled a reversal of American policy. The United States, he stated firmly, had recognized Taiwan as Chinese territory during World War II and would not violate its past agreements. More important, Acheson argued that military aid would not help the Nationalists because the United States could not give "a will to resist and a purpose for resistance to those who must provide it for themselves."[62] On January 12, 1950, Acheson delivered his celebrated speech before the National Press Club in another attempt to defend Truman's China policy. But the address also provides conclusive evidence that the administration judged the survival of the ROK as crucial to the future success of its overall policy in Asia. Subsequently, scholars too often have focused attention solely on Acheson's exclusion of the ROK from the American "defensive perimeter." With the benefit of hindsight, these observers charge that the United States invited a North Korean invasion.[63] Such an appraisal obscures the real significance of the address as a definitive statement of American policy objectives and expectations in Asia. In Korea, the Truman administration still sought to prove that the United States could halt Soviet expansion without an unqualified commitment of power.

In his speech, Acheson explained that the people of Asia were involved in a struggle to overcome essentially two major threats—economic privation and foreign domination. Asian leaders believed that the resolution of these two problems would require the achievement of self-government. The United States, Acheson claimed, always had worked to foster independence for the nations of Asia, while the Soviet Union wanted to deprive these people of control over their own affairs. Washington therefore opposed communism not for selfish reasons but because it was the "spearhead of Russian imperialism." If the United States expected to defeat Moscow's strategy for expansion, the secretary of state stressed, it was vital to avoid any action that might obscure the true nature of Soviet intentions. For example, Asians would interpret American reliance on military means to counter Communist aggression as evidence of imperialism.[64]

Acheson also noted that American military capabilities in Asia were limited. Beyond Japan, the Ryukyus, and the Philippines, he observed, "it must be clear that no person can guarantee these areas against military attack." As a result, in the event of open aggression "the initial reliance must be on the people attacked to resist it and then upon . . . the United Nations which so far has not proved a weak reed to lean on by any people who are determined to protect their independence against outside aggression." Admittedly, Acheson's remarks implied that the United States did not plan to defend the ROK with military power. Yet the secretary of state based his assessment on the assumption that South Korea would not face open armed aggression. For Acheson, the military threat was not as immediate as the challenge of "subversion and penetration."[65] This conviction permitted the administration to adopt a strategy emphasizing the development of local strength and self-reliance as the best means for dealing with domestic violence and political agitation. Truman and his advisors believed that the United States could achieve peace and stability beyond the "defensive perimeter" in Asia without an open-ended commitment of American power because they judged the Soviet threat in that area to be essentially limited in nature.

Acheson's Press Club speech demonstrates how the Truman administration looked to Korea for proof that Asian nations could avert Soviet domination without an unqualified guarantee of American military protection. Acheson asserted that communism thrived on economic dislocation and social upheaval. If Asian nations developed strong democratic institutions and stable economies, they could withstand Communist political pressure. The United States, the secretary of state continued, could contribute to political and economic stability in Asia through providing economic aid, technical knowledge, and administrative advice. But American help alone was not enough. Acheson insisted that Asian leaders themselves had to demonstrate the will to improve conditions and develop the capacity for self-defense. He pointed to China in an effort to substantiate his argument. Chiang Kai-shek, Acheson contended, had failed to satisfy popular needs and wants. As a result, the Chinese people "brushed him aside."[66]

Acheson then specifically mentioned South Korea as an area where the United States was providing limited assistance and thereby fostering the emergence of a strong democracy. In the ROK, he stated confidently, there existed "a very good chance" for successful resistance to Communist expansion and it did not require an express pledge of American military protection. The administration's strategy in Korea would succeed, Acheson predicted, because in contrast to China the South Koreans not only wanted American aid but would use it effectively. It would be "utter defeatism and utter madness" for the United States to withhold such assistance. The secretary of state indicated the importance of South Korea to Truman's policy in Asia when he concluded that "we have a greater opportunity to be effective" in Korea than anywhere else on the Asian mainland.[67]

Acheson's address actually was nothing more than the public enunciation of a strategy that the Truman administration had pursued in Korea with varying degrees of intensity since 1946. As Muccio later explained, the Press Club speech signified no major policy departure; Truman and his advisors always had considered economic assistance as more effective than military power for influencing events in Asia.[68] At least the administration's approach was realistic, since it acknowledged the importance of nationalism in the postwar world. Active and direct American interference in the internal affairs of Asian nations would be foolish and counterproductive because it would alienate people hostile to any hint of imperialism. Acheson's speech reflected Washington's recognition that Asian nationalism was the most effective weapon against Soviet expansion. In the long run, American economic assistance would help build prosperity in Asia, thereby persuading the people to shun the Communist model for political, economic, and social development.[69] For the most part, Truman's critics and the general public never understood the true nature of the administration's policy assumptions and expectations in Korea and elsewhere in Asia.[70]

Acheson abruptly discovered that his efforts to marshal political support for Truman's approach in Asia had failed. One week after his Press Club speech, the House defeated by a single vote its version of the bill providing economic assistance to the ROK for the remainder of fiscal 1950. Most observers agreed that congressional unhappiness over the triumph of communism in China was responsible for the outcome.[71] Rejection of the Korean aid bill shocked Rhee, who had anticipated easy passage after reading Acheson's plea for a continuation of the aid program. ECA officials in Seoul expressed similar disappointment. Bunce warned that while aid would continue for the immediate future, the pipeline soon would run dry and force the termination of several critical programs. Simultaneously, South Korea's legislature adopted a resolution appealing to the United States for continued economic assistance. In Washington, Ambassador Chang conveyed his anguish to Butterworth that the defeat of the aid bill combined with the Press Club speech signified an American decision to abandon the ROK. Butterworth assured Chang that the United States was not wavering in its commitment to South Korea's survival and the administration intended to pressure Congress for a reversal of its position.[72]

Immediately after the House vote, Truman issued a public statement expressing "concern and dismay" over the rejection of the Korean aid bill and urging a quick reconsideration of the matter. With the president's endorsement, Acheson sent a personal letter to Congress asking it to reverse its action on the aid program. Korea, the secretary of state alleged, represented a test of American intentions and the world community would interpret "our conduct in Korea as a measure of the seriousness of our concern with the freedom and welfare of peoples maintaining their independence in the face of great obstacles." Democratic leaders in Congress responded at once to the administration's appeals. Tom Connally, chairman of the Senate Foreign Relations Committee, announced that the Senate authorization bill for aid to Korea would provide the necessary means to rectify the situation. South Korea, he declared, was a "testing ground for democracy" that was badly in need of a "psychological lift."[73]

Even leading Republican senators criticized the House vote as ill advised. During discussions with Acheson, Senator Arthur H. Vandenberg voiced agreement when the secretary of state confessed that he was "shocked at the stupidity of the Republicans in the House." Vandenberg promised to work for rapid and decisive action to repair the damage.[74] To overcome opposition to Truman's program, the Senate Foreign Relations Committee amended its bill to include provisions for more aid to Chiang Kai-shek's government and termination of all assistance to the ROK on June 30, 1950. Although Acheson disliked these changes, congressional consent for aid to Korea was unlikely without the conditions. On February 1, the House Committee on Foreign Affairs voted to recommend passage of the administration's program with the Senate revisions. In its report, the committee advised the House to avoid overemphasis in consideration of the measure on "the situation with respect to civil liberties in South Korea" because the "ultimate aspiration rather than the present fact may be of greater importance."[75]

Truman's congressional allies thus had arranged a compromise with critics of the administration in the House. On February 9, the House passed the amended version of the Korean aid bill by a wide margin. The next day, the Senate gave unanimous consent to the measure without debate. In the end, the administration had persuaded most congressmen that without American aid to the ROK, millions of Asians would lose faith in their ability to resist Communist domination. As Representative Jacob Javits of New York stated succinctly at the time, "all of Asia is watching this test case."[76] Less than three weeks later, Budget Director Frank Pace, Jr., formally requested $100 million in aid to the ROK for fiscal 1951. Subsequently, Hoffman appeared before the House Committee on Foreign Affairs and urged approval for the second year of the aid program. Since the ROK had made "spectacular progress" toward economic recovery, he reasoned, it deserved additional assistance.[77]

Administration officials wisely sought to avoid the delays that had beset the Korean aid program since the summer of 1949. To encourage early approval for a second year of assistance, Acheson made a personal appearance before the House committee. During his testimony, he told these congressmen that with American help, the ROK would build enough strength to "serve as a nucleus for the eventual peaceful unification of the entire country on a democratic basis."[78] Truman even sent a personal letter to the House committee urging favorable action on the administration's program. Communism, he argued, thrived on poverty, misery, and insecurity. Therefore, foreign aid was the "keystone of our protection" because it would help people around the globe to achieve economic independence and political freedom. On March 31, the House complied with Truman's request and voted its approval for a second year of economic assistance to South Korea.[79]

Acheson was rightly suspicious that congressional passage of the aid bill would cause Rhee to relax his efforts to curb inflation. During February, Drumright cabled Washington that despite constant prodding, the "Republic of Korea does not recognize grave consequences [of] continued deficit spending." While Rhee denied the existence of a financial crisis, other cabinet members thought the situation was beyond control.[80] In reply, Acheson instructed Muccio to remind

Rhee that Congress would reappraise the aid program during June 1950. The administration viewed with "great concern and disapprobation" the refusal of South Korean leaders to accept responsibility for the ROK's difficulties, the official distortion of the facts surrounding the financial situation, and Rhee's tendency to disregard the advice of the ECA. When congressional hearings opened to consider the budget for fiscal 1951, Acheson expected proof of the ROK's progress toward controlling inflation and correcting administrative weaknesses.[81]

Following discussions with Rhee, Drumright informed Acheson that the ROK's president had received criticism of his policies with "extraordinary good heart and gave assurances that he is with us 100 percent in seeking measures to curb inflation." On March 4, however, Prime Minister Yi Pŏm-sŏk, in a letter to ECA Director Hoffman, disclaimed the existence of a financial crisis. That same month, several members of the legislative assembly visited the United States and manifested similar indifference. During a meeting with Acheson, they expressed the hope that "the American defense line in the Far East could be stretched to include South Korea." Economic advisor Bunce, who was in Washington for consultations, blamed Rhee's closest advisors for this failure "to appreciate the nature and gravity of the inflationary threat in Korea." Worse still, Rhee's authoritarianism and incompetence were preventing any improvement in economic conditions. Bunce suggested that Washington might have to deliver an ultimatum threatening to cut off all assistance. State Department officials now decided to recall Muccio for discussions. Upon returning to Seoul, Muccio would present Rhee with new and stronger demands for reform, among them a threat to withhold military aid in order to force compliance.[82]

Meanwhile, Congress's initial rejection of the Korean aid bill had sparked a renewal of political friction in the ROK. Rhee's critics in the legislature charged that the president's dictatorial and undemocratic practices not only were preventing the development of popular support but now had undermined the ROK's image in the United States. Unless the legislative branch acted to halt the trend toward centralization of political power in the hands of the executive, many South Korean leaders feared that Washington eventually would terminate all assistance. Accordingly the legislature, in February 1950, began to consider an amendment to the constitution that would make the cabinet responsible to the legislative assembly. Rhee heaped scorn on the proposal, arguing that it would weaken unjustifiably the power of the president and produce chaotic changes in the administrative apparatus of the ROK. He then inaugurated an intensive campaign of threats and propaganda to defeat the amendment. When the legislative assembly voted on the measure in March, the amendment failed to obtain the two-thirds majority necessary for passage. More than sixty delegates cast blank ballots, however, to protest the Rhee government's manipulation of the outcome.[83]

Far more aggravating for the United States, the legislature recently had rejected Rhee's proposals regarding land reform while refusing to act on his recommendations for handling the financial crisis. To break the deadlock, Rhee proposed an amendment to the constitution providing for the creation of a second house in the legislative assembly. A unicameral legislature, he claimed, was "extraordinarily dangerous" and hampered the achievement of genuine political stability in South Korea. Also, Rhee urged the adoption of another amendment to permit popular election of the president of the ROK. Finally, he recommended a postponement of legislative elections scheduled for May 1950 until the assembly had passed his budget and tax proposals as well as the new election law. Criticism of Rhee's announcement was immediate and widespread, forcing the president to abandon temporarily his position on postponing elections in the ROK.[84]

South Korea's problems now reached a dramatic climax. In a letter to Yi Pŏm-sŏk dated March 23, Hoffman chided the prime minister for unwarranted optimism regarding the economic situation in South Korea. The ROK had to take steps to increase taxes and reduce spending; stopgap measures were not enough to restore confidence in the government and the economy. "Unless I am convinced that a forthright, immediate effort will be made to control inflation in Korea," Hoffman threatened, "I must consider the advisability of requesting a lesser" amount of economic aid. In response, Rhee demanded that the legislative assembly act positively on his budget and tax proposals without further delay. On April 1, he formally announced a postponement of legislative elections until November. Holding elections on schedule would only divert the legislature's attention away from South Korea's financial problems. If the assembly approved his recommendations for reform and thereby ensured a continuation of American assistance, Rhee promised to reverse his decision.[85]

For the Truman administration, the political deterioration in South Korea was intolerable. American leaders wanted economic reform, but not at the price of sacrificing the appearance of democracy in the ROK. Thus Acheson moved swiftly to force Rhee to obtain approval for his financial proposals without postponing the elections. On April 3, Assistant Secretary of State Dean Rusk presented Ambassador Chang with a message for Rhee that amounted to an ultimatum. Unless the ROK instituted the "drastic measures required to curb the growing inflation," Washington would reexamine and readjust the ECA program for South Korea. If the ROK's financial crisis persisted, further American assistance could not be effective. The note also reminded the Rhee government that "United States aid, both military and economic, . . . has been predicated upon the existence and growth of democratic institutions" within the Republic of Korea. Therefore, Washington deplored the decision to postpone the May elections. In response, Chang promised to convey the message to Rhee but defended the president's actions. Delaying the elections was necessary because the legislature had refused to pass the budget. Rusk disagreed, pointing out that postponement was inconsistent with democratic principles and would alienate friends of the ROK at the United Nations. International approval was a vital source of strength that South Korea could not afford to sacrifice.[86]

After presenting this stern warning to the ROK, Washington announced that Muccio would return to the United States to discuss South Korea's political and economic progress and problems. Prior to departure, Muccio met with Rhee and pleaded for an expeditious implementation of economic reforms. The ambassador then stated that the use of arbitrary arrest and torture coupled with a postponement of the elections spoke volumes about the undemocratic character of his regime. There were no explanations that would suffice in defense of these actions. When Rhee asked what Washington wanted him to do, Muccio's reply was simple. The United States expected the South Koreans to hold the elections on schedule and to agree on a budget including higher taxes to eliminate the deficit.[87] On April 7, Rhee appeared before the legislature and discussed the possible loss of American aid. He appealed for rapid passage of his budget proposal while promising not to delay the May elections. Drumright reported that the South Koreans had received the American message as "the stern warning which it was intended to be." Although the press thought the ROK had suffered harsher treatment than it deserved, he predicted that the legislature would act quickly to satisfy American demands.[88]

South Korea's political leaders were acutely aware that they would pay a stiff price for defying the United States. On April 11, the ROK's home minister formally announced that the government would sponsor elections the following month. Meanwhile, Rhee was exerting added pressure on the legislature to approve his reform proposals. Upon his departure from Seoul, Muccio applauded these actions. Subsequently, the legislative assembly approved Rhee's budget proposal, which included provisions for a sharp increase in taxes and higher charges for public services.[89] While some observers commended the ROK for its courage, others confessed doubts about the future of democracy and economic growth in South Korea. After all, events in the ROK appeared to resemble closely the ominous situation in China three years earlier.[90] Nevertheless, the Truman administration still hoped that South Korea would improve its performance, thereby restoring faith in the promise of containment in Asia through economic means.

CHAPTER 10

Fulfillment of a Commitment

Despite vexing political and economic problems in South Korea during the spring of 1950, the Truman administration was confident that the ROK could survive. This optimistic attitude depended on the basic assumption that local Communist parties, rather than organized military forces, acted as the primary vehicles of Soviet expansion. American leaders also believed, as one White House staff member explained, that "communism as a force in the domestic politics of all countries feeds on economic, social and national insecurities [and] fades as these lessen."[1] Thus, Truman's strategy in Asia deemphasized military techniques and focused instead on fostering economic and social stability. Yet American officials doubted that any single nation could provide unilaterally the strength necessary to counter all potential Soviet military thrusts. Such an effort, Undersecretary Webb stated publicly in May 1950, would lead inevitably to economic suicide. The "free world" could create the strength required for its protection, he argued, only "if all nations which have an identity of interests contribute as best they can through self-help and mutual aid to the common strength of the whole group."[2]

Some American leaders had started to question the wisdom of this restrained approach when the Soviet Union acquired the atomic bomb in 1949. In January 1950, Truman authorized the building of a hydrogen bomb and ordered his advisors to undertake a reappraisal of American foreign policy. These decisions represented an escalation of concern, but not a change in the overall approach of the administration.[3] Early in April, Truman's advisors submitted a report emphasizing the necessity for the United States and its allies to build additional political, economic, and military strength to counter the growing danger of Soviet expansionism. To obtain more specific information on the nature and costs of such a policy, the president referred the paper to the NSC. The now famous NSC-68 called for a drastic increase in American military capabilities, arguing that the

Soviet threat was global in scope because local Communist movements operated in accordance with Moscow's directions. NSC-68 advanced the conclusion that only the adoption of a $50 billion defense budget would enable the United States to counter effectively this dire threat to international stability.[4]

Truman was reluctant, however, to accept extreme assumptions and conclusions about the nature of the Soviet challenge. Not only did the president refuse to implement NSC-68, he invited his advisors to raise questions regarding the validity of any aspect of the document. Several administration officials subsequently expressed alarm over the lack of clarity and precision in NSC-68's assessment of the danger. In response, Truman professed that the program under consideration "definitely was not as large in scope as some of the people seemed to think."[5] Rather than trying to build a consensus endorsing an expanded military capacity, the president was contemplating instead a further reduction in defense spending to balance the budget. Truman's position must have delighted his economic advisors, who believed that the projected expenditures in NSC-68 were outrageously high. Certainly, Congress would not authorize new taxes in a time of financial retrenchment, while the administration appreciated the political benefits of concentrating its limited funds on domestic programs. Truman and most of his closest advisors acknowledged that the Soviet threat might be both military and global in nature, but they refused to act on their suspicions and take positive steps to produce the power necessary to meet such a challenge.[6]

Significantly, events in South Korea after April 1950 encouraged the belief in Washington that the administration's restrained approach was beginning to pay dividends. One source of optimism was the continued involvement of the United Nations in Korean affairs. In February 1950, the UNCOK had attempted to contact representatives of the DPRK at the 38th parallel, but North Korean troops fired on members of the commission. Nervous about the possibility of an imminent invasion, the UNCOK recommended that the United Nations send trained military observers to monitor developments on the peninsula. Secretary General Trygve Lie complied, dispatching a team of eight experts with instructions to report on any circumstances pointing to the outbreak of conflict in Korea. For the United States, this decision constituted a major victory. American officials in Seoul, however, were unhappy with the UNCOK's persistent efforts to establish contacts with North Korea, knowing that this undertaking would offend the Rhee government. In April, the commission asked Lie to request Soviet cooperation during his upcoming visit to Moscow in gaining access to North Korea to verify Soviet withdrawal. Rather than risking a "very unfortunate controversy," Muccio did not inform Rhee of this planned *démarche*.[7]

For Muccio, it was much more important to persuade the UNCOK to cooperate with the ROK and to supervise the May elections for seats in the legislative assembly. On April 24, Rhee invited the commission to observe the balloting and certify the legitimacy of the outcome. Despite the initial reticence of China's delegate, the UNCOK ultimately voted to supervise the elections, much to the relief of the United States. But the commission would have a smaller staff and fewer facilities for observation than it mustered two years earlier. At best, it could perform only a cursory role in the elections. Meanwhile, Rhee had instituted a new campaign of political repression to weaken those groups opposing his policies. During May, police arrested more than a thousand people on charges of subversion and conspiratorial contact with North Korea, including fifty candidates and one member of the legislature. That same month, Rhee appointed a new head for the police force and ordered him to replace any disloyal subordinates. Drumright protested these actions, arguing that Rhee had to avoid any evidence of a desire to "rig the elections."[8]

Nevertheless, more than two thousand candidates ran for election to the legislature, the vast majority as independents. The main issues in the campaign centered on dissatisfaction with Rhee's leadership and the legislature's control over the cabinet. Muccio cabled Washington that the political atmosphere was "freer than 1948." Although he anticipated the defeat of most incumbents, the ambassador predicted that the elections "will not prove a decisive victory for any contesting group." On election day, an atmosphere of law and order prevailed, permitting the UNCOK to certify the results as legitimate.[9] Despite Rhee's resort to violence and intimidation, more than ninety percent of all eligible voters cast ballots. More significant, few of Rhee's followers gained election; in fact, the most popular candidates were those who had been victims of police repression. Chronic political unrest and economic dislocation also influenced the outcome.[10] For Washington, the elections provided a glimmer of hope that genuine political freedom eventually would triumph south of the 38th parallel. The Truman administration could claim with some justification that in contrast to North Korea, the ROK was making progress toward a working democracy. Not only had the Rhee government permitted elections; it had accepted an unfavorable outcome at that.[11]

Then a new crisis erupted to complicate the administration's efforts to strengthen the ROK. Early in May, Senator Connally, in a published interview, had observed that whenever the Soviet Union "takes a notion she can just overrun Korea just like she will probably overrun Formosa when she gets ready to do it." Since the fall of the ROK was inevitable and Korea was "not absolutely essential," Connally believed the United States should prepare to abandon the peninsula. Rusk immediately urged Webb to remind the senator that his statements betrayed "an attitude of defeatism which the Department does not share and which it has consistently endeavored to counteract." At a press conference on May 3, Acheson commented on Connally's remarks, stating that the administration had indicated on many occasions the importance it attached to South Korea. Not only had the United States participated in the formation of the ROK, but it was "now giving them very substantial economic help, military assistance and advice." Even so, Drumright reported from Seoul that Connally's interview had "shaken to an appreciable extent" South Korea's confidence in American protection should North Korea stage an invasion. The general public had "received with acclaim" Acheson's clarification, however, while President Rhee seemed reassured.[12]

Despite Connally's remarks, the South Korean elections had a favorable impact on Congress. Late in May, the House and the Senate overwhelmingly passed a compromise bill for an extension of the Korean aid program through fiscal 1951.[13] Having secured continued economic assistance, administration officials shifted attention to military aid. Muccio remained convinced that the United States had to expand the military capabilities of the ROK to protect "our stake" in South Korea.[14] KMAG Commander Roberts strongly endorsed Muccio's position, observing that "the cheapest thing big industrial America can do is to furnish other people the product of our factories and resources in order that they may shoot . . . first and well for Uncle Sugar." When the MDAP survey team visited the ROK in December 1949, South Korean officials dwelt on the necessity for more military assistance to offset the increasing size and power of the North Korean army.[15] After study, the MDAP survey team concluded that the ROK warranted additional aid. In its report, it recommended approval of Muccio's proposal to double the amount of the Korean military aid program to $20 million, focusing the expenditures on patrol boats, combat aircraft, and heavier artillery.[16]

When Muccio returned to Washington in April 1950, he lobbied vigorously for more military aid to South Korea, pointing to a "growing sense of responsibility" in the ROK, particularly with respect to training in the constabulary army. He stressed that the South Koreans "have the will and the ability to defend themselves," but Washington had to provide the "missing component" of military and economic aid. "Korea is a symbol of U.S. interest in Asia," Muccio insisted, and needed only a small amount of additional assistance to preserve its freedom and independence. Defense Department officials resisted Muccio's recommendations, arguing that NSC-8/2 did not envision any increase in military aid.[17] Even if NSC-8/2 were revised, the United States lacked sufficient funds, equipment, and trained personnel to satisfy these requests. Muccio answered that all he wanted was "merely a few defensive combat planes, for morale purposes." If the United States could not provide more aid under the MDAP, South Korea would raise taxes to finance an expanded military program, thereby weakening its chances for economic recovery.[18]

South Korea's military capabilities represented an agonizing dilemma for the administration because of Rhee's publicly stated intention to achieve reunification at any price. On March 1, the ROK's president had announced that South Korea would not ignore forever the cries of distress from the people in North Korea. Despite advice from the ROK's "friends across the seas," Rhee pledged that "we shall respond."[19] After the May elections, the State Department nevertheless proposed an increase of $6 million in military aid to South Korea. The JCS promptly registered sharp dissent, asserting that it was difficult to justify additional funds on military grounds because "Korea is of little strategic value to the United States." It would approve the plan only "if political considerations are overriding." But the JCS insisted that the United States should not provide the ROK with more military aid unless it was vital to South Korea's morale and internal stability.[20]

By June 1950, the administration appeared close to making a decision to enlarge military assistance to the ROK significantly. Although South Korea was not crucial to the national security of the United States, Truman and his advisors still judged the ROK's survival to be an important American interest. In his report of June 1 to Congress on the progress of the MDAP, the president indicated his belief that the United States could halt Soviet expansion in Korea and elsewhere in the world if it created the capacity for local self-defense. Although he employed globalist rhetoric, Truman did so to build congressional support for the continuation of an essentially limited policy designed to avert the direct application of American military power. Communist imperialism, he claimed, "seeks to gain its ends by intimidation, by fomenting disorders, and by attempts to force internal collapse." Therefore, the United States could counter the Soviet strategy of expansion through providing economic aid, relying on the United Nations, and creating local military strength.[21]

Administration officials definitely were aware of the danger of an invasion from North Korea. Nevertheless, they firmly believed that once Congress approved a boost in military aid for the ROK, the Rhee government would be sufficiently strong to discourage an attack from the north. But Washington would not provide South Korea with the military capability to attempt forcible reunification, fearing as well that the ROK's economy could not tolerate greater expenditures on defense.[22] Ultimately, Truman and his advisors thought the ROK would be able to defend itself without extensive American aid or advice. As early as April 1950, Roberts, acting on instructions from the Army Department, had ordered the gradual curtailment of the KMAG's advisory functions in the ROK.[23] Reports from Seoul suggested that the constabulary army now had received enough training to withstand a North Korean attack. In one cable, Muccio bragged that the South Koreans benefited from superior "training, leadership, morale, marksmanship and better small arms equipment." During May, Edgar A. J. Johnson of the ECA declared publicly that the ROK's army was capable of repelling an invasion force from the north twice its size. When Roberts left Korea the following month, he stated unequivocally that the ROK had the "best damn army outside the United States."[24]

For Muccio, South Korea's survival required more than just military and economic assistance. He complained, for example, that the administration, in its public pronouncements, frequently omitted South Korea when mentioning those nations of "especial" interest to the United States. It was imperative for Washington to avoid any hint that the ROK had "been written off as expendable." Early in June, the ambassador wrote a letter to MacArthur admonishing Secretary of Defense Johnson for deciding not to come to South Korea while in Japan for talks later that month. Rhee and his advisors were "rather bitter" because American leaders seemed "more interested in developing and sustaining their recent enemy than their long friends." He implored MacArthur to convince Johnson that a visit of only one day would assuage fears in the ROK of American abandonment. Muccio restated these opinions in a letter to Rusk. The "visits of the five Senators and ten Representatives to Korea last autumn, and that of Dr. Jessup last January," the ambassador observed, "had an excellent effect both in informing the visitors and in affecting Korean judgment about United States intentions and in raising Korean morale." Evidence of "strong continued interest" was as important as financial aid for the successful achievement of American aims in Korea.[25]

Possibly in response to Muccio's advice, Truman dispatched his recently appointed special counsel on foreign affairs, John Foster Dulles, to Korea as part of his mission to Japan "regarding the possibilities of negotiating a Japanese Peace Treaty." Dulles left the United States on June 14 and four days later personally surveyed the situation at the 38th parallel. At that time, he congratulated the ROK for the "great strides" it had made toward achieving democracy and economic prosperity.[26] In his address to the South Korean legislature, Dulles said that the ROK was "in the front line of freedom." South Korea had created a stable government, a loyal military force, and improving economic conditions, proving that the task of resisting Soviet expansionism was not hopeless. Dulles then reaffirmed Washington's confidence in the power of containment as a liberating force when he declared: "As you establish here in South Korea a wholesome society of steadily expanding well-being, you will set up peaceful influences which will disintegrate the hold of Soviet Communism on your fellows in the north and irresistibly draw them into unity with you." Dulles concluded his remarks with a pledge of American support for the "Great Korean Experiment," promising that "you will never be alone so long as you continue to play your part in the great design of human freedom."[27]

After studying conditions in South Korea, Dulles was genuinely optimistic about the ROK's future. In one private letter, he noted that the "British Minister, who had had wide experience in eastern countries, . . . had never seen as encouraging an experiment in democracy." William R. Matthews of the *Arizona Daily Star,* a close friend of Dulles who accompanied him on the trip, was similarly impressed. What the Koreans had accomplished, he thought, was "unbelievable." The general public manifested a high degree of "vitality and ambition," while the ROK army was committed to defending the nation. In fact, Matthews believed the South Korean military force "could within the next year take the offensive and take over North Korea." After meeting privately with Rhee, Matthews offered the rather startling conviction

> that the Republic of Korea will within a year launch the offensive to take over North Korea and unite the country. The President . . . said it had to be done whether it provoked war or not. He thought it could be done within a few days, because the people of North Korea will rise up to help out, the minute they see liberation is under way.

Matthews pointed to the confidence of American representatives in Seoul as another indication of rising optimism in South Korea. Far from being a lost cause, the ROK would "hold the line" against Soviet expansion with minimal American assistance.[28]

Once Rhee had sufficient military power, there could be little doubt that he would attempt forcible reunification. South Korea's military capabilities in the spring of 1950, however, precluded such an operation. The constabulary army was comprised of approximately 100,000 troops but possessed equipment for a force only two-thirds that size. While much of the ROK's military equipment was unserviceable and replacement parts were in short supply, the United States purposely had limited the stock of ammunition.[29] By contrast, the DPRK had created an army of about 135,000 well-trained and highly organized troops. In July 1949, around 10,000 seasoned and experienced Korean soldiers had returned from China after helping the Communists defeat the Kuomintang. Far more important, during April and May 1950 the Soviet Union had provided the DPRK with a large number of trucks to increase the mobility of the army. Concurrently, Moscow had shipped for the first time the tanks, heavy artillery, and airplanes that gave North Korea a decisive temporary edge. Since the ROK would not receive the new equipment allocated under the MDAP for several months, the DPRK's superiority, in terms of war-making potential in June 1950, was beyond question.[30]

North Korea's political leaders were just as determined as Rhee to reunify the Korean peninsula. During the spring of 1950, the DPRK attempted to accomplish this objective through peaceful means. On June 7, the "Fatherland Front" issued a public statement denouncing the May elections in South Korea and ridiculing the ROK as an

American-sponsored police state. Furthermore, it proposed a meeting to discuss peaceful unification and the formation of a committee
to organize an election early in August for delegates to a national legislature. The proposal called for the exclusion of Rhee and Yi Pŏm-
sŏk from participation, however, while prohibiting the UNCOK from
observing the elections. Predictably, the ROK scornfully rejected the
plan, announcing its intention to boycott the proceedings. Muccio
dismissed it as "purely [a] propaganda campaign" to offset the
Communist failure to prevent the recent elections. But the acting
chairman of the UNCOK, A. B. Jamieson of Australia, greeted the
proposal with enthusiasm, recommending in a public broadcast a
meeting to discuss possible international consultation and observation.[31]

On June 10, North Korean representatives met with members of
the UNCOK at the 38th parallel. They presented the commission
with copies of a DPRK appeal to the South Korean people to support
the proposal of the Fatherland Front but would not discuss the matter
in detail. After an exchange of gunfire and considerable confusion,
the North Koreans ruled out any United Nations participation in
the process leading to reunification. The following day, three men
crossed the 38th parallel and entered South Korea carrying a "Peace
Manifesto." South Korean troops promptly arrested these representatives of the Fatherland Front, indicating again the ROK's unswerving
hostility to any North Korean proposal for reconciliation. Muccio
urged Rhee to free the three without delay, however, thereby avoiding support for "North Korean propaganda."[32]

In all probability, the DPRK anticipated a favorable public reception for its initiatives in the south. After all, the May elections had
resulted in a repudiation of Rhee's leadership. Furthermore, as Muccio confessed at the time, the "superficial reasonableness" of North
Korea's proposals "may be attractive to a large body [of] South Korea
public opinion." According to one report, a group of South Koreans
had submitted a petition to the Rhee government on June 3 calling
for reunification on any terms and bearing the signatures of more
than five million people. The DPRK undoubtedly hoped that public
opinion would compel Rhee either to accept its proposal for reunification or risk an insurrection. In a final demonstration of its sincerity,
the Fatherland Front, on June 19, proposed a merger of the two legis-
latures for the purpose of drawing up a new constitution and supervising nationwide elections. For Muccio, this latest overture "conceiv-

ably might . . . serve as [a] preliminary step toward all-out war, although [this] seems improbable."[33]

Having failed to achieve reunification peacefully, the DPRK now decided to use force. On the morning of June 25, 1950, the North Korean army launched a massive assault southward across the 38th parallel along six invasion routes. From the start, South Korea could provide only token resistance to the larger and better-equipped northern force. The DPRK probably did not make the final decision for war until the last two weeks before the attack, when it ordered its army into position. On the eve of the invasion, North Korea's leaders apparently thought that their "peace strategy" still might succeed. Captured North Korean documents revealed later that the DPRK did not even recall its military forces from weekend pass until the night before the attack. Despite such short notice, North Korea's leaders must have been confident that the DPRK army would overwhelm the militarily inferior ROK forces. More important, they undoubtedly expected the South Korean people to welcome the invasion and join in a rebellion to oust the Rhee regime from power. Indeed, the North Korean army halted briefly after crossing the parallel, consuming three full days before traveling the short distance to Seoul.[34]

Scholars have spent considerable time discussing the question of Russian involvement in the outbreak of the Korean War. Until writers gain access to archival materials either in the Soviet Union or North Korea, Moscow's role in the events leading to the DPRK's decision to invade South Korea obviously will remain a matter of speculation. But one conclusion seems almost beyond dispute: If North Korea had not been willing to pursue reunification of the peninsula regardless of cost, there would have been no invasion. Those who stress Soviet responsibility for the Korean War assign far too little importance to the domestic origins of the conflict. Both Koreas were obsessed with ending the partition and merely were waiting for the first opportunity to stage a "war of liberation."[35] By June 1950, two main factors probably convinced the North Koreans that a strategy of subversion and infiltration would not bring the collapse of the ROK. First, the May elections seemed to represent progress toward the achievement of a viable political system in South Korea. Second, economic conditions in the ROK recently had experienced a marked improvement, while the Rhee government had implemented strong measures to resolve the financial crisis.[36]

Perhaps more important, Washington's proposal for greater military assistance to the ROK may have created considerable anxiety in Pyongyang. The recent Soviet shipment of military supplies had provided the DPRK with a decisive but temporary military advantage. Further delay would only raise the odds against a successful invasion.[37] In opting for forcible reunification, North Korea's leaders therefore were acting in their own interests regardless of Soviet desires. While hardly an incontrovertible source, the memoirs of Nikita Khrushchev substantiate this interpretation. According to Khrushchev, Kim Il Sung traveled to Moscow in the fall of 1949 and applied heavy pressure on Stalin to sponsor an invasion of South Korea. Kim predicted that at the "first poke" militarily, the people of South Korea would rise up and oust the Rhee government from power. "Naturally," Khrushchev explains, "Stalin couldn't oppose this idea," since it would undermine Moscow's reputation as a staunch defender of revolutionary movements. If Stalin rejected Kim's plan, Khrushchev reasons, there was the clear possibility that the DPRK would launch an invasion in defiance of the will of the Soviet Union.[38]

In its assessment of the Korean War, the Truman administration devoted no attention whatsoever to the domestic origins of the conflict. Truman and his advisors were certain that the Soviet Union had ordered the invasion. Acheson, for example, later declared dramatically that Stalin's "dagger thrust pinned a warning notice to the wall which said: 'Give up or be conquered!' " For Truman, as Ernest R. May has shown, the lessons of the 1930s had created an axiom that dominated his thinking. Manchuria, Ethiopia, and Munich had proved that appeasement, far from halting aggression, only guaranteed a future war under even more difficult circumstances.[39] As the president remarked privately two days after the attack, the United States had to act decisively because:

> Korea is the Greece of the Far East. If we are tough enough now, if we stand up to them like we did in Greece three years ago, they won't take any next steps. But if we just stand by, they'll move into Iran and they'll take over the whole Middle East. There's no telling what they'll do, if we don't put up a fight now.

For American leaders, the North Korean assault was aimed not at the limited goal of reunification but instead at achieving the first step in the Soviet blueprint for world conquest.[40] Within a few days after the invasion, the administration had jettisoned the policy of restraint Acheson had outlined in his Press Club speech and embraced an approach rooted in a globalist assessment of the nature of the Soviet challenge.[41]

North Korea's attack on South Korea convinced the Truman administration that Moscow had altered its tactics for expansion and now would engage in open military aggression to extend the area of Soviet control. It followed logically that the United States could not expect to preserve world peace and stability if it continued to restrict its involvement in international affairs to providing economic aid, technical advice, and limited military assistance. A global military threat of such monumental proportions seemed to demand a drastic alteration of American foreign policy."[42] Nevertheless, the administration adopted a course of action commensurate with its own estimation of the danger only with considerable reluctance. The president could have dispatched combat troops to the peninsula immediately to crush the aggressor swiftly and thereby demonstrate the extent of Washington's resolve. Instead, Truman hoped that South Korea could defend itself without such assistance. If the ROK had been able to repel the North Korean assault alone, the administration might well have gained renewed confidence in its Asian strategy and continued to pursue a limited approach.

Press reports of the North Korean invasion arrived in Washington on the evening of June 24. Responding to a request for confirmation, Muccio cabled that "it would appear from the nature of the attack . . . that it constitutes [an] all-out offensive against ROK."[43] State Department officials promptly contacted Assistant Secretary Rusk and newly appointed Secretary of the Army Frank Pace, Jr. Rusk then notified Acheson, who was not in the capital over the weekend. The secretary of state approved without hesitation Rusk's recommendation that the State Department begin to formulate a United Nations resolution dealing with this "breach of peace" in Korea for consideration at an emergency session of the Security Council.[44] This decision was entirely consistent with past American policy. The Army Department's contingency plan of June 1949 had called for referral of such an incident to the United Nations. Moreover, Acheson had said in his Press Club speech that in the event of open military aggression, the nation under attack should rely first upon its own defenses and then on the international organization.

That same evening, Acheson telephoned Truman, who was at his home in Independence. The president at once agreed with the secretary of state that the United States should provide help to South Korea only in conjunction with the United Nations. Truman also decided not to return to the capital immediately because he did not want to "alarm the people."[45] Since chief American delegate Warren Austin was vacationing in Vermont, Assistant Secretary of State John D. Hickerson contacted Secretary General Lie and briefed him on the reports from Korea. "My God, Jack," exclaimed Lie in reply, "this is war against the United Nations!" Hickerson then explained that Ambassador Ernest A. Gross would call later and officially submit the matter to the international organization for consideration. Lie said he would convene an emergency session of the Security Council, but he cautioned that the United Nations could not act until it had received a report from the UNCOK.[46] The administration's request for international action on the Korean incident was to some extent the outgrowth of a desire to avert a direct and unilateral application of American military power. United Nations support for the ROK would bolster the morale of the South Koreans and greatly improve the ability for local self-defense.

News from Seoul following the attack cast grave doubts on whether the United States could limit its involvement in the conflict. Muccio reported that North Korea's air superiority constituted an "exceedingly serious threat," as enemy aircraft began strafing Seoul and Kimpo airfield on the afternoon of the invasion. "Future course of hostilities," he warned, "may depend largely on whether US will or will not give adequate air assistance." Muccio by then had appealed to MacArthur for additional equipment and ammunition. After complying with this request without the administration's authorization, MacArthur forwarded to Washington his assessment of the Korean situation in the first of a series of teleconferences:

> There is no evidence to substantiate a belief that the north Koreans are engaged in a limited objective offensive or in a raid. On the contrary, the size of the north Korean forces employed, the depth of penetration, the intensity of the attack, and the landings made miles south of the parallel on the east coast indicate that the north Koreans are engaged in an all-out offensive to subjugate south Korea.

Although the South Koreans were shocked, MacArthur reported that the morale of the ROK army was good, while the general public was "fairly stable." In reply, Army Chief of Staff General J. Lawton Collins conveyed Washington's gratitude for MacArthur's "superb and timely action" in providing more military aid to the ROK.[47]

Meanwhile, the United States had requested formally that the Security Council meet in emergency session to review the crisis in Korea. It was important, administration officials thought, for the American public to learn of the North Korean attack and the initiative at the United Nations simultaneously.[48] Despite this emphasis on international action, however, it was clear that South Korea's survival would depend entirely on the extent of Washington's commitment to prevent the DPRK army from conquering the entire peninsula. During the morning of June 25 (Washington time), the State Department finished work on a resolution. In its final form, the American proposal labeled the North Korean attack an unprovoked "act of aggression." It provided that the Security Council would call upon North Korea to cease fire and withdraw from South Korea, while requesting that all nations withhold any assistance to the North Korean regime. Furthermore, it would instruct the UNCOK to monitor compliance with the resolution.[49] Later that day, Acheson telephoned the president and advocated his return to the capital without delay. Truman agreed, instructing Acheson to arrange a meeting of his top advisors for that evening at Blair House.[50]

When the Security Council met that same afternoon, several delegates spoke against Washington's proposal. They argued that there was not enough information to substantiate the charge that North Korea was guilty of aggression. The UNCOK's preliminary report indicated that the Korean incident was assuming the character of a full-scale war, but it recommended possible United Nations mediation alone. Moreover, the attack was scarcely "unprovoked" and the conflict appeared to be a civil war. For many representatives, a decision of this magnitude required more time for consultation with home governments. To overcome these worries, Lie exercised strong leadership and delivered an impassioned speech, which stated in part: "The present situation is a serious one and is a threat to international peace. The Security Council is, in my opinion, the competent organ to deal with it. I consider it the clear duty of the Security Council to take steps necessary to re-establish peace in that area." Over Yugoslavia's objections, the Security Council passed the American proposal with only minor changes.[51] Truman and his advisors hoped that adverse world opinion would force the North Korean army to retreat without necessitating Washington's resort to direct military means.

Truman's policy of relying on the United Nations worked only because the Soviet delegation was not present at the Security Council and therefore unable to veto the American resolution.[52] It is highly unlikely, however, that in the absence of a United Nations sanction the United States would have remained inactive following the North Korean attack. Yet Washington gladly exploited the Soviet boycott to give the impression that the entire world community was united in its determination to resist Soviet-inspired aggression. Truman also recognized that if he stressed the principle of collective security, he would generate more domestic political support for his policies.[53] But the administration's approach unquestionably misled the American people regarding the nature of the conflict. Kennan, who had resigned his position as head of the Policy Planning Staff just prior to the North Korean attack, argued later that he was aware at the time of the dangers of international involvement in the Korean crisis. He purportedly urged Truman to act unilaterally, avowing that the United States possessed both the power and the right to intervene in Korea alone. "This was, finally, a civil conflict," Kennan recalls in his memoirs, "not an international one; and the term 'aggression' in the usual international sense was . . . misplaced."[54]

Few of Truman's diplomatic advisors shared Kennan's viewpoint. At the same time, some American leaders believed that the United States should be ready to implement drastic measures to ensure South Korea's survival. In a cable from Tokyo, Dulles encouraged the administration to prepare to defend the ROK regardless of cost:

> It is possible that the South Koreans may themselves contain and repulse the attack and, if so, this is the best way. If, however, it appears that they cannot do so, then . . . United States forces should be used. . . . To sit by while Korea is overrun by unprovoked armed attack would start a disastrous chain of events leading most probably to world war.

MacArthur, in requesting authorization to send more supplies to South Korea, also commented that the situation was grave and might require American military intervention.[55]

In Moscow, American diplomatic representatives were even more vehement in urging Washington to be decisive. Members of the embassy staff insisted that although Moscow did not favor a major war, "this aggressive military move against [the ROK] represents clear-cut Soviet challenge which in our considered opinion US should answer firmly and swiftly as it constitutes direct threat to our leadership [of the] free world against Soviet Communist imperialism." Any delay would hasten the collapse of South Korea and embolden Moscow to embark on similar adventures elsewhere in the international community with "calculably grave unfavorable repercussions." If, by contrast, the United States acted with speed and resolve, the Soviets might forsake further aggressive action. The "Kremlin's Korean adventure," the cable concluded,

> thus offers us opportunity to show that we mean what we say by talking of firmness and at the same time to unmask present important Soviet weaknesses before eyes of world and particularly Asia where popular concept [of] Soviet power [is] grossly exaggerated as result [of] recent Soviet political and propaganda successes [in] that area.[56]

Ignoring such advice, American leaders showed a preference for restraint in searching for an appropriate response to the Korean crisis. In preparation for the first meeting at Blair House, the State Department formulated a list of policy alternatives that included such limited options as sending South Korea all essential equipment regardless of current programs and permitting the officers in the KMAG to remain with the constabulary army.[57] If necessary, the United States would use naval and air power to establish a protective zone around Seoul and the port of Inchon to permit the successful evacuation of all American personnel. In its report, the State Department outlined as well a more positive course. If South Korea's survival demanded drastic measures, the United States might commit ground forces "to stabilize the combat situation including if feasible the restoration of original boundaries at 38 degree parallel." Significantly, the State Department recommended that MacArthur send a survey team to South Korea forthwith to determine the *minimum* amount of assistance required to enable the ROK to defend itself without at the same time undermining the security of Japan. Acheson cabled Muccio that he hoped South Korea could hold on until the administration had an opportunity to study these options.[58]

Early that evening, Truman returned to Washington. Acheson, Johnson, and Webb were at the airport to greet the president and brief him on the most recent reports from Seoul. Once the car doors had closed, Webb recalled later, Truman declared that this was "a challenge that we must meet. By God, I'm going to let them have it." Johnson then pledged his support for a firm stand, knowing, according to Webb, that Acheson opposed precipitate action. To avoid a possible argument at that time, Webb summarized the State Department's proposal, urging the president to hear it out before making any decisions. Truman agreed, but Webb was still troubled over the implications of the president's remarks. Upon arrival at Blair House, Webb followed Truman into the cloakroom and closed the door. "Knowing from my Bureau of Budget days that the President had always given me a large amount of freedom to express the results of staff work," Webb explained that he and Acheson preferred a restrained approach. He asked the president to resist the temptation to approve drastic steps until the United Nations had a chance to act on the Korean incident.[59]

During informal discussions before dinner, Johnson urged General Omar N. Bradley, chairman of the JCS, to read a memorandum that MacArthur had prepared stressing the strategic importance of preventing the Communists from seizing Taiwan. After Bradley had finished, Truman deferred consideration of the matter until after the meal.[60] During dinner, conversation centered on the global nature of the Soviet challenge in Korea. These American leaders easily agreed that the North Korean attack was equivalent to Hitlerite aggression and appeasement was not a viable alternative. Many of the participants feared the possibility of a wider war. If the North Korean army was unable to subdue the ROK's forces, the Soviet Union or China might enter the conflict. Everyone shared the hope that the South Koreans could defend themselves without the necessity for drastic American assistance.[61]

Following dinner, Acheson summarized the State Department's recommendations. He also suggested that Truman order the Seventh Fleet into the Taiwan Straits to prevent an attack either on the island or the Chinese mainland. Bradley registered his immediate support for Acheson's proposals. He thought that the United States had to draw a line against Soviet expansionism sometime and Korea "was as good an occasion . . . as anywhere else." Yet Bradley advocated only the use of American air and naval power to halt the North Korean advance. He advised against the dispatch of ground forces to Korea because he doubted that Moscow wanted war with the United States and, presumably, unlimited American involvement would compel the Soviets to intervene militarily.[62]

Naval Chief of Staff Admiral Forrest P. Sherman seconded Bradley's assessment but stated defiantly that if the Soviets wanted war, "they will have it." Sherman wanted to avoid a total commitment of American power, however. He favored instead an increase of American advisory personnel in the ROK and reliance on air power to delay the North Korean advance. Air Force Chief of Staff General Hoyt S. Vandenberg then reminded his colleagues that while a limited approach was feasible, the United States was not prepared to counter Soviet military power if Stalin chose to enter the Korean conflict. Frank Pace, Jr., Francis P. Matthews, and Thomas K. Finletter, the secretaries of the army, navy, and air force, respectively, all agreed that in the absence of Soviet military intervention, American air power was sufficient to preserve South Korea's survival. Truman's civilian advisors, while acknowledging the need for some kind of prompt action, were unanimous in opposing the use of American combat troops.[63]

These comments reinforced Truman's original inclination to follow Webb's cloakroom advice and approve the State Department's recommendations for a limited initial response to the Korean crisis. He decided to authorize the shipment of all necessary supplies to the ROK, the dispatch of a survey team to Seoul, and the transfer of the Seventh Fleet from the Philippines to Japan. Moreover, Truman instructed Finletter to make preparations for the destruction of all Soviet airbases in Asia; the State and Defense departments would formulate contingency plans for reacting to the next probable location of Soviet aggression. After approving a press release, the president told his advisors to stress in their public comments that the United States was acting under international authority and would limit its military involvement to protecting the American evacuation from South Korea. Truman said he would consider a more drastic course only if North Korea defied the United Nations resolution.[64] These decisions at the first Blair House meeting showed how reluctant Truman and his advisors were to implement extreme measures during the first hours after the DPRK's assault. Although it perceived the invasion as part of the Soviet design for world conquest, the administration nevertheless had not lost confidence in South Korea's capacity for self-defense.

Subsequent reports from Seoul provided some reason for optimism. After receiving new instructions based on the decisions at Blair House, MacArthur's chief of staff invited officials in Washington to "come over and join the fight. We are delighted with your lines of action and this aid should turn the trick." Muccio cabled Rusk that the South Koreans were "holding their own" and there was evidence of North Korean disengagement. By the morning of June 26 (Washington time), Acheson could inform congressional leaders that "things seemed to be in pretty good shape."[65] But it soon became obvious that despite Washington's show of concern, the ROK army could not halt the North Korean advance. Later that day, Muccio ordered most of the embassy staff to evacuate Seoul.[66] At the same time, the ambassador apprised Washington of his intention to "remain Seoul with limited staff until bitter end." Drumright tried to "argue the Ambassador out of making a martyr of himself," but Muccio wanted to avoid charges that the United States had betrayed the ROK. Acheson quickly cabled Muccio that it would be inadvisable for him to be taken hostage and he should evacuate Seoul at once. Thus, on the morning of June 27 (Korean time), Muccio left Seoul, leaving the KMAG behind.[67]

Meanwhile, Truman had held a second meeting at Blair House on the night of June 26 (Washington time) to discuss the deepening crisis. Once again, Acheson opened the conversations and recommended removing all restrictions on the use of naval and air power in Korea. The president approved this proposal, but he emphasized that American operations should not extend north of the 38th parallel. Acheson then raised the issue of Taiwan. Truman now decided that the Seventh Fleet should move into the Taiwan Straits. But this action did not signal an end to the administration's desire to limit its involvement in the Chinese civil war. Curiously, the president suggested that the United States propose a restoration of Japanese control over Taiwan. Acheson cautioned Truman that it would be unwise to "get mixed up" in China's administration of the island. Truman agreed, declaring disdainfully that he would not give the government of Chiang Kai-shek "a nickel" because previous American aid had been "invested in United States real estate."[68]

Truman and his advisors touched briefly on policy at the United Nations. Acheson explained that the United States would submit a new resolution to the Security Council the next day. After Hickerson read the draft, Truman stressed the importance of unqualified international support for the American plan. When Rusk raised the possibility of a Soviet veto, the president remarked that such an event would be beneficial, since it would help "to lay a base for our action in Formosa." Discussions then shifted to the battlefield situation in Korea. General Collins reported pessimistically that the ROK was on the verge of total collapse. Acheson commented that if Korean attempts at self-defense failed, the United States had to intervene more directly. Johnson disagreed, insisting that the United States had done enough. Truman spoke in favor of Acheson's position, declaring somewhat vaguely that "we must do everything we can for the Korean situation—for the United Nations." Bradley and Collins, assuming that Truman had just indicated his willingness to commit combat ground forces, reminded the president that such a decision would entail the need for mobilization. In reply, both Truman and Acheson voiced the hope that the United States could avoid this drastic step.[69]

Truman's decisions at the second Blair House meeting represented only a minor change in tactics. Air and naval power still were the basic ingredients in the American response. The president continued to place faith in South Korea's ability to defend itself with limited assistance. Collins transmitted new instructions to Tokyo authorizing MacArthur to "offer fullest possible support to South Korean forces so as to permit these forces to reform." In addition, "KMAG personnel should remain with Korean forces to insure continued and effective South Korean resistance."[70] At noon the next day, Truman informed the American people of his decisions with respect to Korea. Pursuant to the Security Council resolution of June 25, he had ordered American air and sea units "to give the Korean government troop cover and support." Furthermore, the United States would "neutralize" Taiwan and increase the amount of economic and military aid to Indochina and the Philippines. These actions were necessary, Truman explained dramatically, because the Korean attack "makes it plain beyond all doubt that the international communist movement is prepared to use armed invasion to conquer independent nations."[71]

That afternoon, the Security Council again considered the Korean issue. The UNCOK had cabled its report on the incident, informing the United Nations that North Korea had ignored the June 25 resolution. Further calls for a ceasefire and mediation, it reported, would be pointless.[72] The American delegation lost little time seizing upon the UNCOK report to push through a resolution legitimizing the previous actions of the United States. Austin read Truman's statement denouncing North Korea for aggression and a flagrant disregard of the will of the United Nations. He then formally requested that "the Members of the United Nations furnish such assistance to the Republic of Korea as may be necessary to repel the armed attack and to restore international peace and security in the area." Earlier that day, Soviet delegate Jacob Malik had rejected Lie's appeal to attend the Security Council session. As a result, the United States again was able to obtain international approval for its proposal.[73]

Truman met with State Department officials that evening to consider the possibility of Soviet military intervention in the conflict. Administration officials were afraid that in the event South Korea successfully defended itself, Moscow might feel obliged to assist its Communist client in completing the conquest of the peninsula. During the NSC meeting the next morning, American leaders agreed that the decision to assist in defending the ROK did not involve a commitment to engage in war with the Soviet Union. Truman then mentioned the "need to resurvey our policy papers so far as the Soviet Union is concerned." Johnson responded that work on such a reassessment was near completion. The Defense Department had given general approval to a State Department paper regarding possible Soviet intervention, but it was mulling over some changes in phrasing. Truman told his advisors that the report had to be kept secret to avoid alarming the general public. Finletter then recommended approval for air strikes against supply lines and bases in North Korea. Although Truman authorized Vandenberg to study this proposal, he withheld consent, presumably because he feared Soviet intervention would follow any military action in North Korea.[74]

North Korea was doing quite well without the help of the Red Army.[75] Nevertheless, MacArthur ordered the commander of the KMAG to "repair to your former locations. Momentous decisions are in the offing. Be of good cheer." In accordance with instructions, he also dispatched a survey team to the ROK under the command of Brigadier General John H. Church.[76] After talks with Muccio at Suwŏn late on the evening of June 27, Church set about reorganizing the ROK army. Evidently he experienced notable success, since Muccio sent a rather encouraging cable to Washington the following morning:

Situation had deteriorated so rapidly [that] had not President's decision plus arrival General Church party become known here, doubtful
any organized Korean resistance would have continued through night.
Combat aid decision plus Church's orders have had great moral effect.

Ambassador Muccio was optimistic that the forthcoming American
air strikes would demoralize the North Korean forces and make it
possible for the ROK army to reform south of the Han River.[77]

By the afternoon of June 28, North Korean forces had occupied
Seoul. Subsequent cables from South Korea indicated that the Rhee
government was "seriously dispirited" as the constabulary army continued to retreat. In his report to MacArthur, Church advised that
extreme measures were essential "if situation is to be stabilized." At
least two American combat teams would be needed to restore the line
along the 38th parallel.[78] In response, MacArthur decided to survey
the situation personally. While en route to Suwŏn on the morning of
June 29, he authorized bombing missions north of the parallel,
although his instructions specifically prohibited this measure.[79] Upon
arrival, MacArthur conferred with the ROK's chief of staff and then
drove northward to observe the battlefield situation at the Han River.
He concluded that South Korea's position was indeed desperate.
During a meeting with Muccio and Rhee (who had flown to Suwŏn
from Taejŏn), MacArthur mentioned without elaborating that he had
arrived at a number of momentous decisions.[80] Yet after returning to
Tokyo, the general cabled a decidedly optimistic report to Washington. Despite fifty percent casualties, MacArthur explained, the South
Korean army was beginning to regroup at Taejŏn and soon might be
able to halt the North Korean advance without drastic military assistance from the United States.[81]

A new sense of optimism characterized discussions at the NSC
meeting late on the afternoon of June 29. In addition to MacArthur's
report, Washington had received word from Moscow that the Soviet
Union had announced its intention to avoid involvement in the
Korean dispute.[82] This information encouraged the belief that the
United States could ensure the survival of the ROK without having to
forsake its policy of restraint. Yet Truman and his advisors still worried
about the possibility of Soviet intervention; they wanted to avoid any
action that might ignite a major war. Having reached agreement with
the State Department, Johnson read and recommended approval for
the proposed JCS directive to MacArthur. The key provision stated

that in the event "substantial Soviet forces actively oppose our present operations in Korea, United States forces should defend themselves, should take no action on the spot to aggravate the situation and should report the situation to Washington."[83]

While Johnson was reading the directive, Truman interrupted. There should be no implication, he stated emphatically, that the United States was going to war with the Soviet Union at this time. His remarks revealed his continuing devotion to caution in responding to the Korean crisis: "We must be damn careful. We must not say that we are anticipating a war with the Soviet Union. We want to take any steps we have to to push the North Koreans behind the line . . . but I don't want to get us over-committed to a whole lot of other things that could mean war." Johnson said he understood and finished the directive. He then explained that the JCS believed it was essential for the United States to establish a beachhead in South Korea in case a total evacuation of American personnel became necessary. Pace urged approval but noted that he had "considerable reservations" about placing any limitations on MacArthur. Truman retorted that restrictions were indispensable if the United States expected to avert a wider war. American military involvement, he avowed, was designed to do no more than "keep the North Koreans from killing the people we are trying to save."[84]

Apparently, the president wanted the freedom to reconsider his decision to punish the aggressor in Korea if the price of American intervention was an open military clash with the Soviet Union. Acheson's comments revealed similar concern over the danger of an escalation of hostilities. While he approved of MacArthur's decision to launch air strikes north of the parallel, the secretary of state pointed to the potentially catastrophic consequences of accidental flights into Manchuria. However, Moscow's public posture of neutrality apparently removed many of the misgivings Acheson had regarding an unqualified commitment of American power in defense of South Korea. If necessary, Acheson stated firmly, the United States should use combat ground forces. "It would be a great disaster," he argued, "if we were to lose now." Truman agreed with Acheson that Moscow did not want a direct military clash with the United States in Korea, remarking prophetically that "the Russians are going to let the Chinese do the fighting for them." When the president closed the meeting, he told Johnson to have MacArthur submit daily reports so that

Washington would be kept fully informed about developments in Korea.[85]

That evening, the JCS dispatched new instructions to Tokyo authorizing MacArthur to employ "such army combat and service forces as to insure the retention of a port and air base in the general area [of] Pusan-Chinhae." MacArthur could engage purely military targets in North Korea if this was necessary for the reduction of South Korean casualties. "Special care will be taken," the JCS emphasized, "to insure that operations in North Korea stay well clear of the frontiers of Manchuria or the Soviet Union." Washington cautioned MacArthur that the United States did not want war with Russia. The administration's instructions concluded that if the Soviets intervened militarily, American forces should implement defensive measures alone and MacArthur should report the situation to Washington without delay.[86]

Before dawn on June 30 (Washington time), the JCS received MacArthur's report on his inspection of the battlefield situation in Korea. The general noted that the ROK army lacked leadership and was in a state of utter confusion because of the absence of plans for an orderly withdrawal. The attack had been a total surprise; effective resistance seemed impossible. The North Korean army, on the other hand, was well equipped and highly trained, boasting some of the best combat units MacArthur had ever seen. "It is now obvious," the general charged, "that this force has been built as an element of Communist military aggression." Without decisive action, MacArthur predicted, North Korea probably would conquer the entire peninsula. "The only assurance for the holding of the present line, and the ability to regain later the lost ground," he advised Washington, "is through the introduction of US ground combat forces into the Korean battle area." MacArthur recommended immediate authorization for the dispatch of one regimental combat team to the front line and the introduction of two additional divisions as soon as practicable for use in a counteroffensive. A more limited American military operation, he warned, would be either "needlessly costly in life, money, and prestige" or even "doomed to failure."[87]

American officials received MacArthur's recommendations with alarm. His previous report had led the administration to believe that it could avoid the use of ground troops. Collins advised Tokyo that a decision of such magnitude required "several hours for consideration." He asked MacArthur if the instructions of the prior night would not suffice to meet the situation temporarily. MacArthur replied that these orders did not provide enough latitude for effective action. "Time is of the essence," he stated categorically, "and a clear-cut decision without delay is imperative." Collins still hestitated, explaining that the tenor of prior discussions at the White House "clearly indicated to me that the President would wish carefully to consider with his top advisors before authorizing introduction of American combat forces into battle area." Finally he agreed to comply with MacArthur's request, promising an answer in thirty minutes.[88] Collins then contacted Pace and summarized MacArthur's proposals. At just before five o'clock that same morning, Pace telephoned Truman and apprised him of the situation. The president's initial reaction suggested a lingering desire again to avoid drastic steps. "Do we have to decide tonight?" he asked. Pace then told the president that in MacArthur's judgment the ROK would fall without American military intervention. To prevent South Korea's collapse, Truman decided to authorize the commitment of one regimental combat team. He deferred action on the use of two combat divisions until later that morning.[89]

There can be no doubt that MacArthur's emphatic request for authority to use combat ground forces was the crucial element in Truman's decision. The president removed the final restrictions on Washington's commitment to defend the ROK only after MacArthur had reported that South Korea was thoroughly incapable of defending itself. Several hours after his telephone conversation with Pace, Truman convened a meeting with his major advisors. By this time, Washington had received word from Muccio confirming MacArthur's assessment. The ambassador reported that South Korea's army was in shambles, its people demoralized, and its government near disintegration.[90] After soliciting comments, the president found that a consensus existed on the necessity for unrestricted use of American ground troops in the Korean conflict. Truman and his advisors agreed that nothing less than the future peace and security of the world community was at stake in Korea. If North Korea conquered the ROK, they believed, the Soviet Union would instigate new acts of armed aggression elsewhere in the world. Eventually, unrestrained Communist expansion would endanger the national security of the United States as well.[91]

For North Korea's leaders, Washington's decision to commit

ground forces in the Korean conflict probably came as a surprise, but it may not have been entirely unexpected. Admittedly, the DPRK had reason to think that the United States would not use military means to prevent the demise of the ROK, since Acheson had placed South Korea outside the American "defensive perimeter."[92] On the other hand, Kim Il Sung and his colleagues must have recognized that such a blatant challenge would demand a firm response. Yet North Korea accepted the risk of American military action because it feared the consequences of postponing the invasion, while anticipating a quick and easy victory. As Khrushchev recalls in his memoirs, "we were inclined to think that if the war were fought swiftly . . . then intervention by the USA could be avoided."[93] Because Truman delayed his decision for military intervention, Kim Il Sung's prediction was almost correct.

For American officials, the attack on South Korea signaled a drastic alteration in Soviet tactics. Nevertheless, caution and restraint characterized Washington's initial reaction to the Korean crisis. Only when the DPRK threatened to overrun all of Korea did Truman decide to defend the ROK regardless of cost. American policy in Korea before the invasion explains the administration's reluctance to commit combat ground troops. By 1949, Truman and his advisors had concluded that with American economic aid, technical advice, and military assistance, South Korea would develop the capacity for self-defense and thereby deter an attack from the north. Containment in Korea, they believed, was possible in the absence of an unqualified guarantee of military protection from the United States because the Soviet challenge in Asia was essentially limited in nature. As Acheson explained later: "The view was generally held that since the Communists had far from exhausted the potentialities for obtaining their objectives through guerrilla and psychological warfare, political pressure and intimidation, such means would probably continue to be used rather than overt military aggression." Despite evidence that an act of armed aggression was imminent in the spring of 1950, American leaders therefore dismissed the ROK as a probable target. As a result, the DPRK's invasion not only surprised but thoroughly shocked administration officials.[94]

While American policy in Korea prior to the attack explains Truman's initial hesitancy, it also made the decision to dispatch ground troops to Korea a near certainty once the ROK proved incapable of defending itself. North Korea's attack represented an unmistakable challenge to American credibility and prestige throughout the world. If Washington allowed South Korea to fall, few nations would place faith in future pledges of support from the United States.[95] Of far greater importance, however, was Truman's unwillingness to abandon an objective that the United States had pursued for almost a decade. Since Pearl Harbor, American leaders had tried to foster the emergence in Korea of an independent and prosperous nation possessing a strong government that reflected the will of the people. To permit the Communists to conquer South Korea after the United States had expended so much in energy and resources to prevent just such an outcome simply was not a viable alternative. Predictably, Truman chose to commit ground forces in the conflict to ensure the survival of the ROK. In the end, American military intervention in the Korean War constituted no reversal of policy, but merely the fulfillment of a commitment.

Conclusion

In his farewell address, Harry S. Truman pointed to the decision to commit combat ground forces in the Korean War as "the most important in my time as president."[1] While some experts on the Truman era might quibble with the president's assessment, military intervention in Korea represents a watershed in the history of American diplomacy after World War II. Prior to June 25, 1950, the Truman administration was uncertain regarding the nature and magnitude of the Soviet threat to the national security of the United States. It therefore sought to counter the perceived challenge of Soviet ideology and power through a reliance on limited means.[2] North Korea's attack on South Korea had a dramatic impact on the administration's assumptions. "Here for the first time since the end of World War II," Truman observed later, "the Communists openly and defiantly embarked upon military force and invasion." Soviet expansionist ambitions now seemed global in scope and much more dangerous, demanding an extreme response from the United States. Truman's dispatch of ground troops to Korea symbolized the final break with a restrained approach. American leaders were convinced that the security of the United States now required an unqualified commitment of power for the preservation of world stability.[3]

American foreign policy in Korea from 1941 to 1950 provides a telling example of how the United States, before the outbreak of the Korean War, attempted to rely on limited means to accomplish its aims in postwar international affairs. Throughout these years, Washington pursued the achievement of a reconstructed Korean nation that reflected the American model of political, economic, and social development. American leaders never abandoned this objective, although they sought to attain it without a full commitment of power and prestige. While the United States traditionally had been indifferent to Korea's fate, in the aftermath of Pearl Harbor Roosevelt and his advisors acknowledged at once the importance of the Korean peninsula to the maintenance of postwar peace in Asia. Realistically, the administration advocated the creation of a four-power trusteeship for the achievement of Korea's independence. When Truman became president in 1945, however, Soviet expansionism in Eastern Europe had begun to alarm American officials. Consequently, Truman temporarily discarded the trusteeship formula and attempted to liberate Korea unilaterally. After Stalin sent the Red Army into Korea ahead of schedule, Truman hastily gained Soviet acceptance of Korea's division into zones of military occupation at the 38th parallel.

Following the Soviet-American partition of Korea, Truman never wavered in his commitment to the achievement of reunification under a government favorable to the United States. At the Moscow Conference in December 1945, the administration resurrected the trusteeship idea and obtained Soviet support for this solution to the Korean problem. But when Moscow refused to accept Washington's interpretation of this agreement, Truman rejected further negotiations and began to search for some way to break the Korean deadlock without resorting to military means. George F. Kennan's containment policy ultimately provided Truman with the answer to his predicament. Initially, the administration believed that economic aid would force Moscow to accept a settlement in Korea on American terms. When the Soviets failed to retreat, Truman's policy shifted to the creation of a separate government capable of self-defense. If successful, this strategy would eventuate in the emergence of a strong, democratic, Western-oriented nation, thereby permitting a safe American withdrawal in the absence of an unqualified guarantee of military protection.

Truman's commitment to South Korea's survival was much greater than most scholars acknowledge. Rather than seeking to desert the ROK, the administration consistently provided it with economic assistance, technical advice, and military aid during the period before June 25, 1950. By early 1949, Truman and his advisors had come to view South Korea as the test case of containment in Asia. South Korea's survival was important because it would resolve two major problems. First, the administration hoped to atone for its perceived failure in China and eliminate Republican carping at Truman's foreign policy. Second, Truman needed proof that the United States could halt Soviet expansion in Asia without a reliance on force of arms. Thus, in Korea, containment promised to achieve a great deal at home and abroad at relatively low cost in terms of men and material. American expectations in Korea were even grander, however, since Truman and his advisors believed that containment would act as a liberating force. Once the North Koreans recognized the benefits of American economic and diplomatic support, they presumably would overthrow the Soviet puppet regime and seek reunification under the South Korean government. Such an eventuality would inflict a significant defeat on the Soviet Union and register a key victory for the principle of national self-determination.

Rather than fulfilling the promise of containment, throughout its first two years of existence South Korea was politically divided and economically weak. Even so, the administration's commitment to the survival of the ROK remained intact. Late in December 1949, for example, Truman approved NSC-48/2, which declared that the United States "should continue to provide for the extension of political support and economic, technical and military aid to the democratically-elected Government of the Republic of Korea."[4] Much to the gratification of American officials, conditions in the ROK experienced a marked improvement during the spring of 1950. Then suddenly the DPRK attacked South Korea. Containment through economic means alone appeared to be inadequate, since the Soviet Union now sought to conquer the world militarily. Despite its dire assessment, the administration did not abandon its limited approach until the ROK showed that it was utterly incapable of self-defense. With North Korea on the verge of total victory, Truman reluctantly decided to defend the ROK regardless of cost.

Significantly, the Truman administration considered North Korea's invasion as a vindication of its containment policy in South Korea. Shortly after the attack, John Foster Dulles spoke for the administration when he claimed that one thing was certain: "[The North Koreans] did not do this purely on their own but as part of the world strategy of international communism." South Korea, he argued, was making remarkable progress toward political freedom and economic stability just before the invasion. For the Soviet Union, this "promising experiment in democracy" in Asia was a source of embarrassment, as well as "a dangerous salient on the otherwise Communist-dominated mainland of North Asia." Stalin and his colleagues had "found that they could not destroy it by indirect aggression, because the political, economic, and social life of the Republic was so sound that subversive efforts, which had been tried, had failed."[5] American leaders therefore concluded that the very success of containment in Korea had forced Moscow to alter its tactics. Since Asians would reject communism if given a free choice, they reasoned, Stalin had turned to open military conquest to expand the area of Soviet control.[6]

Moscow's resort to armed force for the destruction of "wholesome" nations appeared to justify, if not demand, an American willingness to employ its military power to counter the new Soviet strategy. As Dulles explained at the time, "the Korean affair shows that communism cannot be checked merely by building up sound domestic economies."[7] Indeed, this policy had only encouraged military aggression. Washington now fretted that the Soviet Union would initiate similar thrusts into such areas as Indochina and Yugoslavia. Still more alarming, if Stalin had attacked South Korea because of its political and economic progress, there was a strong possibility of "Soviet application [of] similar reasoning to Western Europe."[8] "Since international communism may not be deterred by moral principles backed by *potential* might," Dulles concluded, "we must back those principles with military strength-in-being, and do so quickly."[9]

North Korea's attack therefore convinced Truman and his top advisors that only superior conventional military power—and the willingness to use it against a Communist aggressor—would deter Soviet expansionism in the future. Predictably, the adoption and implementation of NSC-68 now appeared not only logical but imperative if the United States was to preserve its national security. As Acheson recalled later, "Korea moved a great many things from the realm of theory . . . into the realm of actuality and . . . urgency." The Korean War, the secretary of state confessed, "was in part an opportunity to adopt openly a policy urgently recommended in private for some months previously."[10] After June 1950, American foreign policy assumed a decidedly militaristic flavor. Foreign military assistance, for example, experienced a sharp increase as Indochina, Taiwan, and the Philippines in particular received large amounts of such aid. The change in the American approach toward affairs in Europe was possibly more profound. Before Korea, NATO's development had been rather slow, casual, and inefficient. Following American military intervention in the conflict, the United States sent combat forces to Europe and created a unified command while strenuously advocating the rearmament of West Germany.[11]

Washington's obsession with military preparedness after the outbreak of the Korean War constituted a dramatic reversal in the Truman administration's policy on defense spending. Korea ushered in a new era of large military budgets, as leaders in Congress approved sharp increases in expenditures for defense with scarcely a whimper.[12] The American people accepted this remarkable transformation without protest largely because of Truman's globalist assessment of the meaning of the Korean conflict. The president portrayed the Soviet Union as the very embodiment of perfidy and evil, a nation whose leaders were determined to impose the Communist system in piecemeal fashion on an unwanting world. As a result, the general public became convinced that the Communist movement was monolithic and the Munich analogy was valid. On the other hand, Truman's rhetoric gave the impression that the United States was in the vanguard of a new worldwide crusade to defend the principles of peace and democracy. If the American people chose not to accept complete responsibility for halting further Soviet expansion, the results would be catastrophic.[13]

Truman's rhetorical justification for American intervention in the Korean War fostered public support for his policies, at least early in the conflict. But his actions had a regrettable impact on the subsequent course of Soviet-American relations. While the Truman Doctrine speech started the process of hardening the attitudes of American leaders toward the efficacy of negotiations with Moscow, the war in Korea convinced them that Stalin did not want a diplomatic settlement. After June 1950, American diplomacy became steadily more rigid, as the nation's leaders pursued policies and programs with noticeably greater inflexibility.[14] Acheson set the tone for the future of American foreign policy when he insisted in 1951 that world stability after Korea would require a constant reaffirmation of the viability of collective security. If Russia was unable to expand, eventually it would become frustrated and, as George Kennan had predicted, either "mellow" or "wither away." Thus Acheson could claim that "time is on our side, if we make good use of it."[15] Acheson's analysis, however, spawned the unrealistic hope that the United States could gain diplomatic victories through a strategy of stalemate and inaction. In reality, an unwillingness to accept anything less than a perpetuation of the status quo removed any chance for a reduction of the tension and hostility in Soviet-American relations.

Truman's decision to commit combat troops in the Korean War therefore marked a crucial turning point in postwar American diplomacy. Previously, the United States had sought to counter the expansion of Soviet influence in the world through pursuing a policy that corresponded to Kennan's original conception of containment. As John Lewis Gaddis explains, Kennan believed that the United States could meet the Soviet challenge most effectively through "strengthening local forces of independence and by getting them to assume part of the burden."[16] Truman's policy before the North Korean attack was sensible because it recognized the superior strength of nationalism over communism as a force in international affairs. Furthermore, it acknowledged the obvious limitations on the power of the United States to control events in Asia. But South Korea's inability to defend itself destroyed the administration's confidence in the feasibility of a restrained approach. The failure of its limited policy in Korea convinced Truman and his advisors that the prospects for halting Communist expansion elsewhere in the world were slim indeed without positive guarantees of American military protection.

In the final analysis, the Korean War shattered the last vestiges of uncertainty and vacillation in the minds of administration officials regarding Soviet intentions. American leaders never doubted for a moment that Stalin had ordered the invasion in a determined effort to extend the area of Soviet control. Truman and his advisors defined the North Korean attack for the American people as part of the design of "world communism" for global conquest, although Korea's postwar history indicated that a civil war was in fact probable. After June 1950, any evidence of political instability in the world thus assumed the character of a new Soviet threat to international peace and security that the United States could tolerate only at grave risk. Increasingly, Washington came to rely on military intervention, rather than nationalism and indigenous hostility to Russian domination, as the best method for combating the vague threat of "international communism." As a result, following the Korean War, American leaders rarely took into account the relationship between ends and means in the formulation of policies for dealing with revolutionary violence and instability in the international community.[17] Ultimately, Truman's decision to commit combat ground forces in Korea would mark the beginning of a reluctant American crusade to preserve worldwide peace and stability through military means.

Notes

Full references to sources cited in the notes are given in the Selected Bibliography.

Introduction

1. Ernest R. May, *"Lessons" of the Past: The Use and Misuse of History in American Foreign Policy,* pp. 3–18; John Lewis Gaddis, *The United States and the Origins of the Cold War, 1941–1947,* pp. 23–25; John W. Spanier, *American Foreign Policy Since World War II,* pp. 19–20.

2. Intelligence Report, "Political Strategy for the Far East," October 28, 1944, OSS Records, RA 2666; see also Ronald Steel, *Pax Americana*, pp. 21–22.

3. E. Grant Meade, *American Military Government in Korea*, p. 44.

4. Frank Baldwin, "Introduction," in Frank Baldwin, ed., *Without Parallel: The American-Korean Relationship Since 1945*, p. 3.

5. John Lewis Gaddis, "Was the Truman Doctrine a Real Turning Point?" *Foreign Affairs* 52 (January 1974): 391.

6. George F. Kennan, *Memoirs 1925–1950*, pp. 354–367; John Lewis Gaddis, "Containment: A Reassessment," *Foreign Affairs* 55 (July 1977): 876.

7. George F. Kennan, "The Sources of Soviet Conduct," *Foreign Affairs* 25 (July 1947): 581.

8. Jonathan Daniels, *The Man of Independence*, p. 368.

9. Arthur C. Bunce to James K. Penfield, January 20, 1948, Dept. of State Records, 895.00/1–2048.

10. U.S. Dept. of State, *The Fight Against Aggression in Korea*, p. 1.

CHAPTER I: *An End to Indifference*

1. Glenn D. Paige, *The Korean People's Democratic Republic*, p. 18; see also Gregory Henderson, *Korea: The Politics of the Vortex*, p. 121; Robert R. Simmons, *The Strained Alliance: Peking, Pyongyang, Moscow and the Politics of the Korean Civil War*, pp. 4–10.

2. George M. McCune and Arthur L. Grey, Jr., *Korea Today*, p. 26; James F. Schnabel, *Policy and Direction: The First Year*, p. 4.

3. U.S. Dept. of State, *A Historical Summary of United States–Korean Relations 1834–1962*, pp. 3, 41.

4. Robert K. Sawyer and Walter G. Hermes, *Military Advisors in Korea: KMAG in Peace and War*, p. 4; Schnabel, *Policy and Direction*, pp. 3–4; Robert T. Oliver, *Syngman Rhee: The Man Behind the Myth*, p. 33.

5. Dept. of State, *A Historical Summary*, p. 6.

6. Henderson, *Korea*, p. 121; Simmons, *The Strained Alliance*, pp. 12–14.

7. Dept. of State, *A Historical Summary*, pp. 54–55; Norman A. Graebner, *Ideas and Diplomacy: Readings in the Intellectual Tradition of American Foreign Policy*, p. 344.

8. Henderson, *Korea*, pp. 76–78; Paige, *The Korean People's Democratic Republic*, pp. 18–19; McCune and Grey, *Korea Today*, p. 26.

9. Dept. of State, *A Historical Summary*, p. 8; Schnabel, *Policy and Direction*, p. 4.

10. Chong-sik Lee, *The Politics of Korean Nationalism*, p. 154; David J. Dallin, *Soviet Russia and the Far East*, pp. 256–257; Harold M. Vinacke, *The United States and the Far East, 1945–1951*, p. 57.

11. Lee, *The Politics of Korean Nationalism*, pp. 230–231; McCune and Grey, *Korea Today*, p. 16; Simmons, *The Strained Alliance*, p. 14.

12. Dae-sook Suh, "A Preconceived Formula for Sovietization: The Communist Takeover of North Korea," in Thomas T. Hammond, ed., *The Anatomy of Communist Takeovers*, p. 476; Leland M. Goodrich, *Korea: A Study of U.S. Policy in the U.N.*, p. 9; Joungwon A. Kim, *Divided Korea: The Politics of Development, 1945–1972*, p. 36. Some writers have argued that the United States should have recognized the KPG as the legitimate heir to political authority in Korea. See, for example, Oliver, *Syngman Rhee*, pp. 136–143; Richard C. Allen, *Korea's Syngman Rhee: An Unauthorized Portrait*, pp. 49–50; Soon-sung Cho, *Korea in World Politics 1940–*

1950: An Evaluation of American Responsibility, p. 90. Shortly after its formation, however, the KPG began to suffer from bitter factional disputes and quickly lost all organizational support inside Korea. By 1921, the KPG was defunct and its claim to legitimacy during World War II bore no relationship to the reality of the Korean independence movement. See Henderson, *Korea,* pp. 79–86; Lee, *The Politics of Korean Nationalism,* pp. 150–164.

13. William L. Langer, "Korean Independence Movement," May 14, 1942, Dept. of State Records, 895.01/60–21/26.

14. Korean radicals formed a Communist party in 1921. Since the Soviet Union alone provided assistance to the revolutionary movement in Korea during the interwar years, the Korean Communist party enjoyed increasing popularity. By the eve of World War II, it had far outstripped the KPG in terms of influence and power inside Korea. See Henderson, *Korea,* pp. 314–319; Lee, *The Politics of Korean Nationalism,* pp. 158, 178–179.

15. Han Kil-su to Cordell Hull, May 13, 1941, Dept. of State Records, 895.00/727; Edward Lim to Hull, ibid., 895.00/730.

16. Cho So-ang to Hull, June 6, 1941, ibid., 895.00/729; Lee, *The Politics of Korean Nationalism,* p. 228.

17. Bruce Cumings has exaggerated the aggressiveness of Roosevelt's postwar intentions in Asia, arguing that trusteeship "was meant to accommodate postwar American security concerns, open the colonies to American commerce and tutelage, and corral communist and anticolonial revolution." In reality, the president's motives were essentially defensive. Rather than pursuing "hegemony in the postwar world," as Cumings contends, Roosevelt wanted to prevent any other nation from achieving precisely this objective without having to fight a new war. See Bruce Cumings, *The Origins of the Korean War: Liberation and the Emergence of Separate Regimes, 1945–1947,* pp. 129–130.

18. William R. Langdon memorandum, February 20, 1942, Dept. of State Records, 895.01/79.

19. Ibid.; Franklin D. Roosevelt, "Radio Address by the President of the United States on Washington's Birthday," *DSB* 6 (February 28, 1942): 188.

20. Kim Ku to Franklin D. Roosevelt, December 9, 1942, Dept. of State Records, 895.01/48; Cho So-ang to Clarence Gauss, February 4, 1942, ibid., 895.01/78; Stanley K. Hornbeck memorandum, April 20, 1942, ibid., 895.01/102.

21. Sumner Welles, "Policy Regarding 'Free Movements' in the United States," *DSB* 5 (December 13, 1941): 519–520.

22. Charles I. Faddis to Hull, December 8, 1941, Dept. of State Records, 895.01/49; Hull to Guy Gillette, January 6, 1942, ibid., 895.01/59; John W. Staggers, Jay Jerome Williams, and Frederick Harris to Hull, January 9, 1942, ibid., 895.01/60; Samuel Wilder King to Hull, January 19, 1942, ibid., 895.01/63; Syngman Rhee to Hull, February 7, 1942, *FRUS 1942,* I, 859; Adolph A. Berle to Rhee, February 19, 1942, ibid., 862; Rhee to Berle, March 24, 1942, ibid., 865.

23. Charles M. Dobbs, *The Unwanted Symbol: American Foreign Policy, the Cold War, and Korea, 1945–1950,* p. 10.

24. Alger Hiss memorandum, December 18, 1941, Dept. of State Records, 895.01/60–5/26; Hornbeck memorandum, December 20, 1941, ibid., 895.01/54; see also Oliver, *Syngman Rhee,* p. 178.

25. Laurence E. Salisbury memorandum, December 23, 1941, Dept. of State Records, 895.01/52¹/₂; Staggers to Han, January 30, 1942, ibid., 895.01/60–10/26; Hornbeck and Welles to Han, February 9, 1942, ibid., 895.01/92.

26. "Korean Liberty Conference" memorandum, March 3, 1942, ibid., 895.01/84; *NYT,* March 2, 1942, p. 7.

27. Welles press conference comments, March 2, 1942, *FRUS 1942,* I, 864; *NYT,* March 3, 1942, p. 7.

28. James H. R. Cromwell to Hull, May 5, 1942, Dept. of State Records, 895.01/ 123. Upon hearing of Cromwell's resort to blackmail, Han Kil-su immediately exploited the situation and attempted to discredit the KPG. In a series of letters, Han charged Rhee with a "selfish greed for power" and dismissed the KPG's threats as "childish and ridiculous." All "true Korean patriots," he insisted, would fight Japan to the death and did not expect to receive independence on "a silver platter." See Han to Hull, July 3, 1942, ibid., 895.01/137; Han to Hornbeck, July 24, 1942, ibid., 895.01/157; Han to Hull, August 15, 1942, ibid., 895.00/836.

29. Hull to Cromwell, May 20, 1942, ibid., 895.01/137; Cordell Hull, "The War and Human Freedom," *DSB* 7 (July 25, 1942): 639–646.

30. Cromwell to Berle, July 17, 1942, Dept. of State Records, 895.01/153; Cromwell to Berle, July 27, 1942, ibid., 895.01/165; Berle to Cromwell, July 31, 1942, ibid., 895.01/165; JCS report 73, August 9, 1942, JCS Records, CCS 092 Korea (8–5–42), RG 218; JCS to General Joseph Stilwell, August 15, 1942, ibid.

31. JCS memorandum, September 25, 1942, JCS Records, CCS 092 Korea (8–5–42), RG 218; General George C. Marshall memorandum, August 11, 1942, ibid.; JCS to Berle, September 24, 1942, ibid. Hornbeck completely agreed with the assessment of Roosevelt's military advisors. Moreover, he privately expressed admiration for the "organized bands of embittered, resolute, daring, and physically effective Korean insurgents" operating in Siberia and Manchuria, who were willing to fight without any American assistance. By comparison, the old conservatives at Chungking appeared self-seeking and ambitious. See Hornbeck memorandum, August 13, 1942, Dept. of State Records, 895.01/98.

32. Maxwell M. Hamilton to Berle, July 23, 1942, Dept. of State Records, 895.01/ 156A; Arthur B. Emmons III memorandum, August 14, 1942, ibid., 895.01/156A; Harold B. Quarton memorandum, August 15, 1942, ibid., 895.01/157.

33. Gauss to Hull, January 3, 1942, ibid., 895.01/56; Salisbury memorandum, March 14, 1942, ibid., 895.01/86; Far Eastern Affairs memorandum, March 17, 1942, ibid., 895.01/81.

34. Gauss to Hull, March 25, 1942, ibid., 895.01/104; Welles to Gauss, March 25, 1942, *FRUS 1942, China,* 730; Gauss to Welles, March 28, 1942, ibid., 730–731; *NYT,* March 1, 1942, p. 10.

35. T. V. Soong to Roosevelt, April 8, 1942, *FRUS 1942,* I, 868–869; Welles to Gauss, April 11, 1942, Dept. of State Records, 895.01/96.

36. Hornbeck to Welles, April 11, 1942, Dept. of State Records, 895.01/96²/₃.

37. Roosevelt to Welles, April 8, 1942, *FRUS 1942,* I, 867; Welles to Roosevelt, April 13, 1942, ibid., 870–872.

38. George M. Elsey memorandum, August 6, 1948, Dept. of State Records, 895.01/8–648; Hamilton memorandum, April 25, 1942, ibid., 895.01/118¹/₂.

39. Gauss to Welles, April 10, 1942, Dept. of State Records, 895.01/96; Hornbeck memorandum, March 27, 1942, ibid., 895.01/101; Gauss to Hull, April 18, 1942, *FRUS 1942,* I, 872–873.

40. Hull to Roosevelt, April 29, 1942, *FRUS 1942,* I, 873; Hull to Gauss, May 1, 1942, Dept. of State Records, 895.01/99.

41. Gauss to Hull, May 7, 1942, Dept. of State Records, 895.01/112; Gauss to Hull, May 16, 1942, ibid., 895.01/130.

42. Han to Hornbeck, April 20, 1942, ibid., 895.01/102; memorandum of conversation, n.d., ibid., 895.01/60–23/26; memorandum of conversation, n.d., ibid., 895.01/60–25/26.

43. Hull to Gauss, May 8, 1942, *FRUS 1942,* I, 876–877; Gauss to Hull, May 13, 1942, ibid., 877; Gauss to Hull, June 19, 1942, ibid., 877–878.

44. Gauss to Hull, August 18, 1942, *FRUS 1942, China,* 738–739; Gauss to Hull, November 5, 1942, ibid., 174; *NYT,* October 12, 1942, p. 9; *NYT,* March 13, 1943, p. 5; Gauss to Hull, January 7, 1943, *FRUS 1943, China,* 842–843.

45. Gauss to Hull, December 19, 1942, *FRUS 1942, China,* 748; Gauss to Hull, June 19, 1942, Dept. of State Records, 895.01/148; Roy P. McNair, Jr., to War Department, December 11, 1942, ibid., 895.01/228; McNair report, January 12, 1943, ibid., 895.01/216; Gauss to Hull, January 15, 1943, ibid., 895.01/213; Lee, *The Politics of Korean Nationalism,* pp. 222–224.

46. Gauss to Hull, December 9, 1942, Dept. of State Records, 895.01/197. In October, Cho So-ang announced publicly that factionalism in the exile movement had disappeared and all Koreans now supported the KPG. He also wrote a personal letter to Hull dismissing as a "misunderstanding" the suggestion that the KPG would not fight Japan in the absence of American recognition. See *NYT,* October 26, 1942, p. 2; Cho So-ang to Hull, October 1, 1942, Dept. of State Records, 895.01/183. Nevertheless, reports of disunity in the Korean independence movement continued to reach Washington from Chungking. See Gauss to Hull, November 25, 1942, Dept. of State Records, 895.01/199; Han to George Atcheson, December 4, 1942, ibid., 895.01/198; Roy P. McNair, Jr., "Analysis of Political Parties," October 28, 1942, OSS Records, report 24638.

47. John Carter Vincent memorandum, May 1942, Dept. of State Records, 895.01/148; see also Michael Schaller, *The U.S. Crusade in China, 1938–1945,* p. 90.

48. Owen Lattimore to Chiang Kai-shek, draft letter, December 18, 1942, *FRUS 1942, China,* 186–187.

49. Division of Far Eastern Affairs memorandum, October 10, 1942, Dept. of State Records, 895.00/840.

50. Franklin D. Roosevelt, "Radio Address on the 7th Anniversary of the Philippines Commonwealth Government, November 15, 1942," *Public Papers, Roosevelt,* XI, p. 475.

51. *NYT,* December 23, 1945, p. 6; Gauss to Hull, December 29, 1942, Dept. of State Records, 895.01/207; Vincent to Hull, May 11, 1943, ibid., 895.01/256.

52. Rhee to Preston Goodfellow, October 10, 1942, Dept. of State Records, 895.01/231; Goodfellow to War Department, February 17, 1943, ibid.; Oliver, *Syngman Rhee,* p. 185.

53. Hamilton memorandum, February 26, 1943, Dept. of State Records, 895.01/218.

54. Herbert Feis, *Churchill, Roosevelt, Stalin: The War They Waged and the Peace They Sought,* pp. 214–215.

55. Lord Halifax to Hull, February 4, 1943, reel 30, folder 216, box 59, Cordell Hull papers.

56. Feis, *Churchill, Roosevelt, Stalin,* p. 120; Hull memorandum, March 22, 1943, *FRUS 1943,* III, p. 28–34; Cordell Hull, *The Memoirs of Cordell Hull,* II, p. 1236.

57. U.S. draft declaration, March 9, 1943, *FRUS 1943,* I, 747–749; Hull, *Memoirs,* II, pp. 1235–1236; Harry Hopkins memorandum, March 22, 1943, *FRUS 1943,* III, 34–36.

58. Hull memorandum, March 27, 1943, *FRUS 1943,* III, 37; Henry L. Stimson and McGeorge Bundy, *On Active Service in Peace and War,* pp. 599–600; Hull, *Memoirs,* II, pp. 1234, 1595–1596.

59. Hopkins memorandum, March 27, 1943, *FRUS 1943,* III, 38–39; Hull memorandum, March 29, 1943, ibid., 40–41.

60. Anthony Eden, *The Reckoning,* p. 595; Franklin D. Roosevelt, "The Eight Hundred and Eighty-eighth Press Conference (Excerpts), March 30, 1943," *Public*

Papers, Roosevelt, XII, 131–132; Welles memorandum, March 29, 1943, *FRUS 1943, China,* 845–846.

61. Memorandum on International Trusteeship, April 15, 1943, *FRUS, The Conferences at Washington and Quebec, 1943,* 720–726.

62. *NYT,* April 8, 1943, p. 11; Territorial Committee minutes, July 16, 1943, reel 49, folder 336, box 85–86, Hull papers.

63. Hornbeck memorandum, August 19, 1943, reel 23, folder 159, box 51–52, Hull papers; Hornbeck to Hull, October 4, 1943, reel 24, folder 160, box 52–53, ibid.

64. Rhee to Roosevelt, May 15, 1943, Dept. of State Records, 895.01/257; see also Rhee to Gauss, October 18, 1943, ibid., 895.01/305; Korean exile petition to Roosevelt, June 11, 1943, ibid., 895.01/269.

65. *NYT,* September 7, 1943, p. 8; Atcheson to Hull, August 20, 1943, Dept. of State Records, 895.01/286; Hornbeck memorandum, September 28, 1943, *FRUS 1943, China,* 133–135; Hornbeck to Hull, October 1, 1943, reel 24, folder 160, box 52–53, Hull papers.

66. Department of State minutes, August 20, 21, 1943, *FRUS, Washington and Quebec,* 914, 919; Leo Pasvolsky memorandum, August 18, 1943, ibid., 717; conference notes, August 21, 1943, ibid., 926–927; Hull, *Memoirs,* II, pp. 1237–1238.

67. Pasvolsky memorandum, October 3, 1943, *FRUS 1943,* I, 542–543; Hull, *Memoirs,* II, pp. 1304–1305, 1596.

68. Feis, *Churchill, Roosevelt, Stalin,* pp. 214–215; Hull, *Memoirs,* II, pp. 1304–1305. Admiral William D. Leahy never accepted the wisdom of universal application of trusteeship, particularly for Japanese-mandated islands; see Leahy, *I Was There,* pp. 210, 258. Secretary of War Henry L. Stimson and Army Chief of Staff General George C. Marshall agreed; see conference notes, October 29, 1943, *FRUS 1943,* I, 666–667.

69. Memorandum of conversation, November 11, 1943, *FRUS, The Conferences at Cairo and Teheran,* 1943, 257. Harry Hopkins advised Roosevelt that it was consistent with Soviet policy to expect Stalin's concurrence; see Hopkins memorandum, November 23, 1943, ibid., 376.

70. Conference notes, November 23, 1943, ibid., 325; China memorandum, November 24, 1943, ibid., 334; Roosevelt–Churchill meeting notes, November 24, 1943, ibid., 389.

71. "Conference of President Roosevelt, Generalissimo Chiang Kai-shek, and Prime Minister Churchill in North Africa," *DSB* 9 (December 4, 1943): 393. Great Britain's draft for the Cairo Declaration introduced the phrase "in due course." In the original American draft, Hopkins had used the words "at the earliest possible moment," while Roosevelt had substituted the phrase "at the proper moment." See the British draft declaration, n.d., *FRUS, Cairo and Teheran,* 404; American draft declaration, n.d., ibid., 400.

72. Cumings, *The Origins of the Korean War,* p. 106; see also Herbert Feis, *The China Tangle: The American Effort in China from Pearl Harbor to the Marshall Mission,* pp. 252–254.

73. Conference notes, November 30, 1943, *FRUS, Cairo and Teheran,* 566; Pacific War Council notes, January 12, 1944, ibid., 869; *NYT,* December 2, 1943, p. 3.

74. Franklin D. Roosevelt, " 'Keep Us Strong in Our Faith That We Fight for a Better Day for Mankind'—Christmas Eve Fireside Chat on Teheran and Cairo Conferences, December 24, 1943," *Public Papers, Roosevelt,* XII, 555–556.

75. *NYT,* December 6, 1943, p. 6; *NYT,* December 15, 1943, p. 22; *NYT,* March 2, 1944, p. 8; Gauss to Hull, December 7, 1943, *FRUS 1943,* III, 1096.

76. For a contrary view see Dobbs, *The Unwanted Symbol*, p. 58; Cho, *Korea in World Politics*, p. 23.

77. Department of State memorandum, March 29, 1944, *FRUS 1944*, V, 1225–1242. These three papers directly contradict Charles M. Dobbs's contention that prior to the spring of 1945, American officials had made few plans regarding Korea and had engaged in only theoretical and "idle musings" about trusteeship; see Dobbs, *The Unwanted Symbol*, pp. 24, 29, 31.

78. "Korean Political Problems," PWC-124a, May 4, 1944, Postwar Committee Documents, 120–140, box 380, Edward R. Stettinius, Jr., papers.

79. "Composition of Korean Occupation Forces," PWC-125, March 29, 1944, ibid.; "Japanese Technical Personnel," PWC-126, March 29, 1944, ibid.

80. PWC-105, April 4, 1944, Postwar Committee Documents, 100–120, box 380, ibid.; Postwar Programs Committee minutes, 27th meeting, May 3, 1944, Postwar Programs Committee minutes, February 1–May 31, 1944, box 32, ibid.

81. "Korea: Participation in UNRRA," July 14, 1944, State Department miscellaneous file, Political Committee Documents, 1944, box 378, ibid.; Policy Committee minutes, 72nd meeting, July 7, 1944, Policy Committee minutes, box 378, ibid.; see also Joseph Ballantine to Han, February 14, 1944, Dept. of State Records, 895.01/317A.

82. Hull to Gauss, March 28, 1944, *FRUS 1944*, V, 1290; Gauss to Hull, April 13, 1944, ibid., 1290–1291; Gauss to Hull, May 19, 1944, ibid., 1292–1294; Gauss to Hull, June 3, 1944, ibid., 1294; Gauss to Hull, June 1, 1944, Dept. of State Records, 895.01/343; Rhee to Dumbarton Oaks Conference participants, August 18, 1944, ibid., 895.01/8–2144; Rhee to Roosevelt, September 11, 1944, ibid., 895.01/9–1144; Edward R. Stettinius, Jr., to Roosevelt, October 27, 1944, box 216, Stettinius papers.

83. Gauss to Hull, May 4, 1944, Dept. of State Records, 895.01/333; Gauss to Hull, May 15, 1944, enclosure, ibid., 895.01/337.

84. O. Edmund Clubb memorandum, May 19, 1944, *FRUS 1944*, VI, 790–791; John S. Service memorandum, April 7, 1944, ibid., 780; Gauss to Hull, June 29, 1944, Dept. of State Records, 895.01/6–2944.

85. Leahy, *I Was There*, pp. 250–259, "Russia, China, and the Far Eastern Settlement," June 5, 1944, OSS Records, RA 2211; intelligence report, September 22, 1944, ibid., RA 2211.15.

86. Hull, *Memoirs*, II, pp. 1599, 1706; E. F. Cress to JCS, July 27, 1944, Dept. of the Army Records, OPD 336 Korea TS, RG 319.

87. Berle to Joseph C. Grew, July 21, 1944, Dept. of State Records, 895.01/7–2144; see also War Department memorandum, November 12, 1943, Dept. of the Army Records, OPD 381 China, sec. IV (8 Nov 43), RG 319; memorandum for the JCS, December 9, 1943, ibid. American military leaders refused to approve Berle's plan; see JCS memorandum, July 31, 1944, Dept. of State Records, 895.01/7–2144.

88. Hornbeck to Hull, July 18, 1944, reel 49, folder 371, box 85–86, Hull papers; see also "Political Strategy for the Far East," October 28, 1944, OSS Records, RA 2666.

89. Policy Committee minutes, 47th meeting, May 19, 1944, Policy Committee Minutes, box 370, Stettinius papers; Stettinius to Grew, May 5, 1944, box 216, ibid.; Langdon to Hull, August 1, 1944, *FRUS 1944*, VI, 495; Service memorandum, September 23, 1944, ibid., 587.

90. Stettinius to Gauss, August 3, 1944, Memos to Hull, box 730, Stettinius papers.

91. W. Averell Harriman to Roosevelt, October 10, 11, 15, 17, 1944, *FRUS, The Conferences at Malta and Yalta, 1945*, 362–365, 368–371; General John R. Deane to

JCS, October 15, 17, 1944, ibid., 366–368, 371–374; Harriman to Roosevelt, December 15, 1944, ibid., 378–379; Feis, *The China Tangle*, pp. 228–232.

92. Stimson and Bundy, *On Active Service in Peace and War*, p. 603; Leahy, *I Was There*, p. 293; Feis, *The China Tangle*, pp. 232–233; Grew to Stettinius, January 22, 1945, Japan, box 721, Stettinius papers; intelligence report, December 7, 1944, OSS Records, report 105310.

93. Briefing book paper, "Inter-Allied Consultation—Korea," n.d., *FRUS, Malta and Yalta*, 358–361.

94. Charles E. Bohlen minutes, February 8, 1945, ibid., 770.

95. Franklin D. Roosevelt, "The Nine Hundred and Ninety-second Press Conference—Held En Route from Yalta (Excerpts), Aboard the U.S.S. Quincy, February 23, 1945," *Public Papers, Roosevelt*, XIII, 562–564; see also Schaller, *The U.S. Crusade in China*, p. 212. James F. Byrnes, who was present at Yalta and soon would become secretary of state, later argued mistakenly that Roosevelt and Stalin had agreed to a Korean trusteeship only "if a transition period were necessary"; see Byrnes, *Speaking Frankly*, p. 221.

96. Joseph C. Grew and Walter Johnson, eds., *Turbulent Era: A Diplomatic Record of Forty Years 1904–1945*, II, p. 1444; Charles E. Bohlen, *The Transformation of American Foreign Policy*, p. 36; Cho, *Korea in World Politics*, pp. 32–33.

97. Tyler Dennett, "In Due Course," *Far Eastern Survey* 14 (January 17, 1945): 1–3.

98. Arthur C. Bunce, "The Future of Korea: Part I," *Far Eastern Survey* 23 (April 19, 1944): 67–70; see also Arthur C. Bunce, "The Future of Korea: Part II," *Far Eastern Survey* 23 (May 17, 1944): 85–88.

99. Dennett, "In Due Course," p. 4.

CHAPTER 2: *Captive of the Cold War*

1. Akira Iriye, *The Cold War in Asia: A Historical Introduction*, pp. 74, 113, 126–127.

2. Robert M. Slusser, "Soviet Far Eastern Policy, 1945–50: Stalin's Goals in Korea," in Yonosuke Nagai and Akira Iriye, eds., *The Origins of the Cold War in Asia*, pp. 131–133; Suh, "A Preconceived Formula for Sovietization," p. 488.

3. Several scholars have noted that Moscow's initial actions in northern Korea after occupation were rather haphazard, indicating the absence of a premeditated plan for "sovietization." On this point see Chong-sik Lee, "Kim Il-song of North Korea," *Asian Survey* 7 (June 1967): 378; Suh, "A Preconceived Formula for Sovietization," p. 475; Simmons, *The Strained Alliance*, p. 25.

4. Yalta communiqué, "Territorial Trusteeship," *FRUS, The Conference of Berlin (Potsdam), 1945*, II, 1568.

5. Ballantine memorandum, February 5, 1945, *FRUS 1945*, VI, 1018–1020; Erle R. Dickover memorandum, January 24, 1945, Dept. of State Records, 895.01/1–2445.

6. Ballantine memorandum, February 17, 1945, *FRUS 1945*, VI, 1021; John Carter Vincent to Stettinius, February 8, 1945, *FRUS 1945*, VII, 854.

7. Stettinius to Patrick J. Hurley, February 20, 1945, *FRUS 1945*, VI, 1022–1023; see also Major General H. A. Craig summary, February 13, 1945, Dept. of the Army Records, OPD 381, CTO, RG 319.

8. Rhee to Stettinius, May 15, 1945, *FRUS 1945*, VI, 1028; see also intelligence report, June 25, 1945, OSS Records, report 3201.

9. Intelligence report, February 27, 1945, OSS Records, report 120760; intelligence report, March 1, 1945, ibid., report 116077.

10. Atcheson to Stettinius, March 1, 1945, *FRUS 1945,* VI, 1024; Grew to Hurley, March 20, 1945, ibid., 1025.

11. Stimson and Bundy, *On Active Service in Peace and War,* pp. 556–557; cabinet meeting minutes, March 9, 1945, in Walter Millis, ed., *The Forrestal Diaries,* p. 33; James V. Forrestal memorandum, March 30, 1945, ibid., pp. 37–38.

12. Rhee to Stettinius, March 8, 1945, Dept. of State Records, 500.CC/3–845; Han to Stettinius, March 9, 1945, ibid., 500.CC/3–945; *NYT,* March 1, 1945, p. 3.

13. SWNCC papers 76, 77, 78, 99, 101, March 19, 1945, JCS Records, CCS 383.21 Korea (3–19–45), sec. I, RG 218.

14. Franklin D. Roosevelt, "The Nine Hundred and Ninety-eighth Press Conference (Excerpts), April 5, 1945," *Public Papers, Roosevelt,* XIII, 609–610.

15. Gaddis, *The United States and the Origins of the Cold War,* pp. 172–173; Lisle A. Rose, *Dubious Victory: The United States and the End of World War II,* II, pp. 96–99; Robert H. Ferrell, "Truman's Foreign Policy: A Traditional View," in Richard S. Kirkendall, ed., *The Truman Period as a Research Field: A Reappraisal, 1972,* p. 26.

16. President Truman made this decision on April 18, 1945, during discussions with Edward R. Stettinius, Jr., James V. Forrestal, and Stimson, his secretaries of state, navy, and war respectively; see "International Trusteeship" memorandum, April 18, 1945, Memoranda for the President, box 735, Stettinius papers. Subsequently, Stettinius agreed only to the principle of trusteeship and rejected a Soviet request to discuss specifics; see Andrei Gromyko to Stettinius, June 20, 1945, *FRUS, Berlin,* II, 633; Stettinius to Gromyko, June 23, 1945, ibid., 634.

17. Alonzo L. Hamby, *Beyond the New Deal: Harry S. Truman and American Liberalism,* pp. 115, 353–354; Daniels, *The Man of Independence,* pp. 368–369; see also Richard J. Barnet, *Intervention and Revolution: The United States in the Third World,* p. 27.

18. Bruce Cumings argues cogently that in the aftermath of Roosevelt's death, the balance shifted away from American leaders favoring an internationalist approach toward "those who preferred classic nationalist methods: the use of military force and occupation, direct confrontation with the Soviets, and the establishment of definite territorial boundaries." He fails to mention, however, that Stalin already had adopted an identical approach in Eastern Europe convincing Truman of the necessity to respond in kind. See Cumings, *The Origins of the Korean War,* p. 130.

19. Harry S. Truman, *Memoirs,* vol. I: *Year of Decisions,* pp. 76–79; Gaddis, *The United States and the Origins of the Cold War,* pp. 201–203.

20. Gaddis, *The United States and the Origins of the Cold War,* p. 206.

21. Schaller, *The U.S. Crusade in China,* p. 224; David S. McLellan, "Commentary," in Kirkendall, *The Truman Period as a Research Field,* p. 153; Alonzo L. Hamby, *The Imperial Years: The United States Since 1939,* p. 110; George Curry, *James F. Byrnes,* p. 313.

22. Truman, *Year of Decisions,* pp. 79–82.

23. Gaddis, *The United States and the Origins of the Cold War,* pp. 198–206; Rose, *Dubious Victory,* pp. 104–105; see also Wilson D. Miscamble, "Anthony Eden and the Truman–Molotov Conversations," *Diplomatic History* 2 (Spring 1978): 167–180.

24. William D. Leahy, diary entry, April 23, 1945, Diaries 1945, box 5, William D. Leahy papers.

25. James V. Forrestal memorandum, May 12, 1945, in Millis, *The Forrestal Diaries,* p. 56; Herbert Feis, *Contest over Japan,* pp. 27–28.

26. Grew and Johnson, *Turbulent Era*, II, pp. 1456–1457.

27. Herbert Feis, *The Atomic Bomb and the End of World War II*, p. 13.

28. Grew memorandum, May 15, 1945, *FRUS, Berlin*, I, 14; Grew and Johnson, *Turbulent Era*, II, pp. 1445–1446, 1462–1464.

29. Grew and Johnson, *Turbulent Era*, II, pp. 1458–1459; see also Rose, *Dubious Victory*, pp. 132–133; Feis, *The Atomic Bomb and the End of World War II*, p. 7.

30. Grew to John J. McCloy, May 21, 1945, Dept. of the Army Records, OPD 363 TS (5 June 45), RG 319; Grew to Forrestal, May 21, 1945, *FRUS 1945*, VII, 882–883.

31. Memorandum of conversation, May 28, 1945, *FRUS, Berlin*, I, 47; see also Herbert Feis, *Between War and Peace: The Potsdam Conference*, pp. 114–116.

32. Dewitt C. Poole memorandum, May 20, 1945, *FRUS 1945*, VII, 870–873; Joseph C. Grew, "Review of Policy Regarding Korea," *DSB* 12 (June 10, 1945): 1058–1059; Elsey to Truman and Leahy, July 1, 1945, *FRUS, Berlin*, I, 309–310; Feis, *The Atomic Bomb and the End of World War II*, pp. 164–165. Britain agreed completely with Washington's nonrecognition policy toward the KPG. See John M. Allison, *Ambassador from the Prairie or Allison Wonderland*, p. 96; Winant to Stettinius, July 2, 1945, Dept. of State Records, 711.95/7–245.

33. E. F. Cress to JCS, May 31, 1945, JCS Records, CCS 383.21 Korea (3–19–45), sec. I, RG 218; Feis, *The China Tangle*, p. 288; Grew and Johnson, *Turbulent Era*, II, pp. 1466–1468.

34. At the same time, Admiral King reminded Truman that Soviet aid was no longer indispensable and therefore the United States did not have to "beg" for Stalin's assistance. See Briefing book paper 598, "Objectives and Strategy Japan," June 18, 1945, *FRUS, Berlin*, I, 904–905; see also Feis, *The Atomic Bomb and the End of World War II*, p. 8.

35. Leahy notes, June 18, 1945, Diaries 1945, box 5, Leahy papers; Feis, *The Atomic Bomb and the End of World War II*, p. 11.

36. JCS memorandum, June 19, 1945, *FRUS, Berlin*, I, 910–911; Feis, *The China Tangle*, p. 296.

37. State Department policy paper, June 22, 1945, *FRUS 1945*, VI, 561–564.

38. Briefing book paper 605, "Relationship of the Soviet Union to the War Against Japan," n.d., *FRUS, Berlin*, I, 924–927; Briefing book paper 606, n.d., ibid., 927; Briefing book paper 251, June 29, 1945, ibid., 310–311; Briefing book paper 252, July 4, 1945, ibid., 311–313.

39. Briefing book paper 253, July 4, 1945, ibid., 314; Leahy notes, n.d., ibid., 314–315.

40. Chandler to George A. Lincoln, July 6, 1945, Dept. of the Army Records, OPD 014.1 TS, sec. III, RG 319.

41. Harriman to James F. Byrnes, July 3, 1945, *FRUS 1945*, VII, 914; Harriman to Truman, July 9, 1945, *FRUS, Berlin*, I, 234.

42. Stimson and Bundy, *On Active Service in Peace and War*, p. 637; see also Gaddis, *The United States and the Origins of the Cold War*, pp. 244–245; Barton J. Bernstein, "American Foreign Policy and the Origins of the Cold War," in Barton J. Bernstein, ed., *Politics and Policies of the Truman Administration*, p. 32.

43. Stimson to Truman, July 16, 1945, *FRUS, Berlin*, II, 631.

44. Walter Brown notes, July 17, 18, 1945, file 54 (1), James F. Byrnes papers.

45. Walter Brown notes, July 20, 1945, ibid.; Harry S. Truman, diary entry, July 18, 1945, in Robert H. Ferrell, ed., *Off the Record: The Private Papers of Harry S. Truman*, p. 54; see also Gar Alperovitz, *Atomic Diplomacy: Hiroshima and Potsdam*, pp. 103–106; Bernstein, "American Foreign Policy and the Origins of the Cold War," p. 35; Schaller, *The U.S. Crusade in China*, pp. 256–258.

46. Conference notes, July 22, 1945, *FRUS, Berlin*, II, 264–266; Truman, *Year of*

Decisions, pp. 373–374; see also Bruce Cumings, "American Policy and Korean Liberation," in Baldwin, *Without Parallel,* p. 41.

47. Cumings, *The Origins of the Korean War,* p. 113; Cho, *Korea in World Politics,* p. 44.

48. Leahy, diary entry, July 22, 1945, Diaries 1945, box 5, Leahy papers; Leahy, *I Was There,* pp. 404–408.

49. Soviet trusteeship proposal, document 733, July 20, 1945, *FRUS, Berlin,* II, 632; Yalta communiqué, "Territorial Trusteeship," ibid., 1568.

50. Stimson, diary entry, July 23, 1945, ibid., 260n.

51. Ibid.; Feis, *The Atomic Bomb and the End of World War II,* p. 89.

52. Combined Chiefs of Staff report, July 24, 1945, *FRUS, Berlin,* II, 1462–1469; Tripartite Military Meeting minutes, July 24, 1945, ibid., 344–353; see also Feis, *The Atomic Bomb and the End of World War II,* pp. 89–90; Carl Berger, *The Korean Knot: A Military-Political History,* p. 42.

53. Truman, *Year of Decisions,* p. 383; Soviet-American Chiefs of Staff Meeting minutes, July 26, 1945, *FRUS, Berlin,* II, 410–415.

54. Marshall to MacArthur, July 25, 1945, Dept. of the Army Records, OPD 014.1 TS, sec. III, RG 319; H. A. Craig to John E. Hull, July 25, 1945, ibid.; Truman, *Year of Decisions,* pp. 433–434; Schnabel, *Policy and Direction,* p. 7.

55. Roy E. Appleman, *South to the Naktong, North to the Yalu (June–November 1950),* pp. 2–3; Feis, *The China Tangle,* p. 326.

56. Council of Foreign Ministers Meeting minutes, July 23, 1945, *FRUS, Berlin,* II, 282–283.

57. Soviet draft proposal on trusteeship, n.d., ibid., 1594–1595; Council of Foreign Ministers Meeting minutes, August 1, 1945, ibid., 550–551.

58. State Department minutes, August 1, 1945, ibid., 593; Charles Yost memoranda, August 7, 9, 1945, ibid., 604–606, 636–637; Potsdam protocol, August 1, 1945, ibid., 1493.

59. "Potsdam Declaration," *DSB* 13 (July 29, 1945): 137–138; Forrestal memorandum, July 28, 1945, in Millis, *The Forrestal Diaries,* p. 78.

60. Editor's note, *FRUS, Berlin,* II 1474–1475n.

61. Feis, *Contest over Japan,* p. 9.

62. Byrnes, *Speaking Frankly,* p. 212.

63. Sutherland to Marshall, July 28, 1945, Dept. of the Army Records, OPD 014.1 TS, sec. III, RG 319; Memorandum for the JCS, August 1, 1945, ibid.; Marshall to Wedemeyer, August 9, 1945, Dept. of the Army Records, OPD 371 TS, Korea, RG 319.

64. Truman, *Year of Decisions,* p. 444; Feis, *The China Tangle,* p. 337; see also Schaller, *The U.S. Crusade in China,* pp. 263–264.

65. SWNCC Meeting minutes, August 11, 1945, *FRUS 1945,* VI, 634–637; Schnabel, *Policy and Direction,* p. 9; J. Lawton Collins, *War in Peacetime: The History and Lessons of Korea,* p. 25n. In his memoirs, John M. Allison contends that Brigadier General George A. Lincoln, who "was then supposed to be the Korean expert," was responsible for the decision to divide Korea at the 38th parallel; see Allison, *Ambassador from the Prairie,* pp. 116–117. In a passage contained in the original draft but deleted from the final manuscript, however, Allison admits that "I will not vouch for the story but it seems probable." See page proofs, *Ambassador from the Prairie,* folder 2, box 1, John M. Allison papers.

66. Memorandum for the Chief of Staff, August 11, 1945, Dept. of the Army Records, OPD 014.1, sec. III, RG 319.

67. Edwin W. Pauley to Truman, August 11, 1945, PSF (Pauley), Harry S. Truman papers.

68. Quoted in Truman, *Year of Decisions*, pp. 433–434.

69. SWNCC Meeting minutes, August 12, 1945, *FRUS 1945*, VI, 645; Schnabel, *Policy and Direction*, p. 10.

70. JCS memorandum, August 14, 1945, *FRUS 1945*, VI, 657–658; Feis, *The Atomic Bomb and the End of World War II*, p. 151.

71. Truman, *Year of Decisions*, p. 445. Later historical accounts have for the most part accepted Truman's description of the origins of the 38th parallel decision without hesitation. See Arthur L. Grey, Jr., "The Thirty-Eighth Parallel," *Foreign Affairs* 29 (April 1951): 485–487; Max Beloff, *Soviet Foreign Policy in the Far East, 1944–1951*, p. 156; Berger, *The Korean Knot, p. 47*; Kim, *Divided Korea*, p. 31; Iriye, *The Cold War in Asia*, p. 126; Cabell Phillips, *The Truman Presidency: The History of a Triumphant Succession*, p. 292. During the immediate postwar years, many observers believed that the Allies had agreed to the 38th parallel division at Yalta or at Potsdam. See *NYT*, September 29, 1945, p. 14; *NYT*, October 18, 1945, p. 4; *NYT*, October 20, 1945, p. 10; McCune and Grey, *Korea Today*, pp. 42–43; Meade, *American Military Government in Korea*, pp. 91–92; Oliver, *Syngman Rhee*, pp. 201–202; see also Collins, *War in Peacetime*, p. 25; Matthew B. Ridgway, *The Korean War*, pp. 42–47.

72. John Lewis Gaddis, "Korea in American Politics, Strategy, and Diplomacy, 1945–1950," in Nagai and Iriye, eds., *The Origins of the Cold War in Asia*, p. 278. Bruce Cumings appropriately labels the American occupation of southern Korea "the first postwar act of containment"; see Cumings, *The Origins of the Korean War*, p. 131. See also May, *"Lessons" of the Past*, pp. 53–55; Gabriel Kolko, *The Politics of War: The World and United States Foreign Policy, 1943–1945*, pp. 601–604.

73. War Department memorandum, n.d., Dept. of the Army Records, OPD 014.1, sec. III, RG 319; Feis, *The China Tangle*, p. 338; Schnabel, *Policy and Direction*, p. 11.

74. Stalin to Truman, August 12, 16, 1945, *FRUS 1945*, VI, 634, 667–668; Truman, *Year of Decisions*, p. 444; James E. Webb testimony, U.S. Congress, House, Committee on Foreign Affairs, *Korean Aid*, p. 118.

75. Shannon McCune, "The Thirty-Eighth Parallel in Korea," *World Politics* 1 (January 1949): 227; Harry J. Middleton, *The Compact History of the Korean War*, p. 25; John C. Caldwell, *The Korea Story*, p. 10; Grey, "The Thirty-Eighth Parallel," p. 485.

76. Dept. of State, *The Fight Against Aggression in Korea*, p. 3; Walter G. Hermes, *Truce Tent and Fighting Front*, p. 5; see also Gaddis, "Korea in American Politics, Strategy, and Diplomacy," p. 278.

77. Goodrich, *Korea*, p. 13; Dobbs, *The Unwanted Symbol*, p. 29. Dean Rusk later confessed his surprise that Moscow agreed to terms which clearly did not reflect the Soviet Union's superior military position. See Dean Rusk to G. Bernard Noble, July 12, 1950, *FRUS 1945*, VI, 1039.

78. Slusser, "Soviet Far Eastern Policy," p. 137; Martin Lichterman, "To the Yalu and Back," in Harold Stein, ed., *American Civil-Military Decisions: A Book of Case Studies*, p. 634.

79. Ironically, the Japanese proposed a similar line for the division of Korea into spheres of influence to Tsarist Russia in 1896. See Collins, *War in Peacetime*, p. 25; Beloff, *Soviet Foreign Policy in the Far East*, p. 156; McCune, "The Thirty-Eighth Parallel in Korea," p. 226.

80. Grey, "The Thirty-Eighth Parallel," p. 486; Cumings, "American Policy and Korean Liberation," pp. 46–47.

81. Stalin to Truman, August 16, 1945, *FRUS 1945*, VI, 667–668; Truman to Sta-

lin, August 17, 1945, ibid., 670; Harriman to Byrnes, August 23, 1945, ibid., 689–690; Harriman to Truman, August 27, 1945, ibid., 695–696.

82. Harry S. Truman, "The President's News Conference of *August* 16, 1945," *Public Papers, Truman,* I, 226.

83. Cumings, *The Origins of the Korean War,* p. xxiii.

84. Steel, *Pax Americana,* p. 126; McLellan, "Commentary," p. 159.

85. Lee, *The Politics of Korean Nationalism,* pp. 271–273; Kim, *Divided Korea,* pp. 20–21; Baldwin, "Introduction," p. 5.

86. Meade, *American Military Government in Korea,* pp. 32–33; Lee, "Kim Il-song of North Korea," p. 378; Beloff, *Soviet Foreign Policy in the Far East,* p. 158. Several scholars have noted that factionalism afflicted the Korean Communist party as much as other political groups in Korea. Furthermore, Soviet support was inconsistent and halting at best. For example, the Korean Communist party was expelled from the Comintern in 1928 because of "deviationism." See John W. Washburn, "Soviet Russia and the Korean Communist Party," *Pacific Affairs* 23 (March 1950): 59–61; Dallin, *Soviet Russia and the Far East,* pp. 51–52.

87. Henderson, *Korea,* pp. 320–322.

88. Richard E. Lauterbach, "Hodge's Korea," *Virginia Quarterly Review* 23 (June 1947): 350; Cumings, "American Policy and Korean Liberation," pp. 54–55; Henderson, *Korea,* pp. 114–115; Kim, *Divided Korea,* pp. 48–49. Japanese Governor Nobuyuki Abe's selection of a leftist to lead the provisional government in Korea had much to do with his expectation that the Soviet Union would occupy the entire peninsula. See Dobbs, *The Unwanted Symbol,* p. 35.

89. Henderson, *Korea,* pp. 115–118; Dallin, *Soviet Russia and the Far East,* p. 258; Cho, *Korea in World Politics,* pp. 70–72; Berger, *The Korean Knot,* p. 52; Allen, *Korea's Syngman Rhee,* p. 74; Meade, *American Military Government in Korea,* pp. 71–72.

90. Lauterbach, "Hodge's Korea," pp. 350–351; McCune and Grey, *Korea Today,* p. 46; Henderson, *Korea,* p. 119; Cumings, *The Origins of the Korean War,* pp. 85–88; Beloff, *Soviet Foreign Policy in the Far East,* p. 158.

91. Assistant Chief of Staff memorandum, August 12, 1945, Dept. of the Army Records, OPD 014.1 TS, sec. IV, RG 319; Brief of JCS study, August 15, 1945, ibid.; Sawyer and Hermes, *Military Advisors in Korea,* p. 3.

92. MacArthur to JCS, August 22, 1945, *FRUS 1945,* VI, 1037n.; draft memorandum to JCS, n.d., ibid., 1037–1038; SWNCC to MacFarland, August 24, 1945, ibid., 1038n.

93. SWNCC to JCS, September 2, 1945, JCS Records, CCAC 014, sec. I, RG 218; JCS to MacArthur, September 2, 1945, ibid.; MacArthur proclamation, September 7, 1945, *FRUS 1945,* VI, 1043; *NYT,* September 9, 1945, p. 1.

94. JCS to Lieutenant General John R. Hodge, August 5, 1945, JCS Records, CCAC 014, Korea, sec. I, RG 218; Meade, *American Military Government in Korea,* p. 225.

95. H. Merrell Benninghoff to Byrnes, September 15, 1945, *FRUS 1945,* VI, 1049–1052; Meade, *American Military Government in Korea,* p. 44; Cumings, *The Origins of the Korean War,* p. 111.

96. Hagwon Sunoo and William N. Angus, "American Policy in Korea: Two Views," *Far Eastern Survey* 25 (July 31, 1946): 230; U-Gene Lee, "American Policy Toward Korea 1942–1947: Formulation and Execution" (Ph.D. dissertation, Georgetown University, 1973), pp. 167–168; Hodge to War, September 29, 1945, Dept. of the Army Records, OPD 014.1 TS, sec. V, RG 319.

97. Leahy, diary entry, September 29, 1945, Diaries 1945, box 5, Leahy papers; MacArthur to War, September 18, 1945, PSF 41 (Korea), Truman papers.

98. Vincent to Acheson, October 1, 1945, *FRUS 1945,* VI, 1066–1067; Benninghoff to Byrnes, October 1, 1945, ibid., 1065–1066.

99. Vinacke, *The United States and the Far East,* p. 59; Cho, *Korea in World Politics,* p. 156; Pauline Tompkins, *American-Russian Relations in the Far East,* p. 319; Goodrich, *Korea,* pp. 16–17; Baldwin, "Introduction," pp. 6–8.

CHAPTER 3: *In Search of a Settlement*

1. *NYT,* November 25, 1945, IV, p. 8.

2. That both the United States and the Soviet Union could possess legitimate interests in Korea after World War II would seem to be an assertion beyond serious dispute. Nevertheless, Bruce Cumings charges that the United States was guilty of an "unprecedented expression of ambition" in attempting "to project its power onto the Asian mainland and to challenge the Soviet Union in a country that touched Soviet borders, one in which the Russians had long had an interest." See Cumings, *The Origins of the Korean War,* p. 116. At the other extreme, Charles M. Dobbs contends that "the Soviets had done little to deserve" a voice in the postwar reconstruction of Korea because Russia "had made no significant contribution to the defeat of Japan." See Dobbs, *The Unwanted Symbol,* p. 65.

3. *NYT,* September 29, 1945, p. 14; Meade, *American Military Government in Korea,* pp. 4–5; Kim, *Divided Korea,* pp. 3–8.

4. McCune and Grey, *Korea Today,* p. 271; Baldwin, "Introduction," p. 3; Lauterbach, "Hodge's Korea," p. 349.

5. Intelligence report, n.d., OSS Records, report XL10423; "Review of Korea's Postwar Economy," *Far Eastern Economic Review* 11 (August 23, 1951): 230–237; McCune, "The Thirty-Eighth Parallel in Korea," p. 228; Schnabel, *Policy and Direction,* p. 12; see also McCune and Grey, *Korea Today,* p. 59.

6. Lee, *The Politics of Korean Nationalism,* p. 229; Andrew J. Grajdanzev, "Korea Divided," *Far Eastern Survey* 14 (October 10, 1945): 281–283; McCune and Grey, *Korea Today,* p. 128.

7. Cumings, *The Origins of the Korean War,* pp. 39–67; U.S. Dept. of Commerce, "Economic Conditions in South Korea, 1947," *International Reference Service* 5 (December 1948): 1–3.

8. Memorandum for the President, n.d., PPF 3920 (John R. Hodge), Truman papers; see also Dobbs, *The Unwanted Symbol,* pp. 33–34.

9. Quoted in John Gunther, *The Riddle of MacArthur: Japan, Korea and the Far East,* p. 180.

10. C. Clyde Mitchell, *Korea: Second Failure in Asia,* p. 15; Henderson, *Korea,* pp. 212–214.

11. T. Fehrenbach, *This Kind of War: A Study in Unpreparedness,* p. 39; Meade, *American Military Government in Korea,* p. 88.

12. SWNCC memorandum, September 10, 1945, *FRUS 1945,* VI, 1044–1045; *NYT,* September 10, 1945, p. 1; *NYT,* September 11, 1945, pp. 1, 22.

13. Harry S. Truman, "The President's News Conference of *September* 12, 1945," *Public Papers, Truman,* I, 318; SWNCC memorandum, September 11, 1945, JCS Records, CCAC 014 Korea (8–28–45), sec. I, RG 218; *NYT,* September 12, 1945, p. 24; *NYT,* September 14, 1945, p. 1. At the press conference on September 12, Truman also stated that the use of Japanese personnel was a theater decision. In reality, Hodge was following orders from Washington. See State Department memorandum, "Japanese Capitulation," n.d., file 569 (2), Byrnes papers.

14. Acheson to Truman, September 14, 1945, OF 471, Truman papers; Harry S.

Truman, "Statement by the President on the Liberation of Korea, *September* 18, 1945," *Public Papers, Truman,* I, 324–325; *NYT,* September 21, 1945, p. 20.

15. Meade, *American Military Government in Korea,* p. 151.

16. Ibid., pp. 228–229; Steel, *Pax Americana,* p. 269; Tae-ho Yoo, *The Korean War and the United Nations: A Legal and Diplomatic Historical Study,* p. 49.

17. Benninghoff to Byrnes, September 15, 1945, *FRUS 1945,* VI, 1049–1052; Langdon to Byrnes, November 26, 1945, ibid., 1135; Denna Frank Fleming, *The Cold War and Its Origins,* II, p. 590.

18. Meade, *American Military Government in Korea,* p. 235; Cho, *Korea in World Politics,* p. 73; Henderson, *Korea,* p. 130.

19. Bertram D. Sarafan, "Military Government: Korea," *Far Eastern Survey* 15 (November 20, 1946): 349–350; Berger, *The Korean Knot,* p. 50; Meade, *American Military Government in Korea,* p. 227. Bruce Cumings overstates the case when he argues that American occupation officials pursued an "activist, conscious, dynamic . . . policy of seeking a Korea . . . oriented toward and responsive to American interests." For Cumings, these officials wanted only "loyal allies who could be counted upon to stem the tide of domestic revolution in Korea"; See Cumings, *The Origins of the Korean War,* pp. 136, 143. In reality, Hodge rightly emphasized the maintenance of internal stability in southern Korea while viewing with trepidation the presence of Soviet troops north of the 38th parallel. Given the established pattern of Russian behavior in Eastern Europe, initial American occupation policies were neither surprising nor thoroughly unreasonable. Cumings himself admits that "Hodge could not simply manufacture both 'responsible' and anticommunist Korean leadership. He had to find his allies where he could." From the start, American occupation officials "saw the whole People's Republic apparatus as a creature of Soviet designs"; ibid., pp. 183, 187.

20. Quoted in Lauterbach, "Hodge's Korea," p. 354; Benninghoff to Byrnes, September 29, 1945, *FRUS 1945,* VI, 1061–1065.

21. Benninghoff to Atcheson, October 9, 1945, *FRUS 1945,* VI, 1069; Henderson, *Korea,* p. 130; Meade, *American Military Government in Korea,* p. 61; Sunoo and Angus, "American Policy in Korea," p. 228.

22. MacArthur to War, September 29, 1945, Dept. of the Army Records, OPD 381 CTO, RG 319; Benninghoff to Atcheson, October 9, 1945, *FRUS 1945,* VI, 1070; *NYT,* October 10, 1945, p. 7; *NYT,* October 14, 1945, p. 10.

23. U.S. Dept. of State, *North Korea: A Case Study in the Techniques of Takeover,* p. 13; Suh, "A Preconceived Formula for Sovietization," p. 477; Henderson, *Korea,* p. 325.

24. Cumings, *The Origins of the Korean War,* pp. 385–386.

25. McCune and Grey, *Korea Today,* p. 52; Kim, *Divided Korea,* p. 88; Cumings, "American Policy and Korean Liberation," p. 55; Simmons, *The Strained Alliance,* p. 24.

26. Benninghoff to Byrnes, September 26, 29, 1945, *FRUS 1945,* VI, 1059–1060, 1061–1065; Hodge to MacArthur, September 24, 1945, ibid., 1054–1057.

27. Walter S. Robertson to Washington, September 25, 1945, ibid., 1057; Acheson memorandum, September 26, 1945, Dept. of State Records, 895.01/9–2645.

28. Harriman to Washington, September 3, 1945, Dept. of State Records, 895.01/9–345.

29. Acheson to Robertson, September 27, 1945, *FRUS 1945,* VI, 1060; Acheson to Hurley, September 21, 1945, ibid., 1053–1054; Byrnes to Hurley, October 16, 1945, ibid., 1092–1093; "Travel to Korea," *DSB* 13 (October 21, 1945): 643; *NYT,* October 20, 1945, p. 10.

30. Oliver, *Syngman Rhee,* pp. 210–211; Henderson, *Korea,* p. 128. According to

Bruce Cumings, Preston Goodfellow received promises of certain economic concessions and trading rights in postwar Korea as payment for facilitating Rhee's return.
"Let us be frank," Cumings concludes, "Hodge, MacArthur, Goodfellow, and Rhee
conspired against established State Department policy." See Cumings, *The Origins
of the Korean War,* pp. 188–189.

31. MacArthur to War, October 19, 1945, Dept. of the Army Records, OPD 381
CTO, RG 319; Atcheson to Byrnes, October 15, 1945, *FRUS 1945,* VI, 1091–1092.

32. *NYT,* October 18, 1945, p. 4; Henderson, *Korea,* pp. 128–129; Kim, *Divided
Korea,* pp. 57–58; Oliver, *Syngman Rhee,* pp. 213–214.

33. *NYT,* October 21, 1945, p. 30; see also Dobbs, *The Unwanted Symbol,* p. 47;
Cumings, *The Origins of the Korean War,* p. 191.

34. Jay Jerome Williams to Byrnes, November 5, 1945, Dept. of State Records,
740.00119 Control (Korea)/11–545; Vincent memorandum, November 11, 1945,
ibid., 740.00119 Control (Korea)/11–1145.

35. Byrnes to Truman, November 13, 1945, ibid., 740.00119 Control (Korea)/11–1345; Truman to Byrnes, November 16, 1945, ibid., 740.00119 Control
(Korea)/11–1645.

36. War Department memoranda, September 18, 30, 1945, Dept. of the Army
Records, OPD 014.1 TS, sec. V, RG 319; Marshall to MacArthur, October 1, 1945,
FRUS 1945, VI, 1067–1068.

37. JCS 1483/12, October 3, 1945, JCS Records, CCAC 014 Korea, sec. II, RG
218; JCS to Hodge, October 4, 1945, ibid.; MacArthur to JCS, October 11, 1945,
FRUS 1945, VI, 1071–1072; Hodge to War, October 12, 1945, Dept. of the Army
Records, OPD 336 Korea, sec. I, RG 319.

38. Hodge to Benninghoff, October 16, 1945, Dept. of the Army Records, OPD
336 Korea, sec. I, RG 319; T. N. Dupuy to Lincoln, October 29, 1945, ibid.; Lincoln
to Hull, November 1, 1945, ibid.

39. Hull to Lincoln, October 3, 1945, ibid., OPD 320.2 PTO, RG 319; War
Department memorandum, October 8, 1945, ibid.; War to MacArthur, October 27,
1945, ibid.; Robert P. Patterson to Byrnes, November 1, 1945, *FRUS 1946,* I, 1111.

40. Draft proposal on Korean trusteeship, October 13, 1945, file 569 (2), Byrnes
papers; SWNCC to Byrnes, October 22, 1945, *FRUS 1945,* VI, 1093–1096; SWNCC
to JCS, October 24, 1945, ibid., 1096–1103; see also Berger, *The Korean Knot,*
p. 57.

41. John Carter Vincent, "The Post-War Period in the Far East," *DSB* 13 (October
21, 1945): 644–648.

42. Truman, *Year of Decisions,* pp. 521–522; see also Byrnes to Harriman,
November 9, 1945, *FRUS 1945,* VI, 1118–1119; Gilmer to Hull, November 7, 1945,
Dept. of the Army Records, OPD 336 Korea, sec. I, RG 319.

43. Byrnes to Harriman, November 3, 7, 1945, *FRUS 1945,* VI, 1106–1109,
1112–1113.

44. Harriman to Molotov, November 8, 1945, *FRUS 1945,* II, 627; Harriman to
Byrnes, November 12, 1945, *FRUS 1945,* VI, 1121–1122; SWNCC Meeting minutes, November 6, 1945, in Millis, *The Forrestal Diaries,* pp. 107–108.

45. Hull to Russell L. Vittrup, November 10, 1945, Dept. of the Army Records,
OPD 336 Korea, sec. I, RG 319.

46. Trusteeship proposal, November 6, 1945, file 596 (2), Byrnes papers; Blakes-
lee to Vincent, November 14, 1945, Dept. of State Records, 740.00119 Control
(Korea)/11–1445.

47. Vincent to Vittrup, November 7, 1945, *FRUS 1945,* VI, 1113–1114; War to
MacArthur, October 22, 1945, JCS Records, William D. Leahy file, Korea 1946–
1947, RG 218.

48. Charles M. Dobbs offers a different, though unconvincing, assessment. The

State Department, he argues, favored trusteeship not only because it saw Korea as a "back-burner" issue but also because it was still "chasing the illusion of postwar cooperation with the Soviet Union." Worse still, "Washington officialdom sought to overlook Korea, thinking that the problem might solve itself or disappear." See Dobbs, *The Unwanted Symbol,* pp. 53–55.

49. Leahy, diary entry, November 11, 1945, Diaries 1945, box 5, Leahy papers; Truman, *Year of Decisions,* p. 540; see also "Joint Policy Declaration," November 13, 1945, file 569 (2), Byrnes papers.

50. "United States Forces in Korea," *DSB* 13 (November 18, 1945): 812–813.

51. *NYT,* November 3, 1945, p. 5; Rhee to Byrnes, November 4, 1945, *FRUS 1945,* VI, 1110–1111; Ben C. Limb to Vincent, November 7, 1945, ibid., 1115–1117.

52. Hodge to War, November 2, 1945, *FRUS 1945,* VI, 1106; MacArthur to Marshall, November 5, 1945, ibid., 1112; MacArthur to Marshall, October 29, 1945, Dept. of the Army Records, OPD 336 Korea, RG 319.

53. John J. McCloy to Acheson, November 13, 1945, *FRUS 1945,* VI, 1122–1124.

54. Vincent to Acheson, November 16, 1945, *FRUS 1945,* VI, 1127–1128; Hull to Hodge, November 21, 1945, Dept. of the Army Records, OPD 336 Korea, RG 319; embassy report, October 25, 1945, ibid.; *NYT,* November 20, 1945, p. 4; *NYT,* December 4, 1945, p. 2; McNair to War, November 16, 1945, OSS Records, report XL31447.

55. Langdon to Byrnes, November 18, 20, 1945, *FRUS 1945,* VI, 1129–1133; Hodge to MacArthur, November 25, 1945, ibid., 1133–1134.

56. Langdon to Byrnes, November 26, 1945, ibid., 1134–1136; *NYT,* November 22, 1945, p. 11; *NYT,* November 27, 1945, p. 3; *NYT,* December 2, 1945, p. 36; *NYT,* December 6, 1945, p. 3.

57. Byrnes to Langdon, November 29, 1945, *FRUS 1945,* VI, 1137–1138; Langdon to Byrnes, December 11, 14, 1945, ibid., 1142–1144.

58. Memorandum for JCS, December 11, 1945, JCS Records, CCS 383.21 Korea (3–19–45), sec. III, RG 218; SWNCC policy paper, November 29, 1945, file 569 (3), Byrnes papers.

59. MacArthur for Hodge to JCS, December 16, 1945, *FRUS 1945,* VI, 1144–1148.

60. Moscow Conference minutes, December 16, 1945, *FRUS 1945,* II, 617–621. During negotiations at Moscow, American military leaders pestered Byrnes about the need to break the Soviet-American deadlock over Korea. Secretary of War Robert P. Patterson, for example, reminded the State Department that the situation in Korea was deteriorating rapidly and therefore demanded positive steps. The JCS also complained that it was unable to issue adequate directives to Hodge and was urgently in need of advice. For Forrestal, the only answer in Korea was for the United States to propose mutual military withdrawal and immediate independence. If Moscow demurred, each nation could implement a five-year trusteeship in its own zone under the supervision of the United Nations. See Patterson to Acheson, December 19, 1945, Dept. of the Army Records, OPD 336 Korea, RG 319; James C. Dunn to Byrnes, December 19, 1945, JCS Records, CCS 014.1 TS, Korea, RG 218; Forrestal memorandum, December 19, 1945, in Millis, *The Forrestal Diaries,* p. 125. Despite such pressure, the State Department refused to waver in its pursuit of a bilateral agreement. See Acheson to Langdon, December 20, 1945, Dept. of State Records, 740.00119 Control (Korea)/12–2045; War to MacArthur, December 20, 1945, JCS Records, Leahy file, Korea 1946–1947, RG 218.

61. American proposal on Korea, December 17, 1945, *FRUS 1945,* II, 641–643; Moscow Conference minutes, December 18, 19, 20, 1945, ibid., 639, 660, 697–698.

62. Soviet proposal on Korea, December 20, 1945, ibid., 699–700.

63. Moscow Conference minutes, informal meeting, December 21, 1945, ibid., 716–717; Feis, *Contest over Japan,* p. 84; Goodrich, *Korea,* p. 21. Some scholars have insisted that Moscow's support for trusteeship was insincere, but they provide no evidence to substantiate this contention. See Cho, *Korea in World Politics,* p. 97; Dallin, *Soviet Russia and the Far East,* pp. 226–227.

64. Moscow Conference minutes, informal meeting, December 22, 1945, *FRUS 1945,* II, 717; Byrnes, *Speaking Frankly,* pp. 221–222.

65. Langdon to Byrnes, December 30, 1945, Dept. of State Records, 740.00119 Control (Korea)/12–3045; Arthur B. Emmons III to Byrnes, December 30, 1945, *FRUS 1945,* VI, 1152–1153; Hodge to MacArthur, December 30, 1945, ibid., 1154.

66. Hodge to War, December 30, 1945, Dept. of the Army Records, OPD 336 Korea, RG 319; General Dwight D. Eisenhower to MacArthur, December 30, 1945, *FRUS 1945,* VI, 1154–1155; Hodge to War, December 31, 1945, JCS Records, Leahy file, Korea 1946–1947, RG 218; *NYT,* December 31, 1945, p. 1.

67. *NYT,* December 28, 1945, p. 12; Hodge to War, December 31, 1945, Dept. of State Records, 740.00119 Control (Korea)/12–3045; Kim, *Divided Korea,* p. 62.

68. James F. Byrnes, "Report by the Secretary of State on the Meeting of Foreign Ministers," *DSB* 13 (December 30, 1945): 1035–1036; Allison, *Ambassador from the Prairie,* p. 118. After engaging in an exercise of strained logic, Bruce Cumings concludes that the text of the Moscow agreement "implied that a trusteeship might not be necessary." In fact, the accord specifically called for a five-year period of outside supervision prior to complete independence. When Cumings asserts that Byrnes had advanced "an acceptable interpretation" of the Moscow agreement, he distorts its clear meaning. See Cumings, *The Origins of the Korean War,* pp. 217, 220.

69. Memorandum of conversation, January 4, 1946, Dept. of State Records, 740.00119 Control (Korea)/1–446.

70. Leahy, diary entry, December 26, 1945, Diaries 1945, box 5, Leahy papers; Truman, *Year of Decisions,* pp. 547–550; Daniels, *The Man of Independence,* pp. 308–310.

71. Truman, *Year of Decisions,* p. 552; William Hillman, ed., *Mr. President: The First Publication from the Private Diaries, Private Letters, Papers, and Revealing Interviews of Harry S. Truman,* pp. 21–23; Daniels, *The Man of Independence,* p. 310.

72. Langdon to Byrnes, December 30, 1945, Dept. of State Records, 740.00119 Control (Korea)/12–3045; *NYT,* January 2, 1946, p. 2.

73. *NYT,* January 3, 1946, pp. 2, 18; *NYT,* January 4, 1946, p. 20; Hodge to War, January 3, 1946, JCS Records, CSS 383.21 Korea (3–19–45), sec. III, RG 218; see also Kim, *Divided Korea,* p. 62.

74. Lloyd C. Gardner, "Introduction," in Lloyd C. Gardner, ed., *The Korean War,* p. 15; Goodrich, *Korea,* p. 53.

75. Memorandum, December 27, 1945, Trips Overseas, General Correspondence 1945–1947, box 23, Robert P. Patterson papers; Robert P. Patterson, diary entries, January 13, 14, 1946, ibid.

76. Memorandum on press conference questions, January 13, 1946, ibid.; Patterson, diary entries, January 13, 14, 1946, ibid.; *NYT,* January 11, 1946, p. 4; *NYT,* January 13, 1946, p. 18.

77. Patterson, press conference remarks, January 26, 1946, Press Conferences, ibid.

78. Beloff, *Soviet Foreign Policy in the Far East,* pp. 160–161; *NYT,* January 4, 1946, p. 20; *NYT,* January 18, 1946, p. 18.

79. "American and Soviet Commands in Korea Plan Administrative Coordination," *DSB* 14 (January 27, 1946): 111–112; *NYT,* January 11, 1946, p. 4; JCS to Hodge, December 29, 1945, JCS Records, Leahy file, Korea 1946–1947, RG 218;

JCS to MacArthur, January 5, 1946, *FRUS 1946,* VIII, 607; Hodge to Byrnes, January 12, 1946, ibid.

80. *NYT,* January 16, 1946, p. 2; *NYT,* January 17, 1946, p. 17; Benninghoff to Byrnes, February 15, 1946, *FRUS 1946,* VIII, 634–636; U.S. Dept. of State, *The Record on Korean Unification 1943–1960: Narrative Summary with Principal Documents,* pp. 5–6.

81. Paul R. Goode to Hull, January 29, 1946, Dept. of the Army Records, P&O 337, case 5, RG 319; U.S. Dept. of State, *Korea's Independence,* p. 4.

82. Hodge to War, January 25, 1946, JCS Records, CCS 383.21 Korea (3–19–45), sec. III, RG 218.

83. Hodge to War, January 18, 1946, *FRUS 1946,* VIII, 611–612; Hodge to War, February 19, 1946, JCS Records, CCAC 014 Korea (8–28–45), sec. III, RG 218; *NYT,* February 7, 1946, p. 17; *NYT,* February 8, 1946, p. 12.

84. Hodge to War, January 22, 1946, JCS Records, CCS 383.21 Korea (3–19–45), sec. III, RG 218.

85. Dupuy memorandum, February 13, 1946, Dept. of the Army Records, P&O 091 Korea TS, sec. III, cases 3–15, box 21, RG 319.

86. James C. Dunn to SWNCC, January 4, 1946, *FRUS 1946,* VIII, 605–606; Benninghoff to Byrnes, January 7, 1946, ibid., 608.

87. Dupuy memorandum, February 19, 1946, Dept. of the Army Records, P&O 014.1 TS, sec. I, case 1, box 6, RG 319; Acheson to Benninghoff, January 12, 1946, *FRUS 1946,* VIII, 610.

88. Benninghoff to Byrnes, January 23, 1946, *FRUS 1946,* VIII, 615–616; *NYT,* January 14, 1946, p. 2; Kim, *Divided Korea,* p. 63.

89. *NYT,* January 20, 1946, p. 19.

90. Benninghoff to Byrnes, January 22, 1946, *FRUS 1946,* VIII, 613–614.

91. *NYT,* January 23, 1946, p. 15; *NYT,* January 27, 1946, p. 19; Berger, *The Korean Knot,* pp. 62–63.

92. *NYT,* January 24, 1946, p. 19; Hodge to War, January 25, 1946, JCS Records, Leahy file, Korea 1946–1947, RG 218.

93. George F. Kennan to Byrnes, January 25, 1946, *FRUS 1946,* VIII, 617–620.

94. Dean G. Acheson, "Administration of Korea," *DSB* 14 (February 3, 1946): 155; *NYT,* January 26, 1946, p. 7; Vincent to Benninghoff, January 25, 1946, Dept. of State Records, 740.00119 Control (Korea)/1–2546.

95. Harriman to Byrnes, January 25, 1946, *FRUS 1946,* VIII, 622.

96. Feis, *Contest over Japan,* p. 98; see also Byrnes, *Speaking Frankly,* p. 222. For a contrary view, see Dobbs, *The Unwanted Symbol,* pp. 64, 74–75.

97. Richard D. Burns, "James F. Byrnes (1945–1947)," in Norman A. Graebner, ed., *An Uncertain Tradition: American Secretaries of State in the Twentieth Century,* p. 243; Curry, *James F. Byrnes,* p. 306; Hamby, *Beyond the New Deal,* pp. 113–114.

CHAPTER 4: *Patience with Firmness*

1. Gaddis, *The United States and the Origins of the Cold War,* pp. 284, 313; Curry, *James F. Byrnes,* p. 309; Feis, *Contest over Japan,* p. 124; H. Bradford Westerfield, *Foreign Policy and Party Politics: Pearl Harbor to Korea,* p. 211.

2. William Reitzel, Morton A. Kaplan, and Constance G. Coblenz, *United States Foreign Policy, 1945–1955,* p. 89; see also Joseph Marion Jones, *The Fifteen Weeks (February 21–June 5, 1947),* p. 11.

3. Walter Treumann to Lieutenant Colonel Enders, February 23, 1946, Alpha Correspondence, Korea Documents 1946, Charles W. Thayer papers; Kim, *Divided Korea,* p. 92; Suh, "A Preconceived Formula for Sovietization," p. 486.

4. In these elections, there was only one candidate for each position; the vote was for or against, as is common in Communist countries. Lee, "Kim Il-song of North Korea," pp. 377–378; John N. Washburn, "Russia Looks at North Korea," *Pacific Affairs* 20 (June 1947): 154–155; Wilbert B. Dubin, "The Political Evolution of the Pyongyang Government," *Pacific Affairs* 23 (December 1950): 384; Kim, *Divided Korea*, p. 91; Henderson, *Korea*, p. 326. For a contrary interpretation of Kim Il Sung's qualifications as a popular nationalist leader and wartime guerrilla fighter, see Cumings, *The Origins of the Korean War*, pp. 395, 399, 420.

5. McCune and Grey, *Korea Today*, p. 180; Mitchell, *Korea*, pp. 16–17; Dallin, *Soviet Russia and the Far East*, pp. 286–288.

6. Washburn, "Russia Looks at North Korea," p. 156; McCune and Grey, *Korea Today*, pp. 201–202; Suh, "A Preconceived Formula for Sovietization," pp. 480, 487–488; Kim, *Divided Korea*, p. 96.

7. Langdon to Byrnes, August 23, 1946, *FRUS 1946*, VIII, 728.

8. Jon Halliday, "The United Nations and Korea," in Baldwin, *Without Parallel*, p. 122; Cho, *Korea in World Politics*, p. 131; Dept. of State, *North Korea*, pp. 6–7, 57; Lauterbach, "Hodge's Korea," p. 358.

9. Kim, *Divided Korea*, pp. 54–55, 66–67; Henderson, *Korea*, pp. 142–143; Cumings, "American Policy and Korean Liberation," p. 74.

10. Sawyer and Hermes, *Military Advisors in Korea*, pp. 10–11.

11. MacArthur to War, November 26, 1945, Dept. of the Army Records, OPD 014.1 TS, sec. V, RG 319.

12. MacArthur to Eisenhower, November 26, 1945, *FRUS 1945*, VI, 1136; Patterson to Byrnes, November 1, 1946, *FRUS 1946*, I, 1111.

13. JCS to MacArthur, January 9, 1946, JCS Records, Leahy file, Korea 1946–1947, RG 218.

14. Sawyer and Hermes, *Military Advisors in Korea*, p. 12; Kim, *Divided Korea*, p. 67; Henderson, *Korea*, p. 141.

15. Bonesteel memorandum, February 23, 1946, Dept. of the Army Records, P&O 091 Korea, sec. I, cases 1–14, box 87, RG 319; Eisenhower to MacArthur, February 23, 1946, *FRUS 1946*, VIII, 638–639; see also U.S. Dept. of State, *Korea 1945 to 1948: A Report on Political Developments and Economic Resources with Selected Documents*, pp. 29–31; Lauterbach, "Hodge's Korea," pp. 360–361.

16. MacArthur to JCS, February 2, 1946, *FRUS 1946*, VIII, 628–630.

17. Hodge to War, January 22, 1946, ibid., 613.

18. Benninghoff to Byrnes, January 28, 1946, ibid., 627; *NYT*, January 29, 1946, p. 1; *NYT*, February 9, 1946, p. 10.

19. Benninghoff to Acheson, January 13, 1946, *FRUS 1946*, VIII, 611; Benninghoff to Byrnes, February 15, 1946, ibid., 630.

20. Glenn D. Paige, "Korea," in Cyril E. Black and Thomas P. Thornton, eds., *Communism and Revolution: The Uses of Political Violence*, p. 221; *NYT*, February 19, 1946, p. 12.

21. War to Hodge, February 6, 1946, Dept. of the Army Records, P&O 091 Korea TS, sec. III, cases 3–15, box 21, RG 319; SWNCC policy paper, January 28, 1946, *FRUS 1946*, VIII, 624–627.

22. MacArthur to JCS, February 12, 1946, *FRUS 1946*, VIII, 632–633; Dupuy memorandum, February 13, 1946, Dept. of the Army Records, P&O 091 Korea TS, sec. III, cases 3–15, box 21, RG 319; Leahy, diary entry, February 21, 1946, Diaries 1946, box 5, Leahy papers; W. Averell Harriman, January 10, 1980, Oral History Interview Transcript, p. 12, Truman Library; *NYT*, February 3, 1946, p. 23.

23. JCS to MacArthur, February 28, 1946, *FRUS 1946*, VIII, 644.

24. Hodge to War, February 24, 1946, ibid., 641; draft memorandum, February

28, 1946, Dept. of State Records, 740.00119 Control (Korea)/2–2846. At this juncture, George F. Kennan's now famous "long telegram" may have had some impact on Washington's policy in Korea. Charles M. Dobbs contends that after "adopting the ideology of containment" early in 1946, "the U.S. government redefined the situation [in Korea] and considered intelligence only as it fit a preconceived notion of the emerging bipolar struggle. There would be no shadings of gray until it was too late. The damage was wrought by well-meaning, but sadly close-minded men." See Dobbs, *The Unwanted Symbol,* pp. 77–78.

25. War to Hodge, March 1, 1946, JCS Records, CCAC 014 Korea, sec. III, RG 218. The parallels between United States policy in southern Korea and China are obvious.

26. Hodge to Byrnes, March 22, 1946, *FRUS 1946,* VIII, 652–653. For a complete text of both speeches, see McCune and Grey, *Korea Today,* pp. 276–281.

27. *NYT,* March 21, 1946, p. 24.

28. John Z. Williams to Vincent, March 25, 1946, Dept. of State Records, 501.BB Korea/3–2546.

29. Williams to Hugh Borton, April 2, 1946, ibid., 501.BB Korea/4–246.

30. Ibid.; *NYT,* March 31, 1946, p. 14.

31. Byrnes to Patterson, April 1, 1946, *FRUS 1946,* VIII, 655–656.

32. Patterson to Byrnes, April 10, 1946, Dept. of State Records, 740.00119 Control (Korea)/4–1046.

33. Williams to Borton, April 2, 1946, ibid., 501.BB Korea/4–246; Byrnes to Langdon, April 5, 1946, *FRUS 1946,* VIII, 657–658.

34. *NYT,* April 11, 1946, p. 13; *NYT,* April 17, 1946, p. 24; Langdon to Byrnes, April 30, 1946, *FRUS 1946,* VIII, 662–663.

35. Vincent to Byrnes, April 12, 1946, Dept. of State Records, 501.BB Korea/4–1246; Byrnes to Langdon, April 16, 1946, *FRUS 1946,* VIII, 660–661.

36. Langdon to Byrnes, August 30, 1946, Dept. of State Records, 711.00/8–3046; "Durly" [sic] to Charles W. Thayer, April 11, 1946, Alpha Correspondence, Korea Documents 1946, Thayer papers.

37. "Communiqué Issued by U.S.–Soviet Joint Commission on April 18, 1946," *DSB* 16 (January 26, 1947): 173.

38. Hodge to War, April 20, 1946, Dept. of the Army Records, P&O 091 Korea, sec. I, cases 1–14, box 87, RG 319.

39. Ibid.; Acheson to Moscow, Nanking, and Paris embassies, April 25, 1946, *FRUS 1946,* VIII, 661.

40. *NYT,* April 11, 1946, p. 13; *NYT,* April 23, 1946, p. 11; *NYT,* April 27, 1946, p. 5; Langdon to Byrnes, April 14, 1946, *FRUS 1946,* VIII, 660.

41. Hodge to War, May 7, 1946, JCS Records, Leahy file, Korea 1946–1947, RG 218; Hodge to War, May 9, 1946, *FRUS 1946,* VIII, 665–667.

42. *NYT,* April 26, 1946, p. 8; *NYT,* May 8, 1946, p. 10; *NYT,* May 9, 1946, p. 15; Langdon to Byrnes, April 30, 1946, *FRUS 1946,* VIII, 663; Langdon to Byrnes, May 8, 1946, ibid., 677.

43. Langdon to Byrnes, May 8, 1946, *FRUS 1946,* VIII, 667–674.

44. Acheson to Seoul, May 18, 1946, ibid., 680; Hull and Bonesteel to MacArthur and Hodge, May 11, 1946, Dept. of the Army Records, P&O 014.1 TS, sec. I, case 1, box 6, RG 319; see also *NYT,* May 11, 1946, p. 26.

45. SWNCC memorandum, May 22, 1946, *FRUS 1946,* VIII, 680–681; Walter Bedell Smith to Byrnes, May 18, 1946, ibid., 680; Borton to Williams, May 21, 1946, Dept. of State Records, 740.00119 Control (Korea)/5–2146.

46. Langdon to Byrnes, May 24, 1946, *FRUS 1946,* VIII, 685–688.

47. Byrnes to Langdon, May 25, 1946, ibid., 689; War to Langdon, May 25, 1946,

Dept. of State Records, 740.00119 Control (Korea)/5–2546; *NYT,* May 24, 1946, p. 12.

48. Smith to Byrnes, July 1, 1946, Dept. of State Records, 740.00119 Control (Korea)/7–146; *NYT,* May 16, 1946, p. 15; Beloff, *Soviet Foreign Policy in the Far East,* p. 163.

49. Edwin Pauley statement, December 7, 1945, PSF (Pauley), Truman papers; Truman to Pauley, December 21, 1945, ibid.; Pauley to Truman, March 22, 1946, ibid.

50. Harry S. Truman, "The President's Press Conference of *May* 2, 1946," *Public Papers, Truman,* II, 224–225; Pauley to Byrnes, May 10, 1946, Confidential, White House Messages, Traffic 1946, box 3, Robert L. Dennison papers; memorandum, n.d., ibid.; Byrnes to Pauley, May 15, 1946, ibid.

51. Edwin W. Pauley, diary notes, June 20, 1946, PSF (Pauley), Truman papers; Carter to Wolfe, May 30, 1946, Confidential, White House Messages, Traffic 1946, box 3, Dennison papers.

52. Edwin W. Pauley, "Survey of Resources in Manchuria and Korea and the European Reparations Program," *DSB* 15 (August 4, 1946): 233–234; Pauley to Truman, June 22, 1946, *FRUS 1946,* VIII, 706–708.

53. Ibid.; Truman to Acheson, July 3, 1946, PSF (Cabinet File), State Department, folder 2 (Acheson), box 160, Truman papers.

54. John H. Hilldring memorandum, June 6, 1946, *FRUS 1946,* VIII, 692–698.

55. Truman to Pauley, July 16, 1946, *FRUS 1946,* VIII, 713–714. Charles M. Dobbs is mistaken when he states that Pauley's report "fell on largely deaf ears"; see Dobbs, *The Unwanted Symbol,* p. 205.

56. War to MacArthur, July 17, 1946, JCS Records, Leahy file, Korea 1946–1947, RG 218.

57. Thayer to Hodge, July 17, 1946, Alpha Correspondence, Korea Documents 1946, Thayer papers.

58. War Department memorandum, July 25, 1946, Dept. of the Army Records, P&O 091 Korea, sec. I, cases 1–14, box 87, RG 319.

59. Hilldring to SWNCC, July 25, 1946, *FRUS 1946,* VIII, 719; SWNCC to JCS, August 2, 1946, JCS Records, CCS 383.21 Korea (3–19–45), sec. VIII, RG 218.

60. Dupuy memorandum, August 3, 1946, Dept. of the Army Records, P&O 091 Korea, sec. I, cases 1–14, box 87, RG 319.

61. Dupuy memorandum, June 13, 1946, ibid., P&O 091 Korea, sec. II, case 15, box 87, RG 319; Craig memorandum, June 4, 1946, ibid., P&O 014.1 TS, sec. I, case 1, box 6, RG 319. Similarly, the Navy Department had been hesistant to furnish the necessary personnel to establish a Korean coast guard. See Hodge to War, August 8, 1946, ibid., WDSCA 014 Korea, 11 June 1946, sec. III, box 249, RG 165.

62. Truman to Patterson, August 12, 1946, ibid., CSA 091 Korea, RG 335; JCS memorandum, August 2, 1946, ibid.; Forrestal to Truman, August 14, 1946, OF 471, Truman papers.

63. Benjamin Weems, "Behind the Korean Elections," *Far Eastern Survey* 17 (June 23, 1948): 143; Lee, *The Politics of Korean Nationalism,* p. 141; Kim, *Divided Korea,* pp. 28–29.

64. *NYT,* June 22, 1946, p. 2; *NYT,* July 2, 1946, p. 17.

65. Henderson, *Korea,* p. 134.

66. Langdon to Byrnes, July 3, 1946, *FRUS 1946,* VIII, 710–711; Kim, *Divided Korea,* pp. 69–70. Hodge placed a young first lieutenant named Leonard Bertsch in charge of creating this centrist political coalition. According to former American military governor Archibald V. Arnold, Bertsch soon was "running furiously in all directions trying to gather up Korean support sufficient to bring about a coalition, a

Korean legislature and death to the Commie." See Archibald V. Arnold to Thayer, August 20, 1946, Alpha Correspondence, Korea Documents 1946, Thayer papers; see also Cumings, *The Origins of the Korean War*, pp. 254–256.

67. Memorandum of conversation, July 16, 1946, *FRUS 1946*, VIII, 715–716; *NYT,* July 10, 1946, p. 5; McCune and Grey, *Korea Today*, p. 6.

68. Langdon to Byrnes, July 28, 1946, *FRUS 1946*, VIII, 720–721; Langdon to Byrnes, August 2, 1946, ibid., 722–723; Joseph E. Jacobs to Marshall, July 31, 1947, Dept. of State Records, 895.00/7–3147.

69. Dean G. Acheson, "Anniversary of Korean Liberation," *DSB* 15 (August 25, 1946): 384. Communist involvement in a counterfeiting operation also hampered party efforts to build popular appeal; see *NYT,* July 30, 1946, p. 7.

70. Archer L. Lerch to Shoemaker, September 16, 1946, Correspondence, General 1946–1947, box 1, Edgar A. J. Johnson papers; *NYT,* August 25, 1946, p. 28; *NYT,* September 15, 1946, p. 7; *NYT,* September 19, 1946, p. 13; McCune and Grey, *Korea Today*, p. 74; Sawyer and Hermes, *Military Advisors in Korea*, pp. 22–26.

71. Langdon to Byrnes, August 23, 1946, *FRUS 1946*, VIII, 726–729; Bunce to Byrnes, August 26, 1946, ibid., 731–733. Bunce already had endorsed Pauley's recommendations late in June 1946 in an article he prepared for publication in *Pacific Affairs*. Bunce charged in his essay, entitled "Can Korea Be Free?" that Hodge's affection for the extreme conservatives and his tolerance of opposition to trusteeship were primarily responsible for American problems in southern Korea. Soviet distrust of the United States therefore was justified and only a reversal of past policy would lead to a settlement. Not surprisingly, Hodge blocked publication of the article. Acheson, on the other hand, was impressed with Bunce's ability and urged Byrnes to recommend his appointment as the first ambassador to Korea. See Langdon to Byrnes, June 13, 1946, Dept. of State Records, 740.00119 Control (Korea)/6–1346; Acheson memorandum, August 9, 1946, ibid., 740.00119 Control (Korea)/8–946.

72. Langdon to Byrnes, October 9, 17, 1946, *FRUS 1946*, VIII, 743–748.

73. Ibid.; Langdon to Byrnes, November 1, 1946, ibid., 757–759.

74. Langdon to Byrnes, November 2, 1946, ibid., 760; Langdon to Byrnes, December 10, 1946, ibid., 779–780.

75. "Proposal for Reopening Joint Commission," *DSB* 16 (January 26, 1947): 168–173; Bunce to Edwin Martin, December 31, 1946, Dept. of State Records, 895.00/12–3146.

76. *NYT,* September 29, 1946, p. 53; *NYT,* September 7, 1946, p. 16; memorandum of conversation, October 9, 1946, *FRUS 1946*, VIII, 741–742. For detailed coverage of revolutionary violence in southern Korea during the autumn of 1946 and the American response, see Cumings, *The Origins of the Korean War*, pp. 351–381.

77. *NYT,* August 4, 1946, p. 5; *NYT,* September 30, 1946, p. 12; Sarafan, "Military Government," p. 352; Henderson, *Korea*, pp. 142–144; Cumings, *The Origins of the Korean War*, pp. 201–205.

78. *NYT,* October 8, 1946, p. 10; *NYT,* October 10, 1946, p. 12; *NYT,* October 11, 1946, p. 10; Langdon to Byrnes, November 1, 1946, *FRUS 1946*, VIII, 754–756; Kim, *Divided Korea*, p. 67.

79. Langdon to Byrnes, November 3, 1946, *FRUS 1946*, VIII, 761–762.

80. *NYT,* October 16, 1946, p. 8.

81. Langdon to Byrnes, November 3, 14, 1946, *FRUS 1946*, VIII, 763, 767; Meade, *American Military Government in Korea*, p. 189.

82. Bunce to Martin, February 2, 1947, Dept. of State Records, 895.00/2–247.

83. Langdon to Byrnes, August 30, 1946, ibid., 711.00/8–3046; Henderson, *Korea*, pp. 153–154; McCune and Grey, *Korea Today*, pp. 78–80; Mitchell, *Korea*, p. 18; Halliday, "The United Nations and Korea," p. 115.

84. Meade, *American Military Government in Korea,* pp. 186–187.

85. Ibid., p. 186; Henderson, *Korea,* p. 153.

86. Langdon to Byrnes, November 24, 1946, *FRUS 1946,* VIII, 770; Langdon to Byrnes, December 5, 27, 1946, ibid., 773–774, 780–781; "Korea: A Chronology of Principal Events, 1945–1950," *World Today* 6 (August 1950): 321.

87. Langdon to Byrnes, November 27, 1946, *FRUS 1946,* VIII, 772; *NYT,* December 13, 1946, p. 12; Berger, *The Korean Knot,* pp. 70–71.

88. *NYT,* December 6, 1946, p. 18; *NYT,* December 11, 1946, p. 18; Louise Yim to Byrnes, November 1946, file 569 (3), Byrnes papers.

89. Langdon to Byrnes, December 12, 1946, *FRUS 1946,* VIII, 775–778.

90. State Department memorandum, December 13, 1946, Dept. of State Records, 740.00119 Control (Korea)/12–1346; MacArthur for Hodge to War for Rhee, December 21, 1946, Dept. of the Army Records, WDSCA 014 Korea, sec. IV, 11 June 1946, box 249, RG 165.

91. Hodge to Byrnes, December 31, 1946, *FRUS 1946,* VIII, 785–786; Bunce to Martin, December 31, 1946, Dept. of State Records, 895.00/12–3146.

92. MacArthur was particularly outspoken in urging the movement of American occupation forces from Korea to Japan. See Major General Lauris Norstad memorandum, November 26, 1946, Dept. of the Army Records, P&O 337 TS, sec. I, cases 2–24, box 73, RG 319.

93. Clark Clifford's "Russian Report," completed in September 1946, provides strong evidence that the administration had not lost confidence in its "get tough" approach. Any sign of vacillation or indecision, Truman's special counsel advised, would only encourage further Soviet aggression and reduce congressional support for a hard-line policy. See George M. Elsey, April 4, 1970, Oral History Interview Transcript, II, p. 263, Truman Library; Hamby, *Beyond the New Deal,* p. 118; Gaddis, *The United States and the Origins of the Cold War,* pp. 319–321, 339–341. The *New York Times* called for a strong and unyielding American stand in Korea, arguing that this Asian nation represented "a testing ground for the kind of settlements we would like to see elsewhere"; See *NYT,* September 1, 1946, IV, p. 6.

94. Susan M. Hartmann, *Truman and the 80th Congress,* p. 48.

CHAPTER 5: *An Avenue for Escape*

1. Joint Staff Planners memorandum, "Estimate of Probable World Political Situation Up to 1956," October 9, 1946, JCS Records, CCS 092, RG 218.

2. On the importance of maintaining credibility in American policy toward Korea, see William Whitney Stueck, Jr., *The Road to Confrontation: American Policy Toward China and Korea, 1947–1950,* pp. 28–30.

3. MacArthur to Eisenhower, October 28, 1946, *FRUS 1946,* VIII, 750–751; Hodge to Patterson, November 5, 1946, John R. Hodge, General Correspondence, 1945–1947, box 20, Patterson papers; Hodge to War, January 17, 1947, Korea–General file, box 1, Johnson papers.

4. War Department memorandum, October 29, 1946, Dept. of the Army Records, P&O 092 TS, sec. V-A, pt. I, case 85, box 31, RG 319; Vincent to Byrnes, October 29, 1946, *FRUS 1946,* VIII, 751–752; Ernest Gross to Borton, January 6, 1947, Dept. of State Records, 740.00119 Control (Korea)/1–647.

5. Norstad memorandum, January 4, 1947, Dept. of the Army Records, P&O 091 Korea, sec. III, cases 16–50, box 87, RG 319; Hodge to War, January 17, 1947, ibid., WDSCA 014 Korea (1 Nov 46–31 Jan 47), sec. V, box 249, RG 165; MacArthur to War, January 22, 1947, ibid.

6. Lincoln to Howard C. Peterson, January 23, 1947, ibid., P&O 092 TS, 1946–1948, case 85, RG 319; Vincent to Marshall, January 27, 1947, *FRUS 1947,* VI, 601–603.

7. Forrestal memorandum, January 29, 1947, in Millis, *The Forrestal Diaries,* pp. 241–242; Memorandum of the Special Inter-Departmental Committee, February 25, 1947, *FRUS 1947,* VI, 609–618.

8. Dallin, *Soviet Russia and the Far East,* pp. 291–292; McCune and Grey, *Korea Today,* p. 173; Kim, *Divided Korea,* pp. 105–106.

9. Langdon to Marshall, January 17, 1947, *FRUS 1947,* VI, 598–600; John R. Hodge, "Activities of Dissident Korean Groups," *DSB* 16 (February 2, 1947): 210; *NYT,* January 23, 1947, p. 15.

10. Langdon to Marshall, January 21, 1947, Dept. of State Records, 740.00119 Control (Korea)/1–2147; Jacobs to Marshall, August 21, 1947, ibid., 740.00119 Control (Korea)/8–1247.

11. *NYT,* January 24, 1947, p. 13; Rhee to MacArthur, January 20, 1947, Private Correspondence, VIP file, folder 43, box 9, RG 10, Douglas MacArthur papers.

12. Hodge to State, January 26, 1947, Dept. of the Army Records, WDSCA 014 Korea (1 Nov 46–31 Jan 47), sec. V, box 249, RG 165.

13. Hodge to MacArthur for War, January 20, 1947, ibid.

14. Memorandum of the Special Inter-Departmental Committee, February 25, 1947, *FRUS 1947,* VI, 609–618.

15. Ibid.; Vincent and Hilldring to Marshall, February 28, 1947, ibid., 618–619.

16. Langdon to Marshall, February 20, 1947, ibid., 607–608; Bunce to Martin, February 24, 1947, Dept. of State Records, 895.00/2–2447.

17. Marshall to MacArthur, February 7, 1947, *FRUS 1947,* VI, 606; Patterson to Truman, February 19, 1947, OF 471, Truman papers.

18. Harry S. Truman, *Memoirs,* vol. II: *Years of Trial and Hope,* p. 323; *NYT,* February 25, 1947, p. 1.

19. Patterson to Hodge, February 24, 1947, John R. Hodge, General Correspondence, 1945–1947, box 20, Patterson papers; U.S. Congress, Senate, Joint Committee on Armed Services and Foreign Relations, *Military Situation in the Far East,* III, p. 2008.

20. *NYT,* February 26, 1947, pp. 2, 24.

21. Jones, *The Fifteen Weeks,* pp. 90–91.

22. John H. Hilldring, "Korea—House Divided," *DSB* 16 (March 23, 1947): 544–547.

23. Harry S. Truman, "Recommendations on Greece and Turkey," *DSB* 16 (March 23, 1947): 536.

24. Leahy, diary entry, March 12, 1947, Diaries 1947, box 5, Leahy papers; Selig Adler, *The Isolationist Impulse: Its Twentieth Century Reaction,* p. 406; W. W. Rostow, *The United States in the World Arena: An Essay in Recent History,* p. 208; Robert H. Ferrell, *George C. Marshall,* pp. 74–75.

25. Gaddis, "Was the Truman Doctrine a Real Turning Point?" p. 389; Gaddis Smith, *Dean Acheson,* p. 47; Hartmann, *Truman and the 80th Congress,* p. 54.

26. Truman, "Recommendations on Greece and Turkey," p. 536.

27. Truman, *Years of Trial and Hope,* p. 106; Leahy, diary entry, February 27, 1947, Diaries 1947, box 5, Leahy papers; Gaddis, *The United States and the Origins of the Cold War,* pp. 317, 352; Eric F. Goldman, *The Crucial Decade—And After: America 1945–1960,* p. 59; Westerfield, *Foreign Policy and Party Politics,* p. 222; Athan Theoharis, *Seeds of Repression: Harry S. Truman and the Origins of Mac-Carthyism,* pp. 56–57.

28. Hartmann, *Truman and the 80th Congress,* p. 106; Gaddis, "Was the Truman Doctrine a Real Turning Point?" p. 398; Norman A. Graebner, "Global Containment: The Truman Years," *Current History* 57 (August 1969): 77; Gabriel A. Almond, *The American People and Foreign Policy,* p. 12; Steel, *Pax Americana,* p. 23. Even Joseph Marion Jones refers to containment as "not an illogical extension of lend lease"; see Jones, *The Fifteen Weeks,* p. 21.

29. SWNCC Ad-hoc Committee Report on Truman Doctrine, February 21, 1947, *FRUS 1947,* VI, 727–730; see also Gaddis, "Containment: A Reassessment," p. 876.

30. *NYT,* March 21, 1947, p. 12; *NYT,* March 25, 1947, p. 8. During his testimony, Acheson indicated the limited nature of the Truman Doctrine when he stressed that the administration did not intend to help every nation. Although the principle was clear, action would depend on each individual case. See Jones, *The Fifteen Weeks,* pp. 191–193; Gaddis, *The United States and the Origins of the Cold War,* p. 352. Yet Truman and his advisors definitely planned to request economic aid for Korea. Thus, John Gaddis is mistaken when he seems to suggest that from the outset Truman had excluded Korea from his strategy for containing Soviet expansion. See Gaddis, "Korea in American Politics, Strategy, and Diplomacy," p. 281.

31. Hodge to Seoul, March 3, 1947, Dept. of the Army Records, P&O 312.1, sec. XII-A. case 467, RG 319; Eversull report, April 1, 1947, ibid., P&O 091 Korea, sec. III, cases 16–50, box 87, RG 319; Sergeant Harry H. Savage to Truman, March 31, 1947, Dept. of State Records, 895.01/3–3147.

32. Seoul to Hodge, March 6, 1947, Dept. of the Army Records, P&O 312.1, sec. XII-A, case 467, RG 319; Orlando Ward to Paul J. Mueller, April 1, 1947, Far East Command Records, Ward memorandum folder, box 1, RG 6, MacArthur papers.

33. Hilldring to Vincent, March 25, 1947, Dept. of State Records, 740.00119 Control (Korea)/3–2547; Vincent to Hilldring, March 27, 1947, ibid., 740.00119 Control (Korea)/3–2747; Acheson to Patterson, March 28, 1947, *FRUS 1947,* VI, 621–623.

34. Patterson to Acheson, April 4, 1947, *FRUS 1947,* VI, 626–627; Forrestal memorandum, April 25, 1947, in Millis, *The Forrestal Diaries,* p. 265; Patterson to Peterson, April 7, 1947, Dept. of the Army Records, P&O 091 Korea, sec. II, case 15, box 87, RG 319.

35. *NYT,* April 1, 1947, p. 17; *NYT,* April 6, 1947, p. 43; *NYT,* April 11, 1947, p. 18.

36. Harry S. Truman, "The President's News Conference of *April* 3, 1947," *Public Papers, Truman,* III, 191; Harry S. Truman, "The President's News Conference of *May* 15, 1947," ibid., 247.

37. Vincent to Acheson, April 8, 1947, Dept. of State Records, 740.00119 Control (Korea)/4–847. Charles M. Dobbs erroneously contends that the crisis in Greece and Turkey "caused President Truman to drop the economic plan for south Korea" and also seek "to reconvene the Joint Commission." See Dobbs, *The Unwanted Symbol,* p. 85.

38. Marshall to Acheson, April 2, 1947, *FRUS 1947,* VI, 624–625; Acheson to Marshall, April 5, 1947, ibid., 628–629.

39. Coral Bell, *Negotiation from Strength: A Study in the Politics of Power,* p. 21; Alexander DeConde, "George C. Marshall (1947–1949)," in Graebner, *An Uncertain Tradition,* p. 252.

40. Dallin, *Soviet Russia and the Far East,* p. 304; Cho, *Korea in World Politics,* p. 158.

41. "U.S. Urges Reconvening of Joint U.S.–U.S.S.R. Commission," *DSB* 16 (April 20, 1947): 716–717; *NYT,* April 13, 1947, p. 47.

42. Molotov to Marshall, April 19, 1947, *FRUS 1947,* VI, 633–634.

43. Marshall to Molotov, May 2, 1947, ibid., 638–639.

44. Molotov to Marshall, May 8, 1947, ibid., 640–642; Marshall to Molotov, May 12, 1947, ibid., 643; Langdon to Marshall, May 11, 1947, ibid., 639–640; see also "Soviet Position on Resumption of Joint Commission on Korea," *DSB* 16 (May 18, 1947): 995–996.

45. Harry S. Truman, "The President's Special Conference with the Association of Radio News Analysts, *May* 13, 1947," *Public Papers, Truman,* III, 240; *New Republic,* May 5, 1947, pp. 25–27; *Time,* May 30, 1947, pp. 30–31; *Life,* May 19, 1947, p. 32. The *New York Times* in particular applauded the administration's decision to ask for economic aid to southern Korea. "The best way to meet Communism North of the Thirty Eighth Parallel," one editorial advised, "is to strengthen democracy south of the border, to show there that the latter is the better way of life, to prove that life, liberty and happiness can be better pursued in a democratic society than a totalitarian one." See *NYT,* April 13, 1947, IV, p. 8; *NYT,* April 23, 1947, p. 24; *NYT,* April 25, 1947, p. 7.

46. Forrestal memorandum, May 7, 1947, in Millis, *The Forrestal Diaries,* p. 273. Some American officials in Seoul were justifiably skeptical about the chances for success at the Joint Commission. After all, the Soviets had not accepted meekly the American position and, under the Marshall–Molotov compromise, the Soviet delegation still would be able to exclude those groups opposed to trusteeship. Perhaps worse, when negotiations resumed the United States would find itself in the awkward position of being obliged to endorse Soviet opposition to consultation with those very groups whose freedom of speech it had demanded during previous sessions. See *NYT,* May 1, 1947, p. 15; *NYT,* May 12, 1947, p. 20; Beloff, *Soviet Foreign Policy in the Far East,* p. 168.

47. Rhee to Truman, March 13, 1947, *FRUS 1947,* VI, 620; Rhee to Truman, March 26, 1947, OF 471, Truman papers. Robert T. Oliver claims that the State Department had decided in December 1946 to sponsor Rhee after finally realizing that Hodge's opposition to Rhee was undemocratic and favorable to Soviet aims in Korea. MacArthur allegedly played a pivotal role in this shift, since he persuaded his good friend John H. Hilldring to speak on behalf of Rhee. See Oliver, *Syngman Rhee,* pp. 232–233. In reality, Truman's diplomatic advisors had not changed their negative attitude toward Rhee. When Rhee requested an interview with Patterson, for example, State Department officials urged rejection of the request, observing that he "was one of the most dangerous figures in Korean political life" and "had done more than any other Korean to make it difficult for the U.S. Army in Korea." See Major General Albert E. Brown to War, March 14, 1947, Dept. of the Army Records, WDSCA 014 Korea (1 Feb to 30 Apr 47), sec. VI, box 250, RG 165; War Department Intelligence Division memorandum, March 26, 1947, ibid., CSA 091 Korea, case 8, RG 335; Penfield memorandum, March 28, 1947, Dept. of State Records, 895.01/3–2847.

48. *NYT,* May 14, 1947, p. 10; *NYT,* May 18, 1947, p. 31; *NYT,* May 17, 1947, p. 7; Hodge to War, May 17, 1947, Dept. of the Army Records, WDSCA 014 Korea (1 May to 30 Jun 47), sec. VII, box 250, RG 165; Langdon to Marshall, May 17, 18, 1947, *FRUS 1947,* VI, 644–645.

49. Langdon to Marshall, May 21, 1947, Dept. of State Records, 740.00119 Control (Korea)/5–2147; *NYT,* May 19, 1947, p. 3.

50. Langdon to Marshall, May 21, 1947, *FRUS 1947,* VI, 646–647; Rhee to MacArthur, May 23, 1947, Private Correspondence, VIP file, folder 43, box 9, RG 10, MacArthur papers.

51. Hilldring to Hodge, May 21, 1947, Dept. of State Records, 740.00119 Control (Korea)/5–2147; Marshall to Langdon, May 23, 1947, *FRUS 1947*, VI, 648–649.

52. Langdon to Marshall, May 23, 24, 30, 1947, *FRUS 1947*, VI, 649–653, 655–657; *NYT,* May 29, 1947, p. 1; *NYT,* May 30, 1947, p. 4.

53. Langdon to Marshall, June 1, 4, 6, 7, 9, 11, 1947, *FRUS 1947*, VI, 658–663, 665–673; *NYT,* June 1, 1947, p. 18; *NYT,* June 2, 1947, p. 3; *NYT,* June 3, 1947, p. 10; *NYT,* June 5, 1947, p. 18; *NYT,* June 8, 1947, p. 27; George C. Marshall, "Hope Expressed for Early Provisional Government for Korea," *DSB* 16 (June 22, 1947): 1249.

54. Lincoln to Norstad, May 12, 1947, Dept. of the Army Records, P&O 092 TS, sec. V-A, pt. I, case 85, box 31, RG 319.

55. JCS to SWNCC, May 5, 1947, *FRUS 1947*, VI, 737–739.

56. Frederick J. Lawton to Truman, June 3, 1947, OF 471, Truman papers; State Department draft speech, June 3, 1947, ibid.; Bell, *Negotiation from Strength*, p. 23.

57. Tang Tsou, *America's Failure in China, 1941–1950*, pp. 446–453.

58. Acheson to Marshall, June 27, 1947, Dept. of State Records, 740.00119 Control (Korea)/6–2747; Acheson to "Jim" [Webb], Aug. ? [*sic*], 1950, Memoranda of Conversations, May–June 1950, box 65, Dean G. Acheson papers; see also Walter Lippman, *The Cold War: A Study in U.S. Foreign Policy*, pp. 45–46.

59. Hodge to Hilldring, May 26, 1947, *FRUS 1947*, VI, 651–652; *NYT,* May 20, 1947, p. 24; *NYT,* May 26, 1947, p. 12; *NYT,* June 7, 1947, p. 7; *Time*, June 2, 1947, p. 34.

60. Jacobs to Marshall, June 20, 1947, *FRUS 1947*, VI, 677; *NYT,* June 14, 1947, p. 8.

61. *NYT,* June 17, 1947, p. 13; *NYT,* June 24, 1947, p. 17; *NYT,* June 25, 1947, p. 20.

62. Hodge to Marshall, June 19, 1947, *FRUS 1947*, VI, 675; Hodge to War, June 27, 1947, Dept. of the Army Records, WDSCA 014 Korea (1 May to 30 Jun 47), sec. VII, box 250, RG 165.

63. Jacobs to Marshall, June 26, 1947, *FRUS 1947*, VI, 679; Hodge to Marshall, June 26, 1947, ibid., 679–680.

64. For a contrary view, see Dobbs, *The Unwanted Symbol*, p. 100.

65. Jacobs to Marshall, July 3, 4, 1947, *FRUS 1947*, VI, 687–689; *NYT,* July 6, 1947, p. 22.

66. Jacobs to Marshall, June 28, 1947, *FRUS 1947*, VI, 680–682; Marshall to Jacobs, July 2, 1947, ibid., 682.

67. Jacobs to Marshall, July 7, 1947, ibid., 690–691; "Joseph E. Jacobs Appointed Political Adviser to USAF in Korea," *DSB* 16 (June 15, 1947): 1178.

68. Jacobs to Marshall, July 8, 1947, ibid., 693–695; *NYT,* July 6, 1947, p. 22.

69. Hodge to Marshall, July 10, 1947, *FRUS 1947*, VI, 697–700; *NYT,* July 12, 1947, p. 4.

70. Hodge to Marshall, July 17, 1947, *FRUS 1947*, VI, 708–709; Jacobs to Marshall, July 19, 1947, ibid., 709–710; Jacobs to Marshall, July 31, 1947, Dept. of State Records, 895.00/7–3147; Jacobs to Marshall, August 6, 1947, ibid., 895.00/8–647; *NYT,* July 20, 1947, p. 34; *NYT,* July 27, 1947, p. 7; *The Nation*, September 6, 1947, pp. 228–229.

71. Jacobs to Marshall, June 20, 1947, *FRUS 1947*, VI, 676–677; Jacobs to Marshall, July 21, 1947, ibid., 710–711; Kim, *Divided Korea*, pp. 78–79.

72. Marshall to Jacobs, July 14, 1947, *FRUS 1947*, VI, 701–703; Borton to Jacobs, July 25, 1947, Dept. of State Records, 740.00119 Control (Korea)/7–2547.

73. Borton memorandum, July 24, 1947, Dept. of State Records, 895.00/7–2447;

Hodge to War, July 27, 1947, ibid., 740.00119 Control (Korea)/7–2747; Hodge to War, July 27, 1947, JCS Records, CCS 383.21 Korea (3–19–45), sec. XI, RG 218.

74. Jacobs to Marshall, July 30, 1947, *FRUS 1947*, VI, 736; Jacobs to Marshall, August 2, 1947, ibid., 737; *NYT,* August 8, 1947, p. 8; *Time*, August 4, 1947, p. 16. For Hodge, further negotiations at the Joint Commission would be "absurd." He therefore advised Washington to sponsor the extreme right openly and approve a new campaign to "stamp out communism . . . even at the cost of bloodshed." See War Department summary, August 1, 1947, Dept. of the Army Records, P&O 092 Korea TS, sec. V-A, pt. I, case 85, box 31, RG 319; Hodge to Marshall, August 6, 7, 1947, *FRUS 1947*, VI, 744–745.

75. John M. Allison memorandum, July 29, 1947, *FRUS 1947*, VI, 734–735.

76. Ibid.; Ad-hoc Committee to SWNCC, August 4, 1947, ibid., 735–741.

77. Hilldring memorandum, August 6, 1947, ibid., 742; Hilldring to Lovett, August 8, 1947, Dept. of State Records, 895.00/8–847; "Statement by Chief Commissioner of the American Delegation," *DSB* 17 (August 10, 1947): 296–297.

78. Marshall to Smith, August 11, 1947, *FRUS 1947*, VI, 748–749; "U.S. Requests Report from Joint Commission," *DSB* 17 (August 24, 1947): 398–399.

79. Robert A. Lovett to Jacobs, August 15, 1947, *FRUS 1947*, VI, 754; "Denial of Change of Policy Toward Korea," *DSB* 17 (August 24, 1947): 399.

80. Jacobs to Marshall, August 14, 17, 21, 1947, *FRUS 1947*, VI, 753–755, 760–761; Hodge to War, August 25, 1947, JCS Records, CCS 383.21 Korea (3–19–45), sec. XI, RG 218.

81. Jacobs to Marshall, August 14, 19, 1947, *FRUS 1947*, VI, 753–754, 756–757; Hodge to Marshall, August 20, 1947, ibid., 757–760.

82. Lovett to Jacobs, August 23, 1947, ibid., 764–765; "Letter from the Soviet Minister of Foreign Affairs to the Secretary of State," *DSB* 17 (September 7, 1947): 475.

83. Jacobs to Marshall, August 20, 22, 25, 26, 1947, *FRUS 1947*, VI, 760, 762–763, 766–769.

84. Allison to Lovett, August 26, 1947, Dept. of State Records, 740.00119 Control (Korea)/8–2647; Lovett to Smith, August 21, 1947, *FRUS 1947*, VI, 771–774; "Letter from the Acting Secretary of State to the Soviet Foreign Minister," *DSB* 17 (September 7, 1947): 473–475.

85. Smith to Marshall, August 28, 1947, *FRUS 1947*, VI, 775–776; Lovett to Jacobs, September 4, 1947, ibid., 779.

86. Molotov to Marshall, September 4, 1947, ibid., 779–781; "Korean Question to Be Referred to General Assembly," *DSB* 17 (September 28, 1947): 623–624.

87. Truman, *Years of Trial and Hope*, pp. 324–325; Acheson comments, February 13, 1954, Princeton Seminars Transcript, reel 1, tape 1, pp. 7–9, Acheson papers.

88. Jacobs to Marshall, September 8, 1947, *FRUS 1947*, VI, 763; see also *NYT,* September 10, 1947, p. 26.

89. Kim, *Divided Korea*, pp. 78–79; Henderson, *Korea*, pp. 135–136.

90. Denis Stairs, *The Diplomacy of Constraint: Canada, the Korean War, and the United States*, pp. 5–6; Cho, *Korea in World Politics*, p. 205; Tsou, *America's Failure in China*, p. 557; Goodrich, *Korea*, pp. 37–41; Henderson, *Korea*, pp. 148–150.

91. Dean Rusk to Gross, May 9, 1947, Dept. of State Records, 895.00/5–947; Reitzel, Kaplan, and Coblenz, *United States Foreign Policy*, pp. 176–177; Halliday, "The United Nations and Korea," p. 119; Stueck, *The Road to Confrontation*, pp. 89–90.

92. Gaddis, "Korea in American Politics, Strategy, and Diplomacy," pp. 282–283; Stairs, *The Diplomacy of Constraint*, p. 17; Vinacke, *The United States and the Far East*, p. 65.

CHAPTER 6: *A House Divided*

1. Rusk to Gross, May 9, 1947, Dept. of State Records, 895.00/5–947; Reitzel, Kaplan, and Coblenz, *United States Foreign Policy,* pp. 176–177.

2. Robert G. Wesson, "The United Nations in the World Outlook of the Soviet Union and the United States," in Alvin Z. Rubinstein and George Ginsburgs, eds., *Soviet and American Policies in the United Nations,* pp. 6–7; Stueck, *The Road to Confrontation,* pp. 88–89.

3. Lincoln Bloomfield, *The United Nations and U.S. Foreign Policy: A New Look at the National Interest,* p. 182; Halliday, "The United Nations and Korea," pp. 120–121; Goodrich, *Korea,* pp. 38–39.

4. Lovett to Molotov, September 16, 1947, *FRUS 1947,* VI, 790; George C. Marshall, "A Program for a More Effective United Nations," *DSB* 17 (September 28, 1947): 619–620; *NYT,* September 18, 1947, pp. 8, 24.

5. Lovett to Warren R. Austin, September 18, 1947, *FRUS 1947,* VI, 794–795.

6. Marshall memorandum, July 8, 1947, Confidential, State Department, Correspondence, 1946–1947, White House Central Files, folder 9, box 34, Truman papers; "Lt. Gen. A. C. Wedemeyer Heads Mission to Study Conditions in China and Korea," *DSB* 17 (July 20, 1947): 149.

7. W. Walton Butterworth to Marshall, January 6, 1947, *FRUS 1947,* VII, 10; JCS to SWNCC, June 9, 1947, ibid., 839–846; Clubb memorandum, August 3, 1947, ibid., 705; Wedemeyer to Marshall, August 8, 1947, ibid., 713; A. Bland Calder to Wedemeyer, August 13, 1947, ibid., 722.

8. Wedemeyer to J. Leighton Stuart, September 3, 1947, *FRUS 1947,* VI, 765; U.S. Congress, Senate, Committee on Armed Services, *Report to the President, September 1947,* By Lt. Gen. A. C. Wedemeyer, pp. 1–23.

9. Wedemeyer Report, September 19, 1947, *FRUS 1947,* VI, 796–803.

10. Jacobs to Marshall, September 19, 1947, ibid., 804–807.

11. Francis B. Stevens memorandum, September 9, 1947, ibid., 784–785.

12. Ibid.; SWNCC to JCS, September 15, 1947, Korean Documents, box 10, David Lloyd papers.

13. Forrestal to Marshall, September 26, 1947, Korean Documents, box 10, Lloyd papers; JCS to SWNCC, September 26, 1947, *FRUS 1947,* VI, 817–818.

14. Kennan to Butterworth, September 24, 1947, *FRUS 1947,* VI, 814; McClintock to Rusk, September 9, 1947, Dept. of State Records, 895.00/9–1647; "Chronology of Action by the National Security Council and the NSC Staff on U.S. Policy Toward Korea" (Korea–Classified Background Materials), Miscellaneous, box 77, George M. Elsey papers; Leahy to Truman, n.d. (China–Foreign 1948), PSF 32, Truman papers. According to Charles M. Dobbs, Wedemeyer's "visit was for naught because by the time Wedemeyer could submit his report, the government in Washington had decided to take the Korean issue to the United Nations"; see Dobbs, *The Unwanted Symbol,* p. 208. In fact, the administration did subsequently follow Wedemeyer's recommendations. Had it not been for congressional opposition, the provisions of the Wedemeyer report would have experienced a more rapid and complete implementation. See memorandum, May 2, 1951, OF: Wedemeyer Mission, Truman papers.

15. Dupuy to Norstad, October 2, 1947, Dept. of the Army Records, P&O 091 Korea, case 106, box 89, RG 319; Economic Report on Korea, ibid.; Army Department memorandum, September 23, 1947, ibid.

16. Jacobs to Marshall, September 26, 1947, *FRUS 1947,* VI, 816–817; *NYT,* September 27, 1947, p. 1.

17. Bunce to Martin, September 28, 1947, Dept. of State Records, 740.00119

Control (Korea)/9–2847; State Department memorandum, September 24, 1947, ibid., 740.00119 Control (Korea)/9–2447; Cabinet Meeting, September 29, 1947, in Millis, *The Forrestal Diaries,* pp. 321–322; Butterworth to Lovett, October 1, 1947, *FRUS 1947,* VI, 820; Acheson testimony, *Military Situation in the Far East,* p. 2010.

18. Molotov to Marshall, October 10, 1947, *FRUS 1947,* VI, 827–828; Lovett to Smith, October 17, 1947, ibid., 836–837.

19. Austin to Lie, October 17, 1947, ibid., 832–835; Warren R. Austin, "The Problem of the Independence of Korea," *DSB* 17 (October 26, 1947): 820–822; *NYT,* October 18, 1947, p. 14.

20. Jacobs to Marshall, October 18, 20, 1947, *FRUS 1947,* VI, 837, 842–843; *NYT,* October 21, 1947, p. 11.

21. Austin to Marshall, October 29, 1947, *FRUS 1947,* VI, 849.

22. Jacobs to Marshall, August 17, 23, 1947, ibid., 755, 763; Jacobs to Marshall, September 12, 30, 1947, ibid., 787–788, 819; Jacobs to Lovett, September 9, 1947, Dept. of State Records, 895.00/9–947; *NYT,* September 11, 1947, p. 15.

23. Jacobs to Marshall, August 7, 1947, ibid., 745–746; Jacobs to Marshall, September 20, 1947, ibid., 809; Jacobs to Marshall, October 8, 9, 1947, ibid., 824–827; *NYT,* October 8, 1947, p. 11.

24. Rhee to Korean Commission, October 18, 1947, *FRUS 1947,* VI, 838–839; Jacobs to Marshall, October 10, 29, 1947, ibid., 829–830, 848–849.

25. Benjamin F. Taylor memorandum, May 2, 1947, Dept. of the Army Records, P&O 091 Korea, sec. V, case 65, box 88, RG 319; Lincoln memorandum, May 20, 1947, ibid., P&O 091 Korea, sec. I, cases 1–14, box 87, RG 319; Dupuy memorandum, May 9, 1947, ibid., P&O 092 TS, sec. V-A, pt. I, case 85 only, box 31, RG 319.

26. Lincoln memorandum, May 7, 1947, ibid., P&O 091 Korea, sec. I, cases 1–14, box 87, RG 319; Dupuy memorandum, October 15, 1947, ibid., P&O 091 Korea, sec. III, cases 16–50, box 87, RG 319.

27. S. L. Scott memorandum, October 16, 1947, ibid., P&O 091 Korea TS, sec. I, pt. I, box 20, RG 319; William H. Draper to Hodge, October 26, 1947, ibid., P&O 091 Korea, sec. II, pt. I, case 2 only, box 87, RG 319.

28. Policy Planning Staff report, November 6, 1947, *FRUS 1947,* I, 770–777; editor's note, ibid.

29. Wedemeyer to MacArthur and Hodge, November 10, 1947, *FRUS 1947,* VI, 856; Hodge to JCS, November 21, 1947, Dept. of the Army Records, P&O 091 Korea TS, FW 38, RG 319.

30. R. F. Seedlock memorandum, November 28, 1947, Dept. of the Army Records, P&O 091 Korea TS, sec. I, case 1, box 20, RG 319.

31. Jacobs to Marshall, October 21, 1947, Dept. of State Records, 740.00119 Control (Korea)/10–2147; Jacobs to Marshall, October 24, 1947, ibid., 895.00/10–2447; Jacobs to Marshall, October 10, 1947, *FRUS 1947,* VI, 830; Hodge to JCS, November 3, 1947, ibid., 852–853.

32. Austin to Marshall, November 14, 1947, *FRUS 1947,* VI, 857–859; Seedlock memorandum, November 4, 1947, Dept. of the Army Records, P&O 091 Korea, sec. III, cases 16–50, box 87, RG 319. Before it approved the American-sponsored resolution, the General Assembly rejected both a Soviet proposal for mutual withdrawal and one to permit the appearance of representatives from northern Korea before the United Nations. See *NYT,* October 30, 1947, p. 24; "Korea: A Chronology," p. 322.

33. *NYT,* November 5, 1947, p. 26; Leon Gordenker, *The United Nations and the Peaceful Unification of Korea: The Politics of Field Operations 1947–1950,* p. 31.

34. Marshall to Jacobs, November 17, 1947, *FRUS 1947,* VI, 860–861; Jacobs to Marshall, November 19, 1947, ibid., 861–862.

35. Gordenker, *The United Nations and the Peaceful Unification of Korea*, p. 21; Tompkins, *American-Russian Relations in the Far East*, pp. 330–331.

36. Memorandum of conversation, October 28, 1947, *FRUS 1947*, VI, 552–553.

37. Langdon to Marshall, November 29, 1947, ibid., 865–866; Langdon to Marshall, December 7, 1947, ibid., 871–872; Jacobs to Marshall, November 17, 19, 1947, ibid., 859–860, 863–864; Hodge to Marshall, December 2, 1947, ibid., 866–867; Jacobs to Marshall, November 11, 1947, Dept. of State Records, 895.01/11–1147; *NYT,* November 29, 1947, p. 8.

38. Eisenhower to Marshall, December 3, 1947, *FRUS 1947*, VI, 868; Charles E. Saltzman to Marshall, December 4, 1947, ibid., 869–870; Marshall to Eisenhower, December 4, 1947, ibid., 870.

39. Taylor memorandum, December 8, 1947, Dept. of the Army Records, P&O 091 Korea TS, sec. V, case 31, box 22, RG 319.

40. *NYT,* December 7, 1947, p. 18; Penfield to Hodge, December 11, 1947, Dept. of State Records, 895.00/12–1147; Lovett to Langdon, December 11, 1947, *FRUS 1947*, VI, 876–877.

41. Langdon to Lovett, December 13, 1947, *FRUS 1947*, VI, 877–878; Langdon to Lovett, December 19, 1947, Dept. of State Records, 895.00/12–1947.

42. Langdon to Lovett, December 6, 1947, *FRUS 1947*, VI, 871; Lovett to Langdon, December 15, 1947, ibid., 878; Whitman to Bunce, December 12, 1947, Dept. of State Records, 895.00/12–1247.

43. Stairs, *The Diplomacy of Constraint*, p. 13; Ray Atherton to Marshall, December 27, 1947, *FRUS 1947*, VI, 880–882; see also Dobbs, *The Unwanted Symbol*, pp. 120–128.

44. Samuel Reber memorandum, December 30, 1947, *FRUS 1947*, VI, 886–887; Lovett to MacKenzie King, December 30, 1947, ibid., 883–886.

45. Lovett memorandum, January 3, 1948, *FRUS 1948*, VI, 1079–1081.

46. Truman to King, January 5, 1948, ibid., 1081–1083.

47. Edward T. Wailes to Lovett, January 9, 1948, ibid., 1084; King to Truman, January 8, 1948, Confidential, State Department, Documents, 1947–1948, White House Central Files, folder 11, box 35, Truman papers; Stairs, *The Diplomacy of Constraint*, pp. 16–17.

48. Truman to King, January 24, 1948, *FRUS 1948*, VI, 1086–1087.

49. *NYT,* January 9, 1948, pp. 1, 12; *NYT,* January 10, 1948, pp. 18, 22.

50. Gordenker, *The United Nations and the Peaceful Unification of Korea*, pp. 50–52.

51. *NYT,* January 10, 1948, p. 14; Marshall to Langdon, January 6, 1948, *FRUS 1948*, VI, 1083.

52. *NYT,* January 13, 1948, p. 2; *NYT,* January 14, 1948, p. 10; *NYT,* January 18, 1948, IV, p. 10.

53. Jacobs to Marshall, January 24, 1948, *FRUS 1948*, VI, 1085–1086; *NYT,* January 24, 1948, p. 14; Dallin, *Soviet Russia and the Far East*, p. 309.

54. *NYT,* January 28, 1948, p. 2; Jacobs to Marshall, January 30, 1948, *FRUS 1948*, VI, 1088–1089.

55. Langdon to Marshall, December 30, 1947, Dept. of State Records, 895.01/12–3047. The extreme right quickly resorted to political intimidation to undermine Kim's efforts at building a moderate coalition. See Langdon to Marshall, January 3, 1948, ibid., 895.00/1–348. By early 1948, Hodge had cabled Washington that Rhee and his followers had brought southern Korea to the brink of total anarchy through the use of terrorism, beatings, extortion, and other tactics "comparable to those of Al Capone in Chicago." See Hodge to JCS, January 3, 1948, ibid., 895.00/1–348.

56. Kim Ku may have believed sincerely that separate elections would harden the line partitioning Korea. It would seem more likely, however, that the rightist leader had come to recognize that Rhee, after sweeping the elections, would refuse to share power with his former ally. See Jacobs to Marshall, February 10, 1948, *FRUS 1948,* VI, 1101–1103; Kim, *Divided Korea,* pp. 79–80.

57. Jacobs to Marshall, January 29, 1948, *FRUS 1948,* VI, 1087–1088; Jacobs to Marshall, February 2, 1948, ibid., 1089–1091.

58. *NYT,* February 8, 1948, p. 1; *NYT,* February 11, 1948, p. 10; Jacobs to Marshall, February 8, 1948, *FRUS 1948,* VI, 1095–1097.

59. Gordenker, *The United Nations and the Peaceful Unification of Korea,* p. 66; Jacobs to Marshall, February 9, 1948, Dept. of State Records, 895.00/2–948; Jacobs to Marshall, February 10, 1948, *FRUS 1948,* VI, 1099–1101.

60. Sawyer and Hermes, *Military Advisors in Korea,* pp. 28–29; White House Meeting, February 18, 1948, in Millis, *The Forrestal Diaries,* p. 375.

61. Jacobs to Marshall, January 31, 1948, *FRUS 1948,* VI, 1088–1089; *NYT,* February 14, 1948, p. 10.

62. Jacobs to Marshall, February 24, 1948, *FRUS 1948,* VI, 1129–1131; *Time,* February 23, 1948, p. 34; Dallin, *Soviet Russia and the Far East,* p. 310; Kim, *Divided Korea,* pp. 105–106.

63. Leahy, diary entry, February 16, 1948, Diaries 1948–1950, box 6, Leahy papers.

64. Jacobs to Marshall, February 5, 6, 13, 1948, *FRUS 1948,* VI, 1093–1095, 1109; Goodrich, *Korea,* p. 50.

65. Jacobs to Marshall, February 12, 1948, *FRUS 1948,* VI, 1105–1109; Hodge to Marshall, February 14, 1948, ibid., 1110–1113; Langdon to Marshall, February 17, 1948, ibid., 1114–1116.

66. *NYT,* February 8, 1948, IV, p. 10; *NYT,* February 10, 1948, p. 17; *NYT,* February 13, 1948, p. 20.

67. Marshall to certain diplomatic offices, February 9, 1948, *FRUS 1948,* VI, 1098–1099; Robert L. Butler to Marshall, February 12, 1948, ibid., 1104; Waldemar J. Gallman to Marshall, February 12, 1948, ibid., 1105.

68. Marshall to Austin, February 18, 1948, ibid., 1116–1117; *NYT,* February 20, 1948, p. 1.

69. Marshall to Langdon, February 20, 1948, *FRUS 1948,* VI, 1124; Gordenker, *The United Nations and the Peaceful Unification of Korea,* p. 70.

70. Marshall to London, February 21, 1948, *FRUS 1948,* VI, 1124–1125; London to Marshall, February 23, 1948, ibid., 1125n.; Marshall to New Delhi, February 24, 1948, ibid., 1127–1128; New Delhi to Marshall, February 26, 1948, ibid., 1128n.

71. Austin to Marshall, February 24, 1948, ibid., 1128–1129; *NYT,* February 25, 1948, p. 8. Abstaining were Syria, Colombia, Venezuela, Panama, Egypt, Iraq, Afghanistan, Saudi Arabia, Norway, Denmark, and Sweden. See "Need for Elections in Korea," *DSB* 18 (March 7, 1948): 297–298; *NYT,* March 27, 1948, p. 1.

72. Gordenker, *The United Nations and the Peaceful Unification of Korea,* pp. 71–75; *NYT,* February 27, 1948, p. 20.

73. Langdon to Marshall, February 20, 1948, *FRUS 1948,* VI, 1121–1122; *NYT,* March 3, 1948, p. 13; Stairs, *The Diplomacy of Constraint,* p. 22.

74. *NYT,* March 2, 1948, p. 13; "Korean Elections to Be Held on May 9," *DSB* 18 (March 14, 1948): 344–345.

75. *NYT,* March 9, 1948, p. 12; *NYT,* March 10, 1948, p. 5; Langdon to Marshall, March 10, 11, 1948, *FRUS 1948,* VI, 1146–1149; Gordenker, *The United Nations and the Peaceful Unification of Korea,* p. 79.

76. Langdon to Marshall, March 12, 1948, *FRUS 1948*, VI, 1150–1155; Gordenker, *The United Nations and the Peaceful Unification of Korea*, pp. 83–85; *NYT*, March 13, 1948, p. 8.

77. Langdon to Marshall, March 9, 1948, Dept. of State Records, 895.00/3–948; Marshall to Langdon, March 11, 1948, ibid., 895.00/3–1148.

78. Jacobs to Marshall, March 24, 1948, ibid., 501.BB Korea/3–2448; Jacobs to Marshall, April 4, 1948, ibid., 895.00/4–448; *NYT*, April 4, 1948, p. 11.

79. Langdon to Marshall, March 6, 12, 17, 25, 1948, *FRUS 1948*, VI, 1142–1143, 1151, 1155–1158.

80. Jacobs to Marshall, April 8, 1948, Dept. of State Records, 895.00/4–848; Jacobs to Marshall, April 14, 1948, ibid., 740.00119 Control (Korea)/4–1448.

81. *NYT*, April 14, 1948, p. 8; Jacobs to Marshall, April 13, 1948, Dept. of State Records, 895.00/4–1348; James L. Stewart to Hodge, April 22, 1948, ibid., 895.00/4–2248.

82. Jacobs to Marshall, March 24, 1948, *FRUS 1948*, VI, 1158–1159; *NYT*, April 19, 1948, p. 3. Hodge anticipated that the Soviets would attempt to use the south's dependence on electricity from the north as a diplomatic weapon. Even so, he urged Washington to delay complete payment in electrical equipment, arguing that Moscow would continue to supply electricity to the south as long as it expected to receive the coveted materials in return. While the Army Department approved this proposal, it also pressed the Navy Department to provide power barges for southern Korea in case of an emergency. See Dupuy to Norstad, October 2, 1947, Dept. of the Army Records, P&O 091 Korea, sec. III, case 106, box 89, RG 319; Wedemeyer memorandum, November 26, 1947, ibid., P&O 091 Korea, sec. IV, cases 50–65, box 87, RG 319.

83. Jacobs to Marshall, March 29, 1948, *FRUS 1948*, VI, 1162–1163; Jacobs to Marshall, April 5, 1948, ibid., 1169–1170; *NYT*, March 27, 1948, p. 1; *Time*, April 5, 1948, p. 29.

84. Jacobs to Marshall, April 30, 1948, *FRUS 1948*, VI, 1180; *NYT*, April 21, 1948, p. 14; *NYT*, April 22, 1948, p. 2.

85. Jacobs to Marshall, April 30, 1948, *FRUS 1948*, VI, 1184–1186; Jacobs to Marshall, May 3, 1948, ibid., 1188–1191; *NYT*, May 1, 1948, p. 1; *NYT*, May 6, 1948, p. 15; Gordenker, *The United Nations and the Peaceful Unification of Korea*, p. 311; Paige, "Korea," p. 225.

86. Jacobs to Marshall, May 7, 1948, Dept. of State Records, 895.00/5–748; *Time*, May 17, 1948, p. 33; Dept. of State, *Korea 1945 to 1948*, p. 15; Henderson, *Korea*, p. 157; Dallin, *Soviet Russia and the Far East*, pp. 311–312; McCune and Grey, *Korea Today*, pp. 227–228.

87. Jacobs to Marshall, April 27, 1948, Dept. of State Records, 895.00/4–2748; *NYT*, April 28, 1948, p. 17; Henderson, *Korea*, p. 156; Stairs, *The Diplomacy of Constraint*, p. 25.

88. McCune and Grey, *Korea Today*, pp. 228–230; Gordenker, *The United Nations and the Peaceful Unification of Korea*, pp. 92–93.

89. Jacobs to Marshall, April 27, 1948, Dept. of State Records, 895.00/4–2748; C. Clyde Mitchell, "Land Reform in South Korea," *Pacific Affairs* 22 (June 1949): 151; W. D. Reeve, *The Republic of Korea: A Political and Economic Study*, p. 31; Weems, "Behind the Korean Elections," p. 142.

90. Gordenker, *The United Nations and the Peaceful Unification of Korea*, p. 98; Allen, *Korea's Syngman Rhee*, p. 94.

91. Jacobs to Marshall, April 27, 28, 1948, *FRUS 1948*, VI, 1182–1184; "U.N. Temporary Commission to Observe Elections in South Korea," *DSB* 18 (May 30,

1948): 700; Gordenker, *The United Nations and the Peaceful Unification of Korea,* p. 105.

92. Gordenker, *The United Nations and the Peaceful Unification of Korea,* pp. 88, 95–96; see also Hodge to Marshall, April 8, 1948, Dept. of State Records, 895.00/4-848.

93. Jacobs to Marshall, May 12, 1948, Dept. of State Records, 895.00/5-1248; *NYT,* May 11, 1948, p. 11; *NYT,* May 22, 1948, p. 14; Yoo, *The Korean War and the United Nations,* p. 19; Caldwell, *The Korea Story,* p. 37.

94. Jacobs to Marshall, May 10, 13, 1948, *FRUS 1948,* VI, 1192, 1195–1197; Jacobs to Marshall, May 12, 1948, Dept. of State Records, 895.00/5-1248; *NYT,* May 10, 1948, p. 1; Henderson, *Korea,* pp. 217–218; Kim, *Divided Korea,* p. 81; McCune and Grey, *Korea Today,* p. 229. Incredibly, Soon-sung Cho points to the South Korean elections as a clear indication of political maturity; see Cho, *Korea in World Politics,* p. 208.

95. Yong-jeung Kim, "The Cold War: The Korean Elections," *Far Eastern Survey* 17 (May 5, 1948): 101–102; see also *U.S. News,* May 7, 1948, p. 19; *NYT,* May 3, 1948, p. 20.

96. George C. Marshall, "Korean People Congratulated on Election," *DSB* 18 (May 30, 1948): 700; see also *NYT,* May 10, 1948, p. 20.

97. Gilchrist memorandum, May 19, 1948, Dept. of the Army Records, P&O 091 Korea TS, sec. I, case 1, pt. III-A, box 20, RG 319; Lawson memorandum, May 25, 1948, ibid.; *NYT,* May 21, 1948, p. 7.

98. Dept. of State, *North Korea,* p. 11; see also *Commonweal,* February 13, 1948, p. 447; Kolko, *The Politics of War,* p. 604.

CHAPTER 7: *The Dilemma of Withdrawal*

1. Cho, *Korea in World Politics,* p. 244; Ferrell, *George C. Marshall,* pp. 248–249; Goodrich, *Korea,* pp. 70, 95; Kim, *Divided Korea,* pp. 74–75; Henderson, *Korea,* pp. 149–150; Gordenker, *The United Nations and the Peaceful Unification of Korea,* p. 5.

2. Russell D. Buhite, " 'Major Interests': American Policy Toward China, Taiwan, and Korea, 1945–1950," *Pacific Historical Review* 47 (August 1978): 444–446; Gaddis, "Korea in American Politics, Strategy, and Diplomacy," p. 283.

3. Schuyler to Blum, January 2, 1948, JCS Records, CCS 383.21 Korea (3–19–45), sec. XIV, RG 218; "Chronology of Action by the National Security Council," Elsey papers.

4. Memorandum for Wedemeyer, November 24, 1947, Dept. of the Army Records, P&O 091 Korea TS, sec. III, cases 3–15, RG 319; Schuyler to Arnold, December 30, 1947, ibid., P&O 091 Korea, sec. V, RG 319.

5. Seedlock memorandum, January 31, 1948, ibid., P&O 091 Korea TS, sec. III, cases 3–15, RG 319; Maddocks memorandum, February 9, 1948, ibid., CSA 091 Korea TS, RG 335.

6. Butterworth to Marshall, March 4, 1948, *FRUS 1948,* VI, 1137–1139; Allison memorandum, March 5, 1948, ibid., 1139–1141; see also Niles Bond, December 28, 1973, Oral History Interview Transcript, p. 34, Truman Library; Allison, *Ambassador from the Prairie,* pp. 120–121.

7. Cabinet Meeting notes, March 12, 1948, Notes on Cabinet Meetings (January 9–December 31, 1948), Post Presidential File (Set I), box 1, Matthew J. Connelly papers.

8. Biddle to Wedemeyer, March 5, 1948, Dept. of the Army Records, P&O 091 Korea TS, sec. III, cases 3–15, box 21, RG 319; Herbert Druks, *Harry S. Truman and the Russians 1945–1953*, p. 226.

9. Warner R. Schilling, "The Politics of National Defense: Fiscal 1950," in Warner R. Schilling, Paul Y. Hammond, and Glenn H. Snyder, eds., *Strategy, Politics and Defense Budgets*, p. 41.

10. Army to MacArthur, March 18, 1948, Dept. of the Army Records, P&O 091 Korea TS, sec. I, case 1, box 20, RG 319; "Chronology of Action by the National Security Council," Elsey papers.

11. Sidney Souers to Truman, April 2, 1948, *FRUS 1948*, VI, 1163–1169. Secretary of the Army Kenneth C. Royall was responsible for adding the qualifying phrase "so far as practicable." Also, the JCS doubted whether there was enough time to build a viable South Korean constabulary army. See "Chronology of Action by the National Security Council," Elsey papers.

12. Ibid.; Leahy, diary entry, January 8, 1948, Diaries 1948–1950, box 6, Leahy papers.

13. Percy H. Johnston, Paul G. Hoffman, Robert F. Loree, and Sidney H. Scheuer, U.S. Army Committee Report, April 26, 1948, *Economic Position and Prospects of Japan and Korea and Measures Required to Improve Them*, U.S. Department of the Army.

14. Seedlock memorandum, April 16, 1948, Dept. of the Army Records, P&O 091 Korea TS, sec. IV, cases 16–30, box 22, RG 319; Lovett to Jacobs, April 16, 1948, *FRUS 1948*, VI, 1179–1180.

15. Wedemeyer to J. Lawton Collins, March 5, 1948, Dept. of the Army Records, P&O 091 Korea TS, sec. I, case 1 only, pt. II–A, RG 319; Timberman to Collins, March 11, 1948, ibid.; Army to MacArthur and Hodge, March 18, 1948, ibid., pt. I; Hodge to MacArthur, April 19, 1948, ibid., pt. II–B.

16. U.S. Dept. of Commerce, "Economic Review of the Republic of Korea," *International Reference Service* 6 (June 1949): 1–5; *U.S. News*, February 6, 1948, p. 67; Mitchell, *Korea*, pp. 24–27.

17. Dept. of Commerce, "Economic Conditions in South Korea, 1947," p. 1; Weems, "Behind the Korean Elections," p. 145; Cho, *Korea in World Politics*, p. 235; Mitchell, "Land Reform in South Korea," p. 144; McCune and Grey, *Korea Today*, p. 133.

18. Jacobs to Marshall, May 22, 1948, *FRUS 1948*, VI, 1203–1204; *NYT*, May 14, 1948, p. 1; *NYT*, June 16, 1948, p. 17; *NYT*, June 18, 1948, p. 51; "U.S. Urges Soviet Command to Resume Electric Power to South Korea," *DSB* 19 (July 11, 1948): 50–51.

19. Jacobs to Marshall, June 2, 1948, *FRUS 1948*, VI, 1214–1215; Marshall to Smith, June 24, 1948, ibid., 1127–1129; Smith to Marshall, July 21, 1948, ibid., 1252–1253.

20. Bunce to Marshall, July 22, 1948, ibid., 1254; Jacobs to Marshall, August 7, 1948, ibid., 1268; "U.S. Proposals Regarding Resumption of Delivery of Electric Power to South Korea," *DSB* 19 (August 1, 1948): 147–148.

21. Bunce to Marshall, May 15, 1948, *FRUS 1948*, VI, 1198–1199; *NYT*, May 17, 1948, p. 18; *Time*, May 17, 1948, p. 33; Dept. of State, *Korea 1945 to 1948*, pp. 35–36; Paige, "Korea," p. 225. While the administration fully expected the North Korean regime to shut off electric power, it also recognized that a prolonged reliance on emergency power barges for electricity "would be neither economical nor practical for the Korean economy." See Wedemeyer memorandum, November 26, 1947, Dept. of the Army Records, P&O 091 Korea, sec. IV, cases 50–65, box 87, RG 319; Wedemeyer memorandum, May 4, 1948, ibid.

22. *NYT,* May 29, 1948, p. 4; Jacobs to Marshall, May 19, 1948, *FRUS 1948,* VI, 1201–1202.

23. John R. Hodge, "Suggestions to Korean Assembly on Formation of New Government," *DSB* 18 (June 20, 1948): 800.

24. Lovett to Draper, May 19, 1948, *FRUS 1948,* VI, 1200–1201.

25. William J. Sebald to Benninghoff, May 10, 1948, Dept. of State Records, 501.BB Korea/5–1048; Jacobs to Marshall, June 17, 1948, ibid., 895.00/6–1748; "Temporary Commission Resolution," *DSB* 18 (June 20, 1948): 800.

26. Gordenker, *The United Nations and the Peaceful Unification of Korea,* pp. 128–129, 139–140; Marshall to Jacobs, June 4, 1948, *FRUS 1948,* VI, 1215–1216; Jacobs to Marshall, June 11, 1948, ibid., 1218–1219.

27. Hodge to Marshall, June 28, 1948, *FRUS 1948,* VI, 1229–1230; *NYT,* June 27, 1948, p. 12.

28. Jacobs to Marshall, June 30, 1948, *FRUS 1948,* VI, 1231–1232; Jacobs to Marshall, July 7, 1948, ibid., 1233–1234; *NYT,* June 30, 1948, p. 13; *NYT,* July 1, 1948, pp. 12, 22.

29. *NYT,* July 14, 1948, p. 22; Jacobs to Marshall, July 26, 1948, Dept. of State Records, 895.01/7–2648; Dept. of State, *Korea 1945 to 1948,* pp. 17–18; Paul S. Dull, "South Korean Constitution," *Far Eastern Survey* 17 (September 8, 1948): 205–207.

30. Marshall to Truman, April 27, 1948, *FRUS 1948,* VI, 1183–1184; John J. Muccio, February 10, 1971, Oral History Interview Transcript, pp. 5–6, Truman Library; Seedlock to Wedemeyer, March 15, 1948, Dept. of the Army Records, P&O 091 Korea TS, sec. III, cases 3–15, box 21, RG 319.

31. Butterworth to Lovett, May 11, 1948, *FRUS 1948,* VI, 1192–1194; Gilchrist memorandum, May 13, 1948, Dept. of the Army Records, P&O 091 Korea TS, sec. III, cases 16–30, box 22, RG 319.

32. *NYT,* May 21, 1948, p. 7; Lawson memorandum, June 9, 1948, Dept. of the Army Records, P&O 091 Korea, sec. V, case 66, box 88, RG 319; Royall to Marshall, June 23, 1948, ibid., P&O 091 Korea TS, sec. III, cases 3–15, box 21, RG 319; Saltzman to Lovett, July 30, 1948, *FRUS 1948,* VI, 1265.

33. Marshall to Royall, June 23, 1948, *FRUS 1948,* VI, 1224–1225; Lovett to Royall, July 8, 1948, ibid., 1234–1235.

34. Hodge to General Omar N. Bradley, June 17, 1948, Dept. of the Army Records, P&O 091 Korea, sec. V, case 65, box 88, RG 319; Jacobs to Marshall, July 9, 1948, Dept. of State Records, 501.BB Korea/7–948; Marshall to certain embassies, July 10, 1948, *FRUS 1948,* VI, 1235–1237.

35. Smith to Marshall, June 30, 1948, *FRUS 1948,* VII, 326–327; Smith to Marshall, July 14, 1948, ibid., VI, 1240.

36. Jacobs to Marshall, July 11, 1948, ibid., VI, 1238–1239; *NYT,* July 12, 1948, p. 10.

37. Jacobs to Marshall, July 25, 1948, *FRUS 1948,* VI, 1259–1261; Marshall to Jacobs, July 27, 1948, ibid., 1263–1264; Butterworth memorandum, August 2, 1948, Dept. of State Records, 501.BB Korea/8–248.

38. Hodge to Marshall, April 8, 1948, JCS Records, CCS 383.21 Korea (3–19–45), sec. XV, RG 218; Hodge to MacArthur, May 17, 1948, Private Correspondence, VIP file, folder 73, box 5, RG 10, MacArthur papers.

39. Jacobs to Marshall, July 18, 1948, Dept. of State Records, 501.BB Korea/7–1848; Jacobs to Marshall, July 27, 1948, ibid., 895.01A/7–2748.

40. *NYT,* July 20, 1948, p. 12; *NYT,* July 27, 1948, p. 14.

41. Gaddis, "Korea in American Politics, Strategy, and Diplomacy," p. 279.

42. Dobbs, *The Unwanted Symbol,* pp. 29, 111, 194; Cho, *Korea in World Poli-*

tics, pp. 134–136; Kim, *Divided Korea,* pp. 74–75; Dallin, *Soviet Russia and the Far East,* pp. 298–299; Henderson, *Korea,* p. 121.

43. Cumings, *The Origins of the Korean War,* pp. 135–136, 184–185, 439–440; Joyce Kolko and Gabriel Kolko, *The Limits of Power: The World and United States Foreign Policy, 1945–1954,* p. 277; Halliday, "The United Nations and Korea," pp. 109–110.

44. Jacobs to Marshall, August 16, 1948, Dept. of State Records, 895.00/8–1648; Henderson, *Korea,* pp. 160–161; Kim, *Divided Korea,* pp. 119–120; Reeve, *The Republic of Korea,* p. 29.

45. Jacobs to Marshall, August 6, 10, 1948, *FRUS 1948,* VI, 1266–1268, 1270; Jacobs to Marshall, August 2, 1948, Dept. of State Records, 895.00/8–248; *NYT,* August 6, 1948, p. 4; *NYT,* August 10, 1948, p. 12.

46. Jacobs to Marshall, August 12, 1948, *FRUS 1948,* VI, 1272; Hodge to JCS, August 12, 1948, JCS Records, CCS 383.21 Korea (3–19–45), sec. XVI, RG 218.

47. H.A.B. to Schuyler, August 9, 1948, Dept. of the Army Records, P&O 091 Korea TS, sec. V, case 31, box 22, RG 319.

48. Schuyler memorandum, August 9, 1948, ibid.

49. Lawton to Truman, August 16, 1948, OF 471, Truman papers; Truman to Lawton, August 16, 1948, ibid.; C.V.R.S. to Schuyler, August 20, 1948, Dept. of the Army Records, P&O 091 Korea TS, sec. V, case 31, box 22, RG 319; see also Truman, diary entry, April 3, 1948, in Ferrell, *Off the Record,* p. 129.

50. Lawton to Truman, n.d., OF 471, Truman papers; Truman to Marshall, August 25, 1948, *FRUS 1948,* VI, 1288–1289; Philander P. Claxton, September 1, 1948, Dept. of State Records, 895.50 Recovery/9–148.

51. Saltzman memorandum, September 7, 1948, *FRUS 1948,* VI, 1292–1298; Marshall to Paul G. Hoffman, September 17, 1948, ibid., 1303–1305; Hoffman to Marshall, October 1, 1948, ibid., 1312–1313.

52. Jessup to Marshall, July 26, 1948, ibid., 1262–1263; Marshall to Jessup, July 27, 1948, ibid., 1263–1264.

53. Lovett to Truman, July 28, 1948, ibid., 1264; "Policy Toward New Korean Government," *DSB* 19 (August 22, 1948): 242; *NYT,* August 13, 1948, p. 1.

54. *NYT,* August 15, 1948, p. 1; *NYT,* August 15, 1948, IV, p. 8; *U.S. News,* August 6, 1948, p. 20; *Time,* August 23, 1948, p. 24.

55. Truman to Hodge, June 23, 1948, PPF 3920, Truman papers.

56. Sawyer and Hermes, *Military Advisors in Korea,* pp. 31–32, 35.

57. Butterworth memorandum, August 17, 1948, *FRUS 1948,* VI, 1276–1278.

58. JCS to MacArthur for Hodge, August 27, 1948, JCS Records, CCS 383.21 Korea (3–19–45), sec. XVII, RG 218; Wedemeyer to Forrestal, August 30, 1948, Dept. of the Army Records, P&O 091 Korea TS, sec. I, case 1, pt. III–B, RG 319.

59. *NYT,* August 29, 1948, p. 7. Tragically, Hodge continued to experience bitter frustration after his departure from Korea. Upon his return to Washington, he found that the Army Department did not intend to give him a new assignment and even wanted to withhold one of his distinguished service medals. See Hodge to MacArthur, September 11, 1948, Private Correspondence, VIP file, folder 73, box 5, RG 10, MacArthur papers.

60. Jacobs to Marshall, August 18, 1948, *FRUS 1948,* VI, 1279–1281; Marshall to Austin, August 20, 1948, ibid., 1284; Gordenker, *The United Nations and the Peaceful Unification of Korea,* pp. 141–142.

61. Stuart to Marshall, August 13, 1948, *FRUS 1948,* VI, 1272–1273; Lewis Douglas to Marshall, August 13, 1948, ibid., 1273; Lester Pearson to Julian F. Harrington, August 13, 1948, ibid., 1274–1275; Howard Donovan to Marshall, August 14, 1948, ibid., 1276; Orsen N. Nielson to Marshall, August 18, 1948, ibid., 1281.

62. Jacobs to Marshall, August 18, 1948, ibid., 1282–1283; Hodge to Marshall, August 19, 1948, JCS Records, CCS 383.21 Korea (3–19–45), sec. XVI, RG 218.

63. Hodge to Marshall, August 18, 1948, JCS Records, Leahy file, Korea 1948, RG 218; Hodge to State, August 21, 1948, ibid., CCS 383.21 Korea (3–19–45), sec. XVI, RG 218; *NYT,* August 24, 1948, pp. 6–7.

64. "Military and Security Measures Effective Until Completion of Withdrawal of United States Forces from Korea," *Treaties and Other International Acts,* Series 1918; Jacobs to Marshall, August 24, 1948, *FRUS 1948,* VI, 1287; *NYT,* August 25, 1948, p. 14.

65. John J. Muccio to Marshall, September 3, 1948, *FRUS 1948,* VI, 1287; *NYT,* September 3, 1948, p. 12.

66. *NYT,* September 1, 1948, p. 7; *NYT,* September 11, 1948, p. 4; Dept. of State, *Korea 1945 to 1948,* p. 21; Berger, *The Korean Knot,* p. 82; Kim, *Divided Korea,* pp. 107–108, 166–168.

67. Foy D. Kohler to Marshall, September 19, 1948, *FRUS 1948,* VI, 1306; "Position on Withdrawing Occupying Forces From Korea," *DSB* 19 (October 3, 1948): 440; "Position on Withdrawal of Troops from Korea," *DSB* 19 (October 10, 1948): 456; Truman, *Years of Trial and Hope,* p. 328.

68. *NYT,* September 20, 1948, pp. 1, 24; *NYT,* September 21, 1948, p. 16; *NYT,* September 25, 1948, p. 16; *Time,* September 27, 1948, p. 32; Yoo, *The Korean War and the United Nations,* p. 22.

69. Hodge to Coulter, September 17, 1948, Dept. of the Army Records, P&O 091 Korea, sec. V, case 65, box 88, RG 319.

70. Lovett memorandum, September 23, 1948, *FRUS 1948,* VI, 1309–1311; Marshall memorandum, October 13, 1948, ibid., 1314–1315.

71. *NYT,* October 21, 1948, p. 1; *NYT,* October 25, 1948, p. 12; Muccio to Marshall, October 28, 1948, *FRUS 1948,* VI, 1317–1318; *Time,* November 1, 1948, p. 34.

72. Lieutenant Colonel John C. O'Byrne memorandum, November 15, 1948, Dept. of the Army Records, P&O 091 Korea, sec. V, case 65, box 88, RG 319; *NYT,* October 21, 1948, p. 26; *Time,* November 8, 1948, pp. 32–33.

73. O'Byrne memorandum; *NYT,* October 22, 1948, pp. 1, 10; *NYT,* October 26, 1948, p. 12; *NYT,* October 27, 1948, pp. 9, 26; *Life,* November 15, 1948, pp. 55–58; *Time,* November 1, 1948, p. 34; Sawyer and Hermes, *Military Advisors in Korea,* p. 40.

74. *NYT,* November 6, 1948, p. 6; Henderson, *Korea,* pp. 162–164.

75. *NYT,* October 25, 1948, p. 12; Muccio to Marshall, November 16, 1948, Dept. of State Records, 895.00/11–1648.

76. Muccio to Marshall, October 26, 1948, Dept. of State Records, 895.00/10–2648; Muccio to Marshall, November 4, 1948, ibid., 895.00/11–448; Muccio to Marshall, November 12, 1948, *FRUS 1948,* VI, 1325–1327.

77. Jacobs to Bond, October 22, 1948, Dept. of State Records, 501.BB Korea/10–2248; Jacobs to Marshall, October 18, 1948, ibid., 501.BB Korea/10–1848; Jacobs to Bond, October 27, 1948, ibid., 501.BB Korea/10–2748.

78. *NYT,* November 10, 1948, p. 15; *NYT,* November 13, 1948, p. 6; Muccio to Marshall, November 19, 1948, Dept. of State Records, 895.00/11–1948; Muccio to Marshall, November 9, 1948, *FRUS 1948,* VI, 1323.

79. Muccio to Marshall, November 5, 19, 1948, *FRUS 1948,* VI, 1320–1321, 1331–1332; Rhee to MacArthur, November 29, 1948, Private Correspondence, VIP file, folder 43, box 8, RG 10, MacArthur papers. Representatives in the legislative assembly joined Rhee in pleading for a postponement of American withdrawal and overwhelmingly passed a resolution requesting a continuation of the occupation.

Prime Minister Yi Pŏm-sŏk castigated the United States in public for stripping its forces to an unacceptable level in preparation for withdrawal on a moment's notice. Thus the South Koreans were able to unite, but only in demanding a greater commitment of military protection from the Truman administration. See *NYT,* November 21, 1948, p. 30; *NYT,* November 23, 1948, p. 22; *NYT,* November 24, 1948, p. 3; Muccio to Marshall, November 19, 1948, *FRUS 1948,* VI, 1332–1333; Muccio to Marshall, December 17, 1948, Dept. of State Records, 895.00/12–1748.

80. Claxton memorandum, October 29, 1948, Dept. of State Records, 501.BB Korea/10–2948; Saltzman to Wedemeyer, November 4, 1948, ibid., 501.BB Korea/11–448; Lovett to Marshall, November 5, 1948, *FRUS 1948,* VI, 1319; Saltzman to Wedemeyer, November 9, 1948, ibid., 1324; JCS to MacArthur, November 15, 1948, JCS Records, CCS 383.21 Korea (3–19–45), sec. XVIII, RG 218; JCS memorandum, n.d., ibid.; see also Bond, December 28, 1973, Oral History Interview Transcript, pp. 30–31; U. Alexis Johnson, January 19, 1975, Oral History Interview Transcript, p. 35, Truman Library.

81. Forrestal memorandum, October 5, 1948, in Millis, *The Forrestal Diaries,* pp. 498–499; Leahy, diary entry, November 5, 1948, Diaries 1948–1950, box 6, Leahy papers; Frank Pace, Jr., January 22, 1972, Oral History Interview Transcript, pp. 33–34, Truman Library; Truman, *Years of Trial and Hope,* p. 40; Ferrell, *George C. Marshall,* pp. 242–245; Schilling, "The Politics of National Defense," pp. 191–193, 197–198.

82. Forrestal to Walter G. Andrews, December 13, 1948, in Millis, *The Forrestal Diaries,* pp. 536–538; Buhite, " 'Major Interests'," p. 444.

83. Colonel A. T. MacNamara memorandum, November 8, 1948, Dept. of the Army Records, P&O 091 Korea, sec. V, case 65, box 88, RG 319.

84. E. B. Eichholz to Claxton, November 15, 1948, Dept. of State Records, FW 895.50 Recovery/11–1548.

85. Seedlock memorandum, January 31, 1948, Dept. of the Army Records, P&O 091 Korea TS, sec. III, cases 3–15, box 21, RG 319; U.S. Congress, House, Committee on Appropriations, *Background Information on Korea;* Dept. of State, *Korea 1945 to 1948,* p. 39.

86. U.S. Dept. of State, "Economic Cooperation with Korea Under Public Law 793–80th," *Treaties and Other International Acts,* Series 1908; *NYT,* December 11, 1948, p. 1; *NYT,* December 14, 1948, p. 25; *NYT,* December 17, 1948, p. 10.

87. *Christian Century,* January 12, 1948, p. 36; *NYT,* December 19, 1948, p. 12.

88. Muccio to Marshall, December 18, 1948, Dept. of State Records, 895.00/12–1848; Coulter for Muccio to Marshall, December 20, 1948, ibid., 501.BB Korea/12–2048.

89. Folk memorandum, December 24, 1948, Dept. of the Army Records, P&O 092, sec. X, case 139, RG 319.

90. *NYT,* December 25, 1948, p. 2.

91. Owen T. Jones to Marshall, September 15, 1948, Dept. of State Records, 895.01/9–1548; Channing Liem, "United States Rule in Korea," *Far Eastern Survey* 18 (April 6, 1949): 77–80; *NYT,* August 24, 1948, p. 6.

CHAPTER 8: *Test Case of Containment*

1. Adler, *The Isolationist Impulse,* pp. 370, 403; Truman, *Years of Trial and Hope,* p. 238; George M. Elsey, July 10, 1969, Oral History Interview Transcript, pp. 143–145, Truman Library.

2. Athan Theoharis, "The Rhetoric of Politics," in Bernstein, *Politics and Policies of the Truman Administration*, pp. 210–211; Graebner, "Global Containment," pp. 79–80.

3. McGeorge Bundy, ed., *The Pattern of Responsibility*, p. 22; Smith, *Dean Acheson*, p. 16; Norman A. Graebner, "Dean G. Acheson (1949–1953)," in Graebner, *An Uncertain Tradition*, p. 269.

4. Truman, *Years of Trial and Hope*, p. 330.

5. Rusk to Lovett, September 10, 1948, *FRUS 1948*, VI, 1299–1300; Don C. Bliss to Marshall, September 11, 1948, ibid., 1302; Bond memorandum, September 14, 1948, ibid., 1300–1301.

6. U.S. United Nations position paper, October 22, 1948, ibid., 1315–1316; Butterworth to Lovett, November 5, 1948, ibid., 1319; Jacobs to Bond, October 18, 1948, Dept. of State Records, 501.BB Korea/10–1848.

7. "The United States in the United Nations," *DSB* 19 (November 7, 1948): 576; Gordenker, *The United Nations and the Peaceful Unification of Korea*, pp. 141–142.

8. *NYT*, November 3, 1948, p. 6; Marshall to Lovett, November 16, 1948, *FRUS 1948*, VI, 1327–1330; "The United States in the United Nations," *DSB* 19 (November 21, 1948): 637.

9. *NYT*, November 30, 1948, p. 26; *NYT*, December 4, 1948, p. 2.

10. Dulles to Marshall, December 6, 1948, *FRUS 1948*, VI, 1335; *NYT*, December 7, 1948, p. 17.

11. John Foster Dulles, "U.S. Urges Continuation of Temporary Commission on Korea," *DSB* 19 (December 19, 1948): 758–760; *NYT*, December 8, 1948, p. 22.

12. Dulles to Marshall, December 9, 1948, *FRUS 1948*, VI, 1336; "The United States in the United Nations," *DSB* 19 (December 12, 1948): 728.

13. Dulles to Marshall, December 12, 1948, *FRUS 1948*, VI, 1336–1337; *NYT*, December 10, 1948, p. 24.

14. *NYT*, December 8, 1948, p. 30; *NYT*, December 13, 1948, p. 3; Dulles to Marshall, December 13, 1948, *FRUS 1948*, VI, 1337.

15. Berger, *The Korean Knot*, pp. 84, 88–89; see also Muccio to Marshall, December 13, 1948, Dept. of State Records, 740.00119 Control (Korea)/12–848.

16. Sawyer and Hermes, *Military Advisors in Korea*, pp. 36–37; *Time*, January 10, 1949, p. 19; *NYT*, December 30, 1948, p. 3; *NYT*, January 15, 1949, p. 5.

17. Draper to Saltzman, December 22, 1948, *FRUS 1948*, VI, 1341–1343; Zierath memorandum, January 6, 1949, Dept. of the Army Records, P&O 091 Korea TS, sec. V, case 31, box 22, RG 319.

18. *NYT*, December 31, 1948, p. 4; Muccio to Acheson, January 6, 1949, Dept. of State Records, 895.00/1–649.

19. Max Bishop to Butterworth, December 17, 1948, *FRUS 1948*, VI, 1337–1340; J. Leighton Stuart to Marshall, December 29, 1948, *FRUS 1948*, VII, 695.

20. Army Department memorandum, January 10, 1949, Dept. of the Army Records, P&O 091 Korea TS, sec. I, cases 5–16, box 162, RG 319; W. A. Rudlin memorandum, January 19, 1949, Dept. of State Records, 501.BB Korea/1–1949; Coulter to JCS, January 11, 1949, JCS Records, CCS 383.21 Korea (3–19–45), sec. XIX, RG 218; Butterworth to Lovett, January 10, 1949, *FRUS 1949*, VII, pt. 2, 942–943.

21. Saltzman to Draper, January 25, 1949, *FRUS 1949*, VII, pt. 2, 944–945. Acheson wanted to discuss only the political and military aspects of formulating a new position on Korea while avoiding the specific issue of withdrawal. See Acheson to Royall, January 25, 1949, Background file, Department of State, PSF–Korean War Documents, box 1, Truman papers.

22. MacArthur to JCS, January 19, 1949, Dept. of the Army Records, P&O 091 Korea TS, sec. V, case 31, box 22, RG 319.

23. Ibid.; Army Department memorandum, January 10, 1949, ibid., P&O 091 Korea TS, sec. I, cases 5–16, box 162, RG 319; *NYT,* March 2, 1949, p. 22; see also Ridgway, *The Korean War,* p. 12.

24. *NYT,* January 1, 1949, p. 4; memorandum of conversation, January 5, 1949, *FRUS 1949,* VII, pt. 2, 940–941.

25. *NYT,* February, 5, 1949, p. 5; *NYT,* February 9, 1949, p. 15; Army Department memorandum, February 8, 1949, Dept. of the Army Records, CSA 091 Korea TS, RG 335; Truman, *Years of Trial and Hope,* p. 329.

26. Royall memorandum, February 8, 1949, *FRUS 1949,* VII, pt. 2, 956–958; Muccio memorandum, February 25, 1949, ibid., 958–959.

27. Army Department memorandum, February 8, 1949, Dept. of the Army Records, CSA 091 Korea TS, RG 335.

28. NSC–8/1, March 16, 1949, ibid., P&O 091 Korea, sec. I–A, RG 319.

29. Ibid.; see also Royall to Acheson, January 25, 1949, ibid., P&O 091 Korea TS, box 163, RG 319.

30. NSC–8/2, March 22, 1949, *FRUS 1949,* VII, pt. 2, 969–978; "Chronology of Action by the National Security Council," Elsey papers. In approving NSC–8/2, the Truman administration merely reaffirmed a commitment to implement a program for economic aid and technical advice for Korea that it had initially begun to consider early in 1947. Lewis McCarroll Purifoy is therefore incorrect when he contends that it was the emergence of McCarthyism early in 1950 that caused the State Department to make "plans to provide various forms of assistance to small states on China's periphery, particularly Korea . . . , by way of demonstrating to critics that the department was as determined to 'stop the expansion of Communism' in Asia as in Europe." See Purifoy, *Harry Truman's China Policy: McCarthyism and the Diplomacy of Hysteria, 1947–1951,* pp. 149–150.

31. Maddocks to Army Chief of Staff, March 7, 1949, Dept. of the Army Records, P&O 091 Korea TS, sec. I, box 163, RG 319; Maddocks to Secretary of the Army, March 22, 1949, ibid.; Sawyer and Hermes, *Military Advisors in Korea,* p. 38. While accepting the revisions in NSC–8/1, Acheson emphasized in discussions with Truman's other top advisors that "the success of the policy set forth therein may well be dependent upon the adequacy of the transfer of military equipment and supplies . . . in furnishing the Korean Government with effective security forces equipped to fill immediately the gap left by the withdrawal of U.S. occupation forces and to bridge the critical period until military assistance to be provided under pending legislation begins to flow." See NSC Meeting minutes, March 22, 1949, NSC Meetings 28–37 (December 2, 1948–April 7, 1949), PSF–National Security Council Documents, box 205, Truman papers.

32. "United States Recognizes Republic of Korea," *DSB* 20 (January 9, 1949): 59–60; *NYT,* January 2, 1949, p. 1.

33. Muccio to Acheson, February 9, 1949, Dept. of State Records, 501.BB Korea/2-949; John P. Gardiner memorandum, February 7, 1949, *FRUS 1949,* VII, pt. 2, 953–955.

34. *NYT,* February 13, 1949, p. 47; *NYT,* February 19, 1949, p. 4; Seoul to Acheson, February 15, 1949, Dept. of State Records, 501.BB Korea/2-1549.

35. Muccio to Marshall, December 7, 1948, Dept. of State Records, 895.00/12-748; Seoul to Acheson, February 18, 1949, ibid., 501.BB Korea/2-1849; *NYT,* February 22, 1949, p.3; Gordenker, *The United Nations and the Peaceful Unification of Korea,* p. 153.

36. Everett F. Drumright to Acheson, February 12, 1949, *FRUS 1949*, VII, pt. 2, 960–961.

37. Gregory Henderson memorandum, March 7, 1949, Dept. of State Records, 501.BB Korea/3–749; David Mark memorandum, March 12, 1949, ibid., 501.BB Korea/3–1249; Muccio to Acheson, April 18, 1949, ibid., 895.00/4–1849; Gordenker, *The United Nations and the Peaceful Unification of Korea*, pp. 155–156.

38. *NYT*, February 3, 1949, p. 12; *NYT*, February 12, 1949, p. 13; *NYT*, February 17, 1949, pp. 3, 22; "Korean Membership in the United Nations," *DSB* 20 (February 20, 1949): 227; "The United States in the United Nations," *DSB* 20 (February 27, 1949): 253–254.

39. "The United States in the United Nations," *DSB* 20 (April 17, 1949): 492.

40. Drumright to Acheson, March 17, 1949, *FRUS 1949*, VII, pt. 2, 967. The Young Group also opposed the Korean-American Financial and Property Settlement and Rhee's plan to give the United States the Banto Hotel for its embassy. See Drumright to Acheson, February 11, 1949, Dept. of State Records, 740.00119 Control (Korea)/2–1149.

41. Drumright to Acheson, February 11, 1949, enclosures, Dept. of State Records, 740.00119 Control (Korea)/2–1149.

42. Muccio to Acheson, February 26, 1949, ibid., 895.01/2–2649.

43. *NYT*, March 13, 1949, p. 52; Acheson memorandum, March 24, 1949, Dept. of State Records, 895.20 Missions/3–2449.

44. Drumright to Acheson, March 15, 1949, *FRUS 1949*, VII, pt. 2, 966; Drumright to Acheson, March 14, 1949, Dept. of State Records, 895.00/3–1449.

45. Acheson to Seoul, April 5, 1949, Dept. of State Records, 895.20 Missions/4–549.

46. Muccio to Acheson, April 5, 1949, ibid., 740.00119 Control (Korea)/4–549; Muccio to Acheson, April 9, 12, 1949, *FRUS 1949*, VII, pt. 2, 981–982, 986–987.

47. Gardiner memorandum, April 6, 1949, Dept. of State Records, 501.BB Korea/4–649; memorandum of conversation, April 8, 1949, ibid., 740.00119 Control (Korea)/4–849.

48. Muccio to Acheson, April 14, 1949, *FRUS 1949*, VII, pt. 2, 988; Rhee to Muccio, April 14, 1949, ibid., 990–991; Acheson to Muccio, April 15, 1949, ibid., 992; Muccio to Acheson, April 16, 1949, ibid., 992n.

49. Butterworth to Acheson, April 18, 1949, ibid., 992–993; *NYT*, April 19, 1949, pp. 1, 24; Muccio to Acheson, April 18, 1949, Dept. of State Records, 501.BB Korea/4–1849.

50. Muccio to Acheson, April 30, 1949, Dept. of State Records, 895.001 Rhee/4–3049; Muccio to Acheson, May 7, 1949, ibid., 501.BB Korea/5–749; *NYT*, April 30, 1949, p. 4; *NYT*, May 7, 1949, p. 4; Muccio to Acheson, April 26, 1949, *FRUS 1949*, VII, pt. 2, 995–997.

51. Acheson to Muccio, April 28, 1949, *FRUS 1949*, VII, pt. 2, 997–998; Muccio to Acheson, May 2, 1949, ibid., 1000–1003; "Korean Military Advisory Group Established," *DSB* 20 (June 19, 1949): 786–787; see also *NYT*, May 8, 1949, p. 29.

52. Muccio memorandum, May 2, 1949, *FRUS 1949*, VII, pt. 2, 1003–1005.

53. Muccio to Acheson, May 7, 1949, ibid., 1011–1012; Acheson to Muccio, May 9, 1949, ibid., 1014–1016; Acheson to Muccio, May 9, 1949, Dept. of State Records, 740.00119 Control (Korea)/5–949; Muccio to Acheson, June 13, 1949, ibid., 895.00/6–1349.

54. Muccio to Acheson, May 9, 12, 1949, *FRUS 1949*, VII, pt. 2, 1013, 1021–1022; Muccio memorandum, May 10, 1949, ibid., 1016–1018.

55. Muccio to Acheson, April 29, 1949, ibid., 998–999; Muccio to Acheson, May

3, 1949, ibid., 1005–1006; Louis A. Johnson to Acheson, May 4, 1949, ibid., 1007; Lawson to Secretary of the Army, April 29, 1949, Dept. of the Army Records, P&O 091 Korea TS, sec. I-A, bk. 2, box 163, RG 319.

56. Muccio to Acheson, May 6, 11, 1949, *FRUS 1949,* VII, pt. 2, 1008–1009, 1018–1019; Acheson to Johnson, May 10, 1949, ibid., 1016.

57. Gordon Gray to Acheson, April 29, 1949, ibid., 999; Acheson to Muccio, May 9, 1949, ibid., 1014–1015; Butterworth to Maddocks, May 13, 1949, ibid., 1022–1023; Muccio to Acheson, May 13, 1949, Dept. of State Records, 501.BB Korea/5-1349.

58. Muccio to Acheson, May 17, 1949, *FRUS 1949,* VII, pt. 2, 1029–1030.

59. Muccio to Acheson, May 19, 20, 1949, ibid., 1030–1031, 1033–1034; memorandum of conversation, May 21, 1949, Dept. of State Records, 740.00119 Control (Korea)/5-2149.

60. *NYT,* May 29, 1949, p. 17; Muccio to Acheson, June 3, 1949, Dept. of State Records, 740.00119 Control (Korea)/6-349.

61. Muccio to Acheson, May 26, 1949, *FRUS 1949,* VII, pt. 2, 1034–1035; John C. Ross to Acheson, June 1, 1949, ibid., 1036–1037; memorandum of conversation, June 4, 1949, Dept. of State Records, 740.00119 Control (Korea)/6-449; Rhee to MacArthur, May 22, 1949, Private Correspondence, VIP file, folder 43, box 9, RG 10, MacArthur papers.

62. Muccio to Acheson, May 31, 1949, *FRUS 1949,* VII, pt. 2, 1035–1036; James E. Webb to Muccio, June 3, 1949, ibid., 1037–1038.

63. Muccio to Acheson, June 6, 1949, ibid., 1039; Muccio to Acheson, June 7, 1949, Dept. of State Records, 501.BB Korea/6-749; Drumright to Acheson, July 5, 1949, ibid., 895.00/7-549. For a detailed discussion of Rhee's maneuvers regarding the formation of a "Pacific Pact," see Dobbs, *The Unwanted Symbol,* pp. 171–175.

64. Army Department memorandum, June 27, 1949, *FRUS 1949,* VII, pt. 2, 1046–1057. Muccio already had recommended that American warships should visit South Korea periodically as a show of concern. On July 8, 1949, a cruiser and two destroyers arrived at Pusan for a three-day "goodwill visit." See Bolte memorandum, June 23, 1949, Dept. of the Army Records, CSA 091 Korea TS, RG 335; *NYT,* July 9, 1949, p. 5.

65. Army Department memorandum, July 27, 1949, 1052–1054.

66. Ibid., 1054.

67. Ibid., 1054–1055.

68. Ibid., 1055–1057; see also JCS to CSA, June 23, 1949, JCS Records, CCS 383.21 Korea (3–19–45), sec. XX, RG 218.

69. "U.S. Policy Toward Korea," *DSB* 20 (June 19, 1949): 781. The Truman administration also submitted to Congress a request for nearly $2 million to finance "an informational, cultural, educational and exchange of persons program" for the ROK. See Webb to Souers, June 6, 1949, NSC Meeting 36–March 22, 1949, NSC Meetings 28–37 (December 2, 1948–April 7, 1949), PSF-National Security Council Documents, box 205, Truman papers.

70. Acheson to John Kee, May 11, 1949, Memoranda of Conversations, May–June 1950, box 65, Acheson papers; Webb to Truman, June 4, 1949, Memorandum–Congress, Korea file, Charles S. Murphy papers.

71. Harry S. Truman, "Request to Congress for Continuing Economic Assistance," *DSB* 20 (June 19, 1949): 781–783.

72. Ibid. Given the substantive provisions and rhetorical justifications of Truman's speech, it is difficult to accept the argument that McCarthyism was primarily responsible for Washington's increasing commitment to South Korea. Nevertheless, Lewis

McCarroll Purifoy contends that "only 'McCarthyism' had the demonic power to force the administration to reverse policies" and to manifest a "rising passion for adventures on the Asian continent"; see Purifoy, *Harry Truman's China Policy,* p. 167. For a similar interpretation regarding the relationship between McCarthyism and Truman's Korea policy, see Dobbs, *The Unwanted Symbol,* p. 177.

73. Louis L. Gerson, *John Foster Dulles,* p. 56; David S. McLellan, *Dean Acheson: The State Department Years,* pp. 191–192; Tsou, *America's Failure in China,* pp. 489, 499; Westerfield, *Foreign Policy and Party Politics,* pp. 306–307.

CHAPTER 9: *Promise and Performance*

1. *NYT,* June 29, 1949, p. 11; *NYT,* June 30, 1949, p. 9; "Korea," *DSB* 20 (July 4, 1949): 848; Drumright to Acheson, July 11, 1949, Dept. of State Records, 895.00/7–1149.

2. Drumright to Acheson, January 7, 1949, Dept. of State Records, 895.00/1–749; Drumright to Acheson, February 9, 1949, ibid., 895.00/2–949; Muccio to Acheson, January 27, 1949, *FRUS 1949,* VII, pt. 2, 947–952; Roberts to Wedemeyer, May 2, 1949, Dept. of the Army Records, P&O 091 Korea, sec. III, cases 41–60, box 548, RG 319.

3. *NYT,* May 5, 1949, p. 16; Muccio to Acheson, May 19, 1949, Dept. of State Records, 501.BB Korea/5–1949; Muccio to Acheson, June 13, 1949, ibid., 895.00/6–1349.

4. Muccio to Acheson, June 7, 1949, Dept. of State Records, 895.002/6–749; Muccio to Acheson, June 16, 1949, ibid., 895.032/6–1649; Muccio to Acheson, June 18, 1949, ibid., 895.002/6–1849.

5. Gardiner to Acheson, June 20, 1949, Dept. of State Records, 501.BB Korea/6–2049; *NYT,* June 16, 1949, p. 4.

6. *NYT,* June 19, 1949, p. 12; Gordenker, *The United Nations and the Peaceful Unification of Korea,* pp. 164–165.

7. *NYT,* June 22, 1949, p. 3; *NYT,* June 23, 1949, p. 3; Muccio to Acheson, June 22, 1949, Dept. of State Records, 895.00B/6–2249; Muccio to Acheson, June 23, 1949, ibid., 895.00B/6–2349.

8. *NYT,* June 27, 1949, p. 1; *NYT,* June 28, 1949, p. 10; Muccio to Acheson, June 27, 1949, *FRUS 1949,* VII, pt. 2, 1045–1046; Henderson to Acheson, June 29, 1949, Dept. of State Records, 895.00/6–2949; Drumright to Acheson, July 11, 1949, ibid., 895.00/7–1149.

9. Muccio to Acheson, June 25, 1949, Dept. of State Records, 895.00B/6–2549; Drumright to Acheson, July 11, 1949, ibid., 895.00/7–1149; Drumright to Acheson, July 8, 1949, ibid., 895.00B/7–849; Henderson to Acheson, July 9, 1949, ibid., 895.00/7–949.

10. Muccio to Acheson, July 14, 1949, ibid., 501.BB Korea/7–1449; *NYT,* July 8, 1949, p. 1; *NYT,* July 9, 1949, p. 5; Kim, *Divided Korea,* pp. 169–170; Beloff, *Soviet Foreign Policy in the Far East,* p. 178.

11. U.S. Congress, House, Committee on Foreign Affairs, *Korean Aid,* pp. 7–26; *NYT,* June 9, 1949, p. 18.

12. *Korean Aid,* p. 29; see also *NYT,* June 11, 1949, p. 4.

13. *Korean Aid,* pp. 112–117.

14. Ibid., pp. 43–44, 124, 137, 170–173, 180–181; see also *Time,* June 20, 1949, pp. 31–32.

15. Memorandum for Truman, June 18, 1949, Dept. of State Records, 895.50 Recovery/6–1849; *NYT,* June 21, 1949, p. 13.

16. *Korean Aid,* pp. 191–192; "Aid to Korea," *DSB* 21 (July 11, 1949): 37; *NYT,* June 24, 1949, p. 2.

17. Lawton to Truman, June 28, 1949, Correspondence, box 6, Frederick J. Lawton papers; *Background Information on Korea,* pp. 1–2; U.S. Congress, House, Committee on Foreign Affairs, *Aid to Korea; NYT,* July 1, 1949, p. 6.

18. U.S. Congress, House, Committee on Foreign Affairs, *Aid to Korea,* Minority Report.

19. Clark Clifford to Truman, July 8, 1949, "Support for the Korean Aid Program," Official file: Economic Assistance to Korea, Clark M. Clifford papers; Foster memorandum, August 23, 1949, Korea data–general, PSF–Korean War file, box 243, Truman papers; Truman to Acheson, October 17, 1949, Memoranda of Conversations, October–November 1949, box 64, Acheson papers; U.S. Congress, House, Committee on Appropriations, *Supplemental Estimate of Appropriation Continuing for Two Months the Present Program of Assistance to the Republic of Korea; Background Information on Korea,* pp. 28–29; "Supplemental Estimate of Appropriation for Fiscal 1950," *DSB* 21 (July 25, 1949): 117–118.

20. *NYT,* June 8, 1949, p. 7; *NYT,* June 10, 1949, p. 4; *NYT,* July 2, 1949, p. 4; Muccio to Acheson, July 2, 1949, *FRUS 1949,* VII, pt. 2, 1057–1058.

21. *NYT,* July 3, 1949, p. 13; *NYT,* July 19, 1949, p. 8; Muccio to Acheson, July 18, 19, 1949, *FRUS 1949,* VII, pt. 2, 1062–1063.

22. Acheson to Muccio, July 19, 1949, *FRUS 1949,* VII, pt. 2, 1063; Muccio to Acheson, July 21, 23, 1949, ibid., 1065–1066; *NYT,* July 23, 1949, p. 4.

23. *NYT,* July 12, 1949, p. 3; *NYT,* July 26, 1949, p. 16; Acheson memorandum, July 11, 1949, *FRUS 1949,* VII, pt. 2, 1058–1059.

24. Drumright to Acheson, August 10, 1949, Dept. of State Records, 895.00/8–1049; Muccio to Acheson, August 16, 1949, ibid., 895.001 Rhee/8–1649.

25. Harry S. Truman, "The President's News Conference of *August* 11, 1949," *Public Papers, Truman,* V, 421; Truman to Rhee, September 26, 1949, *FRUS 1949,* VII, pt. 2, 1084–1085.

26. Harry S. Truman, "Special Message to the Congress on the Need for a Military Aid Program, *July* 25, 1949," *Public Papers, Truman,* V, 398. When the United States withdrew from Korea, it transferred to the ROK military equipment valued at $110 million based on 1949 replacement costs. See *Background Information on Korea,* pp. 33–34; see also "Report on Military Assistance Rendered to Foreign Countries Since V-J Day," *DSB* 21 (September 26, 1949): 479; Acheson to Souers, July 19, 1949, NSC Meeting 36–March 22, 1949, NSC Meetings 28–37 (December 2, 1948–April 7, 1949), PSF–National Security Council Documents, box 205, Truman papers.

27. "Chronology of Action by the National Security Council," Elsey papers; Lawson memorandum, July 19, 1949, Dept. of the Army Records, P&O 091 Korea TS, sec. I, cases 5–16, box 162, RG 319.

28. Roberts to Bolte, September 13, 1949, Dept. of the Army Records, P&O 091 Korea, sec. III, cases 41–60, box 548, RG 319; Seoul to Acheson, June 16, 1949, Dept. of State Records, 740.00119 Control (Korea)/6–1649.

29. Lawson memorandum, July 19, 1949, Dept. of the Army Records, P&O 091 Korea TS, sec. I, cases 5–16, box 162, RG 319; Major General R. E. Duff for Bolte to Army Chief of Staff, September 12, 1949, ibid., P&O 091 Korea TS, sec. I-E, bk. 1, box 163, RG 319; Gray to Johnson, September 13, 1949, ibid., CSA 091 Korea TS, RG 335.

30. For Roberts, the South Korean soldier "has many qualities I'd like to transfer to American soldiers, [such as] attentiveness, stoicism, a desire to learn, a ready willingness to die if ordered, tenacity. His weaknesses are his desire to kick civilians around . . . , his sadistic tendencies and his leaders. These soldiers actually seem to

revel in disagreeable weather and hardships." "If they can only fight as well as they parade," he concluded sarcastically, "we are 'in'." See Roberts to Bolte, August 19, 1949, ibid., P&O 091 Korea, sec. III, cases 41–60, box 548, RG 319; Drumright to Acheson, July 11, 1949, Dept. of State Records, 895.00/7–1149; Sawyer and Hermes, *Military Advisors in Korea*, pp. 58–65.

31. Muccio to Acheson, July 26, 1949, *FRUS 1949*, VII, pt. 2, 1066–1067; Muccio to Acheson, September 16, 1949, ibid., 1079–1080; Muccio to Acheson, October 13, 19, 1949, ibid., 1086–1089; Muccio to Acheson, November 8, 10, 18, 1949, ibid., 1094–1096, 1099–1100.

32. Muccio to Acheson, November 4, 1949, ibid., 1093–1094; Webb to Muccio, November 28, 1949, ibid., 1101–1102. When Congress approved the MDAP in 1949, it provided for $10,970,000 in military aid to South Korea. This figure, however, was substantially less than the president's request. See editor's note, ibid., 1086.

33. Muccio to Acheson, December 1, 1949, ibid., 1102–1104.

34. Muccio to Acheson, December 7, 1949, ibid., 1005–1006; John Z. Williams memorandum, December 7, 1949, ibid., 1004–1005; see also Rhee to MacArthur, December 2, 1949, Private Correspondence, VIP file, folder 43, box 8, RG 10, MacArthur papers.

35. Acheson to Muccio, December 9, 1949, *FRUS 1949*, VII, pt. 2, 1107; Muccio to Acheson, December 16, 19, 1949, ibid., 1108–1110.

36. Webb to Muccio, June 3, 1949, ibid., 1038; Muccio to Acheson, June 11, 1949, ibid., 1040–1041; "Korea," *DSB* 21 (July 18, 1949): 48; *NYT,* July 12, 1949, p. 3; *NYT,* July 13, 1949, p. 18.

37. Acheson to Muccio, July 11, 1949, Dept. of State Records, 501.BB Korea/7–1149; Acheson to Muccio, July 19, 1949, ibid., 501.BB Korea/7–1949; Muccio to Acheson, July 22, 1949, ibid., 501.BB Korea/7–2249.

38. Muccio to Acheson, July 23, 1949, *FRUS 1949*, VII, pt. 2, 1065–1066.

39. Muccio to Bond, July 25, 1949, Dept. of State Records, 501.BB Korea/7–2549; Muccio to Bond, August 4, 1949, ibid., 501.BB Korea/8–449; Muccio to Bond, August 6, 1949, ibid., 501.BB Korea/8–649; *NYT,* August 27, 1949, p. 5.

40. Muccio to Bond, August 20, 1949, *FRUS 1949*, VII, pt. 2, 1068–1069.

41. *NYT,* September 9, 1949, p. 1; *NYT,* September 10, 1949, p. 7; Muccio to Bond, September 12, 1949, Dept. of State Records, 501.BB Korea/8–3149.

42. Acheson to Moscow, September 13, 1949, Dept. of State Records, 501.BB Korea/9–1349; see also "U.S. Position on Problems Confronting Fourth General Assembly," *DSB* 21 (October 3, 1949): 490, 494.

43. "Korea," *DSB* 21 (October 3, 1949): 499; *NYT,* September 30, 1949, p. 5.

44. Charles Fahy, "The Position of Korea in International Affairs Today," *DSB* 21 (October 24, 1949): 625–626; see also Bloomfield, *The United Nations and U.S. Foreign Policy*, p. 171.

45. "Korea," *DSB* 21 (October 10, 1949): 539; *NYT,* October 4, 1949, p. 5.

46. Charles Fahy, "The Problem of the Independence of Korea," *DSB* 21 (November 7, 1949): 694–695. On the new commission, Turkey replaced Syria. See United Nations Resolution, October 21, 1949, *FRUS 1949*, VII, pt. 2, 1090–1092; *NYT,* October 14, 1949, p. 26; *NYT,* October 22, 1949, p. 6; "The United States in the United Nations," *DSB* 21 (October 31, 1949): 662; "Admission of New Members," *DSB* 22 (January 2, 1950): 35–36.

47. Muccio to Acheson, October 7, 1949, Dept. of State Records, 895.00/10–749; Gordenker, *The United Nations and the Peaceful Unification of Korea*, pp. 24–25.

48. Muccio to Acheson, October 17, 1949, *FRUS 1949*, VII, pt. 2, 1087–1088; *NYT,* October 6, 1949, p. 13; *NYT,* October 18, 1949, p. 20.

49. Drumright to Acheson, September 13, 1949, Dept. of State Records, 895.00/

9–1349; Muccio to Acheson, October 7, 1949, ibid., 895.00/10–749; *NYT,* September 6, 1949, p. 15; *NYT,* September 16, 1949, p. 15; Muccio to Acheson, November 3, 1949, Dept. of State Records, 895.00/11–349; Muccio to Acheson, November 7, 1949, ibid., 895.00/11–749; Henderson, *Korea,* pp. 165–166.

50. Henderson to Acheson, November 28, 1949, Dept. of State Records, 895.00/11–2849; Muccio to Acheson, December 2, 1949, ibid., 895.00/12–249.

51. "Economic Development in South Korea," *Far East Economic Review* 7 (October 20, 1949): 519–521; "Review of the Economy of the Republic of Korea," *Far East Economic Review* 10 (January 11, 1951): 41–47; see also *The Nation,* August 13, 1949, pp. 151–153; *Business Week,* September 17, 1949, pp. 116–118.

52. Muccio to Acheson, November 7, 1949, Dept. of State Records, 895.00/11–749; *NYT,* September 12, 1949, p. 15; *NYT,* September 13, 1949, p. 17; *NYT,* January 1, 1950, p. 74; U.S. Dept. of Commerce, "Economic Review of the Republic of Korea, 1949," *International Reference Service* 7 (July 1950): 5–7.

53. Muccio to Acheson, November 14, 1949, *FRUS 1949,* VII, pt. 2, 1096–1098.

54. Butterworth to Acheson, December 16, 1949, ibid., 1110–1112; Butterworth to Muccio, December 13, 1949, Dept. of State Records, 895.51/12–1349.

55. Acheson to Muccio, December 30, 1949, *FRUS 1949,* VII, pt. 2, 1112–1114; ECA report, December 31, 1949, Dept. of State Records, 895.51/12–3149; see also *NYT,* January 4, 1950, p. 74.

56. Drumright to Acheson, January 28, 1950, *FRUS 1950,* VII, 20–22; *NYT,* January 13, 1950, p. 3; *NYT,* January 14, 1950, p. 1.

57. Jessup memorandum, January 14, 1950, *FRUS 1950,* VII, 1–3; Drumright to Acheson, January 28, 1950, ibid., 18–20; editor's note, ibid., 11n.; *NYT,* January 15, 1950, p. 2.

58. Muccio to Acheson, January 18, 1950, *FRUS 1950,* VII, 8–11.

59. Jessup memorandum, January 14, 1950, ibid., 5–7.

60. Wedemeyer testimony, *Military Situation in the Far East,* p. 2296; Johnson testimony, ibid., pp. 2578–2579; Bundy, *The Pattern of Responsibility,* p. 185; Tsou, *America's Failure in China,* pp. 534–535; Purifoy, *Harry Truman's China Policy,* pp. 142–147; Ernest R. May, "The Nature of Foreign Policy: The Calculated Versus the Axiomatic," *Daedalus* 91 (Fall 1962): 656–667.

61. "United States Policy Toward Formosa," *DSB* 22 (January 16, 1950): 79.

62. Ibid., pp. 79–81. Acheson later stated that only American military intervention could have prevented the destruction of Chiang Kai-shek's regime on Taiwan early in 1950. If Washington had intervened, however, Truman and his advisors feared that this measure would discredit the United States in Asia and thereby help the Soviet Union. According to Acheson, the administration announced its intention to avoid involvement in the Chinese civil war in order to tell the people of Asia to "Keep your chin up; it doesn't matter; this isn't important." See Acheson testimony, *Military Situation in the Far East,* pp. 1672–1675.

63. John W. Spanier, *The Truman-MacArthur Controversy and the Korean War,* p. 20; Glenn D. Paige, *The Korean Decision June 24–30, 1950,* p. 351; Robert Leckie, *Conflict: The History of the Korean War, 1950–1953,* pp. 36–37; David Rees, *Korea: The Limited War,* p. 14; Richard Rovere and Arthur M. Schlesinger, Jr., *The General and the President and the Future of American Foreign Policy,* p. 101; Robert T. Oliver, *Why War Came in Korea,* pp. 233–234; Berger, *The Korean Knot,* p. 97; Phillips, *The Truman Presidency,* p. 293.

64. Dean G. Acheson, "Crisis in Asia: An Examination of United States Policy," *DSB* 22 (January 16, 1950): 111–113.

65. Ibid., pp. 115–116. Both MacArthur and the JCS agreed with Acheson's assessment that South Korea was beyond the American "defensive perimeter." See Collins, *War in Peacetime,* p. 31; George F. Kennan comments, February 13, 1954,

Princeton Seminars Transcript, reel 1, tape 2, p. 2, Acheson papers. In his memoirs, Acheson dismissed charges that he had given the North Koreans a "green light" to invade the ROK as "specious, for Australia and New Zealand were not included either and the first of all our mutual defense agreements was made with Korea." See Dean G. Acheson, *Present at the Creation: My Years in the State Department,* p. 358; see also McLellan, *Dean Acheson,* pp. 209–210.

66. Acheson, "Crisis in Asia," pp. 113–115, 116–117.

67. Ibid., p. 117; see also Acheson comments, February 13, 1954, Princeton Seminars Transcript, reel 1, tape 2, p. 2, Acheson papers.

68. Muccio, February 10, 1971, Oral History Interview Transcript, p. 16; see also Reitzel, Kaplan, and Coblenz, *United States Foreign Policy,* p. 2.

69. Tsou, *America's Failure in China,* p. 536; Dobbs, *The Unwanted Symbol,* p. 181; May, "The Nature of Foreign Policy," pp. 661–662.

70. Smith, *Dean Acheson,* p. 137; Gaddis, "Korea in American Politics, Strategy, and Diplomacy," pp. 284–285.

71. *NYT,* January 20, 1950, p. 1; *NYT,* January 21, 1950, p. 16; *Background Information on Korea,* pp. 18–22; *Christian Century,* February 1, 1950, p. 132; see also Michael A. Guhin, *John Foster Dulles: A Statesman and His Times,* p. 98; Paige, *The Korean Decision,* p. 35; Tsou, *America's Failure in China,* p. 538. For a contrary view, see Purifoy, *Harry Truman's China Policy,* p. 194.

72. *NYT,* January 20, 1950, p. 4; *NYT,* January 21, 1950, p. 5; Williams memorandum, January 20, 1950, *FRUS 1950,* VII, 11–14; Drumright to Acheson, January 21, 1950, Dept. of State Records, 795.00/1–2150.

73. "Regret Expressed Over House Action on Aid to Korea," *DSB* 22 (February 6, 1950): 212; *NYT,* January 22, 1950, p. 1.

74. Acheson Memorandum, January 21, 1950, Memoranda of Conversations, January–February 1950, box 65, Acheson papers; Lucius Battle memorandum, January 21, 1950, ibid.; *NYT,* January 21, 1950, p. 1.

75. *NYT,* January 25, 1950, p. 1; *NYT,* January 31, 1950, p. 2; *NYT,* February 1, 1950, p. 12; *NYT,* February 2, 1950, pp. 3, 26; U.S. Congress, House, Committee on Foreign Affairs, *Economic Assistance to Certain Areas in the Far East.*

76. "Economic Assistance to Certain Areas of the Far East," *DSB* 22 (March 13, 1950): 405; *NYT,* February 8, 1950, p. 11; *NYT,* February 10, 1950, p. 1; *NYT,* February 11, 1950, pp. 6, 14; U.S. Congress, House, Committee on Foreign Affairs, *Providing for Foreign Economic Assistance;* U.S. Congress, House, Committee of Conference, *Conference Report on Foreign Economic Assistance Act of 1950;* U.S. Congress, Senate, Committee of Conference, *Conference Report on Foreign Economic Assistance Act of 1950.*

77. U.S. Congress, House, Committee on Appropriations, *Supplemental Estimate for Assistance to the Republic of Korea;* U.S. Congress, House, Committee on Foreign Affairs, *A Bill to Amend the Economic Cooperation Act of 1948;* U.S. Congress, Senate, Committee on Foreign Relations, *Foreign Economic Assistance, 1950.*

78. *A Bill to Amend the Economic Cooperation Act of 1948,* pp. 356–357. Acheson delivered the same presentation to the Senate Committee on Foreign Relations. See Dean G. Acheson, "Continued Aid to Korea Requested," *DSB* 22 (March 20, 1950): 454–455; *NYT,* March 8, 1950, p. 6.

79. Harry S. Truman, "Letter to the Chairman, House Committee on Foreign Affairs, Urging Enactment of the Foreign Assistance Act, March 25, 1950," *Public Papers, Truman,* VI, 228–229; *NYT,* March 31, 1950, p. 18.

80. Acheson to Muccio, February 3, 1950, *FRUS 1950,* VII, 25–26; Drumright to Acheson, February 10, 1950, ibid., 26–28.

81. Acheson to Muccio, February 14, 1950, ibid., 28–29.

82. Drumright to Acheson, February 21, 1950, ibid., 29–30; Bond memoran-

dum, March 15, 1950, ibid., 30–33; Acheson memorandum, March 22, 1950, Memoranda of Conversations, March–April 1950, box 65, Acheson papers.

83. *NYT,* January 24, 1950, p. 8; *NYT,* February 2, 1950, p. 3; *NYT,* February 8, 1950, p. 12; *NYT,* March 10, 1950, p. 14; *NYT,* March 12, 1950, p. 17; *NYT,* March 14, 1950, p. 10; U.S. Dept. of State, *The Conflict in Korea: Events Prior to the Attack on June 25, 1950,* p. 22; Kolko and Kolko, *The Limits of Power,* p. 567.

84. *NYT,* February 1, 1950, p. 13; *NYT,* March 15, 1950, p. 16; *NYT,* March 22, 1950, p. 17; Gordenker, *The United Nations and the Peaceful Unification of Korea,* p. 170; Muccio to Acheson, March 31, 1950, Dept. of State Records, 795.00/3-3150.

85. *NYT,* March 31, 1950, p. 4; *NYT,* April 1, 1950, p. 5; *NYT,* April 4, 1950, p. 26; John W. Foster to Seoul, March 27, 1950, *FRUS 1950,* VII, 36–37.

86. Bond memorandum, April 3, 1950, *FRUS 1950,* VII, 40–43; Acheson to Chang, April 3, 1950, ibid., 43–44; "U.S. Concerned Over Korea's Mounting Inflation," *DSB* 22 (April 7, 1950): 602. Muccio recommended the inclusion of the section demanding the holding of elections in South Korea on schedule. See Muccio to Acheson, April 1, 1950, *FRUS 1950,* VII, 39–40.

87. *NYT,* April 8, 1950, p. 1; Muccio to Acheson, April 4, 1950, *FRUS 1950,* VII, 44–45.

88. Drumright to Acheson, April 28, 1950, *FRUS 1950,* VII, 52–58.

89. *NYT,* April 12, 1950, p. 3; *NYT,* April 16, 1950, p. 36; *NYT,* April 18, 1950, p. 13; *NYT,* April 24, 1950, p. 5; W. G. Hackler memorandum, April 27, 1950, *FRUS 1950,* VII, 48–49.

90. *NYT,* April 27, 1950, p. 28; *Christian Century,* April 19, 1950, p. 485; *U.S. News,* April 7, 1950, pp. 24–26; Dorothy Woodman, "Korea, Formosa, and World Peace," *Political Quarterly* 21 (October 1950): 368; Bundy, *The Pattern of Responsibility,* p. 30; see also Kolko and Kolko, *The Limits of Power,* p. 569.

CHAPTER 10: *Fulfillment of a Commitment*

1. Richard E. Neustadt to Stephen J. Spingarn, June 8, 1950, International Affairs, Foreign Policy file, box 18, Stephen J. Spingarn papers.

2. Webb comments, May 15, 1950, "Freedom Budget Panel," Speech file, Frank Pace, Jr., papers.

3. Paul Y. Hammond, "NSC-68: Prologue to Rearmament," in Schilling, *Strategy, Politics, and Defense Budgets,* pp. 289–292; Bell, *Negotiation from Strength,* pp. 36–37.

4. Truman, *Years of Trial and Hope,* pp. 311–312; Charles S. Murphy, May 19, 1970, Oral History Interview Transcript, p. 184, Truman Library; Hammond, "NSC-68," pp. 308–309, 320, 326, 329–330.

5. Truman to Lawton, May 23, 1950, Memoranda for HST, Agendas and Notes, box 6, Lawton papers; Herbert Feis and Paul Nitze comments, October 10, 1953, Princeton Seminars Transcript, reel 2, tape 2, pp. 11–12, Acheson papers.

6. Hammond, "NSC-68," pp. 331–332, 345, 362, 370; Rostow, *The United States in the World Arena,* p. 225; Westerfield, *Foreign Policy and Party Politics,* p. 340. One administration official later complained that throughout the spring of 1950, NSC-68 "was being . . . nibbled to death by the ducks." See Adrian Fisher comments, October 10, 1953, Princeton Seminars Transcript, reel 2, tape 2, p. 11, Acheson papers.

7. *NYT,* February 17, 1950, p. 13; *NYT,* February 26, 1950, p. 32; Muccio to Acheson, May 3, 1950, *FRUS 1950,* VII, 66; Drumright to Acheson, May 5, 1950, ibid., 68–74.

8. *NYT,* March 3, 1950, p. 10; *NYT,* May 12, 1950, p. 3; *NYT,* May 26, 1950, p. 9; *NYT,* May 27, 1950, p. 4; Drumright to Acheson, May 1, 2, 1950, *FRUS 1950,* VII, 58–61, 63–64; Gordenker, *The United Nations and the Peaceful Unification of Korea,* pp. 179–181, 203–205; Henderson, *Korea,* p. 258.

9. *NYT,* May 30, 1950, p. 18; Muccio to Acheson, May 27, 1950, *FRUS 1950,* VII, 89–92; "The United States in the United Nations," *DSB* 22 (June 19, 1950): 1021; U.S. Dept. of State, *United States Policy in the Korean Crisis,* pp. 18–19.

10. *NYT,* May 28, 1950, p. 23; *NYT,* May 31, 1950, p. 8; *NYT,* June 1, 1950, p. 10; *NYT,* June 4, 1950, IV, p. 2; Henderson, *Korea,* p. 288; Dept. of the Army, *Korea-1950,* p. 8.

11. *NYT,* June 2, 1950, p. 22; Gunther, *The Riddle of MacArthur,* pp. 188–189; Berger, *The Korean Knot,* p. 99; Rees, *Korea,* p. 20.

12. Rusk to Webb, May 2, 1950, *FRUS 1950,* VII, 64–66; editor's note, ibid.; Drumright to Acheson, May 2, 9, 1950, ibid., 66–67, 77–78.

13. *NYT,* May 7, 1950, IV, p. 12; *NYT,* May 23, 1950, p. 2; *NYT,* May 26, 1950, p. 1.

14. Muccio to Acheson, January 25, 1950, *FRUS 1950,* VII, 15–18; Allison to Najeeb Halaby, January 31, 1950, ibid., 24–25; see also Drumright to Acheson, March 16, 1950, ibid., 34–35.

15. Roberts to Wedemeyer, May 2, 1949, Dept. of the Army Records, P&O 091 Korea, sec. III, cases 41–60, box 548, RG 319; Drumright to Acheson, May 11, 1950, *FRUS 1950,* VII, 83–84.

16. Roberts memorandum, January 25, 1950, Dept. of the Army Records, P&O 091 Korea, sec. IV, case 60, box 549, RG 319; Bond and Lawson memorandum, February 8, 1950, ibid.

17. W. G. Hackler memorandum, April 27, 1950, *FRUS 1950,* VII, 48–51; see also Acheson to Muccio, April 13, 1950, ibid., 45–46; Drumright to Acheson, April 20, 1950, ibid., 46–47.

18. Bond memorandum, May 10, 1950, ibid., 78–81; Acting MDAP Director to Rusk, May 10, 1950, ibid., 82–83; Webb to Seoul, May 19, 1950, ibid., 85–86; Muccio to Acheson, May 23, 1950, ibid., 87–88. At one press conference, Rhee even suggested that the South Koreans would expand their military capabilities by "selling our bodies if necessary." See Drumright to Acheson, January 25, 1950, Dept. of State Records, 795.00/1–2550.

19. *NYT,* March 2, 1950, p. 20; John J. Muccio, December 27, 1973, Oral History Interview Transcript, pp. 14–16, Truman Library.

20. Leven C. Allen to JCS, May 26, 1950, JCS Records, CCS 383.21 Korea (3–19–45), sec. XXI, RG 218; Memorandum for the Secretary of Defense, n.d., ibid.

21. U.S. Congress, House, Committee on Appropriations, *First Semiannual Report on Mutual Defense Assistance Program.*

22. Sawyer and Hermes, *Military Advisors in Korea,* pp. 104, 106, 186; *Military Situation in the Far East,* p. 2115; see also John Dille, *Substitute for Victory,* pp. 18–19; Henderson, *Korea,* p. 341; Leckie *Conflict,* pp. 36–37. During June 1950, Muccio cabled Washington that he believed, "and KMAG concurs, should South Korean forces be strengthened by some measure [in] air defense and heavy artillery, superiority or at least reasonable equality would rest with South vis-à-vis North Koreans." See Muccio to Acheson, June 14, 1950, *FRUS 1950,* VII, 105.

23. Bolte to Roberts, December 28, 1949, Dept. of the Army Records, P&O 091 Korea, sec. IV, case 61, box 549, RG 319; Muccio to Acheson, June 23, 1950, *FRUS 1950,* VII, 121–124; Sawyer and Hermes, *Military Advisors in Korea,* pp. 112–113. Army Department officials decided to order a phased reduction in the size of the KMAG after Roberts reported that the ROK constabulary army, during recent suc-

cessful operations against guerrillas in South Korea, had proved its ability to halt an invasion from the north. For Bolte, these comments from Roberts were especially timely because "currently, the JCS are studying, on a global basis, the possibility of reducing missions, advisory groups and other special assignments." On April 18, MacArthur received word from Washington that it was "increasingly important . . . to economize in terms of personnel and dollars in Korea." Ironically, Roberts developed a plan for a forty percent reduction in the KMAG by January 1, 1951, which arrived in Washington on the day North Korea invaded the ROK. See Roberts to Bolte, March 8, 1950, Bolte to Roberts, March 27, 1950, Dept. of the Army Records, 091 Korea, sec. I, cases 1–20, box 121, RG 319; Duff to MacArthur, April 18, 1950, ibid., sec. I-B, case 4 only, bk. I, subs. 1-, box 121.

24. Quoted in Robert D. Heinl, *Victory at High Tide: The Inchon-Seoul Campaign,* p. 12; *NYT,* May 20, 1950, p. 7. Muccio was much impressed with the ROK constabulary army's systematic destruction of guerrilla forces in North Kyongsang province. "With loss during past three weeks of about 500 men and several hundred weapons," he enthused, "North Koreans may be loath to commit more men and equipment to such adventures." See Muccio to Acheson, April 4, 1950, Dept. of State Records, 795B.00/4-2550. See also Central Intelligence Agency report, June 19, 1950, *FRUS 1950,* VII, 109–111; Collins, *War in Peacetime,* p. 43. According to one report in *Time* magazine, "most observers now rate the 100,000-man South Korean army as the best of its size in Asia"; *Time,* June 5, 1950, p. 26.

25. Muccio to MacArthur, June 4, 1950, Private Correspondence, VIP file, folder 30, box 8, RG 10, MacArthur papers; Muccio to Rusk, May 25, 1950, *FRUS 1950,* VII, 88–89; Muccio to Rusk, June 1, 1950, ibid., 96–97.

26. "John Foster Dulles to Visit Korea and Japan," *DSB* 23 (June 19, 1950): 998; "Statement by John Foster Dulles on Departure for Far East," *DSB* 23 (June 26, 1950): 1061; *NYT,* June 8, 1950, p. 13; *NYT,* June 19, 1950, p. 3; Allison, *Ambassador from the Prairie,* p. 147.

27. John Foster Dulles, "The Korean Experiment in Representative Government," *DSB* 23 (July 3, 1950): 12–13; *NYT,* June 20, 1950, p. 20. According to John M. Allison, who accompanied Dulles on his trip to Korea, administration officials in Washington were responsible for drafting the Dulles speech. See Allison, *Ambassador from the Prairie,* p. 130.

28. Dulles to William L. Holland, August 17, 1950, Korea 1950, John Foster Dulles papers; Dulles to Holland, September 7, 1950, ibid.; William R. Matthews to Dulles, June 20, 1950, Correspondence, box 142, ibid.

29. Appleman, *South to the Naktong, North to the Yalu,* pp. 12–18; Henderson, *Korea,* pp. 149, 341; Heinl, *Victory at High Tide,* pp. 12–13; H. A. DeWeerd, "Strategic Surprise in the Korean War," *Orbis* 6 (Fall 1962): 438.

30. Drumright to Acheson, May 11, 1950, *FRUS 1950,* VII, 83–84; Central Intelligence Agency report, June 19, 1950, ibid., 118–121; Schnabel, *Policy and Direction,* p. 37; Dept. of State, *North Korea,* pp. 17, 114–116; see also Allen S. Whiting, *China Crosses the Yalu: The Decision to Enter the Korean War,* p. 43.

31. Muccio to Acheson, June 9, 10, 1950, *FRUS 1950,* VII, 98–102; *NYT,* June 9, 1950, p. 15; *NYT,* June 10, 1950, p. 4.

32. Muccio to Acheson, June 11, 12, 13, 1950, *FRUS 1950,* VII, 102–104; *NYT,* June 11, 1950, p. 26; "The United States in the United Nations," *DSB* 23 (June 19, 1950): 1021.

33. Muccio to Acheson, June 16, 1950, *FRUS 1950,* VII, 106–107; Schnabel, *Policy and Direction,* p. 9; Dept. of the Army, *Korea-1950,* pp. 7–9; Beloff, *Soviet Foreign Policy in the Far East,* p. 182; Kim, *Divided Korea,* p. 173.

34. Drumright to Allison, July 5, 1950, Topical file 1, folder 3, PSF–Korean War

Documents, box 4, Truman papers; Muccio, February 10, 1971, Oral History Interview Transcript, p. 32; Muccio, December 27, 1973, Oral History Interview Transcript, pp. 10–11; Strobe Talbott, ed., *Khrushchev Remembers*, p. 369; Appleman, *South to the Naktong, North to the Yalu*, pp. 19–20, 34. Some revisionist historians have attempted to prove that Rhee initiated the attack starting the Korean War. These writers argue that during the Dulles visit to the ROK, American leaders and Rhee completed plans for a South Korean invasion of North Korea. See I. F. Stone, *The Hidden History of the Korean War*, pp. 22–27; Karunakar Gupta, "How Did the Korean War Begin?" *China Quarterly* (October–December 1972): 699–716. Scant evidence exists, however, to substantiate such an interpretation. On this point, see Robert R. Simmons, Chong-sik Lee, W. E. Skillend, and Karunakar Gupta, "Comment," *China Quarterly* (April–June 1973): 354–368.

35. Lloyd C. Gardner, "Truman Era Foreign Policy: Recent Historical Trends," in Kirkendall, *The Truman Period as a Research Field*, p. 59; Wilbur W. Hitchcock, "North Korea Jumps the Gun," *Current History* 20 (March 20, 1951): 142; Fleming, *The Cold War and Its Origins*, II, pp. 605–606; Robert R. Simmons, "The Korean Civil War," in Baldwin, *Without Parallel*, pp. 149, 171; Gordenker, *The United Nations and the Peaceful Unification of Korea*, p. 241. For an assessment of the extent of Soviet involvement in the outbreak of the war in Korea, see William Stueck, "The Soviet Union and the Origins of the Korean War," *World Politics* 28 (July 1976): 622–635.

36. William Stueck, "Cold War Revisionism and the Origins of the Korean Conflict: The Kolko Thesis," *Pacific Historical Review* 42 (November 1973): 547; Marguerite Higgins, *War in Korea*, p. 162; "Review of Korea's Postwar Economy," pp. 235–236; Fehrenbach, *This Kind of War*, p. 53; Paige, "Korea," pp. 227–228.

37. Hitchcock, "North Korea Jumps the Gun," p. 142; Stueck, "The Soviet Union and the Origins of the Korean War," p. 631; see also Kolko and Kolko, *The Limits of Power*, pp. 573–578; Simmons, *The Strained Alliance*, p. 114.

38. Talbott, *Khrushchev Remembers*, pp. 367–368.

39. Acheson testimony, *Military Situation in the Far East*, pp. 1715, 1936; Truman, *Years of Trial and Hope*, pp. 333, 464; May, "The Nature of Foreign Policy," pp. 662–663; May, *"Lessons" of the Past*, pp. 73–74, 80–82; Dept. of State Intelligence Estimate, June 25, 1950, *FRUS 1950*, VII, 149.

40. Elsey notes, June 26, 1950, box 71, George M. Elsey papers.

41. Gardner, "Introduction," pp. 7, 11, *Military Situation in the Far East*, p. 971; Fleming, *The Cold War and Its Origins*, II, pp. 602–604.

42. Marshall D. Shulman, *Stalin's Foreign Policy Reappraised*, p. 140; Bundy, *The Pattern of Responsibility*, p. 245.

43. Acheson to Muccio, June 24, 1950, *FRUS 1950*, VII, 125; Muccio to Acheson, June 25, 1950, ibid., 125–126; Albert L. Warner, "How the Korean Decision Was Made," *Harper's* 202 (June 1951): 99. At 6:30 A.M. in Seoul, the KMAG received word from South Korea's duty officer of an "exceptionally strong attack" across the 38th parallel. After three more reports, the KMAG notified Drumright, who "dismissed it as just another rumor." But when the KMAG had confirmed that North Korea was engaged in an invasion in force, Drumright contacted Muccio at 9:30 A.M. See Drumright to Allison, July 5, 1950, Topical file 1, folder 3, PSF–Korean War Documents, box 4, Truman papers. Muccio waited for positive confirmation from the KMAG before cabling news of the attack to Washington at 11:26 A.M. Because of the fourteen-hour time differential, the administration received this information at 9:26 P.M. on June 24. See Elsey memorandum, June 26, 1950, Korea (June 24, 1950), box 71, Elsey papers; Muccio, February 10, 1971, Oral History Interview Transcript, pp. 30–32.

44. Editor's note, *FRUS 1950*, VII, 126–127; Acheson comments, February 13, 1954, Princeton Seminars Transcript, reel 2, tape 1, p. 1, Acheson papers; Frank Pace, Jr., January 21, 1971, Oral History Interview Transcript, p. 67, Truman Library; Elsey memorandum, June 26, 1950, Korea (June 24, 1950), box 71, Elsey papers; Acheson, *Present at the Creation*, pp. 401–402.

45. Acheson, *Present at the Creation*, p. 404; Truman, *Years of Trial and Hope*, p. 332; Eben A. Ayers chronology, June 25, 1950, Diary–1950, box 16, p. 94, Eben A. Ayers papers; Truman to Elsey, June 27, 1950, Korea (June 24, 1950), box 71, Elsey papers; Noble to Elsey, June 29, 1951, ibid.; memorandum of conversation, n.d., ibid.; Rusk memorandum, August 7, 1950, *FRUS 1950*, VII, 128.

46. Trygve Lie, *In the Cause of Peace*, pp. 327–328; John D. Hickerson, June 5, 1973, Oral History Interview Transcript, pp. 93–94, Truman Library; Warner, "How the Korean Decision Was Made," p. 100.

47. Muccio to Acheson, June 25, 1950, *FRUS 1950*, VII, 129; Muccio to MacArthur, June 25, 1950, ibid., 133; teleconference, June 25, 1950, ibid., 135–138; MacArthur to Irwin, June 25, 1950, Acheson briefing book, Korea (June 25, 1950), box 71, Elsey papers; Schnabel, *Policy and Direction*, p. 65.

48. Editor's note, *FRUS 1950*, VII, 128; Acheson to certain embassies, June 25, 1950, ibid., 131; Hickerson, June 5, 1973, Oral History Interview Transcript, p. 95; see also U.S. Dept. of State, *Guide to the U.N. in Korea*, p. 6.

49. United States resolution, June 25, 1950, *FRUS 1950*, VII, 155–156; "U.S. Presents Cease-Fire Resolution to Security Council," *DSB* 23 (July 3, 1950): 3–5.

50. Editor's note, *FRUS 1950*, VII, 143; Truman to Elsey, June 27, 1950, Korea (June 25, 1950), box 71, Elsey papers; Elsey notes, n.d., ibid.; Acheson, *Present at the Creation*, p. 404; Warner "How the Korean Decision Was Made," p. 100.

51. Charles P. Noyes memorandum, June 25, 1950, *FRUS 1950*, VII, 144–147; editor's note, ibid.; Lie, *In the Cause of Peace*, p. 330.

52. Bundy, *The Pattern of Responsibility*, p. 254; Bloomfield, *The United Nations and U.S. Foreign Policy*, p. 13; E. Joan Parr, "Korea—Its Place in History," *Political Quarterly* 23 (October 1952): 358.

53. Edwin C. Hoyt, "The United States Reaction to the Korean Attack," *American Journal of International Law* 55 (January 1961): 49, 55; Coral Bell, "Korea and the Balance of Power," *Political Quarterly* 25 (January–March 1954): 27; Spanier, *The Truman-MacArthur Controversy and the Korean War*, p. 38; Bloomfield, *The United Nations and U.S. Foreign Policy*, pp. 63, 66–67.

54. Kennan, *Memoirs 1925–1950*, p. 490; see also Goodrich, *Korea*, p. 117; Philip E. Mosely, "Soviet Policy and the War," *Journal of International Affairs* 6 (Spring 1952): 107–114; Reitzel, Kaplan, and Coblenz, *United States Foreign Policy*, pp. 266–267.

55. Dulles and Allison to Acheson and Rusk, June 25, 1950, Korea (June 25, 1950), box 71, Elsey papers; MacArthur to J. Lawton Collins, June 25, 1950, Far East Command Records, Korea file 1, folder 4, box 9, RG 6, MacArthur papers.

56. Walworth Barbour to Acheson, June 25, 1950, *FRUS 1950*, VII, 139–140. Ambassador Alan G. Kirk later endorsed this call for a firm stand. See Kirk to Acheson, June 27, 1950, ibid., 199.

57. JCS briefing paper, June 25, 1950, Korea (June 25, 1950), box 71, Elsey papers.

58. Memorandum, June 25, 1950, ibid.; Acheson to Muccio, June 25, 1950, *FRUS 1950*, VII, 156–157.

59. Ayers chronology, June 25, 1950, Diary–1950, pp. 94–95, Ayers papers; Webb to John W. Snyder, April 25, 1975, General Correspondence, 1973–1975, S-folder 2, James E. Webb papers.

60. Beverly Smith, "The White House Story: Why We Went to War in Korea," *Saturday Evening Post* 224 (November 10, 1951): 76; Collins, *War in Peacetime*, p. 13. For the full text of MacArthur's memorandum, see *FRUS 1950*, VII, 161–165.

61. Acheson comments, February 13, 1954, Princeton Seminars Transcript, reel 2, tape 1, p. 3, Acheson papers; Smith, "The White House Story," pp. 78–79.

62. Jessup memorandum, June 25, 1950, Memoranda of Conversations, May–June 1950, box 65, Acheson papers.

63. Ibid.

64. Ibid.; Truman, *Years of Trial and Hope*, pp. 334–335; Acheson, *Present at the Creation*, p. 406; Collins, *War in Peacetime*, p. 14; Schnabel, *Policy and Direction*, p. 69; see also Paige, *The Korean Decision*, pp. 130–143.

65. Muccio to Acheson, June 25, 1950, *FRUS 1950*, VII, 165–166; Acheson to Kee, June 26, 1950, ibid., 170–171; teleconference, June 25, 1950, Korea (June 25, 1950), box 71, Elsey papers; Acheson to Connally, June 26, 1950, Memoranda of Conversations, May–June 1950, box 65, Acheson papers. Nevertheless, Muccio had ordered the evacuation of dependent American women and children. By early morning on the second day of the war, nearly seven hundred people were safely aboard the Norwegian fertilizer ship *Reinholdt* and on their way to Japan. See Muccio to Acheson, June 26, 1950, *FRUS 1950*, VII, 140–141, 154–155, 168; Drumright to Allison, July 5, 1950, Topical file 1, folder 3, PSF–Korean War Documents, box 4, Truman papers; Sawyer and Hermes, *Military Advisors in Korea*, pp. 120–123.

66. One reason why Muccio delayed the evacuation of Seoul was to discourage government officials from fleeing southward. During discussions with Rhee, he emphasized that once the president and his cabinet left the capital, the South Korean people would become demoralized and "much of the battle would be lost." Worse still, "think what history will say of you," the ambassador advised. Terrified at the thought of being captured, Rhee and his cabinet "took off for the tall timber" on the morning of June 27. See Muccio to Acheson, June 26, 1950, *FRUS 1950*, VII, 141–143; Hickerson, June 5, 1973, Oral History Interview Transcript, pp. 101–102; Muccio, February 10, 1971, Oral History Interview Transcript, p. 34.

67. Muccio to Acheson, June 26, 27, 1950, *FRUS 1950*, VII, 170, 173, 184–185; Acheson to Sebald, June 26, 1950, ibid., 178; Drumright to Allison, July 5, 1950, Topical file 1, folder 3, PSF–Korean War Documents, box 4, Truman papers; see also Allison, *Ambassador from the Prairie*, pp. 134–136.

68. Jessup memorandum, June 26, 1950, Memoranda of Conversations, May–June 1950, box 65, Acheson papers.

69. Ibid.; Truman to Elsey, June 27, 1950, Korea (June 26, 1950), box 71, Elsey papers.

70. Teleconference, June 26, 1950, Korea (June 26, 1950), box 71, Elsey papers; Smith, "The White House Story," pp. 80–81; Paige, *The Korean Decision*, p. 167; Leckie, *Conflict*, p. 53.

71. Harry S. Truman, "U.S. Air and Sea Forces Ordered into Supporting Action," *DSB* 23 (July 3, 1950): 5.

72. Muccio to Acheson, June 26, 1950, *FRUS 1950*, VII, 168–169; UNCOK to Lie, June 26, 1950, ibid., 207; Dept. of State, *United States Policy in the Korean Crisis*, pp. 2–3, 19–21.

73. Austin to Acheson, June 27, 1950, *FRUS 1950*, VII, 208–209; "Resolution Adopted by United Nations Security Council," June 27, 1950, ibid., 211; Warren R. Austin, "U.S. Asks Security Council to Assist in Repelling Attack," *DSB* 23 (July 3, 1950): 6–8; Lie, *In the Cause of Peace*, pp. 332–333.

74. Elsey notes, June 27, 1950, Korea (June 27, 1950), box 71, Elsey papers; Acheson to Johnson, June 28, 1950, *FRUS 1950*, VII, 217; memorandum of conversation,

June 28, 1950, Memoranda of Conversations, May–June 1950, box 65, Acheson papers; NSC Meeting minutes, June 28, 1950, NSC Meeting 58–June 28, 1950, NSC Meetings 56–64 (May 4–August 10, 1950), PSF–National Security Council Documents, box 208, Truman papers; Lindsay memorandum, June 28, 1950, JCS Records, CCS 383.21 Korea (3–19–45), sec. XXI, RG 218; Truman, *Years of Trial and Hope,* pp. 340–341.

75. North Korean military forces entered Seoul during the late evening of June 27. By that time, the ROK's military chief of staff had destroyed prematurely the pedestrian bridge across the Han River. Not only were several American advisors then trapped in Seoul, but the "blowing of the bridge was the breaking point for control over the populace . . . , and from that point on panic, confusion and disorder reigned in the city." See Major General Frank E. Lowe, n.d., Report on Mission, Appendix to KMAG report, tab 1, PSF–Frank E. Lowe file, box 246, Truman papers.

76. Appleman, *South to the Naktong, North to the Yalu,* pp. 40–43; Sawyer and Hermes, *Military Advisors in Korea,* p. 133.

77. Muccio to Acheson, June 28, 1950, *FRUS 1950,* VII, 210–211.

78. Appleman, *South to the Naktong, North to the Yalu,* p. 44; Drumright to Acheson, June 29, 1950, *FRUS 1950,* VII, 220–221; Dept. of the Army, *Korea–1950,* p. 13; Church to MacArthur, June 28, 1950, Far East Command Records, Correspondence, folder 1, box 4, RG 6, MacArthur papers.

79. Douglas MacArthur, *Reminiscences,* p. 332; Collins, *War in Peacetime,* pp. 18–19; Schnabel, *Policy and Direction,* p. 74; see also Richard R. Haynes, *The Awesome Power: Harry S. Truman as Commander in Chief,* p. 177.

80. Appleman, *South to the Naktong, North to the Yalu,* pp. 44–45; Drumright to Acheson, June 29, 1950, *FRUS 1950,* VII, 227–228; Major General John H. Chiles, July 27, 1977, Oral History Interview Transcript, pp. 33–34, Truman Library.

81. Acheson notes, June 29, 1950, Korea (June 29, 1950), box 71, Elsey papers; Drumright to Allison, July 5, 1950, Topical file 1, folder 3, PSF–Korean War Documents, box 4, Truman papers; MacArthur to JCS, June 29, 1950, Far East Command Records, Korea file 1, folder 4, box 9, RG 6, MacArthur, papers.

82. Kirk to Acheson, June 29, 1950, *FRUS 1950,* VII, 229–230.

83. NSC Meeting minutes, June 28 [29], 1950, NSC Meeting 59–June 29, 1950, NSC Meeting 56–64 (May 4–August 10, 1950), PSF–National Security Council Documents, box 208, Truman papers; NSC Meeting summary, June 29, 1950, NSC Memoranda for the President (Meeting Discussions, 1948–1953), ibid., box 220, Truman papers; Elsey notes, June 29, 1950, (White House–State–Defense Meeting, 5 P.M., June 29, 1950), box 71, Elsey papers.

84. Ibid.; see also Truman, *Years of Trial and Hope,* pp. 341–342; Paige, *The Korean Decision,* pp. 248–249.

85. Ibid.; Acheson, *Present at the Creation,* pp. 411–412.

86. JCS to MacArthur, June 29, 1950, *FRUS 1950,* VII, 240–241; Babcock to Dulles, November 24, 1950, Conference Dossiers (UN–China 1950), file 473, Dulles papers; Acheson briefing paper, n.d. (White House–State–Defense Meeting, 5 P.M., June 29, 1950), box 71, Elsey papers.

87. MacArthur to JCS, June 30, 1950, *FRUS 1950,* VII, 248–250; Glenn Paige has noted the discrepancy between the contents of this report and the timing of its dispatch. MacArthur returned from Suwŏn fifteen hours before he requested the use of American combat ground forces; see Paige, *The Korean Decision,* p. 239. In all probability, General Church's extremely pessimistic report on the afternoon of June 30 (Korean time) stimulated MacArthur's action. At that time, Church cabled Tokyo that the situation had deteriorated further and the South Korean army could not halt the Communist advance. See Appleman, *South to the Naktong, North to the Yalu,* pp. 56–57.

88. Memorandum, June 30, 1950, Korea (June 30, 1950), box 71, Elsey papers; teleconference, June 30, 1950, *FRUS 1950,* VII, 250–252; Far East Command Records, Korea file 1, folder 4, box 9, RG 6, MacArthur papers.

89. Pace, January 22, 1972, Oral History Interview Transcript, pp. 73–74; Acheson briefing paper, June 30, 1950, box 71, Elsey papers; see also Truman, *Years of Trial and Hope,* p. 342; Paige, *The Korean Decision,* p. 256.

90. William J. Sebald to Acheson, June 30, 1950, *FRUS 1950,* VII, 254–255; Truman, *Years of Trial and Hope,* p. 343; Ayers chronology, June 30, 1950, Diary–1950, box 16, p. 102, Ayers papers; Schnabel, *Policy and Direction,* p. 79.

91. Elsey notes, June 30, 1950, Korea (June 30, 1950), box 71, Elsey papers; Elsey, April 9, 1970, Oral History Interview Transcript, p. 270; Paige, *The Korean Decision,* p. 260.

92. Stueck, "The Soviet Union and the Origins of the Korean War" p. 632; Gaddis, "Korea in American Politics, Strategy, and Diplomacy," pp. 285–286; Whiting, *China Crosses the Yalu,* pp. 38–39; Paige, "Korea," pp. 227–228.

93. Talbott, *Khrushchev Remembers,* p. 368.

94. Acheson testimony, *Military Situation in the Far East,* p. 1991; Truman, *Years of Trial and Hope,* p. 331; Muccio to Acheson, June 29, 1950, *FRUS 1950,* VII, 99–101; see also Schnabel, *Policy and Direction,* p. 64; McLellan, *Dean Acheson,* pp. 268–269. Kennan, Collins, and MacArthur all emphasize that the North Korean attack was a complete surprise. See Kennan, *Memoirs 1925–1950,* p. 485; Collins, *War in Peacetime,* p. 2; MacArthur, *Reminiscences,* p. 327; see also Gaddis, "Korea in American Politics, Strategy, and Diplomacy," p. 286. In May 1950, the ROK's defense minister warned that a North Korean invasion was imminent. See *NYT,* May 11, 1950, p. 14; editor's note, *FRUS 1950,* VII, 85. Rhee had pointed to the threat of an attack from the north so often in the past, however, that American leaders did not assign any particular importance to these recent warnings. See Stueck, *The Road to Confrontation,* p. 168.

95. Truman, *Years of Trial and Hope,* p. 333; Kennan, *Memoirs 1925–1950,* p. 486; Collins, *War in Peacetime,* p. 41. Recently, several writers have stressed that Truman intervened in the Korean War to preserve American credibility and prestige. See Stueck, *The Road to Confrontation,* p. 173; Buhite, " 'Major Interests'," pp. 450–451; Gaddis, "Korea in American Politics, Strategy, and Diplomacy," p. 288. While this interpretation is both important and valid, it is not particularly new. For earlier examples, see Louis J. Halle, *The Cold War as History,* p. 208; Spanier, *The Truman-MacArthur Controversy and the Korean War,* p. 28; Robert E. Osgood, *Limited War: The Challenge to American Strategy,* p. 166; Berger, *The Korean Knot,* p. 108; Fehrenbach, *This Kind of War,* p. 80; Rovere and Schlesinger, *The General and the President,* p. 99; Rostow, *The United States in the World Arena,* p. 235.

Conclusion

1. Harry S. Truman, "The Challenge of the Cold War," *DSB* 28 (January 26, 1953): 127; see also Truman, *Years of Trial and Hope,* p. 463; Francis H. Heller, *The Korean War: A 25-Year Perspective,* pp. 3–9.

2. Gaddis, "Was the Truman Doctrine a Real Turning Point?" p. 391.

3. Truman, *Years of Trial and Hope,* p. 464; see also Acheson comments, October 11, 1953, Princeton Seminars Transcript, reel 6, tape 1, p. 2, Acheson papers; Smith, *Dean Acheson,* pp. 423–424.

4. NSC Meeting minutes, December 29, 1949, NSC Meeting 50–December 29, 1949, NSC Meetings 48–55, PSF–National Security Council Documents, box 207, Truman papers; see also Webb to James S. Lay, Jr., February 10, 1950, NSC Meeting

36–March 22, 1949, NSC Meetings 28–37 (December 2, 1948–April 7, 1949), ibid. Subsequent scholars have noted correctly that the administration failed to publicize the extent of its commitment to the ROK prior to North Korea's invasion. See Stueck, *The Road to Confrontation*, pp. 161–162; Goodrich, *Korea*, p. 100; Paige, *The Korean Decision*, pp. 65–66.

5. John Foster Dulles, "A Militarist Experiment," *DSB* 23 (July 10, 1950): 49–50; John Foster Dulles, "To Save Humanity from the Deep Abyss," *New York Times Magazine*, July 30, 1950, pp. 5, 34; Dulles memorandum, June 29, 1950, *FRUS 1950*, VII, 237.

6. John Foster Dulles, "Korean Attack Opens New Chapter in History," *DSB* 23 (August 7, 1950): 207–210; Dulles, "A Militarist Experiment," pp. 49–50; Dulles, "To Save Humanity from the Deep Abyss," p. 34; see also Theoharis, *Seeds of Repression*, p. 62; Shulman, *Stalin's Foreign Policy Reappraised*, p. 140.

7. John Foster Dulles, "U.S. Military Action in Korea," *DSB* 23 (July 17, 1950): 88–92.

8. Washington to Tokyo, June 27, 1950, Far East Command Records, Korea file 1, folder 4, box 9, RG 6, MacArthur papers; Acheson to certain embassies, June 26, 1950, *FRUS 1950*, VII, 166.

9. Dulles, "To Save Humanity from the Deep Abyss," pp. 34–35; Dulles, "U.S. Military Action in Korea," pp. 90–91.

10. Acheson comments, October 10, 1953, Princeton Seminars Transcripts, reel 2, tape 2, p. 15, Acheson papers. One administration official later observed that "we were sweating over it, and then—with regard to NSC-68—thank God Korea came along." See Barrett comments, October 10, 1953, ibid., reel 3, tape 1, p. 3; see also Nitze comments, October 11, 1953, ibid., reel 6, tape 1, pp. 1–4; Frederick J. Lawton, July 9, 1973, Oral History Interview Transcript, p. 20, Truman Library; Bundy, *The Pattern of Responsibility*, p. 77. Many writers have pointed out that the Korean War provided the stimulus for implementation of NSC-68. On this issue see Gaddis, "Korea in American Politics, Strategy, and Diplomacy," pp. 290–291; Bell, *Negotiation from Strength*, p. 38; Graebner, "Dean Acheson," p. 272; McLellan, "Commentary," p. 156; Simmons, *The Strained Alliance*, pp. 141–142; Walter LaFeber, *America, Russia, and the Cold War, 1945–1966*, p. 104; Bert Cochran, *Harry Truman and the Crisis Presidency*, pp. 348–349.

11. Bundy, *The Pattern of Responsibility*, p. 76; Rostow, *The United States in the World Arena*, p. 257; Rees, *Korea*, p. 445; Charles E. Bohlen, *The Transformation of American Foreign Policy*, p. 114; Gardner, "Introduction," pp. 5, 13; Steel, *Pax Americana*, p. 129; May, "The Nature of Foreign Policy," p. 663; Seyom Brown, "Korea and the Balance of Power," in Allen Guttman, ed., *Korea: Cold War and Limited War*, pp. 249, 258; Norman Kaner, "I. F. Stone and the Korean War," in Thomas G. Paterson, ed., *Cold War Critics: Alternatives to Foreign Policy in the Truman Years*, pp. 247–248.

12. Bundy, *The Pattern of Responsibility*, pp. 77–80; Stueck, *The Road to Confrontation*, pp. 173–174; Bell, *Negotiation from Strength*, p. 17; Graebner, "Dean Acheson," p. 272.

13. Kennan, *Memoirs 1925–1950*, pp. 498–499; Spanier, *The Truman-MacArthur Controversy and the Korean War*, p. 270; Osgood, *Limited War*, pp. 166, 191–192; Theoharis, *Seeds of Repression*, pp. 65–66; Paige, *The Korean Decision*, p. 352; Almond, *The American People and Foreign Policy*, pp. 79, 159; Gardner, "Truman Era Foreign Policy," p. 59; William Appleman Williams, *The Tragedy of American Diplomacy*, p. 273; see also Michael S. Twedt, "The War Rhetoric of Harry S. Truman During the Korean Conflict" (Ph.D. dissertation, University of Kansas, 1969), pp. 232, 242.

14. Norman A. Graebner, *Cold War Diplomacy 1945–1960,* pp. 57–60; Bell, "Korea and the Balance of Power," p. 29; Reitzel, Kaplan, and Coblenz, *United States Foreign Policy,* pp. 302, 323.

15. Quoted in Rees, *Korea,* p. 449; see also Bundy, *The Pattern of Responsibility,* pp. 253–254; May, *"Lessons" of the Past,* pp. 75–76; Higgins, *War in Korea,* p. 17.

16. Gaddis, "Containment: A Reassessment," p. 876.

17. Charles E. Bohlen offers the compelling conclusion that in the absence of the Korean War, "I seriously doubt that we would have any involvements of a military nature in the Pacific." See Bohlen, *The Transformation of American Foreign Policy,* p. 114. John Lewis Gaddis has pointed out that American military capabilities did not match Truman's globalist rhetoric until after the Korean War. As he explains, "despite its sweeping language the Truman administration, between 1947 and 1950, had neither the intention nor the capability of policing the rest of the world; . . . the real commitment to contain communism everywhere originated in the events surrounding the Korean War." See Gaddis, "Was the Truman Doctrine a Real Turning Point?" p. 386; see also Denis Brogan, "The Illusion of American Omnipotence," *Harper's* 205 (December 1952): 22–27; Steel, *Pax Americana,* p. 23; Brown, "Korea and the Balance of Power," p. 255; Baldwin, "Introduction," p. 16; Harry J. Middleton, *The Compact History of the Korean War,* pp. 231–232; Gardner, "Introduction," p. 24.

Selected Bibliography

Primary Sources

MANUSCRIPT AND ARCHIVAL COLLECTIONS

Acheson, Dean G. Harry S. Truman Library. Independence, Mo.
Allison, John M. Harry S. Truman Library. Independence, Mo.
Ayers, Eben A. Harry S. Truman Library. Independence, Mo.
Byrnes, James F. Clemson University Library. Clemson, S.C.
Clifford, Clark M. Harry S. Truman Library. Independence, Mo.
Connelly, Matthew J. Harry S. Truman Library. Independence, Mo.
Dennison, Robert L. Harry S. Truman Library. Independence, Mo.
Dulles, John Foster. Princeton University Library. Princeton, N.J.
Elsey, George M. Harry S. Truman Library. Independence, Mo.
Hull, Cordell. Library of Congress. Washington, D.C.
Johnson, Edgar A. J. Harry S. Truman Library. Independence, Mo.
Lawton, Frederick J. Harry S. Truman Library. Independence, Mo.
Leahy, William D. Library of Congress. Washington, D.C.
Lloyd, David. Harry S. Truman Library. Independence, Mo.
Locke, Edwin A., Jr. Harry S. Truman Library. Independence, Mo.
MacArthur, Douglas A. Douglas A. MacArthur Memorial Library. Norfolk, Va.
Murphy, Charles S. Harry S. Truman Library. Independence, Mo.
Pace, Frank, Jr. Harry S. Truman Library. Independence, Mo.
Patterson, Robert P. Library of Congress. Washington, D.C.
Spingarn, Stephen J. Harry S. Truman Library. Independence, Mo.
Stettinius, Edward R., Jr. University of Virginia Library. Charlottesville, Va.
Thayer, Charles W. Harry S. Truman Library. Independence, Mo.
Truman, Harry S. Harry S. Truman Library. Independence, Mo.
U.S. Department of the Army Archives. Army Staff Files. Record Group 319. National Archives. Washington, D.C.
———. Civil Affairs Section Files. Record Group 165. National Archives. Washington, D.C.
———. Secretary of the Army Files. Record Group 335. National Archives. Washington, D.C.
U.S. Department of State Archives. Record Group 59. National Archives. Washington, D.C.
U.S. Joint Chiefs of Staff Archives. Record Group 218. National Archives. Washington, D.C.
U.S. Office of Strategic Services Archives. Record Group 226. National Archives. Washington, D.C.
Webb, James E. Harry S. Truman Library. Independence, Mo.

MEMOIRS AND PERSONAL ACCOUNTS

Acheson, Dean G. *Present at the Creation: My Years in the State Department.* New York: Norton, 1969.
Allison, John M. *Ambassador from the Prairie or Allison Wonderland.* Boston: Houghton Mifflin, 1973.
Byrnes, James F. *Speaking Frankly.* New York: Harper & Row, 1947.
Collins, J. Lawton. *War in Peacetime: The History and Lessons of Korea.* Boston: Houghton Mifflin, 1969.
Eden, Anthony. *The Reckoning.* Boston: Houghton Mifflin, 1956.
Ferrell, Robert H., ed. *Off the Record: The Private Papers of Harry S. Truman.* New York: Penguin Books, 1980.
Grew, Joseph C., and Johnson, Walter, eds. *Turbulent Era: A Diplomatic Record of Forty Years 1904–1945.* 2 vols. Boston: Houghton Mifflin, 1952.
Hull, Cordell. *The Memoirs of Cordell Hull.* 2 vols. New York: Macmillan, 1948.
Kennan, George F. *Memoirs 1925–1950.* Boston: Little, Brown, 1967.
Leahy, William D. *I Was There.* New York: McGraw-Hill, 1950.
Lie, Trygve. *In the Cause of Peace.* New York: Macmillan, 1955.
MacArthur, Douglas A. *Reminiscences.* New York: McGraw-Hill, 1964.
Millis, Walter, ed. *The Forrestal Diaries.* New York: Viking Press, 1951.
Ridgway, Matthew B. *The Korean War.* Garden City: Doubleday, 1967.
Rosenman, Samuel I., ed. *The Public Papers and Addresses of Franklin D. Roosevelt.* Vols. 11–13. New York: Random House, 1950.
Stimson, Henry L., and Bundy, McGeorge, eds. *On Active Service in Peace and War.* New York: Harper & Row, 1947.
Talbott, Strobe, ed. *Khrushchev Remembers.* Boston: Little, Brown, 1970.
Truman, Harry S. *Memoirs.* Vol. 1: *Year of Decisions.* Garden City: Doubleday, 1955.
————. *Memoirs.* Vol. 2: *Years of Trial and Hope.* Garden City: Doubleday, 1956.

GOVERNMENT DOCUMENTS

U.S. Congress. House. Conference Committee. *Conference Report on Foreign Economic Assistance Act of 1950.* H. Rept. 2117 to accompany H.R. 7797, 81st Cong., 2nd sess., May 19, 1950.
————. Committee on Appropriations. *Supplemental Estimate for Assistance to the Republic of Korea.* H. Doc. 480 and 481, 81st Cong., 2nd sess., February 27, 1950.
————. Committee on Appropriations. *Supplemental Estimate of Appropriation Continuing for Two Months the Present Program of Assistance to the Republic of Korea.* H. Doc. 247, 81st Cong., 1st sess., June 29, 1949.
————. Committee on Foreign Affairs. *Aid to Korea.* 2 pts., H. Rept. 962 on H.R. 5330, 81st Cong., 1st sess., July 1, 1949.
————. Committee on Foreign Affairs. *Background Information on Korea.* H. Rept. 2495 Pursuant to H.R. 206, 81st Cong., 2nd sess., July 11, 1950.
————. Committee on Foreign Affairs. *A Bill to Amend the Economic Cooperation Act of 1948.* Hearings on H.R. 7378, 81st Cong., 2nd sess., February–March, 1950.
————. Committee on Foreign Affairs. *Economic Assistance to Certain Areas in the Far East.* H. Rept. 1571 to accompany S. 2319, 81st Cong., 2nd sess., February 1, 1950.

————. Committee on Foreign Affairs. *First Semiannual Report on Mutual Defense Assistance Program.* H. Doc. 613, 81st Cong., 2nd sess., June 1, 1950.

————. Committee on Foreign Affairs. *Korean Aid.* Hearings on H.R. 5330, 81st Cong., 1st sess., June 1949.

————. Committee on Foreign Affairs. *Providing for Foreign Economic Assistance.* 5 pts. H. Rept. 1802 to accompany H.R. 7797, 81st Cong., 2nd sess., May 22, 1950.

U.S. Congress. Senate. Conference Committee. *Conference Report on Foreign Economic Assistance Act of 1950.* S. Rept. 168 on H.R. 7797, 81st Cong., 2nd sess., May 18, 1950.

————. Committee on Appropriations. *Foreign Aid Appropriations for 1951.* Hearings on Making Appropriations for Foreign Aid for the Fiscal Year Ending June 30, 1951, and for Other Purposes, 81st Cong., 1st sess., 1950.

————. Committee on Appropriations. *Third Deficiency Appropriations Bill for 1949.* Hearings on H.R. 5300: Aid to Korea and Securities and Exchange Commission, 81st Cong., 1st sess., 1949.

————. Committee on Armed Services. *Report to the President, September 1947.* By Lt. Gen. A. C. Wedemeyer, 82nd Cong., 1st sess., 1951.

————. Committee on Foreign Relations. *Aid to the Republic of Korea.* S. Rept. 748 on S. 2319, 81st Cong., 1st sess., July 22, 1949.

————. Committee on Foreign Relations. *Foreign Economic Assistance, 1950.* 2 pts. S. Rept. 1371 on S. 3304, 81st Cong., 2nd sess., 1950.

————. Committee on Foreign Relations. *United States and Korean Problem, Documents 1943–1953.* S. Doc. 74, 83rd Cong., 1st sess., July 30, 1953.

————. Joint Committee on Armed Services and Foreign Relations. *Military Situation in the Far East.* Hearings to Conduct an Inquiry into the Military Situation in the Far East and the Facts Surrounding the Relief of General of the Army Douglas MacArthur from His Assignment in That Area, 81st Cong., 1st sess., 1951.

U.S. Department of the Army. *Economic Position and Prospects of Japan and Korea and the Measures Required to Improve Them.* By Percy H. Johnston, Paul G. Hoffman, Robert F. Loree, and Sydney H. Scheuer. U.S. Army Committee Report, April 26, 1948.

U.S. Department of State. *Department of State Bulletin.* Vols. 5–23. 1941–1950.

————. "Economic Cooperation with Korea Under Public Law 793—80th Congress." *Treaties and Other International Acts.* Series 1908. Washington, D.C., 1949.

————. *Foreign Relations of the United States. The Conference of Berlin (Potsdam), 1945.* 2 vols. Washington, D.C., 1960.

————. *The Conferences at Cairo and Teheran, 1943.* Washington, D.C., 1961.

————. *The Conferences at Malta and Yalta, 1945.* Washington, D.C., 1955.

————. *The Conferences at Washington and Quebec, 1943.* Washington, D.C., 1970.

————. *Diplomatic Papers 1942.* Vol. I: *General, the British Commonwealth, the Far East.* Washington, D.C., 1960.

————. *Diplomatic Papers 1942. China.* Washington, D.C., 1956.

————. *Diplomatic Papers 1943.* Vol. I: *General.* Washington, D.C., 1963.

————. *Diplomatic Papers 1943.* Vol. III: *The British Commonwealth, Eastern Europe, the Far East.* Washington, D.C., 1963.

————. *Diplomatic Papers 1943. China.* Washington, D.C., 1957.

————. *Diplomatic Papers 1944.* Vol. V: *The Near East, South Asia, and Africa—The Far East.* Washington, D.C., 1965.

―――. *Diplomatic Papers 1944*. Vol. VI: *China*. Washington, D.C., 1966.
―――. *Diplomatic Papers 1945*. Vol. II: *General: Political and Economic Matters*. Washington, D.C., 1967.
―――. *Diplomatic Papers 1945*. Vol. VI: *The British Commonwealth, The Far East*. Washington, D.C., 1969.
―――. *Diplomatic Papers 1945*. Vol. VII: *The Far East: China*. Washington, D.C., 1969.
―――. *Diplomatic Papers 1946*. Vol. I: *General: The United Nations*. Washington, D.C., 1973.
―――. *Diplomatic Papers 1946*. Vol. VIII: *The Far East*. Washington, D.C., 1971.
―――. *Diplomatic Papers 1947*. Vol. I: *General: The United Nations*. Washington, D.C., 1973.
―――. *Diplomatic Papers 1947*. Vol. VI: *The Far East*. Washington, D.C., 1972.
―――. *Diplomatic Papers 1947*. Vol. VII: *The Far East: China*. Washington, D.C., 1972.
―――. *Diplomatic Papers 1948*. Vol. VI: *The Far East and Australasia*. Washington, D.C., 1974.
―――. *Diplomatic Papers 1948*. Vol. VII: *The Far East: China*. Washington, D.C., 1973.
―――. *Diplomatic Papers 1949*. Vol. VII: *The Far East and Australasia*. Pt. 2. Washington, D.C., 1976.
―――. *Diplomatic Papers 1950*. Vol. VII: *Korea*. Washington, D.C., 1976.
―――. "Military and Security Measures Effective Until Completion of Withdrawal of United States Forces from Korea." *Treaties and Other International Acts*. Series 1918. Washington, D.C., 1949.
―――. "Mutual Defense Assistance: Agreement Between the United States of America and Korea." *Treaties and Other International Acts*. Series 219. Washington, D.C., 1950.
U.S. President. *Public Papers of the Presidents: Harry S. Truman, 1945-1950*. Washington, D.C., 1961-1964.

NEWSPAPERS AND PERIODICALS

Business Week
Christian Century
Commonweal
Life
Nation
New Republic
New York Times
Saturday Evening Post
Time
U.S. News and World Report

ORAL HISTORY INTERVIEW TRANSCRIPTS

Bond, Niles. December 28, 1973. Harry S. Truman Library. Independence, Mo.
Chiles, John H. July 27, 1977. Harry S. Truman Library. Independence, Mo.
Elsey, George M. February 10, 17, 1964, March 9, 1965, July 10, 17, 1969, April 4, 1970, and July 7, 10, 1970. Harry S. Truman Library. Independence, Mo.
Harriman, W. Averell. January 10, 1980. Harry S. Truman Library. Independence, Mo.

Hickerson, John D. November 10, 1972, January 26, 1973, and June 5, 1973. Harry S. Truman Library. Independence, Mo.
Johnson, U. Alexis. January 19, 1975. Harry S. Truman Library. Independence, Mo.
Lawton, Frederick J. June 17, 1963, and July 9, 1963. Harry S. Truman Library. Independence, Mo.
Muccio, John J. February 10, 18, 1971, and December 27, 1973. Harry S. Truman Library. Independence, Mo.
Murphy, Charles S. May 2, 1963, June 3, 1963, July 24, 1963, May 21, 1969, June 24, 1969, July 15, 25, 1969, and May 19, 1970. Harry S. Truman Library. Independence, Mo.
Pace, Frank, Jr. January 1, 22, 1972, February 17, 25, 1972, and June 26, 1972. Harry S. Truman Library. Independence, Mo.

Secondary Sources

GOVERNMENT PUBLICATIONS

U.S. Department of the Army. *Korea—1950*. Washington, D.C., 1952.
U.S. Department of Commerce. "Economic Conditions in South Korea, 1947." *International Reference Service* 5 (December 1948).
———. "Economic Review of the Republic of Korea." *International Reference Service* 6 (June 1949).
———. "Economic Review of the Republic of Korea, 1949." *International Reference Service* 7 (July 1950).
U.S. Department of State. *The Conflict in Korea: Events Prior to the Attack on June 25, 1950*. Far Eastern Series, no. 45. Washington, D.C., 1951.
———. *The Fight Against Aggression in Korea*. Far Eastern Series, no. 37. Washington, D.C., 1950.
———. *Guide to the U.N. in Korea*. Far Eastern Series, no. 47. Washington, D.C., August 1951.
———. *A Historical Summary of United States-Korean Relations 1834-1962*. Far Eastern Series, no. 115. Washington, D.C., November 1962.
———. *Korea*. Office of Public Affairs. Washington, D.C., August 1951.
———. *Korea 1945 to 1948: A Report on Political Developments and Economic Resources with Selected Documents*. Far Eastern Series, no. 28. Washington, D.C., October 1948.
———. *Korea's Independence*. Far Eastern Series, no. 18. Washington, D.C., October 1947.
———. *North Korea: A Case Study in the Techniques of Takeover*. Far Eastern Series, no. 103. Washington, D.C., January 1961.
———. *The Record on Korean Unification 1943-1960: Narrative Summary with Principal Documents*. Far Eastern Series, no. 101. Washington, D.C., October 1960.
———. *United States Policy in the Korean Crisis*. Far Eastern Series, no. 34. Washington, D.C., July 1950.

BOOKS

Adler, Selig. *The Isolationist Impulse: Its Twentieth Century Reaction*. New York: Collier Books, 1958.
Allen, Richard C. *Korea's Syngman Rhee: An Unauthorized Portrait*. Tokyo: Tuttle, 1960.

Almond, Gabriel A. *The American People and Foreign Policy.* New York: Praeger, 1965.

Alperovitz, Gar. *Atomic Diplomacy: Hiroshima and Potsdam.* New York: Vintage Books, 1967.

Ambrose, Stephen E. *Rise to Globalism: American Foreign Policy 1938-1970.* Baltimore: Penguin Books, 1972.

Appleman, Roy E. *South to the Naktong, North to the Yalu (June-November 1950).* Washington, D.C.: U.S. Dept. of the Army, 1961.

Baldwin, Frank, ed. *Without Parallel: The American-Korean Relationship Since 1945.* New York: Pantheon Books, 1974.

Barnet, Richard J. *Intervention and Revolution: The United States in the Third World.* Cleveland: World, 1968.

Bell, Coral. *Negotiation from Strength: A Study in the Politics of Power.* New York: Knopf, 1963.

Beloff, Max. *Soviet Foreign Policy in the Far East, 1944-1951.* New York: Oxford University Press, 1953.

Berger, Carl. *The Korean Knot: A Military-Political History.* Philadelphia: University of Pennsylvania Press, 1957.

Bernstein, Barton J., ed. *Politics and Policies of the Truman Administration.* Chicago: Quadrangle Books, 1970.

Bloomfield, Lincoln. *The United Nations and U.S. Foreign Policy: A New Look at the National Interest.* Boston: Little, Brown, 1967.

Bohlen, Charles E. *The Transformation of American Foreign Policy.* New York: Norton, 1969.

Bundy, McGeorge, ed. *The Pattern of Responsibility.* Boston: Houghton Mifflin, 1952.

Caldwell, John C. *The Korea Story.* Chicago: Regnery, 1952.

Caridi, Ronald J. *The Korean War and American Politics: The Republican Party as a Case Study.* Philadelphia: University of Pennsylvania Press, 1968.

Cho, Soon-sung. *Korea in World Politics 1940-1950: An Evaluation of American Responsibility.* Berkeley: University of California Press, 1967.

Cochran, Bert. *Harry Truman and the Crisis Presidency.* New York: Funk and Wagnalls, 1973.

Cumings, Bruce. *The Origins of the Korean War: Liberation and the Emergence of Separate Regimes, 1945-1947.* Princeton: Princeton University Press, 1981.

Curry, George. *James F. Byrnes.* Vol. XIV: *American Secretaries of State and Their Diplomacy.* Edited by Samuel Flagg Bemis and Robert H. Ferrell. New York: Cooper Square Publishers, 1965.

Dallin, David J. *Soviet Russia and the Far East.* New Haven: Yale University Press, 1949.

Daniels, Jonathan. *The Man of Independence.* Philadelphia: Lippincott, 1950.

Dille, John. *Substitute for Victory.* Garden City: Doubleday, 1954.

Dobbs, Charles M. *The Unwanted Symbol: American Foreign Policy, the Cold War, and Korea, 1945-1950.* Kent, Ohio: Kent State University Press, 1981.

Druks, Herbert. *Harry S. Truman and the Russians 1945-1953.* New York: Robert Speller and Sons, 1966.

Fehrenbach, T. *This Kind of War: A Study in Unpreparedness.* New York: Macmillan, 1963.

Feis, Herbert. *The Atomic Bomb and the End of World War II.* Princeton: Princeton University Press, 1966.

———. *Between War and Peace: The Potsdam Conference.* Princeton: Princeton University Press, 1960.

————. *The China Tangle: The American Effort in China from Pearl Harbor to the Marshall Mission.* Princeton: Princeton University Press, 1953.

————. *Churchill, Roosevelt, Stalin: The War They Waged and the Peace They Sought.* Princeton: Princeton University Press, 1970.

————. *Contest over Japan.* New York: Norton, 1967.

Ferrell, Robert H. *George C. Marshall.* Vol. XV: *American Secretaries of State and Their Diplomacy.* Edited by Samuel Flagg Bemis and Robert H. Ferrell. New York: Cooper Square Publishers, 1966.

Fleming, Denna Frank. *The Cold War and Its Origins.* 2 vols. Garden City: Doubleday, 1961.

Gaddis, John Lewis. *The United States and the Origins of the Cold War, 1941-1947.* New York: Columbia University Press, 1972.

Gardner, Lloyd C., ed. *The Korean War.* New York: Quadrangle Books, 1972.

Gerson, Louis L. *John Foster Dulles.* Vol. XVII: *American Secretaries of State and Their Diplomacy.* Edited by Samuel Flagg Bemis and Robert H. Ferrell. New York: Cooper Square Publishers, 1967.

Goldman, Eric F. *The Crucial Decade—And After: America, 1945-1960.* New York: Random House, 1960.

Goodrich, Leland M. *Korea: A Study of U.S. Policy in the U.N.* New York: Council on Foreign Relations, 1956.

Gordenker, Leon. *The United Nations and the Peaceful Unification of Korea: The Politics of Field Operations 1947-1950.* The Hague: Martinus Nijhoff, 1959.

Graebner, Norman A. *Cold War Diplomacy 1945-1960.* Princeton: D. Van Nostrand, 1962.

————. *Ideas and Diplomacy: Readings in the Intellectual Tradition of American Foreign Policy.* New York: Oxford University Press, 1964.

————. ed. *An Uncertain Tradition: American Secretaries of State in the Twentieth Century.* New York: McGraw-Hill, 1961.

Guhin, Michael A. *John Foster Dulles: A Statesman and His Times.* New York: Columbia University Press, 1972.

Gunther, John. *The Riddle of MacArthur: Japan, Korea and the Far East.* New York: Harper & Row, 1951.

Guttman, Allen, ed. *Korea: Cold War and Limited War.* Lexington, Mass.: Heath, 1972.

Halle, Louis J. *The Cold War as History.* New York: Harper & Row, 1971.

Hamby, Alonzo L. *Beyond the New Deal: Harry S. Truman and American Liberalism.* New York: Columbia University Press, 1973.

————. *The Imperial Years: The United States Since 1939.* New York: Weybright and Talley, 1976.

Hartmann, Susan M. *Truman and the 80th Congress.* Columbia: University of Missouri Press, 1976.

Haynes, Richard F. *The Awesome Power: Harry S. Truman as Commander in Chief.* Baton Rouge: Louisiana State University Press, 1973.

Heinl, Robert D. *Victory at High Tide: The Inchon-Seoul Campaign.* Philadelphia: Lippincott, 1968.

Heller, Francis H. *The Korean War: A 25-Year Perspective.* Lawrence: Regents Press of Kansas, 1977.

Henderson, Gregory. *Korea: The Politics of the Vortex.* Cambridge: Harvard University Press, 1968.

Hermes, Walter G. *Truce Tent and Fighting Front.* Washington, D.C.: U.S. Dept. of the Army, 1966.

Higgins, Marguerite. *War in Korea.* Garden City: Doubleday, 1951.

Hillman, William, ed. *Mr. President: The First Publication from the Personal Diaries, Private Letters, Papers, and Revealing Interviews of Harry S. Truman.* New York: Farrar, Straus & Giroux, 1952.

Horowitz, David. *Free World Colossus.* New York: Hill & Wang, 1965.

Iriye, Akira. *The Cold War in Asia: A Historical Introduction.* Englewood Cliffs, N.J.: Prentice-Hall, 1974.

Jones, Joseph Marion. *The Fifteen Weeks (February 21–June 5, 1947).* New York: Harcourt Brace Jovanovich, 1955.

Kim, Joungwon A. *Divided Korea: The Politics of Development, 1945–1972.* Cambridge: Harvard University Press, 1975.

Kirkendall, Richard S., ed. *The Truman Period as a Research Field: A Reappraisal, 1972.* Columbia: University of Missouri Press, 1974.

Kolko, Gabriel. *The Politics of War: The World and United States Foreign Policy, 1943–1945.* New York: Harper & Row, 1968.

Kolko, Joyce, and Kolko, Gabriel. *The Limits of Power: The World and United States Foreign Policy, 1945–1954.* New York: Harper & Row, 1972.

LaFeber, Walter. *America, Russia, and the Cold War, 1945–1966.* New York: Wiley, 1967.

Leckie, Robert. *Conflict: The History of the Korean War, 1950–1953.* New York: Putnam's, 1962.

Lee, Chong-sik. *The Politics of Korean Nationalism.* Berkeley: University of California Press, 1963.

Lippman, Walter. *The Cold War: A Study in U.S. Foreign Policy.* Edited by Ronald Steel. New York: Harper & Row, 1972.

McCune, George M., and Grey, Arthur L., Jr. *Korea Today.* Cambridge: Harvard University Press, 1950.

McLellan, David S. *Dean Acheson: The State Department Years.* New York: Dodd, Mead, 1976.

May, Ernest R. *"Lessons" of the Past: The Use and Misuse of History in American Foreign Policy.* New York: Oxford University Press, 1975.

Meade, E. Grant. *American Military Government in Korea.* New York: King's Crown Press, 1951.

Middleton, Harry J. *The Compact History of the Korean War.* New York: Hawthorn Books, 1965.

Mitchell, C. Clyde. *Korea: Second Failure in Asia.* Washington, D.C.: Public Affairs Institute, 1951.

Nagai, Yonosuke, and Iriye, Akira, eds. *The Origins of the Cold War in Asia.* New York: Columbia University Press, 1977.

Oliver, Robert T. *Syngman Rhee: The Man Behind the Myth.* New York: Dodd, Mead, 1955.

————. *Why War Came in Korea.* New York: Fordham University Press, 1950.

Osgood, Robert E. *Limited War: The Challenge to American Strategy.* Chicago: University of Chicago Press, 1957.

Paige, Glenn D. *The Korean Decision June 24–30, 1950.* New York: Free Press, 1968.

————. *The Korean People's Democratic Republic.* Hoover Institution Studies, no. 11. Stanford: Hoover Institution, 1966.

Phillips, Cabell. *The Truman Presidency: The History of a Triumphant Succession.* Baltimore: Penguin Books, 1966.

Purifoy, Lewis McCarroll. *Harry Truman's China Policy: McCarthyism and the Diplomacy of Hysteria, 1947–1951.* New York: New Viewpoints, 1976.

Rees, David. *Korea: The Limited War.* New York: St. Martin's Press, 1964.

Reeve, W. D. *The Republic of Korea: A Political and Economic Study*. London: Oxford University Press, 1963.

Reitzel, William, Kaplan, Morton A., and Coblenz, Constance G. *United States Foreign Policy, 1945-1955*. Washington, D.C.: Brookings Institute, 1956.

Rose, Lisle A. *Dubious Victory: The United States and the End of World War II*. 2 vols. Kent, Ohio: Kent State University Press, 1973.

Rostow, W. W. *The United States in the World Arena: An Essay in Recent History*. New York: Harper & Row, 1960.

Rovere, Richard, and Schlesinger, Arthur M., Jr. *The General and the President and the Future of American Foreign Policy*. New York: Farrar, Straus & Giroux, 1951.

Rubinstein, Alvin Z., and Ginsburgs, George, eds. *Soviet and American Policies in the United Nations*. New York: New York University Press, 1971.

Sawyer, Robert K., and Hermes, Walter G. *Military Advisors in Korea: KMAG in Peace and War*. Washington, D.C.: U.S. Dept. of the Army, 1962.

Schaller, Michael. *The U.S. Crusade in China, 1938-1945*. New York: Columbia University Press, 1979.

Schilling, Warner R., Hammond, Paul Y., and Snyder, Glenn H., eds. *Strategy, Politics, and Defense Budgets*. New York: Columbia University Press, 1962.

Schnabel, James F. *Policy and Direction: The First Year*. Washington, D.C.: U.S. Dept. of the Army, 1972.

Shulman, Marshall D. *Stalin's Foreign Policy Reappraised*. Cambridge: Harvard University Press, 1963.

Simmons, Robert R. *The Strained Alliance: Peking, Pyongyang, Moscow and the Politics of the Korean Civil War*. New York: Free Press, 1975.

Smith, Gaddis. *Dean Acheson*. Vol. XVI: *American Secretaries of State and Their Diplomacy*. Edited by Samuel Flagg Bemis and Robert H. Ferrell. New York: Cooper Square Publishers, 1972.

Spanier, John W. *American Foreign Policy Since World War II*. New York: Praeger, 1971.

————. *The Truman-MacArthur Controversy and the Korean War*. New York: Norton, 1965.

Stairs, Denis. *The Diplomacy of Constraint: Canada, the Korean War, and the United States*. Toronto: University of Toronto Press, 1974.

Steel, Ronald. *Pax Americana*. New York: Viking Press, 1972.

Stone, I. F. *The Hidden History of the Korean War*. New York: Monthly Review Press, 1952.

Stueck, William Whitney, Jr. *The Road to Confrontation: American Policy Toward China and Korea, 1947-1950*. Chapel Hill: University of North Carolina Press, 1981.

Theoharis, Athan. *Seeds of Repression: Harry S. Truman and the Origins of McCarthyism*. Chicago: Quandrangle Books, 1971.

Tompkins, Pauline. *American-Russian Relations in the Far East*. New York: Macmillan, 1949.

Tsou, Tang. *America's Failure in China 1941-1950*. Vol. I. Chicago: University of Chicago Press, 1963.

Vinacke, Harold M. *The United States and the Far East, 1945-1951*. Stanford: Stanford University Press, 1952.

Westerfield, H. Bradford. *Foreign Policy and Party Politics: Pearl Harbor to Korea*. New Haven: Yale University Press, 1955.

Whiting, Allen S. *China Crosses the Yalu: The Decision to Enter the Korean War*. Stanford: Stanford University Press, 1960.

Whitney, Courtney. *MacArthur: His Rendezvous with History.* New York: Knopf, 1956.
Williams, William Appleman. *The Tragedy of American Diplomacy.* New York: Dell, 1972.
Yoo, Tae-ho. *The Korean War and the United Nations: A Legal and Diplomatic Historical Study.* Louvain: Librairie Desbarax, 1965.

ARTICLES

Bell, Coral. "Korea and the Balance of Power." *Political Quarterly* 25 (January–March 1954): 17–29.
Brogan, Denis W. "The Illusion of American Omnipotence." *Harper's* 205 (December 1952): 21–27.
Buhite, Russell D. " 'Major Interests': American Policy Toward China, Taiwan, and Korea, 1945–1950." *Pacific Historical Review* 47 (August 1978): 425–451.
Bunce, Arthur C. "The Future of Korea: Part I." *Far Eastern Survey* 23 (April 19, 1944): 67–70.
———. "The Future of Korea: Part II." *Far Eastern Survey* 23 (May 17, 1944): 85–88.
Dennett, Tyler. "In Due Course." *Far Eastern Survey* 14 (January 17, 1945): 1–14.
DeWeerd, H. A. "Lessons of the Korean War." *Yale Review* 40 (Summer 1951): 592–603.
———. "Strategic Surprise in the Korean War." *Orbis* 6 (Fall 1962): 435–452.
Dubin, Wilbert B. "The Political Evolution of the Pyongyang Government." *Pacific Affairs* 23 (December 1950): 381–392.
Dull, Paul S. "South Korean Constitution." *Far Eastern Survey* 17 (September 8, 1948): 205–207.
Dulles, John Foster. "To Save Humanity from the Deep Abyss." *New York Times Magazine* (July 30, 1950): 5.
"Economic Development in South Korea." *Far Eastern Economic Review* 7 (October 20, 1949): 519–521.
Gaddis, John Lewis. "Containment: A Reassessment." *Foreign Affairs* 55 (July 1977): 873–886.
———. "Was the Truman Doctrine a Real Turning Point?" *Foreign Affairs* 52 (January 1974): 386–402.
Graebner, Norman A. "Global Containment: The Truman Years." *Current History* 57 (August 1969): 77–83.
Grajdanzev, Andrew J. "Korea Divided." *Far Eastern Survey* 14 (October 10, 1945): 281–283.
Grey, Arthur L., Jr. "The Thirty-Eighth Parallel." *Foreign Affairs* 29 (April 1951): 482–487.
Gupta, Karunakar. "How Did the Korean War Begin?" *China Quarterly* (October–December 1972): 699–716.
Hitchcock, Wilbur W. "North Korea Jumps the Gun." *Current History* 20 (March 20, 1951): 136–144.
Hoyt, Edwin C. "The United States Reaction to the Korean Attack." *American Journal of International Law* 55 (January 1961): 45–76.
Kaner, Norman. "I. F. Stone and the Korean War." In *Cold War Critics: Alternatives to Foreign Policy in the Truman Years.* Edited by Thomas G. Paterson. Chicago: Quadrangle Books, 1971.
Kennan, George F. "The Sources of Soviet Conduct." *Foreign Affairs* 25 (July 1947): 566–582.

Kim, Yong-jeung. "The Cold War: The Korean Elections." *Far Eastern Survey* 17 (May 5, 1948): 101–102.

"Korea: A Chronology of Principal Events, 1945–1950." *World Today* 6 (August 1950): 319–330.

Lauterbach, Richard E. "Hodge's Korea." *Virginia Quarterly Review* 23 (June 1947): 349–368.

Lee, Chong-sik. "Kim Il-song of North Korea." *Asian Survey* 7 (June 1967): 349–368.

Lichterman, Martin. "To the Yalu and Back." In *American Civil-Military Decisions: A Book of Case Studies.* Edited by Harold Stein. Birmingham: University of Alabama Press, 1963.

Liem, Channing. "United States Rule in Korea." *Far Eastern Survey* 18 (April 6, 1949): 77–80.

McCune, Shannon. "The Thirty-Eighth Parallel in Korea." *World Politics* 1 (January 1949): 223–232.

McLellan, David S. "Dean Acheson and the Korean War." *Political Science Quarterly* 83 (March 1968): 16–39.

May, Ernest R. "The Nature of Foreign Policy: The Calculated Versus the Axiomatic." *Daedalus* 91 (Fall 1962): 653–667.

Miscamble, Wilson D. "Anthony Eden and the Truman–Molotov Conversations." *Diplomatic History* 2 (Spring 1978): 167–180.

Mitchell, C. Clyde. "Land Reform in South Korea." *Pacific Affairs* 22 (June 1949): 144–154.

Mosely, Philip E. "Soviet Policy and the War." *Journal of International Affairs* 6 (Spring 1952): 107–114.

Oliver, Robert T. "Korea: A Progress Report (I)." *Current History* 17 (July 1949): 133–136.

———. "Korea: A Progress Report (II)." *Current History* 17 (September 1949): 261–264.

———. "The Republic of Korea Looks Ahead (I)." *Current History* 15 (September 1948): 156–161.

———. "The Republic of Korea Looks Ahead (II)." *Current History* 15 (October 1948): 218–221.

———. "Tug of War in Korea." *Current History* 13 (October 1947): 221–225.

Paige, Glenn D. "Korea." In *Communism and Revolution: The Uses of Political Violence.* Edited by Cyril E. Black and Thomas P. Thornton. Princeton: Princeton University Press, 1964.

Parr, E. Joan. "Korea—Its Place in History." *Political Quarterly* 23 (October 1952): 352–367.

"Review of the Economy of the Republic of Korea." *Far East Economic Review* 10 (January 11, 1951): 41–47.

"Review of Korea's Postwar Economy." *Far East Economic Review* 11 (August 23, 1951): 230–237.

Sarafan, Bertram D. "Military Government: Korea." *Far Eastern Survey* 15 (November 20, 1946): 349–352.

Simmons, Robert R., Lee, Chong-sik, Skillend, W. E., and Gupta, Karunakar. "Comment." *China Quarterly* (April–June 1973): 354–368.

Smith, Beverly. "The White House Story: Why We Went to War in Korea." *Saturday Evening Post* 224 (November 10, 1951): 22–23.

Stueck, William. "Cold War Revisionism and the Origins of the Korean Conflict: The Kolko Thesis." *Pacific Historical Review* 42 (November 1973): 537–560.

————. "The Soviet Union and the Origins of the Korean War." *World Politics* 28 (July 1976): 622–635.

Suh, Dae-sook. "A Preconceived Formula for Sovietization: The Communist Takeover of North Korea." In *The Anatomy of Communist Takeovers*. Edited by Thomas T. Hammond. New Haven: Yale University Press, 1975.

Sunoo, Hagwon, and Angus, William N., "American Policy in Korea: Two Views." *Far Eastern Survey* 25 (July 31, 1946): 228–231.

Warner, Albert L. "How the Korean Decision Was Made." *Harper's* 202 (June 1951): 99–106.

Washburn, John N. "Russian Looks at North Korea." *Pacific Affairs* 20 (June 1947): 152–160.

————. "Soviet Russia and the Korean Communist Party." *Pacific Affairs* 23 (March 1950): 59–64.

Weems, Benjamin. "Behind the Korean Elections." *Far Eastern Survey* 17 (June 23, 1948): 142–146.

Woodman, Dorothy. "Korea, Formosa, and World Peace." *Political Quarterly* 21 (October 1950): 364–373.

UNPUBLISHED DISSERTATIONS

Lee, U-Gene. "American Policy Toward Korea 1942–1947: Formulation and Execution." Ph.D. dissertation, Georgetown University, 1973.

Lofgren, Charles A. "Congress and the Korean Conflict." Ph.D. dissertation, Stanford University, 1966.

Morris, William G. "The Korean Trusteeship 1941–1947." Ph.D. dissertation, University of Texas, 1975.

Twedt, Michael S. "The War Rhetoric of Harry S. Truman During the Korean Conflict." Ph.D. dissertation, University of Kansas, 1969.

Index

NAME INDEX

Abe, Noboyuki, 48, 53, 271n. 88
Acheson, Dean G., 122, 242; and aid programs for ROK, 191, 192, 204, 219, 220–222, 229, 300n. 31, 307n. 78; assessment of Truman Doctrine, 284n. 30; attitude toward Nationalist China and Chinese civil war, 217, 219, 220, 306n. 62; criticism of Syngman Rhee and ROK, 206, 224; and implementation of Moscow agreement, 67, 73, 110; National Press Club speech, 217–219, 237, 251, 306n. 65; participation in Blair House meetings, 242–243, 244–245; plans for aid to southern Korea, 108–109; position on use of U.S. combat troops in Korea, 245, 248; pressure on ROK to adopt ECA reform program, 214–215, 221–222, 224; response to outbreak of Korean War, 236, 237, 242, 244; and UNCOK, 189, 211–212; and U.S. commitment to ROK, 229, 251, 306n. 65; and U.S. withdrawal, 189, 190, 192, 299n. 21, 300n. 31; and U.S. occupation policies, 53–54, 57, 62, 72, 109, 281n. 71; and U.S. strategy for halting Soviet expansionism, 175–176, 256, 257
Allison, John M., 120–121, 269n. 65, 310n. 27
An Ho-sang, 77–78
Antonov, Alexei E. (General), 41, 42
Arnold, Archibald V. (Major General), 55, 84, 97, 113, 280n. 66
Atcheson, George, 57
Austin, Warren R., 131, 140, 187, 238, 246

Balasanov, G. M., 81–82, 92–93
Benninghoff, H. Merrell, 62, 71, 79; appraisal of Soviet intentions in Korea, 56; assessment of political situation in southern Korea, 50, 54, 55, 59
Berle, Adolph A., 11–12, 24, 265n. 87

Bevin, Ernest, 64, 65
Bishop, Max, 179, 180
Bolte, Charles L. (Major General), 203, 310n. 23
Bond, Niles, 146, 182, 211
Bonesteel, C. H., III (Colonel), 44
Bradley, Omar N. (General), 242–243, 245
Brown, Albert E. (Major General), as head of U.S. delegation at Joint Commission negotiations, 113, 116–117, 118, 121, 122, 130, 131
Bunce, Arthur C.: comments on SKILA elections, 95; and economic aid to Korea, 94, 105, 220; and Pauley report, 92, 281n. 71; on reform in ROK, 3, 222
Butterworth, W. Walton, 136, 152, 165, 180, 214, 220
Byrnes, James F., 75, 96, 275n. 60, 281n. 71; desire for U.S. occupation of Korea, 39, 43; discussions at Potsdam on trusteeship, 42–43; and Joint Commission negotiations, 82; on Japan's defeat in World War II, 39, 40, 43; participation in the Moscow Conference of 1945, 64–66, 67–68, 72, 276n. 68; and Pauley visit to northern Korea, 87, 88, 92; and trusteeship, 62, 63, 64, 266n. 95

Chang Myŏn, 168, 188, 194, 220, 224
Chang T'aek-sang, 173
Chang Tŏk-su, 136
Chiang Kai-shek, 14, 15, 43, 102; and Chinese influence in Asia, 23; fears of Soviet expansionism, 13, 19, 23, 29, 36; and KPG, 12–13, 23, 56, 62; opposition to negotiations with Soviet Union, 56; position on Korean independence, 14, 20, 21; and reforms in China, 176, 182, 203, 218; support for in U.S. Congress, 197, 199, 203, 220; U.S. support for, 116, 176, 222;

SUBJECT INDEX

About the Author

James Irving Matray earned his doctoral degree in United States history at the University of Virginia, where he specialized in American diplomacy. He holds a master's degree from the University of Virginia and a bachelor's degree from Lake Forest College, where he graduated with honors and was elected to Phi Beta Kappa. Presently an assistant professor of history at New Mexico State University in Las Cruces, he has taught previously at the University of Texas at Arlington, California State College in Bakersfield, Glenville State College in West Virginia, and Delaware State College. His articles have appeared in *Diplomatic History,* the *Journal of American History,* the *Pacific Historical Review,* and *The Historian.* In 1980, he was co-recipient of the Stuart L. Bernath Article Award from the Society for Historians of American Foreign Relations.

A Study from the Center for Korean Studies
University of Hawaii

The Center for Korean Studies was established in 1972 to coordinate and develop the resources for the study of Korea at the University of Hawaii. Its goals are to enhance faculty quality and performance in Korean studies; to develop comprehensive, balanced academic programs; to stimulate research and publications; and to coordinate the resources of the University of Hawaii with those of other institutions, organizations, and individual scholars engaged in the study of Korea. Reflecting the diversity of the academic disciplines represented by affiliated members of the University faculty, the Center seeks especially to promote interdisciplinary and intercultural studies.

Studies from the Center for Korean Studies

Studies on Korea: A Scholar's Guide, edited by Han-Kyo Kim. 1980

Korean Communism, 1945–1980: A Reference Guide to the Political System, by Dae-Sook Suh. 1981

Korea and the United States: A Century of Cooperation, edited by Youngnok Koo and Dae-Sook Suh. 1984

The Reluctant Crusade: American Foreign Policy in Korea, 1941–1950, by James I. Matray. 1985

Production Notes

This book was designed by Roger Eggers. Composition and paging were done on the Quadex Composing System and typesetting on the Compugraphic 8400 by the design and production staff of University of Hawaii Press.

The text typeface and display typeface is Garamond.

Offset presswork and binding were done by Vail-Ballou Press, Inc. Text paper is Glatfelter Offset, basis 50, a "permanent" uncoated paper.